D1531115

An Analysis of the New Financial Institutions

Recent Titles from Quorum Books

From Organizational Decline to Organizational Renewal: The Phoenix Syndrome
Mary E. Guy

Modern Analytical Auditing: Practical Guidance for Auditors and Accountants
Thomas E. McKee

Multiple Use Job Descriptions: A Guide to Analysis, Preparation, and Applications
for Human Resources Managers
Philip C. Grant

Cost-Effective Marketing Research: A Guide for Marketing Managers
Eric J. Soares

Corporate Philosophies and Mission Statements: A Survey and Guide for Corporate
Communicators and Management
Thomas A. Falsey

Strategic Executive Decisions: An Analysis of the Difference Between Theory
and Practice
Michael J. Stahl

Motivating Strategies for Performance and Productivity: A Guide to Human
Resource Development
Paul J. Champagne and R. Bruce McAfee

Innovation Through Technical and Scientific Information; Government and
Industry Cooperation
*Science and Public Policy Program, University of Oklahoma: Steven Ballard,
Thomas E. James, Jr., Timothy I. Adams, Michael D. Devine, Lani L. Malysa,
and Mark Meo*

Transformations in French Business: Political, Economic, and Cultural Changes
from 1981-1987
Judith Frommer and Janice McCormick, eds.

Economics and Antitrust Policy
Robert J. Larner and James W. Meehan, Jr., eds.

A Legal Guide to EDP Management
Michael C. Gemignani

U.S. Commercial Opportunities in the Soviet Union: Marketing, Production, and
Strategic Planning Perspectives
Chris C. Carvounis and Brinda Z. Carvounis

AN *Analysis* OF THE *New* FINANCIAL INSTITUTIONS

Changing Technologies, Financial Structures, Distribution Systems, and Deregulation

A̶LAN G̶ART

Q

QUORUM BOOKS

NEW YORK • WESTPORT, CONNECTICUT • LONDON

Library of Congress Cataloging-in-Publication Data

Gart, Alan.
    An analysis of the new financial institutions : changing
technologies, financial structures, distribution systems, and
deregulation / Alan Gart.
        p. cm.
    ISBN 0-89930-271-8 (lib. bdg. : alk. paper)
    1. Financial services industry—United States. 2. Financial
institutions—United States. 3. Financial services industry.
4. Financial institutions. I. Title.
HG181.G358 1989
332.1 '0973—dc19   88-4933

British Library Cataloguing in Publication Data is available.

Library of Congress Catalog Card Number: 88-4933
ISBN: 0-89930-271-8

First published in 1989 by Quorum Books

Greenwood Press, Inc.
88 Post Road West, Westport, Connecticut 06881

Printed in the United States of America

The paper used in this book complies with the
Permanent Paper Standard issued by the National
Information Standards Organization (Z39.48-1984).

10 9 8 7 6 5 4 3 2 1

Contents

Figures and Tables

TABLES

Preface

Significant changes are taking place in financial markets and within the financial services industry:

1. The United States has become a debtor nation. Net overseas investment was a negative $237 billion in 1986. Japan, on the other hand, had net overseas investment of $180 billion in 1986.

2. The United States banking industry is saddled with $59 billion worth of sour loans made to a growing list of troubled borrowers which include developing countries, farmers, real estate developers, takeover artists, and oil drillers.

3. During the 1980s, we have witnessed a continual increase in the number of commercial bank failures, which have risen from 10 in 1980 to an estimated 250-260 in 1988.

4. When the international agreement among 12 central banks germane to minimal equity-to-asset ratios is combined with huge loan losses on behalf of most large American banks, commercial banks (especially money-center banks) will be under regulatory pressure to increase their equity capital.

5. The world's debtor nations owed an estimated $1.2 trillion at the end of 1987. This total is likely to increase during the remainder of the 1980s. The World Bank has stated that, in terms of creditworthiness, the debtor nations' "position has stubbornly failed to improve. . . . In the five years since 1982, no country involved in rescheduling its debts has significantly reduced its debt ratios" despite the fact that there has been a five-year economic boom in most industrial countries. What is particularly worrying is that adjustment has proved so difficult in a period of prolonged economic expansion and that the lack of progress has itself produced a sort of "debt fatigue."

The international debt crisis intensified during 1987. Money center banks will be under greater pressure to increase their write-offs of LDC (less developed country) loans and to increase their loan loss reserves following a decision in December 1987 by the Bank of Boston, the thirteenth largest U.S. bank, to write off $200 million of its total $1 billion in Third World loans and to set aside $470 million to pay for losses it might sustain on the rest. While other banks, led by Citicorp, announced huge loan loss reserves against about 20 percent of their Latin debt in the spring of 1987, the Bank of Boston's move represented the first time that a major lender had given up on such loans. If Citicorp were to cover its LDC loans to the same extent, it would have to set aside an additional $4.1 billion (or in excess of four years of profit). Also, if Manufacturers Hanover imitated Bank of Boston's actions, it would have to add $3.13 billion to reserves and would then have a common equity-to-assets ratio of only 0.69 percent, well below regulatory standards. Large money-center banks would have to sell assets, shrink balance sheets and asset growth, cut or limit dividends, increase equity offerings, and reduce merger and acquisition activity.

Bank loans to Latin nations at the time of the Bank of Boston action were selling at between 36.5 percent of their original amounts for Argentine loans, to 61 percent for Venezuelan loans. In terms of bank accounts, every dollar added to the loan loss reserves would reduce bank earnings by an equal amount.

In addition, a novel proposal to help reduce the $105 billion foreign debt burden of Mexico was introduced by Mexico, the U.S. Treasury, and J. P. Morgan. However, Mexico's innovative debt-swap plan fell far short of expectations in that the nation's foreign debt was reduced by only $1.1 billion, well below the loan reduction amount originally envisioned. On the other hand, the plan resulted in interest savings for Mexico of $1.54 billion over the next 20 years. The plan, which offered banks the chance to tender discounted debt in exchange for new bonds, attracted 320 bids from 139 banks world-wide, covering $6.7 billion of debt. Mexico accepted bids from 95 of these banks, covering $3.67 billion of its $53 billion of government debt. Mexico replaced the $3.67 billion of bank debt with $2.56 billion of new, 20-year bonds. Mexico accepted bank tenders up to a price of just under 75 cents on the dollar with an average price paid for the debt of just under 70 cents on the dollar.

The new Mexican bonds offered a higher interest rate than existing Mexican government bank debt and were backed by 20-year, zero-coupon U.S. Treasury bonds. The average price Mexico accepted for its debt—about 70 cents on the dollar—indicated that the so-called secondary loan market may be undervaluing Mexican debt. At that time, Mexican debt had traded at 50 cents on the dollar. The Mexican debt-swap plan attracted broad interest because it was presented as a new approach to the billions of dollars of debt that burdens developing countries. Some analysts see the plan as the first concerted attempt by a creditor bank and a heavily indebted country to develop a model for sharing losses on loans between bank creditors and debtor countries, while others suggest it was just a way of allowing smaller banks to get out of the business of lending to Mexico. Another major significance of the plan was that for the first time, the United States took an active role in helping ease pressure on Third World debtors which, unlike Mexico, do not have strong foreign currency reserves to buy the special U.S. bonds to make the plan work. (Venezuela is one exception, however.) Also, the other nations do not have Mexico's special relationship with the United States.

Participants on both sides benefitted from the debt swap. Mexico reduced its total debt and its annual interest payments, while some banks cleared up a portion of their Mexican loan portfolio, writing off a portion of the loans but earning a higher rate of interest on the remainder. The U.S. Treasury also benefitted by marketing some new debt of its own. One of the reasons that more banks did not participate in the swap was that some of the money-center banks were not in a comfortable enough financial/capital position to write off much more debt.

6. Loan portfolios of commercial banks are undergoing significant changes—especially the shift from business debt to mortgage and consumer credit. On the mortgage front, banks have introduced a new "reducible" fixed-rate mortgage instrument with a one-time opportunity to lock in a new, lower rate if prevailing interest rates drop at least two percentage points at any time from the second through fifth years of the plan.

Countervailing trends have been evident among the large bank holding companies (BHCs) in the 1980s. Given the increase in asset risk among the large BHCs the effective capital positions of these BHCs now appear to be weaker than at the beginning of the 1980s, despite the increases in capital to asset ratios. The deterioration in the effective capital positions among the largest BHCs argues for vigorous regulatory efforts to raise further the level of capital in banking and to ensure more rapid adjustments in capital requirements to changes in asset risk in the future.

7. Investment portfolios are also undergoing change. Banks have reduced their holdings of municipal bonds in response to the loss of special tax privileges for banks investing in this market. In addition, banks and thrifts are shifting out of treasury issues into mortgages pass-throughs or mortgage backed securities.

8. Large money-center banks are attempting to generate more off-balance sheet income in order to improve their return on assets. Bank holding companies, in addition to their finance company, factoring, mortgage banking, and credit and debit card services, have begun to diversify into mutual funds, discount brokerage, and insurance. All are active in investment or merchant banking abroad, and as much investment banking activity in this country as the law allows, merger and acquisition activity, and a huge amount of interest rate and foreign currency swap activity.

9. The barriers to interstate banking are breaking down with the formation of nonbank banks and super-regional banks such as NCNB, PNC, CoreStates, Sun Trust, First Union, Fleet Financial, and Banc One. In general, these banks are free of huge foreign loan losses and have sound, well-capitalized franchises in multi-state locations.

10. A great corporate restructuring is underway and it is taking many forms.

Restructuring includes streamlining of costs, internal reorganization, networking arrangements among firms, privatization, leveraged buyouts, stock repurchases, divestitures, consolidations, and mergers and acquisitions in unprecedented numbers.

11. In addition to the formation of gigantic money-center bank holding companies and large super-regionals, the rise of financial conglomerates has been another structural change that is having a large impact on the financial services industry. Not only have the traditional players—the banks, insurance companies, and brokerage firms—expanded in scope, but they have been joined by relatively new players such as Xerox and G.E. For example, Xerox Financial Services sells insurance protection for auto, home, and business from its Crum and Foster subsidiary, life insurance from Xerox Financial Services Life, and mutual funds and unit investment trusts from Van Kampen Merritt. Investment banking services and asset management services are offered by Furman Selz, while leasing is offered through Xerox Credit Corporation.

12. Bad loans wiped out 1987 profits at many money-center banks, agricultural banks, and banks headquartered in Texas. While Latin American, energy and real estate loan problems hurt the money-center banks, vacant office space, an overabundance of hotels and condominiums in the Sunbelt, and a precipitous decline in oil prices contributed to bank problems in Texas and surrounding states. There have been numerous mergers and acquisitions of troubled banks and savings and loans in Texas and surrounding states.

13. Banks continue to face intense competition from nondepository institutions and foreign commercial banks. In just a decade, foreign banks have increased their U.S. commercial and industrial lending from $17 billion to $91 billion, while assets of mutual funds have quadrupled in a decade. Banks have lost their exclusive hold on transaction accounts and have seen net demand deposits decline from over 50 percent of deposits in the 1950s to close to 15 percent in 1988.

14. Profit spreads within the commercial banking industry are shrinking. A key ratio, return on assets (ROA), declined to a miniscule 0.2 percent in 1987, below the 0.7 percent average that prevailed early in the 1980s. With the growth of the commercial paper market, underwriting, and private placements around the globe, pressure on bank lending to large corporations has intensified and margins have been squeezed. The decline in margins has even been extended to letters of credit and into corporate middle-market lending in the United States. Banks are seeking increased sources of fee income, new products and services, and are trying to reduce their fixed costs in attempting to increase their ROA.

15. Deregulation has been one of the salient factors impacting financial institutions during the 1970s and 1980s. The moratorium embodied in the Competitive Equality Banking Act of 1987 prohibited banks from seeking expanded powers in businesses such as securities underwriting, real estate, and insurance until after March 1, 1988. Although congressional views on these issues are uncertain, the banks have found allies in Federal Reserve Board

Chairman Alan Greenspan and in the Comptroller of the Currency, Robert L. Clarke. Greenspan suggested that opening new business ventures to banks would improve their profitability and long-term prospects, provided that safeguards assured that bank deposits would not be used to finance securities operations. Greenspan would support a modernization of the banking system because the banks' traditional role of financial intermediation has eroded significantly as the marketplace has changed. Developments in computer and communications technology have reduced the economic role of commercial banks and enhanced the function of investment banking. The nation's biggest corporate borrowers are selling directly to the credit markets through issues of commercial paper and mortgage-backed securities, and the trend toward direct investor-borrower linkages is growing rapidly. Also, bank entry into securities dealing and underwriting would inject more competition into investment banking and reduce underwriting costs.

After having failed to secure important deregulation from Congress for years, the banking industry has found that the Federal Reserve, the Federal Deposit Insurance Corporation (FDIC), and the Comptroller of the Currency are willing to move for regulatory changes. As a matter of fact, banks such as Citicorp, Chase Manhattan, and Bankers Trust received approval from the Federal Reserve (the Fed) to underwrite commercial paper, mortgage-backed securities, and industrial revenue bonds. The Fed is also seeking comment on a proposal to let bank holding companies engage in certain new real estate activities. While it seems an inopportune time for banks to enter territory where Wall Street firms are retrenching, support appears to be growing in Congress for a revision of the 1933 Glass-Steagall Act, which prohibits banks from underwriting corporate securities.

16. Although the 1982 Garn-St. Germain bill expanded the asset powers of thrift institutions, savings and loans and savings banks remain predominantly mortgage-lending institutions with small portfolios of business and consumer loans.

17. Troubled as business is for many commercial banks, many savings and loans are in worse shape. A third of the nation's 3,147 savings associations lost money in 1987, giving the industry a record net loss of $6.8 billion. The unprofitable institutions lost a total of $13.4 billion, which overwhelmed the $6.6 billion in profits posted by the rest of the industry. The net loss for 1987 exceeded by 50 percent the $4.6 billion that savings institutions lost in 1981, during a period of record high interest rates. The 1987 loss was concentrated in Texas and in the surrounding regions in the energy and agricultural regions of the country. The Federal Home Loan Bank Board (FHLBB) reported that, based on regulatory accounting principles, 345 institutions were insolvent at the end of 1987, and that, based on generally accepted accounting principles, 510 were insolvent. As a matter of fact, the Home Loan Bank Board rescued or liquidated 48 insolvent thrifts in 1987 and planned to close about the same number in 1988.

18. There are many profitable savings and loan associations. These

institutions have complained to the FSLIC that the additional premiums that they are paying for depository insurance will lead them to leave the FHLB system and seek cheaper FDIC insurance. The healthy S&Ls feel that they are paying unfair premiums to help cover the losses of the S&L industry's weak sisters. The FHLBB has responded by offering to reduce deposit insurance premiums for well capitalized thrifts. With its deposit insurance reduction proposal, the FHLBB is trying to demonstrate that they are not going to tax the healthy S&Ls out of existence. In order to keep the industry together under FSLIC insurance, they have to keep the strongest thrifts as members of the FHLB system.

19. In March 1987, the General Accounting Office declared the FSLIC insolvent because it would be unable to meet all its future obligations on insured deposits at failed but not yet closed thrifts. Prior to the passage in 1987 of legislation authorizing a recapitalization, the FSLIC had been unable to take remedial action with respect to these insolvent thrifts, owing to the inadequacy of its resources. Essentially, the FSLIC's current reserves of $2.7 billion are dwarfed by the $40 to $90 billion or so that would be needed to bail out the troubled thrifts. Under the terms of the recapitalization plan approved as part of the Competitive Banking Equality Act, the newly created Financing Corporation could borrow up to $10.8 billion as needed by the FSLIC through issuance of long-term debt to bail out troubled thrifts. The primary job of the FHLBB is to liquidate, sell, or nurse the several hundred institutions that are already insolvent but still open for business. The FHLBB must also maintain the confidence of depositors so that there will not be large deposit runoffs.

20. Despite 184 failed banks in 1987, the FDIC is in much better financial shape than the FSLIC, and closed the year with $18 billion in assets, roughly as much as it had at the beginning of 1987. The regulatory agency paid out a record $3.5 billion in 1987, which was matched by insurance premiums that members pay, plus interest on the agency's investment portfolio.

21. The Pension Benefits Guarantee Corporation (PBGC), established in 1974, guarantees pension benefits to workers. This agency has also run into financial difficulty when companies such as LTV filed for a Chapter 11 bankruptcy reorganization and defaulted on its steel workers pensions, effectively sticking the PBGC with $2.4 billion in unfunded liabilities. The insurance rates had to be increased substantially in 1988 in order to keep losses at tolerable levels.

22. The growth of international financial markets has been accelerated by a flood of innovative products from a creative investment banking industry in the United States. Financial services and markets are globalizing as a result of economic growth, economic volatility and imbalances, the computer, information and technological revolution, deregulation, and a greater reliance on financial markets. Japanese and European commercial and investment banking institutions have expanded their activities and increased their penetration in the U.S. market for financial services.

23. In the 1980s, securitization of loans accelerated markedly in the United

States, as well as in Canada, Australia, and the United Kingdom. The pass-through certificate, the mortgage-backed bond, and the pass-through bond (which pioneered in the United States) have been adopted to the requirements of the domestic financial systems and legal traditions of these other countries.

Product securitization is associated with the rapid creation of mortgage-backed securities for residential mortgages and with bonds backed by mortgages on commercial property and automobile loan and credit card debt. Depository institutions have been able to accomplish three goals through securitization: (1) reduce interest rate risk; (2) limit assets subject to capital requirements; (3) generate fee and servicing income.

Mortgage securitization as a percentage of mortgage originations leaped from approximately 40 percent in 1984 to 81 percent in 1986, before sliding to about 74 percent in 1987. Market securitization has been most notable in the growth of underwriting in place of growth in bank lending. This has been assisted by the provisions of protection against risk. For example, banks guarantee commercial paper and municipal bond issues with letters of credit, while a number of insurance companies provide protection against default on municipal bonds.

24. The structure of the stock market is no longer what it was 20 or even 5 years ago. In the 1960s and throughout most of the 1970s, pension and retirement funds along with insurance companies supplied the overwhelming majority of new equity investment funds. In the 5 years prior to the 1973-1974 stock market break, private pension fund managers placed more than 90 percent of their new investable funds in the equity markets. In the late 1970s and early 1980s pension fund equity investment remained high, but it declined as a percentage of the total.

Although pension fund, mutual fund, foreign institutional and insurance company purchases of equities are still important, institutional purchases are no longer dominant. From 1984 to 1987, the biggest buyers of corporate stock have been corporations themselves. Mergers, share buyback programs, and leveraged buyouts have absorbed nearly one-sixth of the total market value.

In addition, the average ratio of pension fund assets to liabilities for the Fortune 500 companies was about 160 percent at year-end 1987. The sheer size of the pension surplus, its visibility under the Financial Accounting Standards Board FASB87, and the volatility to which it is exposed under current asset allocation policies have caused some companies to reduce the percentage of pension assets held in common stock.

25. State and local governments issued $98.6 billion in municipal debt in 1987, down from $147 billion in 1986 and $201 billion in 1985. Gross spread or underwriting profit in negotiated fixed rate revenue bonds fell to $13.48 per $1,000 in 1987 from $14.98 in 1986. Merrill Lynch Capital Markets led all underwriters, acting as lead manager in 266 issues totaling $8.6 billion, while Salomon Brothers Inc. was in second place with 77 issues totaling $7.7 billion. Despite their large underwriting role, Salomon abandoned the municipal bond business in October 1987 because of its declining profitability.

26. Increased competition in corporate and municipal underwritings has led to a decline in underwriting spreads for investment bankers. The October 1987 stock market crash, underwriting losses, mergers and acquisitions, and overstaffing led many Wall Street firms to layoff employees when profits declined in 1987. As a matter of fact, E. F. Hutton became a casualty within the industry and merged with Shearson Lehman Brothers. In addition, commercial banks have slashed over 10,000 jobs in New York after their dismal profit performance in 1987. In total, at least 20,000 jobs were lost in the financial services industry in New York City alone, ending a period of rapid employment growth.

27. After a few years of operating losses, the property-casualty industry had an estimated 1987 operating profit of $13.7 billion, more than double the $5.4 billion profit of 1986. Underwriting losses declined to approximately $9.8 billion in 1987 from $15.9 billion in 1986. Investment income, interest and dividends earned from assets, reached about $23.5 billion in 1987, a 7.3 percent increase over 1986. Despite expectations of a slowdown in operating profits during the remainder of the 1980s, the industry has recovered from the financial crisis of 1984-1985.

28. In 1987, premiums flowing into the traditional insurance industry (excluding self-insurance, captives, and pension fund deposits) totaled approximately $400 billion. This figure amounted to close to 9 percent of the gross national product of the United States.

29. Insurers have been experimenting with alternative distribution systems for products that do not require a high degree of professional expertise and personal counseling. Common to such alternative marketing approaches is the desire to reach large blocs of consumers as a group rather than individually. These approaches work best with products easily understood by the consumer (for example, term life) and where policies have become standardized and can be viewed as commodities. Insurers are beginning to experiment with sales in bank lobbies and shopping centers, and in the use of technology. Insurance companies are attempting to reach directly into the homes of the buying public through television, the home computer, telephone systems of enhanced capability, and mass mailings. Of critical importance will be an ability to capitalize on technological opportunities for service improvements and cost reductions.

30. The stock market collapse of October 1987 gave clear warning of the vulnerability of important elements of the financial system to sudden shocks. Although only a few small securities firms failed, the market turbulence produced significant problems for specialists, traders, and market makers on the stock exchange. Financial markets gave evidence of fragility and instability that have not entirely disappeared in mid-1988. It is essential that the reexamination of our market mechanisms and regulatory systems go forward to identify any actions that might be needed to safeguard the strength of our financial markets and reduce the risks of economic disruption. October 19, 1987, suggests that there are some gaping holes in the free-market paradigm and that some form of

government regulation in the form of "circuit breakers" may be necessary to temper huge market swings. The trouble comes in getting the warring futures and equity camps and their respective regulators to agree on the details of such matters.

31. The U.S. financial services sector has probably undergone more structural change since 1975 than during all of the period since the Great Depression. Changes in regulation, technology, distribution systems, and financial structure have been in the forefront of these dramatic changes. However, volatile interest rates, double-digit inflation followed by disinflation, and a number of recessions have also contributed to the structural changes.

According to a 1987 Ernst & Whitney survey of over 150 chief executives of the nation's largest insurance companies, most insurers still sell insurance through brokers and agents. However, 28 percent of the companies are also using direct mail, telemarketing, and bank lobby stations. Four out of ten chief executives who said their firms use these alternative distribution systems, said those methods account for more than 10 percent of their total business. In addition, one-fourth of the survey respondents predicted that use of nontraditional distribution methods will account for more than 10 percent of new insurance sales within five years.

32. During 1988 American investors caught a case of leveraged buyout fever despite the bankruptcy of Revco, D.S. Inc. earlier that year. Revco was a large company that had been taken private in a leveraged buyout in 1986. Investment bankers, corporate executives, commercial banks, pension funds and LBO partnerships have all jumped into the lucrative LBO game staked out by such well known firms as Kohlberg Kravis Roberts & Co. In a leveraged buyout, investors borrow huge sums of money to buy companies, hoping to pay off the debt with the companies' cash flow and to profit handsomely by the resale of the entire company or divisions of the company. With a typical leverage of 10-to-1 used in these deals, investors put up $1 in equity for every $10 of borrowed funds. The borrowed funds usually are a combination of bank borrowing, bond issues, and preferred stock issues. Banks tend to provide more than half of the funds at rates well above the prime rate. In addition banks earn lucrative commitment fees. The dollar volume of LBO loans in July 1988 jumped to 40 percent of all commercial loans compared to only 14 percent a year earlier. Mr. Greenspan, Chairman of the Federal Reserve Board, has cautioned banks about making too many LBO loans and has suggested intense scrutiny of the credit quality of LBO borrowers in the light of the enormous amount of leverage and the possibility of a recession in the 1989–1992 period. The record amount of debt being put on the books at firms leaves little room for managerial error and could lead to better corporate management. On the other hand, it could lead to increased plant closings and layoffs as LBO managers run a leaner company when faced with heavy interest costs on their outstanding debt.

There are likely to be repercussions associated with the large number of huge LBO deals. There will be SEC investigations of disclosures to bondholders, particularly in issues where internal management makes an LBO offer and the outstanding bonds are downgraded by the rating agencies. Germane to new bond issues, we are likely to see investor protection against downgradings created by leveraged buyouts in the form of put options available to investors if there is an LBO offer or a large accumulation of the company's stock by an investor. There are also likely to be changes in managerial contracts with some rewards tied to the performance of the company's stock in addition to the traditional reward structure. There is congressional concern about job losses related to LBOs and to the general fortunes being made in management-led buyouts. After all, management is supposed to work for all of the stockholders. There are also some questions concerning possible governmental tax losses related to LBOs. Some pension funds have expressed second thoughts on their LBO investments even though returns have averaged 40 percent up until 1988. It is likely that LBO returns will still be substantial, but will be lower than they have been.

This book will bring the reader up-to-date on the changes in regulation and deregulation, structure and restructuring, mergers and acquisitions, technology, distribution systems, sources and uses of funds, strategies, and the profitability of the institutions that are the dominant players within the financial services industry. Financial innovation has been a dominant force; for example, securitization has had an enormous impact within the investment banking industry, while universal life insurance has had a major impact on the insurance industry. Similarly, money market, NOW, and Super-NOW accounts have played a key role in the liability side of bank balance sheets in the 1980s, while videotex systems and debit cards should have a major impact on financial institutions in the 1990s. Discount brokerage firms and money market funds have also made a major impact within the financial services industry. In addition, this book also provides the latest management thinking about asset and liability management, the apparent consolidation of the financial services industry, and the latest marketing approaches and technological capabilities. It also provides some guidance on managing a financial institution through a changing environment and the regulatory maze. Institutions that survive and prosper will require superior skills in marketing, information systems, and planning and strategic implementation. Choosing the right market segments and the proper products and services, and understanding the most important leverage points in the management of technology and operations will all be part of the basic survival kit, along with more efficient distribution systems.

The chapters describe how the financial services industry developed, where it is today, and what it will be like in the next decade. In addition, the book describes the nature of the competition, the evolution of new products and services, and the impact of deregulation on each segment of the financial services industry. These segments include: commercial banking, international banking, savings and loans, savings banks, credit unions, life insurance companies, property-casualty companies, pension funds, finance companies, leasing companies, investment banking, brokerage firms, investment companies, and money market funds.

Acknowledgments

I would like to thank David Leahigh of Lehigh University for writing the chapter on asset-liability management and Ron Caruso (editor of the *Equipment Financing Journal*) for writing the chapter on leasing companies. The chapter on leasing has been dedicated in memory of Ron Caruso's parents. In addition, I would like to thank the Federal Reserve Bank of New York and Tom Druitt (Goldman Sachs) for inviting me to attend seminars on banking and the money markets that were sponsored by their institutions, as well as Deborah Naulty (Federal Reserve Bank of Philadelphia) and Richard Cohn (Drug Scan) for their invaluable assistance. James Rosenthal (Lehigh University), Ameé Pollack (Franklin and Marshall College), and Steven Gart (University of Pennsylvania) deserve special praise for drawing many of the graphs and figures.

1

Introduction

SEPARATE INDUSTRIES: TRADITIONAL FUNCTIONS

In the past there was a distinct separation between the banking, insurance, and securities industries. Each industry operated within clearly defined parameters, and firms competed against similar entities on an almost level playing field. Prudential competed against MONY, New England Life, Metropolitan Life and other life insurance companies, while State Farm competed against Allstate, Liberty Mutual, and other property and casualty insurers for their main source of insurance premium income. On the banking front, Citibank vied with Chase Manhattan, Chemical Bank, Manufacturers Hanover, and other banking concerns for their share of loans and deposits. In the securities industry, Merrill Lynch competed against Dean Witter Reynolds and other security firms for the investment dollars of consumers. These firms seemed content to operate and compete against similar companies within defined traditional boundaries.[1]

The products marketed by these separate industries reflected their traditional functions. Securities firms dealt primarily with the underwriting and marketing of stocks and bonds. Insurance companies sold traditional life, health, and property and liability insurance to protect against financial loss. Banks concentrated on making short-term loans, and accepting demand, savings, and time deposits. Consumer activity appeared to be segmented, since the consumer usually went to an insurance agent for life and property-casualty insurance needs, and frequented the local bank or thrift to handle checking, savings, and borrowing needs. The stockbroker was consulted when purchases of stocks and bonds were contemplated.

The segmented industries simplified things for the consumer and for firms in the financial services industry. There was a slight overlap in the products and services offered to the public, but it never seemed to create serious problems. For example, savings banks in New York and Massachusetts offered modest amounts of life insurance. For many years, the respective participants appeared to be satisfied with the specialization of function that existed in the financial markets.

REGULATION AND DEREGULATION

Banks and thrifts faced more regulations and restrictions than did insurance companies and brokerage firms. Banks had depository insurance up to $100,000, and paid no interest on demand deposits. On the other hand, banks were not permitted to branch across state lines, underwrite corporate securities, or offer insurance (other than credit life). In addition, banks and thrifts were limited in the interest rates that they could pay on deposits under $100,000 by Regulation Q interest-rate ceilings. (Actually, it was these interest-rate ceilings that helped set off the financial revolution.)

When money and capital market interest rates exceeded the ceilings applicable to bank depository accounts, customers withdrew their deposits and reinvested them directly in higher yielding money market instruments (disintermediation). This led to the establishment of money market funds in the early 1970s when money market rates reached double-digit levels. Banks clamored for an equal playing field and were eventually permitted to offer insured money market accounts to the public without interest-rate ceilings as a result of the passage of the Garn-St. Germain Act in 1982. It took banks and thrifts a decade to gain a level playing field with money market funds.

Even though bank pricing was deregulated by Garn-St. Germain, there has been only limited product or geographical deregulation. Banks and thrifts can now offer discount brokerage services and are permitted to acquire failing out-of-state depository institutions. In 1985, the Supreme Court ruled that regional interstate bank mergers were permissible if the states where the involved banks were headquartered approved reciprocal interstate banking. Also, banks could have insurance companies or insurance agencies sell insurance on the premises of the bank.

INSURANCE AND BROKERAGE DIVERSIFICATION

Insurance companies and brokerage firms were not dormant during this period. Many of the money market funds were established or acquired by insurance companies and brokerage firms. In addition, many brokerage firms began to sell insurance products and annuities, while many life insurance companies began to diversify and purchased stock brokerage firms and investment companies. For example, Prudential acquired Bache, John Hancock acquired Tucker Anthony, Equitable acquired DLJ, and Metropolitan acquired Century 21 as well as a large investment management company. Also, companies such as Sears and American Express went on acquisition binges. Sears bought Dean Witter and Coldwell Banker, and set up a nonbank bank (see chapter 2) in Delaware to offer its "Discover Card" which competes with Visa and Mastercard. These purchases by Sears added to their other holdings in the financial services industry, which included Allstate and Sears Savings Bank. American Express bought Shearson and other brokerage firms as well as IDS to add to its international bank, credit card, travel and entertainment business, and Fireman's Fund. Although the sale of insurance products by stock brokerage firms has been modest, it is expected to increase as more brokerage firms begin to sell insurance, as more brokerage firms are acquired by insurers, and as techniques for cross-selling financial products and services become perfected.

In addition to Sears, other retailers such as J.C. Penney, Montgomery Ward, Kroger, K-Mart, and various other supermarkets and regional retailers have become active in the financial services industry. The managements of traditional financial service companies can probably learn something from retailers who do not distinguish themselves by products but rather by the image of their institutions. Stores like Bloomingdale's seek to create their own following. Since the proliferation of vendors within the financial services industry has made it more difficult for consumers to differentiate among products, the image of the seller is becoming increasingly important. Brand loyalty, the ability of a brand to retain its customers over repeated periods of purchase in retailing, must be considered in a different context within the financial services industry. Another way of looking at brand loyalty is in the variety and number of services that a customer takes from the same institution. For banks, brokerage firms, and insurance companies, the more products and services that a company succeeds in selling individual customers, the more likely the customer will be to remain with that institution. An interesting corollary is that it is more expensive and time-consuming to acquire new customers than to retain old ones.

Changing Distribution Systems

The system of selling insurance through career agency systems and independent agents is often thought to be an expensive means of distribution for many insurance companies. Mass marketers, stockbrokers, and banks have attempted to increase their market share at the expense of insurance agents, while insurance companies have attempted to reduce their distribution costs. Insurers are seeking alternative distribution systems that are more cost-efficient.

It also appears as if the consumer has become more sophisticated, better informed, and more price-conscious. Insurance is being viewed by many consumers as a commodity, like sugar. Brand names such as Domino have become less important than price. The same is becoming true of term insurance.

The winners of the financial services battles will be those with the lowest prices per product, those with the most responsive products, and those who can efficiently serve and deliver products to the consumer. Both banks and insurance companies know that when it comes to money matters, customer loyalty is usually not toward the institution but toward cost, convenience, and service.

Companies such as Metropolitan Life took a major step into direct or mass marketing of insurance with an agreement to sell their products and services through *Reader's Digest*. This distribution arrangement to sell insurance to the magazine's 18 million subscribers supplements the sales force of more than 10,000 insurance agents. In a similar move, Provident Mutual acquired Continental Life Insurance Company, which sells insurance directly to consumers via telemarketing. Direct mail with telemarketing support appears to be an extremely cost-effective way to attain maximum penetration of the consumer marketplace, but only a handful of companies have this capability. It is entirely possible that there could be a thinning of the ranks of insurance agents because of substantial changes in distribution methods involving telecommunications and other technology, mass marketing, and the sale of personal lines of insurance by the banks.

Mergers and Acquisitions

With mounting competition in the financial services industry we can expect to see more mergers and acquisitions as stronger institutions acquire weaker ones and as companies attempt to expand their customer bases in an effort to cross-sell additional products and services to supplement their current distribution systems. In addition, cross-industry mergers should increase as more nonfinancial companies decide to enter the financial service industry because the industry is viewed as one of long-run growth potential. Whoever finds a way to effectively distribute multiple service products to a defined market is likely to be a major winner in the financial services arena. The salient question as managers is not whether you can make a merger, but whether you can make a merger work and whether it can be made at a reasonable price. In the merger process, greater efficiencies are usually achieved with aggressive cost cutting, staff reductions, and the merging of technologies. A key skill will be the ability to undertake successful mergers and to achieve economies of scale.[2]

In 1981, three giants of the financial service industry (Sears, Prudential, and American Express) spent a total of $2 billion buying Dean Witter Reynolds, Bache, and Shearson Loeb Rhoades, respectively. After many years, there is only modest evidence of synergy, and the earnings of Prudential-Bache and Dean Witter Reynolds have been disappointing. Despite their considerable resources, the three acquirers do not seem to have significantly enhanced the brokers' profits. Each of these financial giants still has the building blocks of a marketing powerhouse, but with the exception of American Express, mass marketing and cross-selling have not been very effective so far. For example, 15 percent of Prudential's insurance agents and stockbrokers work together and share sales prospects and commissions. By 1990, Prudential hopes that the number will increase to 50 percent. Even American Express has not developed much fruitful interaction between its highly profitable credit card business and Shearson Lehman Hutton, Inc. So far only Sears has offered an incentive to consumers. If you buy or list a house with Coldwell Banker, you are entitled to a 25 to 30 percent discount on furniture purchased at Sears.

According to Ken Nichols, president of Home Life Insurance Co., some of the acquisitions made by insurance companies and financial conglomerates seem to resemble impulse buying rather than acquisitions that follow strategic plans. Anthony Bianco, *Business Week* securities industry analyst, has stated that "the basic failing of the financial supermarkets is that they were structured not to make money, but to chase a dream—the dream of capturing every financial asset in sight through a mass market for financial services." Although the financial supermarkets may "get it right" someday, most are having problems, and for many of them, restructuring has become a way of life.[3]

Changes in Technology

Technological developments have continued to bring fundamental changes to the financial services industry. The growth of automated teller machines (ATMs) and point-of-sale terminals has altered methods of approving credit transactions and has laid the groundwork for wider use of direct-debit systems, which will provide immediate transfer of funds while taking credit out of the credit card system. ATMs have also enabled banks to shorten branch hours and to build smaller and fewer branches. Individual banks have connected their ATMs with those of other regional and national networks through which customers of any participating institution may transfer and obtain currency. Systems have also been developed to allow bill paying by phone or by home computer.

The use of the home computer is also likely to change not only the way we bank, but the way we shop. We can now use the home computer for bank balance inquiries, funds transfer, bill paying, obtaining financial and other information, select data base access, accessing information systems, purchase and sale of stocks and other securities, stock market prices, theater ticket purchasing, race track betting, the sending of messages, news retrieval, travel schedule guides, catalog shopping, and comparative shopping. This last option could gradually help to change the distribution or marketing system for financial services (particularly in personal lines of insurance for those consumers who want to buy insurance at a cheaper price and are not interested in personalized service). While the use of videotex systems and the home computer are still in their infancy, they are likely to play a big role in future payment, information, and distribution systems within the financial services industry once the costs to the customer are reduced.

Although the videotex systems developed by a major newspaper chain and offered in southern California and southern Florida were not a commercial success, the videotex alliance formed by IBM and Sears has accepted the challenge to offer consumers an affordable technologically attractive system. Videotex is a service that harnesses the power of the personal computer to bring electronic shopping, information, and entertainment into the home. Several dozen local and national companies have signed up to offer services, which range from stock brokerage, insurance and banking, to lodging, travel and shopping for groceries, jewelry, clothing, and a variety of durable goods. For example, the subscriber can shop for groceries at the local Kroger supermarket where items are displayed in a list aisle by aisle. The groceries are paid for by credit card and are delivered to the customer's home. In addition, the computer remembers what the shopper bought on previous electronic visits and asks if these items need to be restocked the next time the customer dials into the supermarket.

The user can also book airline and hotel reservations, read newspapers and encyclopedias, obtain sports scores and movie reviews. Local movie theater and sporting event schedules are also available. On the banking front, a user can check account balances, balance the checkbook and transfer funds from savings to checking. The user can also study stock prices on the Dow-Jones financial wire and execute buy and sell orders for stocks and bonds. With a package deal of $150 that includes the new Prodigy system software, six months of access time, modem and all necessary cables and connectors, this videotex system is given a good chance of becoming commercially successful. Videotex systems allow busy people better ways to manage their time and offer 24 hour per day service every day of the week.

The insurance industry has not experienced much deregulation compared with the banking industry. Financial technology has also taken shorter steps in the insurance industry when compared with the great strides in bank payment systems or in securities trading and information systems. Technology in the insurance business means more than back office mechanization; it is also the development of management information systems, brokerage-insurance company computer interfaces, and the reduction in distribution and operating expenses.

BANKS AND INSURANCE

It appears as though the leasing of lobby space by banks to independent agents or insurance companies could enhance bank revenues. The bank receives rental payments, a percentage of sales, or both, as well as list fees and statement stuffer charges, and it provides a service for its customers. The bank participates in a new source of revenue that is not tied directly to its asset base, and is provided with a window into the insurance industry. In the case of deregulation, the bank is positioned positively. It is also in a position to get closer to an insurer should insurance company acquisitions be approved.

The insurance company or agency can also benefit from this leased space arrangement. The advantages to the insurance company are: gaining a new source of sales, using the depository institution's customer lists, benefiting from the good will and reputation of the bank, and sharing the cost of a major expansion of its distribution system. It offers insurers defensive positioning against possible direct entry of banks into selling insurance, and gives them a window on bank operations and a potential new source of ideas for product development. It also permits insurers to get closer to a particular institution with a view toward more permanent affiliation following deregulation. Furthermore, it allows multi-line insurance companies the use or development of cross-selling, for example, life, auto, and homeowner's insurance.[4]

Many large retail-oriented banks would like to sell insurance directly to the public without involving an insurance company or agency. Some banks, such as Citicorp, would also like to be the insurance underwriter. There is also the strong possibility that banks such as Citicorp would have a competitive cost advantage over insurance companies, since it is estimated that certain large banks will be able to save between 40 and 50 percent of the normal 30-percent distribution costs in the insurance industry. This could mean a savings to consumers of 12 to 15 cents on every premium dollar if these cost savings are passed on to them.[5]

Unfortunately, some independent agents and direct writers could be hurt by the loss of business to banks. Some business will be lost because of price factors, while some will be lost because people tend to have faith and trust in their banker and like the concept of a "financial supermarket." In addition, the banker usually has an advantage over the insurance agent when it comes to regular contact with the consumer. On the other hand, most affluent consumers have been taught over the years by Madison Avenue to shop at different stores for specific products. "Upscale" consumers are likely to deal with numerous financial institutions for specialized products and services. The affluent consumer typically desires personal attention, financial planning, and professional advice. Banks are looking for quick sales and not the in-depth advice that is the forte of the independent agent.

While the management of most insurance companies remain opposed to direct bank sales or underwriting of insurance products, there are some industry supporters. In a strong statement related to the underwriting of life insurance by banks, John Carter, chairman of Equitable Life Assurance Society, has claimed that banks should be kept out of the business of making lifetime promises. "The assets backing a policy have got to be there when it comes to deliver on the promise . . . they can't be in Argentina." On the other hand, E. James Morton, president of John Hancock Mutual Life Insurance Co., favors a level playing field. He feels that if banks are permitted to sell insurance, then insurance companies "must offer banking services as well as insurance services and all the rest."[6]

Congress will eventually determine whether banks will be permitted to underwrite insurance and what role insurance companies will play in the traditional banking functions. Until then, the players in the financial services industry are adding as many new products and services as the law allows.

Further Deregulation Possibilities

As previously mentioned, banks have been able to circumvent restrictions on interstate banking by acquiring out-of-state ailing banks and thrifts, and through regional compacts between states whereby reciprocal agreements allow banks to merge across state borders. In addition, bank holding companies have established nonbank banks in numerous states, which have for the most part concentrated on consumer banking.

Some large banks such as Citicorp, Chase Manhattan, and Bankers Trust have received approval from the Federal Reserve to begin dabbling in new underwriting businesses such as commercial paper, mortgage-backed securities, and industrial revenue bonds. Major money-center banks would like to see the removal of the Glass-Steagall Act of 1933, one of the nation's landmark banking laws, which forbids banks from underwriting any corporate securities.

Alan Greenspan, Federal Reserve Board chairman, has supported the position that banks should be able to engage in the broadest range of securities underwriting. As a safeguard, he recommended that the securities operations be confined to a separate unit of a bank holding company so that the commercial bank would be insulated from any risks involved in the securities business. Most banks accept the necessity for separation and insulation of banking from affiliated securities business to protect federally insured deposits.

Greenspan argued that the repeal of the Glass-Steagall Act would respond to the market changes that have already taken place in the financial marketplace and would allow banks to improve their profitability and long-term prospects. The basic argument for modernizing the banking system is that the bank's traditional role of financial intermediation—acting as a middleman for the exchange of funds—has eroded as the marketplace has changed. Essentially, the biggest borrowers are selling directly to the credit markets through issues of commercial paper and mortgage-backed securities. Unless the laws are changed, the basic competitiveness of banks would continue to be reduced as the trend toward direct investor-borrower linkages continues to expand. What is really needed to keep the markets stable and financial institutions profitable are well-managed and well-capitalized financial service companies, whether they are owned by investment banks, commercial banks, or financial conglomerates.

The argument against the repeal of Glass-Steagall is that a combination of banking and securities underwriting would pose significant risks to the banking system. If a large securities unit of a bank were to run into financial difficulty, the bank's financial resources might be used to bail out the securities unit. Such actions could pose a danger to bank depositors and the entire financial system if the problems were large enough.

The Senate Banking Committee, headed by Senator Proxmire, proposed a compromise that would allow banks to breach the Glass-Steagall Act in stages. Commercial bank holding companies would be able to engage in underwriting many types of securities in separate entities that would be independent of the bank within six months after passage of the bill. These entities would be able to underwrite mutual funds and corporate debt issues, but not corporate equity issues. In 1991, Congress would decide whether banks would also gain the ability to underwrite corporate stock. On March 30, 1988, the Proxmire Bill passed the Senate by an overwhelming 94 to 2 vote. This bill would allow banks to own and operate securities firms and would permit securities firms to enter into the banking business. Also, once banks can offer mutual funds, mutual fund companies would be able to purchase banks. If and when Congress allows banks to underwrite corporate equity, securities firms which do not have extremely large insurance and real estate operations will be permitted to operate and acquire banks. Under the bill, securities firms could own banks, and would not be subject to Federal Reserve capital regulation and monitoring of the consolidated organization so long as 80 percent of the organization's consolidated earnings and assets were derived from securities activities and bank subsidiaries remained adequately capitalized.

Presently, several of the largest securities houses are affiliated with insurance, real estate and even commercial firms. Thus, the current version of the bill would not permit these firms to own banks without major divestiture. The Senate bill prevents acquisitions and mergers among the largest banks and securities firms. It specifically blocks banks with assets of over $30 billion from allying themselves with securities firms with assets of more than $15 billion.

Proxmire, who introduced the bill in the fall of 1987, has argued in conjunction with numerous financial experts that developments in the financial industry have altered the competitive dynamics of banking. The Glass-Steagall Act hinders the banking industry from competing effectively with less regulated institutions such as brokerage firms and insurance companies who already offer many quasi-banking products and services.

SUMMARY

Although there used to be some overlap in the products and services offered to the public, banks, insurance companies, and investment banking firms operated and competed against similar companies within traditionally defined boundaries. However, changes in the economy, regulation, technology, marketing, and a more sophisticated and affluent consumer have brought about significant changes in the product lines and services offered by the "retail" players within the financial services industry. Although some companies continue to specialize in their primary area of expertise, we have begun to see the emergence of financial conglomerates and financial supermarkets offering one-stop shopping for financial services. In addition, the proliferation of vendors within the financial services industry has made it difficult for consumers to differentiate among products. With all of these changes taking place, it is going to be difficult for the consumer to tell the difference between Merrill Lynch and Sears or Prudential and Citicorp from the standpoint of the retail financial services offered to consumers, as the distinctions between all the large players in the financial services industry begin to blur.

There are likely to be at least three large power bases remaining after the continued consolidation of the financial services industry. Established banks and insurance companies will represent two of these power bases. A third large power base will come from the customer-oriented organizations that have access to large numbers of potential customers, such as American Express, Merrill Lynch, Sears, Kroger, and J.C. Penney. In a second scenario, we can visualize a world of banks without branches that increasingly rely on media advertising, credit and debit cards, ATMs, and home computers connected with modems, telephone lines, cable television, or videotex systems. A third scenario would have customer interface taking place more frequently at the place of employment, with a complete extension of the concept of employee benefits. Of course, there will still be opportunities for financial boutiques, financial consultants, and insurance agents to provide personal attention and professional guidance in their chosen specialties to upscale consumers and others who require advice and counsel.

NOTES

1. Virginia Chapter of the Society of Chartered Property and Casualty Underwriters, "Competitive Trends in the Financial Services Industry," *CPCU Journal* (September 1981): 78-79.

2. Gart, *Banks, Thrifts, and Insurance Companies: Surviving the 1980s* (Lexington, Mass.: Lexington Books, 1985), 127.

3. *Business Week,* December 23, 1985, 10.

4. C. A. Klem, "An Outline of Issues in Negotiating Agreements on Insurance Activities in Banks," *Banks in Insurance Report* (April 1985): 20-21.

5. *Society Page,* December 1985, 20.

6. E. J. Morton, "Financial Services Deregulation: A Necessity for the Insurance Industry," *The Sears Sounding Board* (Sears Financial Network, 1984): 5.

APPENDIX: Asset Size and Uses of Funds

The largest of the financial institutions with respect to total assets are the commercial banks. Even though there are almost 15,000 commercial banks in the United States, there are more credit unions. Savings and loan associations and life insurance companies have almost the same level of assets, while private pension plans and state and local pension funds were in the fourth and fifth positions at year-end 1987. Savings banks, investment companies, and finance companies were in close competition for sixth place in total asset size. Property-casualty companies were next in asset size, followed by money market funds, and credit unions. (See Table 1.1.)

While some institutions have diversified their portfolio holdings commensurate with deregulation, banks remain the dominant lender to businesses, while thrift institutions remain the dominant factor in the residential mortgage market. Pension funds hold the most equities among financial institutions, while banks, mutual funds, and property-casualty insurance companies are the major institutional holders of tax-exempt securities. Commercial banks are the leading financial intermediary germane to commercial and industrial loans, and the second largest mortgage lender. They are also a major lender of

Table 1.1

Total Assets of Financial Intermediaries at Year-End (Billions of Dollars)

Financial Intermediary	1960	1970	1975	1980	1985	1987*
Commercial Banks	$257.6	$ 576.2	$ 964.9	$1,703.7	$2,483.8	$2,847.1
Savings Institutions:						
Savings Associations	71.5	176.2	338.2	629.8	1,080.6	1,262.0
Savings Banks	40.6	79.0	121.1	171.6	216.8	260.2
Total	112.1	255.2	459.3	801.4	1,297.4	1,522.2
Life Insurance Companies....	119.6	207.3	289.3	479.2	825.9	1,052.2
Private Pension Funds	38.1	112.0	194.5	383.6	606.3	700.8
State and Local						
Pension Funds	19.7	60.3	104.8	198.1	404.7	529.3
Finance Companies........	27.6	64.1	99.1	202.4	354.4	447.8
Money Market Funds.......	. . .	. . .	3.7	76.4	243.8	316.1
Investment Companies	17.0	47.6	42.2	58.4	251.7	453.8
Credit Unions	6.3	18.0	36.9	69.0	137.2	183.7
Total	$598.0	$1,340.7	$2,194.7	$3,972.2	$6,605.2	$8,053.0

*Preliminary.
Sources: CUNA International, Inc.; Federal Home Loan Bank Board; Federal Reserve Board; Institute of Life Insurance; Investment Company Institute; National Council of Savings Institutions; United States League of Savings Institutions.

consumer credit and have large holdings of tax-exempt bonds and government securities. Savings and loans are the dominant factor in the mortgage markets and hold a substantial volume of mortgage-backed securities, while savings banks are also an important lender in the mortgage markets. The portfolios of savings banks are more diversified than those of savings and loans. Credit unions tend to concentrate on consumer credit, although mortgage credit extensions have grown rapidly in the last few years.

Life insurance companies hold huge portfolios of corporate and foreign bonds, as well as mortgages. They have relatively large holdings of U.S. Government and agency securities and common stocks. Policy loans are another important portfolio component. Property-casualty insurance companies have large holdings of municipal bonds and few holdings of commercial mortgages. Corporate bonds, equities, and Treasury and agency securities are among their other salient holdings.

Private pension funds have extremely large holdings of common shares (over 2/3 of assets). Corporate bonds and credit market instruments such as commercial paper, Treasury bills, and certificates of deposit are other important holdings. State and local pension funds invest primarily in three types of securities. Their investments in common stock, corporate bonds, and U.S. Government securities are about equally distributed.

Finance companies are important lenders to businesses and the consumer. Mortgage loans are also an important component of many finance company portfolios. Although the dominant holding of mutual funds is common stock, the various types of mutual funds have enormous holdings of U.S. Government and agency securities, corporate bonds, and tax-exempt securities. In addition, money market funds hold considerable portfolios of commercial paper, Treasury bills, certificates of deposit, and tax-exempt bills and notes. (See Table 1.2.)

The return on equity and assets differs among the various types of financial institutions (see Tables 1.3 and 7.8, and Figure 8.1). These returns vary over the business cycle. However, over the longer term, investment banking firms, large insurance brokerage firms, and stockholder-owned life insurance companies have had the highest returns on equity.

Table 1.2
Assets Outstanding, Year-End 1986 (Billions of Dollars)

	A	B	C	D	E	F	G	H	I
Treasury Securities	204	12	10	89	18	59	46	-	157
Agency securities	113	166	30	35	9	60	31	-	99
Tax-Exempt Securities	203	1	2	65	-	12	92	-	1
Corporate & Foreign Banks	47	20	16	47	-	321	44	-	269
Corporate Equities	-	-	NA	161	-	83	68	-	606
Mortgages	503	665	119	-	18	193	5	68	23
Consumer Credit	320	51	19	-	79	54*	-	163	-
Business Loans	719	24	10	-		-	-	175	-
Open-Market Paper	11	26		9		26	-	-	52
Other	461	193	33	8	52	97	60	6	(102)
Total	$ 2581	1158	239	414	166	905	346	412	1105

A: Commercial Banks; B: S&Ls; C: Mutual Savings Banks; D: Open-End
Investment Companies; E: Credit Unions; F: Life Insurance Companies;
G: P/C Companies; H: Finance Companies; I: Pension Funds;

Source: Flow of Funds Accounts Financial Assets and Liabilities, Year-
End, 1963-1986, Board of Governors of Federal Reserve System,
September 1987.

* Policy Loans

Table 1.3
Return on Equity at Other Selected Financial Institutions, 1975-1984

Industry	1980 – 1984	1975 – 1984
Commercial Banking	12.2%	12.3%
17 Multinational BHCs.............	13.0[2]	13.1[2,3]
Finance Companies[4]	12.6	11.4
Mortgage Companies[4]	13.1	13.7[5]
Securities	18.7	16.4
Investment Banks.................	26.0	21.5
Other Securities.................	15.8	14.5
Life Insurance	13.4	13.7
Stockholder-owned...............	15.2	15.6
Mutual..........................	10.5	10.6
Property and Casualty Insurance	7.4	10.9[6]
Stockholder-owned...............	7.7	11.2[6]
Mutual..........................	7.4	9.8[6]
Insurance Brokerage		
Large Firms.....................	18.3	22.5[6]
Small Firms.....................	9.2	12.5[6]
Diversified Financial Firms[7]	13.1	14.0

[1] Returns for commercial banks, securities firms, life insurers, and property and casualty insurers are based on average equity. Because of limited availability of data, returns for finance companies, mortgage companies, and insurance brokers are based on year-end equity. By way of comparison, nonfinancial firms (represented by those included in Standard & Poor's 400 stock index) reported average returns of 13.7 percent over 1980-84 and 14.0 percent over 1975-84.

[2] Excludes Crocker and Continental Illinois in 1984.

[3] 1976 – 1984.

[4] Excluding subsidiaries of bank holding companies.

[5] 1978 – 1984.

[6] 1976 – 1984, one complete underwriting cycle.

[7] Aetna Life & Casualty, American Express, Beneficial Corporation, Household International, E.F. Hutton, Merrill Lynch, Transamerica, and Sears Roebuck.

Source: Federal Reserve Bank of New York, *Recent Trends in Commercial Bank Profitability, A Staff Study.* New York: Federal Reserve Bank of New York, 1986.

2

Introduction to Commercial Banking

HISTORICAL BACKGROUND

The first bank in the United States, the Bank of North America, was established in Philadelphia in 1782. The bank was granted the power to issue bank notes which could be exchanged for their equivalent value in metallic coins. Patterned after the success of the Bank of North America, banks were opened in New York and Boston in 1784 and in a number of other cities prior to 1800.

There was both political and economic controversy over the establishment of banks in the United States during the colonial period. In addition to the controversy over whether states or the federal government should charter banks, the commercial sector supported banking, while the agricultural sector opposed it. Business forces favored a strong banking industry that stimulated capital formation and promoted trade by providing capital and a supply of money. Agrarian interests believed that banks favored industry and commerce at the expense of farming interests and frontier areas of the country. They also felt that banks lowered the quality of the nation's money because bank notes and deposits displaced silver and gold coins from circulation.

Banks chartered by individual states were the dominant factors in the American banking scene until the establishment of a national banking system in 1863. The state banks suffered through numerous financial panics, crises of confidence, and business recessions.

Congress had a few broad goals in designing the National Bank Acts: (1) to provide the nation with a safe and uniform currency system; (2) to provide for the establishment of a system of federally chartered banks that would be owned and operated by private individuals; and (3) to provide a new source of loans to finance the Civil War.

The banking acts also established higher minimum capital requirements for the protection of depositors, as well as minimum reserve requirements against the banks' deposits and notes outstanding. A problem with state banking at that time was that some states had poorly designed and enforced banking regulations which often did not adequately protect depositor safety or protect the public against counterfeit notes issued by banks.

The National Banking Act permitted the Treasury Department to establish the Office of the Comptroller of the Currency, whose responsibility was to supervise, administer, and examine national banks. National bank notes were printed by the U.S. Treasury Department to ensure standardization and quality of printing, and to reduce the possibility of counterfeiting, which was a serious problem with over 1,500 state banks that issued nonuniform notes before the Civil War. The national bank notes were redeemable by another bank only at a substantial discount.

The existence of both a national and a state chartered banking system is known as the dual banking system. That distinction exists today. The concepts of reserve requirements and limitations on loans to any one borrower which were established in 1863 also continue today.

Although the National Banking Acts of 1863 and 1864 did not reinstate central banking, they did correct some of the major problems of state banking. Two major shortcomings of these acts were the lack of a flexible or elastic currency supply and the pyramiding of reserves, which was responsible for the tendency of the banking system to precipitate liquidity squeezes. The aforementioned deficiencies often led to financial panics and economic depressions. In 1913, in response to the financial panics of 1873, 1884, 1893, and 1907, Congress established the Federal Reserve System. This marked the return of central banking after an absence of three-quarters of a century following the demise of the Second Bank of the United States. After the passage of the Federal Reserve Act, no major changes were made in the banking system until after the massive bank failures that coincided with or followed the Great Depression of 1929. A number of bank measures were enacted in the postdepression period in order to protect banks and their depositors. For example, Congress prohibited the payment of interest on demand deposits and limited interest payments on bank savings deposits. In addition, Congress gave the Federal Reserve power to impose selective credit controls on margin credit purchases of stocks. This power was granted to help prevent repetitions of the 1929 stock market crash and the ensuing economic decline.

WHAT IS A COMMERCIAL BANK?

The etymology of the word "bank" can be traced to the French word "banque" (meaning chest) and the Italian word "banca" (meaning bench). "Chest" suggests the safekeeping function, while "bench" refers to the table, counter, or place of business of a money changer, and suggests the transaction function. The two basic functions that commercial banks perform are (1) the safekeeping function (providing a safe place to store savings); and (2) the transaction function (furnishing a means of payment for buying goods and services).[1] Banks also perform a lending function, supplying liquidity to the economy. As a matter of fact, in the 1970 amendment to the Bank Holding Company Act of 1956, the U.S. Congress defined a commercial bank as a financial institution that makes commercial loans and accepts demand deposits.

WHAT IS A NONBANK BANK?

This definition is important because by not engaging in either commercial lending or demand deposit activities a corporation can run and operate a quasi-bank without being subject to Federal Reserve regulation as a bank holding company. These quasi-banks are usually referred to as "nonbank banks." Many of these nonbank banks have chosen to forgo commercial lending; these financial institutions have been referred to as consumer banks. Alternatively, another type of limited service bank can make consumer and commercial loans, accept all deposit forms with the exception of demand deposits, and still escape the Bank Holding Company Act definition of a bank. As a matter of fact, both types of limited-purpose banks can be owned by the same parent company, thus offering complementary and complete banking services.

Many retailers, brokerage firms, insurance companies, financial service conglomerates, and industrial companies have taken advantage of the nonbank-bank loophole to enter the banking business. Companies such as Sears, Fidelity Management, Dreyfus, Prudential, Aetna, J.C. Penney, Parker Pen, Merrill Lynch, Dimension Financial Corp., General Electric, Household International, and Chrysler Corporation have all established nonbank banks. Even some bank holding companies, such as Citicorp and Chase Manhattan Corporation, have set up nonbank banks in attractive suburban locations throughout the United States in order to circumvent regulatory restrictions against interstate banking. As of this writing, the nonbank loophole has been closed, but of those nonbank banks that were established before March 1, 1987, some have been permitted to operate. However, there is a restriction on the annual growth of assets of these nonbank banks.

COMMERCIAL BANKS DECLINE IN IMPORTANCE

Prior to December 31, 1980 (earlier for the New England states), commercial banks had a monopoly of the transaction function as they were the only financial institutions to have demand deposit or checking account powers. Currently, commercial banks share this power with savings banks, savings and loan associations, credit unions, money market funds, mutual funds, and brokerage firms that offer check-writing services.

Unlike nonfinancial firms, a bank's assets consist mainly of financial assets as opposed to physical assets. The typical bank has only about 2 percent of its assets tied up in fixed assets such as buildings, equipment, furniture, and fixtures. Most bank assets are in the form of loans to businesses, consumers, and government, and in the form of investments in Treasury, agency, and municipal securities.

Most of a commercial bank's liabilities are in the form of deposits held by consumers, businesses, and government. Two salient aspects of bank deposits are (1) the short-term nature of the deposits and (2) the large volume of deposits and borrowed funds relative to the equity-capital base. Another balance sheet characteristic is that banks have a high degree of financial leverage. Financial leverage is often referred to as capital adequacy and is commonly measured by a bank's capital-to-asset ratio.

Even though commercial banks are still currently the largest of the financial intermediaries, banks have begun to decline in relative importance within the financial services industry. Since 1975, banking's market share of total financial assets held by financial institutions has declined by nearly 20 percent. At the same time, other financial service providers, especially mutual funds, money market funds, and finance companies, have had an increase in market share.

Commercial lending at large banks has declined from a 71 percent share of the short-term credit of domestic nonfinancial corporations in 1975, to about 50 percent in 1987. (See Figure 2.1.) Much of this market share was lost to the lower-priced commercial paper market. Also, the share of commercial bank holdings of outstanding auto loans has declined from over 52 percent in 1980 to under 40 percent in 1987. Much of this decline is related to below-market-rate loans offered by auto-affiliated finance companies.

Another key development in bank lending markets is the trend toward securitization. Banks have traditionally collected funds through deposits and loaned these funds to borrowers. Recent advances in information technology and reductions in underwriting and transactions costs have shifted the underlying cost advantage away from this traditional form of intermediation toward direct funding in the securities markets. The trend toward securitization has spread to mortgages, auto loans, and consumer receivables. It is expected that securities will be issued that will eventually be backed by commercial loans, agricultural loans, foreign loans, and student loans. The bottom line is that the basic nature of some important bank lending markets is changing as traditional lending markets in which banks can participate are shrinking.[2]

Since the Great Depression, the banking industry has functioned remarkably well within its regulatory boundaries. However, the historically comfortable fit between the industry and its regulatory framework has been strained recently as banks face new competitors and changing markets. The Glass-Steagall Act, which imposes sweeping prohibitions on the securities activities of commercial banks, as well as other outdated laws, have prevented banking organizations from introducing new products and services to meet customer needs. Diversified financial service firms have rushed in to fill the void between the services customers want and the service banks can legally provide.[3]

Figure 2.1
Large Bank Commercial Loans as a Percentage of Total Short-Term
Borrowing* of Nonfinancial Corporations, 1975-1985

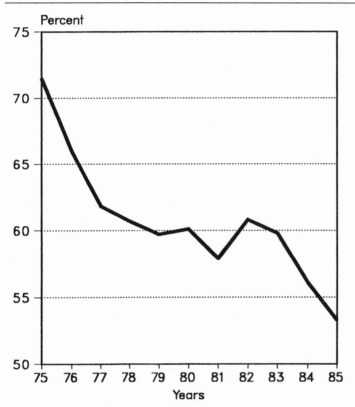

* Short-term borrowing includes: Commercial Paper, Acceptances, Finance
  Company Loans, and Commercial and Industrial Loans at Large Banks
Sources: Federal Reserve Board Flow of Funds Accounts and Federal Reserve
  Bulletin.

While for more than half a century banks were largely regarded as demand
deposit institutions with a peripheral concern for savings and time deposits,
current data reveals that this is no longer the case. In addition, in the past the
typical commercial banker was primarily an asset manager, who loaned and
invested the demand deposits that continuously flowed into the banking system.
Today's banker must be both a liability manager and an asset manager. The
banks must be concerned with the volume of fixed- versus variable-rate loans,
the maturity of these loans, and the mixture, nature, and cost of deposits used to
fund the loan and investment portfolio. Generally speaking, banks find that they
must buy whatever funds they need in a way that combines the principles of
liquidity, safety, and profitability. With a significantly larger share of their

deposit liabilities now interest-rate-sensitive, banks are more exposed to earning swings because of changes in interest rates. Banks have sought to reduce interest-rate risk by more closely matching the maturities of assets and liabilities, by hedging, and by using interest-rate swaps.

In mid-1987, non-interest-bearing demand deposits accounted for about 16 percent of all deposits in the commercial banking system, compared to 74 and 43 percent respectively in 1950 and 1974. These cost-free deposits are no longer the bank's basic source of funds; consumer savings and time accounts, NOW accounts and deregulated money market accounts, along with large CDs (certificates of deposit) and Eurodollar deposits dominate the liability side of most balance sheets of large banks. In addition, bank holding companies utilize large amounts of commercial paper. The higher-cost liabilities have brought with them problems in the management of funds to which the prior generation of bankers was never exposed.

CATEGORIZATION OF BANKS

Prior to the 1980s, banks were generally classified by either geographic presence or business orientation into three major categories:

Geographical Presence:
1. Money-center banks (operating in national and international markets);
2. Major regional banks (operating primarily in regional markets);
3. Local community banks (operating in local markets).

Business Presence:
1. Wholesale banks (e.g., J.P. Morgan and Banker's Trust);
2. Retail banks (most community banks);
3. Wholesale/retail banks (Chase Manhattan and Bank of America).

A wholesale bank has a commercial, corporate focus, while a retail bank focuses on consumer business, with loan and deposit transactions characterized by much smaller size and higher activity than a wholesale bank would typically experience. A wholesale/retail bank is one with a more balanced mix of consumer and corporate accounts.

James H. Wooden, vice president and financial services industry analyst with Merrill Lynch, has suggested another possible configuration or classification of the emerging financial structure in the 1980s. He identified five categories of financial institutions:[4]

1. National nonbank, primarily retail-oriented, financial service firms that would include for example, American Express, Prudential, Merrill Lynch, and Sears;

2. National banks with heavy emphasis on technologically based management and product delivery systems that would include, for example, Bank America, Citicorp, Chase Manhattan, and First Interstate Bancorp;

3. Mostly wholesale commercial banks that perhaps might involve combinations with investment banks should the Glass-Steagall Act change. This would include Morgan

Guaranty, Banker's Trust, Continental Illinois, First Chicago, Northern Trust, and Harris Trust;

4. Strong regional or semiregional holding companies, quite possibly including savings and loans as part of them. These would serve the retail and mid-sized corporate market and would be consolidated units in terms of management structure, with a regional base. These might include PNC, Meritor, NCNB, Wachovia, Corestates, Bank of New England, and other strong regional banks;

5. None of the above: This would include the boutiques and other specialized institutions and select thrift institutions.

Another categorization scheme was developed by D. C. Waite, who classified financial institutions as having Type 1, Type 2, or Type 3 characteristics. Type 1 institutions are heavily capitalized national distribution companies with relatively low debt-to-equity ratios. These companies have well-developed information on costs of individual products and customers. They tend to emphasize cost control and cost reduction. They make rapid price adjustments to bring prices in line with costs. These companies tend to have expertise in managing a broad distribution network with integrated operational capability. Type 1 companies have product development and marketing expertise with the capability to maintain a flow of innovative products. These companies have a clear sense of corporate direction, with effective planning capability, and tend to undertake selective acquisitions to broaden expertise or sales coverage. Major nonbank financial institutions such as Merrill Lynch and American Express, as well as the largest money-center banks, are classified as Type 1 institutions.[5]

Type 2 firms are generally low-cost producers with characteristics that include narrow, simple product lines and require minimal service. They tend to aggressively discount prices relative to conventional producers. There is a line rather than a staff emphasis, with low structural personnel costs. These firms expand through reproduction of low-cost systems and emphasize low prices in their advertising. Examples of Type 2 firms would be discount brokers, no-load mutual funds, new entrants, and some of the major nonbank financial institutions.[6]

Type 3 companies are specialty firms that emphasize product or customer segments rather than geographic niches. These companies have expertise in products or markets that cannot be unbundled easily or have not been highly price-sensitive. Of recent vintage, these firms have deemphasized their remaining price-sensitive products and increased their emphasis on fees for service. They delineate a well-defined market segment, selectively acquire their competitors to deepen rather than broaden expertise, and emphasize information advertising rather than image or price advertising. Type 3 characteristics can be found among small banks and thrifts, second-tier commercial banks (asset size over $1 billion) and nonbank financial institutions (major savings institutions and finance companies). Some of the major money-center banks might also be categorized as Type 3 companies (See Figure 2.2).[7]

Banks can also be classified by their structure. There are unit banks, branch

Figure 2.2
Bank Classification or Categories

```
Charter
     National Bank
     State Bank

Structure
     Unit Bank
     Retail Bank
     Holding Company Bank

Type of Business
     Wholesale Bank
     Retail Bank
     Wholesale/Retail Bank

Geographic Market
     Money-Center or Multinational Bank
     Regional Bank
     Community Bank

Other Characteristics
     Type I      -heavily capitalized national distribution
                  companies
     Type II     -low cost producers with narrow, simple
                  product line
     Type III    -specialty firms that emphasize product or
                  customer segment
```

banks, and holding company banks. Within a holding company, a bank may be either a unit bank or a branch type.

BANK HOLDING COMPANIES

A holding company is a corporation or organization that owns other firms. Commercial banks are either independent or owned by a holding company. Bank holding companies (BHCs) developed as a way to circumvent laws and regulations that were restricting the growth of commercial banks. Another reason for forming BHCs was the tax advantage gained from filing a consolidated tax return. The BHC umbrella has been utilized to avoid geographical restrictions placed on commercial banks and to form or acquire additional subsidiaries in financially related activities.

With full-scale interstate branching still legally prohibited, BHCs have concentrated on expansion in areas of nonbank services not excluded by the McFadden Act (see Glossary). Through acquisitions and new installations, bank holding companies have established factoring companies, consumer and commercial finance companies, leasing companies, real estate investment trusts

(REITs), investment or financial advising firms, courier service, credit and debit card companies, credit life insurance, insurance agencies, industrial banks, nonbank financial institutions such as Merrill Lynch and American Express, as well as the largest money-center banks, are classified as Type 1 institutions.[5] BHCs can engage in these activities anywhere in the United States and are not limited by state laws on branch and unit banking. Some of these locations could be converted into actual branches if enabling legislation were passed. Some bank holding companies have been allowed by the Federal Reserve to acquire savings and loans that were in jeopardy of failure in other states. Equally important, BHCs can compete more effectively with nonbanking companies such as American Express, Prudential-Bache, and Merrill Lynch which are making consumer and business loans, but are not regulated in the same fashion as banks.

In addition to their regular banking businesses, bank holding companies are permitted to expand into closely related nonbanking areas. Table 2.1 lists the domestic nonbank activities permitted by regulation or specific Federal Reserve Board order. Ownership of finance companies and mortgage companies (allowed by the 1971 regulations) are the permitted activities most frequently engaged in by bank holding companies.

Large banks are battling with the investment banking industry and the regulatory authorities over the right to underwrite various mortgage-backed securities and industrial revenue bonds. Banks cannot underwrite most municipal revenue bonds, although the Glass-Steagall Act permits banks to underwrite municipal general obligation bonds and housing and education-oriented revenue bonds. Banks may underwrite the mortgage-backed securities of federally sponsored agencies, but banks may not underwrite privately issued mortgage-backed securities. Even though banks can make, hold, and sell commercial, agricultural, and consumer loans, they cannot underwrite or distribute securities backed by these loans. It is interesting to note that the nonbank subsidiaries of bank holding companies account for only 6.4 percent of total bank holding company assets.

Table 2.2 lists the domestic nonbank activities that have been denied by the Federal Reserve Board, along with the reasons for the denial. This list includes activities in the areas of insurance, real estate, securities, data processing, travel agencies, and providing credit ratings on bonds, preferred stock, and commercial paper.

It should be mentioned that there are one-bank and multibank holding companies. The implementation of BHC functions have for the most part been beneficial to customers as well as the banks themselves. The record of the Federal Reserve in considering requests for acquisition for nonbank entities by BHCs clearly indicates that approval was granted only after benefits to the public such as lower service charges, lower interest rates on loans, and greater choices for sources of a particular service could be identified. The BHC framework offers excellent opportunities for meeting both wholesale and retail banking needs and servicing as wide a clientele as possible, both at home and abroad.

Table 2.1

Domestic Nonbank Activities Permitted by Regulation or Specific Federal Reserve Board Order and Date of Initial Approval

Nonbanking Activities Approved

Year	By Regulation	By Specific Order
1971	– Making and servicing loans – Industrial banking – Trust company functions – Investment or financial advice – Leasing personal or real property – Community development – Data processing (significantly expanded in 1982) – Insurance sales	Operating a "pool reserve plan" for the pooling of loss reserves of banks with respect to loans to small businesses.
1972	– Underwriting credit life, accident and health insurance	Operating a thrift institution in Rhode Island.
1973	– Courier services	Buying and selling gold and silver bullion and silver coin.
1974	– Management consulting to depository institutions (expanded to other than commercial banks in 1982) – Leasing real property	None
1975	– None	Operating a guaranty savings bank in New Hampshire.
1976	– None	None
1977	– None	Operating an Article XII Investment Company under New York State Law.
1978	– None	None
1979	– Issuance and/or sale of money orders (up to $1,000 face value), savings bonds, and travelers checks (issuance of travelers checks added in 1981)	Retail check authorization and check guaranty services. Providing consumer-oriented financial management courses, counseling, and related financial materials.
1980	– Real estate appraising	None
1981	– None	None
1982	– None	Engaging in commercial banking activities overseas through branches of a nonbank Delaware company. Operating a distressed savings and loan association.

Table 2.1 (continued)

Year	By Regulation	By Specific Order
1983	– None	Operating a limited-purpose National bank that conducts credit card activities only.
1984	– Arranging commercial real estate equity financing – Securities brokerage – Underwriting and dealing in government obligations and money market instruments – Foreign exchange advisory and transactional services – Acting as a Futures Commission Merchant ("FCM")	Issuing consumer-type payment instruments having a face value of not more than $10 thousand. Operating a "nonbank bank" through a limited purpose commercial bank charter. FCM brokerage of futures contracts on a municipal bond index, and related futures advisory services. Providing financial feasibility studies for private corporations; performing valuations of companies and a large blocks of stock for a variety of purposes; providing expert witness testimony on behalf of utility firms in rate cases.
1985	– None	FCM brokerage of certain futures contracts on stock indexes, and options on such contracts. Tax preparation services for individuals performed in a nonfiduciary capacity. Credit card authorization services and lost/stolen credit card reporting services. Employee benefits consulting activities. Expanded student loan servicing activities. Issuance and sale of official checks with no limitation on the maximum face value, but subject to certain limitations.
1986	– None	Underwriting and reinsuring home mortgage redemption insurance.

Source: Appendices to the statement by Paul A. Volcker, Chairman, Board of Governors of the Federal Reserve System, before the Subcommittee on Commerce, Consumer and Monetary Affairs, Committee on Government Operations, U.S. House of Representatives, June 1986.

Table 2.2
Domestic Nonbank Activities Denied by the Federal Reserve Board
and Reason for Denial

Year	Activity Denied	Reason
1971	Insurance premium funding ("equity funding") (combined sale of mutual funds and insurance).	Potential for conflict of interest and unsound banking practices.
	Underwriting general life insurance not related to extensions of credit.	No reasonable basis for a finding that activity was closely related to banking.
1972	Real estate brokerage.	Not closely related to banking.
	Land investment and development.	Has not been and is not permissible; not closely related to banking.
	Real estate syndication.	Inconsistent with Glass-Steagall Act. Activities go beyond those of REIT advisor and are not closely related to banking.
	General management consulting.	Conflicts of interest and combining of banking and commerce.
	Property management services generally.	No basis found to support permissibility.
1973	Sale of level term credit life insurance.	Not directly related to an extension of credit.
	Armored car services.	Deferral of a decision by the Board due to lack of interest and evidence presented by bank holding companies at rulemaking.
1974	Underwriting mortgage guaranty insurance.	Not appropriate at the time in light of untested activity, and need of BHCs to slow their rate of expansion and strengthen their existing operations.
	Operating a savings and loan association (except in Rhode Island, or unless the S&L is distressed).	(Related to specific case only). Public benefits do not outweigh adverse effects because of financial strain placed on applicant by funding requirements. (See 1977 below.)
1975	Computer output microfilm service where it is not an output device for otherwise permissible data processing services.	Not a financially related activity.

26

Table 2.2 (continued)

Year	Activity Denied	Reason
1976	Operating a travel agency.	Insufficient historical relationship to general nature of banking to be closely related; not functionally or integrally related to other permissible banking activities.
1977	Operating a savings and loan association (except in Rhode Island, or unless the S&L is distressed.	(Related to specific case only). Elimination of existing competition. (General considerations). Conflict between regulatory frameworks, erosion of institutional rivalry, and deferral to Congress as to proper means of regulating "near bank" thrifts.
1978	Underwriting property and casualty insurance.	Applicant did not meet its burden of proof that activity met National Courier tests.
1980	Real estate advisory activities.	No reasonable basis found for permissibility.
	Underwriting home loan mortgage life insurance (subsequently approved).	Banks have not traditionally engaged in the activity; not integrally related to lending transaction or otherwise functionally or integrally related to banking. More like term life insurance.
	Certain contract, key entry, data processing services.	Services were not data processing or a reasonably necessary incident thereto (alteration of form, not substance, of data).
1982	Offering investment notes with transactional features.	Public confusion regarding uninsured status of notes and lack of diversification of investments. Also, circumvention of Regulation Q.
1985	Providing credit ratings on bonds, preferred stock and commercial paper.	Conflict of interest between a major lender and a rating company are pervasive; particularly serious given relatively few rating companies in industry.
1986	Acting as a specialist in foreign currency options on a security exchange.	Financial risk, insufficient skill and experience to manage risk, and potential for conflicts of interest.
	Title insurance activities.	Violates Garn-St Germain limits on insurance activities.

Source: Appendices to the statement by Paul A. Volcker, Chairman, Board of Governors of the Federal Reserve System, before the Subcommittee on Commerce, Consumer and Monetary Affairs, Committee on Government Operations, U.S. House of Representatives, June 1986.

27

Bank holding companies accounted for approximately 95 percent of domestic commercial banking assets in 1987. The development of bank holding companies reflects a more competitive environment from banks and nonbanks in the battle for consumer financial services and a restrictive legislative and regulative climate. The holding company form of organization allows bank holding companies to engage in some activities that are not permitted to commercial banks and provides for geographic expansion beyond state boundaries.

With the passage of the Garn-St. Germain Act of 1982, the limitation on full-service bank expansion across state lines through the use of holding companies began to erode because banks were permitted to buy large failing banks and any size of troubled thrift in other states. Some states even permitted these savings and loans to be converted into banks. In addition, a number of states passed legislation allowing out-of-state ownership of banks primarily on a reciprocal basis. By mid-1987 more than half of the states had adopted legislation permitting out-of-state banks (usually within a specified region) to merge with or to purchase banks within that state.

One-bank holding companies can be classified into three groups: traditional, conglomerate, and congeneric. Traditional one-bank holding companies are the largest group and are usually closely held corporations set up to control a small bank. However, they may also be involved in insurance, finance, or real estate. Conglomerate one-bank holding companies are nonfinancial organizations that own a bank, like Goodyear Tire and Rubber Company. There are also nonprofit foundations, labor unions, and charitable trusts that own banks. Congeneric one-bank holding companies are organized by large banks to engage in financially related businesses.

One-bank holding companies account for more than 80 percent of the total number of bank holding companies. More than half of the one-bank holding companies are located in states with unit banking laws. The largest number of holding companies are found in states with restrictive banking laws and the smallest number in states that permit statewide branch banking. Multibank holding companies may be used as a substitute for branch banking where there is restrictive legislation on branching. A feature of multibank holding companies lies in their ability to realize many of the benefits and render most of the services of widespread branch banking organizations while retaining the decentralization of management at the local level.

An advantage of expansion of services through holding company subsidiaries is that it insulates the bank from the commercial ventures of the holding company; that is, the obligations of the holding company are not obligations of the bank. They are separate and distinct legal entities. The activities of the holding company do not affect the safety and soundness of the holding company's bank subsidiary or involve the bank's capital.

BRANCHES

A consequence of interstate banking limitations has been a highly fragmented banking system composed of close to 14,531 banks with 42,255 branches, which made a total of 59,786 banking institutions as of May 1987. Many of these banks are small banking organizations serving rural communities. In contrast, most industrial nations have a highly concentrated banking system, composed of a small number of banking organizations with branches throughout the nation. Canada has 11 domestic commercial banks, of which 5 dominate the country's financial structure. In England, a handful of clearing "banks" control 60 percent of all bank deposits with a network of 12,000 branches. In France, where there are 86 commercial banks, the 5 largest control over 75 percent of the deposits.

With thousands of banks operating without branches, the average size of a U.S. bank is usually much smaller than its counterpart in other countries. While about 70 percent of the U.S. banks held assets under $100 million in 1986, most large banks abroad held at least $1 billion in assets. In the United States about 2 percent of all banks are in the over-$1 billion category. While the U.S. banking system is dominated numerically by small banks, there is a heavy concentration of market power in the hands of about two dozen giant-sized institutions. Although competition among banks themselves (and among bank and nonbank financial institutions) has intensified, there does appear to be a gradual consolidation of resources into fewer but larger banking and nonbanking organizations. These institutions are offering a wider variety of products and services in an effort to diversify, to enter new markets, and to open up new sources of potential profitability.

Many small banks still exist because the directors of these banks, who are the principal stockholders, take a paternalistic view of the communities they serve. The salary scales of small banks are low and they do not participate in many of the low-profit-margin activities of some of the giant banks, allowing net profits to make up a higher percentage of assets than at much larger banks. Other reasons for the higher return on assets are that there are often no other banks serving the area, and loan losses are minimal because the board of directors will be thoroughly familiar with the credit standing of all residents in the community.

The ability to operate branch offices is determined by state law. A branch bank is a banking facility not in the main office that is capable of offering services similar to those of the main office; it can make loans and investments, receive deposits, make withdrawals, and carry out other functions of the main bank. The courts have ruled that remote automated teller machines be classified as branches. Given these definitions of a branch bank, state laws can be divided into three main categories: (1) laws that permit statewide branch banking; (2) laws that permit branching within limited geographic areas; and (3) laws that prohibit branch banking. (See Figure 2.3.)

The terms "statewide," "limited," and "unit banking" are conventional

Figure 2.3
State Branch Banking Laws, November 1986

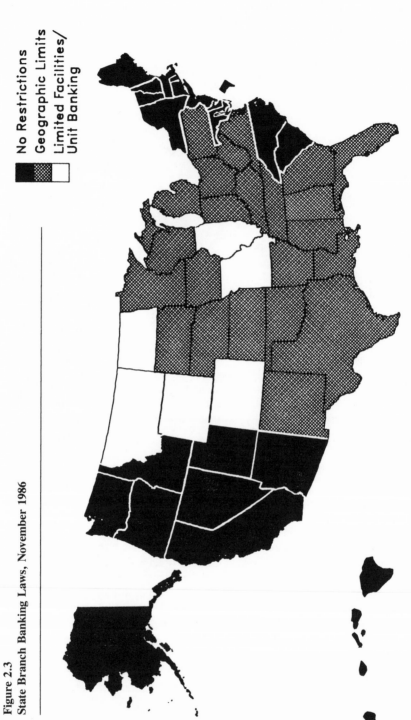

No Restrictions

Geographic Limits

Limited Facilities/
Unit Banking

Source: American Bankers Association, Office of the General Counsel.

ways to classify banking structures. Some of the states that prohibit branch banking and the number of banks in each are Colorado (525), Illinois (1,212), Kansas (609), Missouri (606), Montana (171), North Dakota (180), Oklahoma (522), and Tennessee (285).

The restrictive policies of many states related to branch banking led commercial banks to seek some method of circumventing the regulations in order to serve more customers in more than one locality even when state laws specifically prohibit actual branching. Some states with restrictive branching laws allow group or chain banking to exist. In chain banking, the stock ownership of common directors exerts control over several independent banks, while in group banking, two or more banks are under the control of a holding company, which is not necessarily a commercial bank. Most of these banks are located in the Midwest and the South. Also, some large money-center banks have opened loan production offices throughout the country in cities with major corporate headquarters. Although these loan production offices cannot accept deposits or cash checks, they primarily function to obtain business loans. It is ironic that while some states debate whether a bank can have a branch one-quarter mile from its main office, other banks are branching on a nationwide and international scale by operating domestic loan production offices and Edge corporations (see Chapter 6) in major important export centers of the country where international loans are needed. In addition, the holding company structure permits finance company and mortgage banking offices, as well as credit card loans and facilities throughout the country, even though interstate banking was prohibited by the McFadden Act.

At the end of World War II, the country had less than 5,000 operating branch banks. Commensurate with the prosperity that followed World War II was the spread of branch banking and consolidation of smaller banks into bigger ones through mergers and acquisitions. Between the end of the war and 1970, over 3,000 unit banks were acquired in massive merger movements. Despite the gradual replacement of unit banks by branching systems, the number of banks has expanded gradually. Demographic forces such as migration from Northern states to Southern and Western states and from cities to suburbs, as well as economic forces, stimulated the demand for banking services and opened up new markets.

In addition to increased branching activity, there has been an increase in merger activity. Following merger transactions, the public has generally been charged lower rates on loans and has received modestly higher rates on some type of deposits and reduced service charges on deposits. On the negative side, although the overall bank size rose, contributing to management prestige and salary increases, mergers did little for stockholders except in the acquired bank.

The merger movement is rapidly changing the competitive face of banking as large regional banks move across state lines. While the number of banks is dropping slowly, the concentration of assets appears to be growing more rapidly. This consolidation is evident when the holding companies and not just individual banks are considered. Many of these consolidations have occurred in the Southeastern, Middle-Atlantic and New England states. Holding companies such as PNC, Corestates, NCNB, Wachovia, Sun, Citizens and Southern, Fleet Financial, Banc One, and Bank of New England have grown dramatically in size and have become regional retail powerhouses with intentions of remaining independent of the New York bank holding companies (these will be permitted to expand nationally in the 1990s). New York bank holding companies that wished to expand have set up consumer banks (nonbank banks) across state lines and acquired troubled thrifts or banks in other states permitted under the Garn-St. Germain Bill. The large bank holding companies have also expanded across state borders with loan production offices, consumer finance companies, leasing companies, and commercial finance companies. The aforementioned interstate mergers have substantially lifted the prices of stocks of potential bank acquisition candidates. (See Figures 2.4 and 2.5.)

THE DUAL BANKING SYSTEM

The American banking system is known as a dual system because its main feature is side-by-side federal and state chartering and supervision of commercial banks. This system permits the regulated parties to choose their regulator; national banks can shift to nonmember status and vice versa. Roughly two-thirds of the commercial banks have state charters; however, the one-third with national charters hold more than half of the assets in the commercial banking system. (See Table 2.3.) Federally chartered banks must include "national" or "national association" in their title and must be members of both the FDIC and Federal Reserve System. Thus, only a state bank can be a noninsured bank.

With the exception of one state-owned bank in North Dakota, most commercial banks are owned by public shareholders. There are also approximately 15 private banks in the United States. These banks are partnerships and are not eligible to be members of the Federal Reserve or the FDIC. These private banks are not even examined by federal government bank examiners. In the case of large money-center banks and regional banks, most bank stocks are traded actively. However, the stocks of many smaller banks are not traded actively and are often held by a small number of shareholders.

ASSET AND LIABILITY CONSTRAINTS

Banks are required to hold cash or reserves at the Federal Reserve as a percentage of deposits, with the percentage required for time and savings deposits generally lower than that required for demand deposits (see the next section on reserve requirements). The deregulated money-market-type account that was approved for use on December 14, 1982, has no reserve requirements. With a few trivial exceptions, no equity-type assets can be acquired. Earning

Table 2.3
Status of Insured Commercial Banks, June 30, 1986

	Number of Banks 14,186		Total loans and Investments $1,847,784	
All Commercial Banks	Number	Percent	Amount	Percent
National Banks	4,866	34	$1,088,052	59
State Banks	9,320	66	759,732	41
Federal Reserve Member Banks	5,954	42	1,362,285	74
Non-Member Banks	8,232	58	485,499	26

Source: Board of Governors of the Federal Reserve System:
73rd Annual Report, 1986

assets are confined to debt obligations or loans of domestic and foreign governmental units and agencies, corporations, or individuals.

Banks with national charters may not lend more than 15 percent of their capital to any borrower or invest more than 15 percent in any one security. There are a few exceptions to these limitations. Loans guaranteed by the federal government and loans made to other commercial banks in the federal funds market are exempt from the 15 percent limit, as are investments in Treasury, agency, and general obligation municipal bonds. The quality of the entire earning asset portfolio is subject to regulatory evaluation and comment. Writedowns and writeoffs of doubtful credits can be required. Marketable obligations of adequate credit quality are valued at amortized cost, while other bonds must be carried at market value on the financial statements. For bank government security dealers, dealer-originated positions must be held in a separate trading account at the lower of cost or market figures.

RESERVE REQUIREMENTS OF
DEPOSITORY INSTITUTIONS

Since the 1930s, members of the Federal Reserve System have been required to hold sterile, non-interest-bearing reserves at the Federal Reserve Bank or in vault cash equal to at least a specified fraction of their deposits. The passage of the Depository Institutions Deregulation and Monetary Control Act of 1980 established uniform reserve requirements for all depository institutions. The act provided for an eight-year phase-in of reserve requirements for depository institutions that are not Federal Reserve members and a four-year phase-down for member banks.

Figure 2.4
Interstate Banking Laws, December 1986

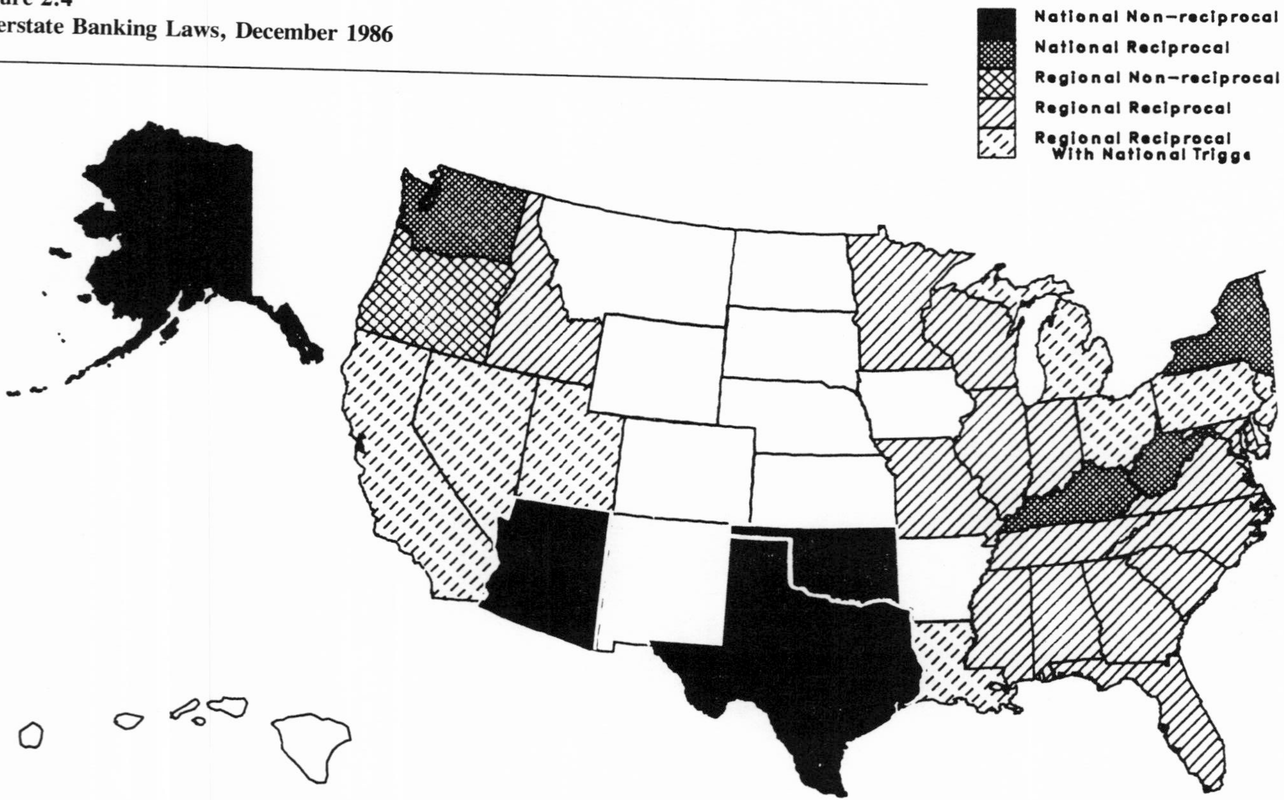

National Non-reciprocal
National Reciprocal
Regional Non-reciprocal
Regional Reciprocal
Regional Reciprocal
With National Trigge

Source: American Bankers Association, Office of the General Counsel.

Figure 2.5
Interstate Banking Laws, December 1986 (eventual outcome as currently enacted)

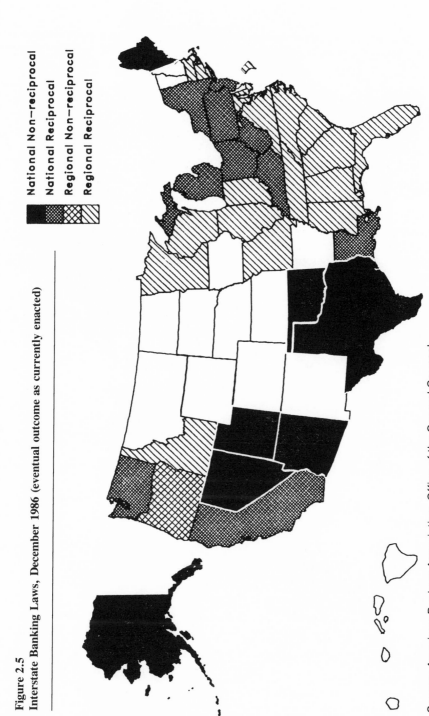

National Non-reciprocal

National Reciprocal

Regional Non-reciprocal

Regional Reciprocal

Source: American Bankers Association, Office of the General Counsel.

Before implementation of the DIDMCA (1980), member-bank reserve requirements were 7 percent of the first $2 million of demand deposits, 9.5 percent on the next $8 million, 11.75 percent on the next $90 million, 12.75 percent on the next $300 million, and 16.25 percent on demand deposits greater than $400 million. Reserves against long-term savings and time deposits (4 years or longer) were only 1 percent, but ordinary savings deposits required 3 percent reserves. Time deposits of between 30 and 179 days had a 6-percent reserve, while those maturing at from 180 days to 4 years had a 2.5-percent reserve requirement. After the passage of the DIDMCA, reserve requirements on transaction accounts at banks with deposits under $40.5 million were set at 3 percent, while reserve requirements were set at 12 percent for banks with deposits in excess of $40.5 million. Nonpersonal time deposits with maturities of less than 1.5 years were given a 3 percent reserve requirement, while those with maturities of greater than 1.5 years have no reserve requirements. All types of Eurocurrency liabilities have a 3 percent reserve requirement. (See table 2.4.)

NOTES

1. J. F. Sinkey, Jr., *Commercial Bank Financial Management: In the Financial Services Industry,* 2nd ed. (New York: Macmillan Publishing Company, 1986), 1-2.

2. American Bankers Association, *Statistical Information on the Financial Services Industry,* 4th ed. (Washington, D.C.: American Bankers Association, 1987), 8.

3. Ibid., 11.

4. Gart, *An Insider's Guide to the Financial Services Revolution* (New York: McGraw-Hill, 1984), 17-19.

5. D. C. Waite, "Deregulation and the Banking Industry," *The Bankers' Magazine,* vol. 165, no. 1 (January-February 1982); 31-32.

6. Ibid.

7. Ibid., 33-34.

Table 2.4
Reserve Requirements of Depository Institutions[1] (Percent of deposits)

Percent of deposits

Type of deposit, and deposit interval[2]	Depository institution requirements after implementation of the Monetary Control Act	
	Percent of deposits	Effective date
Net transaction accounts[3,4]		
$0 million–$40.5 million	3	12/15/87
More than $40.5 million	12	12/15/87
Nonpersonal time deposits[5]		
By original maturity		
Less than 1½ years	3	10/6/83
1½ years or more	0	10/6/83
Eurocurrency liabilities		
All types	3	11/13/80

1. Reserve requirements in effect on Dec. 31, 1987. Required reserves must be held in the form of deposits with Federal Reserve Banks or vault cash. Nonmembers may maintain reserve balances with a Federal Reserve Bank indirectly on a pass-through basis with certain approved institutions. For previous reserve requirements, see earlier editions of the *Annual Report* and of the FEDERAL RESERVE BULLETIN. Under provisions of the Monetary Control Act, depository institutions include commercial banks, mutual savings banks, savings and loan associations, credit unions, agencies and branches of foreign banks, and Edge corporations.

2. The Garn–St Germain Depository Institutions Act of 1982 (Public Law 97–320) requires that $2 million of reservable liabilities (transaction accounts, nonpersonal time deposits, and Eurocurrency liabilities) of each depository institution be subject to a zero percent reserve requirement. The Board is to adjust the amount of reservable liabilities subject to this zero percent reserve requirement each year for the succeeding calendar year by 80 percent of the percentage increase in the total reservable liabilities of all depository institutions, measured on an annual basis as of June 30. No corresponding adjustment is to be made in the event of a decrease. On Dec. 15, 1987, the exemption was raised from $2.9 million to $3.2 million. In determining the reserve requirements of depository institutions, the exemption shall apply in the following order: (1) net NOW accounts (NOW accounts less allowable deductions); (2) net other transaction accounts; and (3) nonpersonal time deposits or Eurocurrency liabilities starting with those with the highest reserve ratio. With respect to NOW accounts and

other transaction accounts, the exemption applies only to such accounts that would be subject to a 3 percent reserve requirement.

3. Transaction accounts include all deposits on which the account holder is permitted to make withdrawals by negotiable or transferable instruments, payment orders of withdrawal, and telephone and preauthorized transfers in excess of three per month for the purpose of making payments to third persons or others. However, MMDAs and similar accounts subject to the rules that permit no more than six preauthorized, automatic, or other transfers per month, of which no more than three can be checks, are not transaction accounts (such accounts are savings deposits subject to time deposit reserve requirements).

4. The Monetary Control Act of 1980 requires that the amount of transaction accounts against which the 3 percent reserve requirement applies be modified annually by 80 percent of the percentage increase in transaction accounts held by all depository institutions, determined as of June 30 each year. Effective Dec. 15, 1987 for institutions reporting quarterly and Dec. 29, 1987 for institutions reporting weekly, the amount was increased from $36.7 million to $40.5 million.

5. In general, nonpersonal time deposits are time deposits, including savings deposits, that are not transaction accounts and in which a beneficial interest is held by a depositor that is not a natural person. Also included are certain transferable time deposits held by natural persons and certain obligations issued to depository institution offices located outside the United States. For details, see section 204.2 of Regulation D.

Source: Federal Reserve Bulletin, 1.15.

3

Commercial Bank Asset Composition

ASSET COMPOSITION

Loans typically dominate the asset portfolios of most commercial banks. These loans include credit extension to households, businesses, and governments for a wide variety of purposes. The largest portion of credit extended by all insured commercial banks in mid-1987 was in the form of commercial and industrial loans which accounted for approximately 34 percent of total loans, while real estate loans and loans to individuals accounted for close to 32 percent and 19.0 percent, respectively. The allocation of loans varies widely among banks of different sizes, locations, management preferences, and market conditions. The credit distribution of smaller banks tends to favor consumer, mortgage, and agricultural loans, while the largest banks tend to have on their books large portions of commercial and industrial loans, foreign loans, and loans to financial institutions and securities brokers and dealers. (See Table 3.1.)

Commercial banks also hold substantial amounts of securities in portfolio. Cash and short-term securities usually comprise much larger portions of total assets than at nonbank financial institutions. U.S. Treasury securities, federal agency securities, repurchase agreements, federal funds sold, and municipal bonds are the key instruments held in most bank investment portfolios. (See Table 3.2.) U.S. Government and tax-free state and local government securities dominate the portfolio. Some large, money-center banks act as dealers in securities issued by state or local governments, or by the federal government or one of its agencies. As a dealer, a bank sometimes takes a large position in a security in which it makes a market.

The substantial holdings of liquid assets in the banks are attributable to the large volume of unstable demand, NOW, and Super-NOW accounts, as well as to the role played by commercial banks in administering the nation's payments

Table 3.1
Portfolio Composition of Insured Commercial Banks
Balance Sheet Items as a Percentage of Assets

Item	A 1983	A 1987	B 1983	B 1987
Interest Earning Assets	90.82	91.10	87.16	88.59
Loans	52.10	52.95	53.10	59.71
Commercial and industrial	14.29	13.22	18.45	18.53
Real estate	18.64	23.78	15.92	22.00
Consumer	12.44	11.51	11.78	14.27
Securities	29.75	28.45	20.85	20.96
U.S. government	18.89	18.71	11.30	11.04
State and local	10.29	7.65	8.68	7.79
Other	0.57	2.09	0.86	2.14
Federal funds sold and repos	5.76	6.46	5.69	4.71
Interest bearing deposits	3.21	3.25	7.52	3.24

Item	C 1983	C 1987	D 1983	D 1987
Interest Earning Assets	81.56	80.63	83.38	85.78
Loans	62.93	58.40	58.63	61.00
Commercial and industrial	32.31	24.22	26.77	24.01
Real estate	9.22	12.52	11.88	16.05
Consumer	4.72	5.99	6.90	11.48
Securities	6.39	6.68	10.45	15.36
U.S. government	2.60	2.33	4.66	7.73
State and local	2.49	2.90	5.24	6.00
Other	1.30	1.45	0.56	1.64
Federal funds sold and repos	2.52	2.51	2.98	2.79
Interest bearing deposits	9.72	8.29	11.40	6.03

A=Banks under $300 million in assets
B=Banks with $300 million to $5 billion in assets
C=Nine money center banks
D=Large banks other than money center banks

Source: Federal Reserve Bulletin, July 1988, pp.415-418.

system. Banks also hold currency and coin to help satisfy the demand for cash, and keep required reserves with the Federal Reserve Banks and balances with their various correspondents banks in both demand and time accounts. Also, cash items in the process of collection can sometimes reach a rather substantial level.

CLASSIFICATION OF LOANS

Commercial loans are classified according to maturity. Short-term loans are made primarily to support working capital needs and have maturities of under

Table 3.2

Selected Assets as a Percentage of Total Assets, All Insured Commercial Banks, 1983-1987

Item	1983	1984	1985	1986	1987
Interest-earning assets.................	85.95	85.74	86.05	86.02	86.62
Loans	56.46	57.66	58.51	57.86	58.36
Securities	17.47	17.57	17.58	18.29	18.57
U.S. government	9.79	9.89	9.50	9.26	10.04
State and local government...	6.84	6.76	6.99	7.49	6.25
Other bonds and stocks	.83	.93	1.08	1.55	2.28
Gross federal funds sold and reverse repurchase agreements	4.34	4.17	4.43	4.72	4.43
Interest-bearing deposits	7.69	6.33	5.53	5.15	5.26
MEMO					
Loss reserves	.63	.70	.80	.92	1.36
Average assets (billions of dollars)	2.245	2.401	2.559	2.753	2.882

Source: *Federal Reserve Bulletin*, July 1988, p. 409.

one year. Term loans are made for equipment purchases and more permanent funding needs and have maturities of more than one year. Although short-term loans have traditionally been emphasized by banks, term loans have become an extremely important component of the loan portfolios of many banks.

In addition to their classification by maturity, loans are also classified by whether they are fixed-amount loans or credit lines. With a fixed-amount loan, the proceeds for the entire loan are borrowed at one time, while with a credit relationship, the company can borrow up to an agreed-upon amount or lending limit. A revolving credit line allows the institution to borrow up to a designated limit, repay, and reborrow over the period for which the credit line is approved. Nonrevolving credit may be used with project and real estate construction loans, with funds dispersed at various stages of completion. A nonrevolving credit line does not permit the borrower the option to repay and reborrow. The major money-center and large regional banks offer standby credit lines as a backup source of repayment to commercial paper issuers. For an agreed-upon fee or compensating balance, the bank guarantees that, if necessary, it will make funds available to the company issuing the commercial paper, so that the commercial paper may be redeemed.

Loans can be either secured or unsecured. An unsecured loan is made with no particular collateral backing the loan, while a secured loan is secured by specific, identified assets of the borrower. Any assets in which the lender can perfect a lien may serve as collateral. The collateral serves as an alternative means of loan payment in case of default. The decision to make the loan secured or unsecured is usually a function of the size of the loan, the financial strength of the borrower, the perceived risks, the type of collateral available, and the costs of using assets as security. Administrative and monitoring costs may limit the benefit of the security to the bank.

There are asset-based loans in which the asset used to secure the loan assumes a key role in the creation of cash flows to repay the loan. Examples of such loans are inventory floor-plan loans and accounts receivable loans. In the former case, the lender looks to the sales of the inventory to generate cash flow for repayment of the loan. Loans are also collateralized by assets such as Treasury bills and bonds or stocks that are pledged as security.

Banks also provide lease financing for the purchase of equipment as an alternative to term lending. A lease differs from a loan in that the bank actually owns the asset and rents it to the lessee. Lease-financing receivables account for about 3 percent of total loans. The return to the bank through leasing is generally higher than the interest that could be earned on loans made to a purchaser, but there are usually increased risks associated with leasing.

Commercial Loans

Commercial loans range from short-term, self-liquidating loans to finance seasonal needs (agricultural or Christmas merchandise) through term loans (maturities exceeding one year) to finance the acquisition of capital assets or loans to supply working capital. These loans can be unsecured or secured by specific collateral.

The seasonal loan is a short-term advance that furnishes working capital for a short period of time and is repaid when inventory and receivables are partially converted into cash at the end of the seasonal upsurge. Although secured seasonal loans have become more prevalent with the decrease in liquidity position of many firms, most seasonal loans made by commercial banks are unsecured.

The working capital loan, a legitimate credit need for many businesses, is usually repaid out of earnings or refinancing. Businesses that carry a large and varied inventory throughout the year or sell in volume on credit, such as retailers, are likely to need working capital loans. Special arrangements used for both seasonal and longer-term working capital loans are referred to as revolving credit. Under a revolving credit plan, the borrower pays a commitment fee on the unused portion of a guaranteed credit line in addition to the agreed-upon rate of interest. This fee compensates the bank for holding money available over a period of up to several years and assures the borrower that funds will be there when needed.

Term loans comprise a large percentage of the commercial and industrial loans at large commercial banks. Term loans are probably the key source for financing plant and equipment needs of firms that are too small to borrow in the capital markets, and represent an example of a bank meeting the credit needs of a customer by relating purpose to payment. In addition to the collateral generally obtained and the provisions for regular amortization, term loans usually contain convenants with minimum working capital levels and net worth-to-debt ratios and which limit withdrawals or dividends from the business during the term of the loan. A term loan should be repaid out of the net cash income of the business with explicit repayment dates, and is generally amortized over the life of the loan. Leasing is a specialized type of lending whereby the bank retains title to the property leased but the client leases the equipment for most of its expected life. Even some prime, corporate customers find it advantageous to lease equipment.

Loans to finance companies that have unusually large amounts of debt in their financial structure must be analyzed as long-term commitments. These companies usually rotate their debt from one bank to another, paying off loans on each line of credit periodically. Another specialized type of loan is factoring. Factoring is a form of lending in which the bank purchases the borrower's accounts receivable, with or without recourse. The rates charged are generally 3 to 6 points above the prime rate in an area of high risk. Many banks acquired commercial finance companies engaged in factoring to help them evaluate these often high-yielding but complicated credits. In another specialty area, rural banks tend to service the financing needs of farmers by making agricultural or equipment loans to farm operators. As rural banks service their agribusiness customers, they face competition from the Farmers Home Administration and

Farm Credit Administration components. In some cases, when loan requests exceed legal lending limits, rural banks arrange loan participations with such federal agencies or with their bigger city correspondents.

Many banks receive loan applications from local small businesses that have primitive financial controls, small loan requirements, and no financial alternatives. Some banks enter into participation or insure some of these loans with the Small Business Administration (SBA) in order to help control the risks of their small-business loans.

The rate charged to the borrower may be fixed or it may fluctuate with other interest rates. In recent years, the trend has been toward greater use of floating-rate loans that fluctuate along with interest rates in the economy. In this case, interest-rate risk is in the hands of the borrower rather than the banker.

Commercial banks are the prime lenders to most business firms. About 1,500 large businesses with strong credit ratings have access to the commercial paper market. Corporate treasurers from these firms can issue unsecured IOUs either directly or through the help of investment bankers on the open market, and have them purchased by institutional investors. Commercial paper rates for the highest-quality borrowers are usually under bank borrowing rates. Banks have also set up loan production offices in this country and representative offices abroad to help generate loans. These offices cannot accept deposits, but can solicit and help service loans. Loans outside the headquarters region help to diversify the portfolio geographically.

Another category of specialized lending for money-center banks and large regional banks is international lending. Since this subject is treated in Chapter 6, the discussion here will be brief. It is important to note that some New York banks earned more than half their profits from international activities prior to 1985.

U.S. international banking activities have grown rapidly since the 1960s in order to help meet the needs of corporate customers, which have become increasingly multinational; to meet the demand by foreign governments for capital; to increase lending activity during periods when public policy tried to constrain domestic expansion; and to diversify bank loan portfolios and other sources of revenue. Banks have engaged in letters of credit and bankers acceptances for years in support of short-term financing for international trade, while over the last 20 years U.S. banks have played an active role in the growth of the syndicated Eurocurrency market for loans.

Foreign lending by U.S. commercial banks grew dramatically in geographical scope and size from the mid-1970s to the early 1980s as U.S. multinational banks helped recycle dollars from oil-exporting to oil-importing nations. However, a global recession and high international interest rates made it extremely difficult for some oil-importing nations to service their foreign debt during the early 1980s. The culmination of these difficulties led to the international debt crisis in 1987 and a decline in U.S. bank lending abroad.

Leasing

Banks entered the leasing business in the early 1960s as a natural adjunct to their normal lending activities. A financial lease is the functional equivalent of a loan since the lessee is obligated to make a stream of payments to the lessor. Much leasing activity is tax-shelter-oriented as the owner of the equipment can take advantage of accelerated depreciation.

Lease financing by banks became popular as a means to finance trains, planes, computers, production, medical and pollution-control equipment, production and material handling machinery, and energy drilling equipment. Leases typically give the lessee firm use of an asset over most of the asset's life, with the option to buy the asset at the expiration of the lease term. In a lease agreement, the lessor owns equipment that it makes available for the lessee's use in return for, at minimum, rental fees. In a financial lease, the only kind offered by banks, the lessor expects to recover the entire acquisition cost of the leased asset plus profit. The lessor's proceeds include tax benefits related to accelerated depreciation, rental income, and salvage value. Financial leases cannot be cancelled, and they are usually net leases, meaning that the lessee is responsible for maintenance, insurance, and applicable taxes.

The most straightforward form of leasing is the direct lease, in which the bank provides 100-percent financing. Banks also get involved in a modified form of lease financing through leasing companies where the bank does not take an ownership position in the asset. The leasing company acquires the asset using funds lent by the bank and then leases the asset to a client. The lessor pledges the asset against its loan through a security agreement and pledges the lease revenues as well.

In leveraged leasing, it is typical for a bank holding company affiliate to act as the lessor, setting up an ownership trust that acquires an asset to be leased. The holding company provides only a small part of the funds for purchase of the asset (for example, 20 percent), while the trust borrows the remaining funds from an institutional investor. The institutions providing the debt funds to the trust do not have recourse to the bank holding company (lessor). They look to the ability of the lessee to make rental payments and to the collateral value of the asset.

The profitability to the bank holding company of leveraged leasing is dependent on the tax benefits of owning the asset as well as the rental income. In relation to the amount of equity dollars invested, these benefits are multiplied by leveraging with debt. Usually the tax benefits of ownership are passed through to the lessee in the form of lower lease rental payments. On the other hand, if the lessee is able to take full advantage of the tax benefits, there is probably little financial advantage in a leveraged lease.

It is difficult to tell from balance sheet figures the extent of leasing activity at a bank holding company because only the lessor's equity in the equipment leased appears as an asset. In a leveraged lease, this equity declines to 0 in a few years because the bank borrows the remaining required funds on a long-term basis. Even if the impact of leasing on the balance sheet is minimal, there may be a substantial effect on the tax position of the bank and on the return earned by the bank's stockholders. Leasing companies and their activities are dealt with more extensively in Chapter 16.

Consumer Loans

Since the end of World War II, consumer lending has grown rapidly at commercial banks to the point where commercial banks have become the dominant financial institution in consumer lending. Such consumer loans have risen from just under 8 percent of all commercial bank loans to close to 17.5 percent in recent years.

Consumer loans include both installment and noninstallment credit. The latter consists of single-payment loans, charge accounts, and service credit. Installment credit, by far the bigger of the two categories of consumer lending, consists of loans to purchase specific goods or services such as cars and appliances, and loans to meet extraordinary or previously incurred expenses. Bank credit card loans outstanding are classified by the Federal Reserve as loans to finance the purchase of goods or services. Most personal installment loans are made by direct negotiation between the bank and the borrower. However, installment sales credit can be direct or indirect. A bank can purchase installment sales contracts from stores.

The potential profitability of bank credit cards comes from these sources:

1. The interest charged to the card user who does not pay the bill on time;
2. A yearly fee that guarantees a credit line; and
3. The discount at which the bank purchases sales slips from the merchant, which can range from 2 to 6 percent.

Most card-issuing banks participate in one or both nationwide card associations: Master Card or VISA. At year-end 1986 there were 99.1 million VISA cards and 79.3 million Master Cards in the United States. A customer may use this card internationally or domestically at all affiliated merchants and banks, and even at automated teller machines in another part of the country.

Many large banks also make consumer loans through their holding-company-affiliated consumer finance companies. A subsidiary of this type offers both geographical and rate diversification (most states have a usury law that sets the maximum rate that a lender can charge on consumer loans). There are also loans to individuals to purchase and carry securities. A bank is often more willing to lend to and to charge a lower rate to an individual willing to pledge marketable securities as loan collateral. On occasion, an individual can borrow more cheaply from a bank than from a brokerage firm in a margin account.

Consumers are also big borrowers of mortgage money to finance the purchase of a home. That subject will be dealt with extensively later in this chapter.

Auto loans, which were formerly made for a maximum of two years, are now being made for up to five years. Also, down payments of 10 or 20 percent were required previously. Today, however, some banks are offering loans without down payments in order to stimulate business. Some banks even offer lower rates for car loans of $20,000 or more in order to develop relationships with upscale customers. During 1986-1987 the captive finance companies of the domestic automobile companies offered lending rates between 1.9 and 6 percent in order to stimulate sales of select car models. This proved extremely popular with the American consumer. These finance companies captured the bulk of consumer auto financing away from the banks. It is not clear at the time of this writing whether this is a harbinger of future consumer borrowing trends.

Although banks may surrender much of the market for new car loans to the captive finance companies of the auto giants if discount loan rates continue, they are expected to remain competitive in the market for used car loans, which are not expected to be subsidized. Banks are also expected to capture a huge percentage of consumer loans which will be collateralized with equity in the borrower's home. These loans are expected to grow in importance because of the nature of the changes in the tax bill that became effective in 1987 and relate to the ability of the taxpayer to deduct interest payments on mortgage loans as an itemized deduction on federal income taxes.

Real Estate Loans

Real estate loans are the second most important loan category in bank portfolios, next to commercial and industrial loans. Banks make loans for construction and land development, conventional system mortgage loans, and loans secured by nonfarming, nonresidential properties. Just about all banks make residential mortgage loans, while most large banks also make specialized loans to developers of large-scale real estate properties. These banks have specialized units that focus on construction loans and loans to real estate investment trusts (REITs). Mortgage loans are a specialized form of consumer and commercial lending that is usually secured by real estate. Most residential mortgage loans are conventional fixed-rate loans that are secured by first mortgages on one-to-four-family residences. However, recently adjustable rate mortgages (ARMs) have become more popular with bank managements who wish to eliminate interest rate risks associated with fixed-rate loans. A number of new mortgage instruments have been introduced such as: unequal payment fixed-rate mortgage instruments, graduated payment mortgages, flexible-payment mortgages, reverse-annuity mortgages, roll-over mortgages, and variable rate mortgages. Real estate loans on average represent close to one-third of all loans at insured banks. However, they vary in importance from bank to bank. Typically, banks under $0.5 billion in assets have a larger proportion of real estate loans than money-center banks.

Commercial banks can make both conventional mortgages and VA (Veteran's Administration) guaranteed or FHA (Federal Housing Administration) insured mortgages, but usually prefer the higher yields and smaller amount of paperwork for conventional mortgages. Conventional mortgages generally have a commitment fee of 2 to 4 points upon takedown of the loan, and there is an active and growing secondary market for these mortgages. Mortgages offer a bank monthly amortization and interest payments, as well as an opportunity to cross-sell the home owner a variety of other banking services. Many banks sell the permanent mortgages in the secondary market, earning the front-end origination fees while continuing to service the mortgage.

Banks make more construction loans than any other financial intermediary. About two-thirds of all banks make this type of loan. A bank typically provides interim or bridge financing to a project developer in a construction loan. Most construction and land development loans are of relatively short duration and are maintained on the books while the project is under development or construction. Usually, but not always, the bank will require the borrower to have obtained a prior commitment to provide long-term mortgage financing for the complete project. In fact, the permanent financing would be used to repay the construction loan. However, some banks will finance the construction of a home or business for a valued customer with the expectation that they will acquire and hold the mortgage on the completed premises.

Commercial mortgage lending is an activity of only a small percentage of commercial banks. The primary consideration in a commercial mortgage loan is the relationship of the income derived from the property to the cost of maintaining it, paying taxes, and servicing the loan. The income from the property is typically the product of leases to tenants with whom the bank probably does not deal directly.

There are a number of restrictions on residential mortgage loans. A national bank may not have its total real estate loans secured by first liens exceeding 100 percent of its paid-in, unimpaired capital plus 100 percent of its unimpaired surplus or 100 percent of its time and savings deposits, whichever amount is larger. In addition to the 100-percent limit on first lien mortgages, national banks can also make junior mortgage loans (secured by other than first liens), but in total these cannot exceed 20 percent of unimpaired capital plus surplus. The maximum loan-to-appraised-value ratio is 90 percent for conventional mortgages; FHA and VA residential mortgages are exempt from these terms.

Accounts Receivable Financing, Factoring, and Inventory Financing

Accounts receivable financing is a form of collateralized lending where the bank lends money against an agreed-upon percentage of accounts receivable assigned to it (50 to 90 percent). The borrower typically continues its regular credit and collection functions since its customers are not notified of the assignment of their debt to the bank. The bank gains access to the readily convertible collateral of weaker customers whose credit and repayments are controlled in that receivable financing permits borrowing only as the borrower generates sales with additional provision of automatic repayment of the loan as collections are received.

In factoring, a bank or a commercial factor actually purchases accounts receivable from its customer at a percentage of their face value. The bank notifies the customer's debtors to remit all payments directly to the bank instead of the original seller of the merchandise. Typically, the customer is required to maintain a cash reserve against losses related to buyers' claims against the customer firm. (See Table 3.3.)

Any loan that is secured by inventory and scheduled to be repaid from the sale of that inventory is considered to be inventory financing. Inventory lending is often higher-risk lending because of the extension of this kind of financing to financially weak firms, and problems encountered relative to the marketability, valuation, and physical control of inventory. There are floating lien, trust receipt (floor plan financing), and warehouse financing forms of inventory lending.

Under the floating lien, the seller is not constrained from selling inventories, so the bank cannot control specific inventory items. This type of financing may be used to provide continuing security on receivables created when inventory is sold. Trust receipt financing involves transitory legal ownership of inventory by the bank. The borrower is usually provided with funds to pay for goods received from suppliers, and holds the goods in trust for the bank by issuing the bank a trust receipt for specifically identifiable goods, such as automobiles. As sales

Table 3.3
Factoring versus Accounts Receivable Financing

	Factoring	Accounts Receivable Financing
Cost	Higher	Lower
Debtor Notification	Yes	No
Credit Function Performed by	Bank	Borrower
Collection Function Peformed by	Bank	Borrower
Account Ownership	Bank	Borrower
Proceeds Allowed via	Purchase	Loan
Cash reserve Required	Yes	No

occur, the borrower either transmits the proceeds to the bank or sells to the bank from the borrower's credit sales.

Warehouse financing facilitates inventory lending by providing controls on the disposition of the inventories. Banks undertake a major risk in warehouse financing because of the difficulty of verifying the quality of goods on which they acquire warehouse receipts.

COMPARATIVE LOAN PORTFOLIOS

The loan portfolios of large money-center banks differ from those of other banks. For example, commercial and industrial loans account for close to 25 percent of the loans made by money-center banks, between 20 and 25 percent of the loans made by large (non-money-center) banks, approximately 19 percent of the loans made by banks with assets of between $300 million and $5 billion, and about 25 percent of the loans made by banks with assets under $300 million. On the other hand, personal loans accounted for between 11 and 15 percent of the loans made by the two smaller categories of banks, while personal loans accounted for close to 12 percent of the loans at the large, non-money-center banks and about 6 percent of the loans at the money-center banks. Also, lease financing accounts for a larger percentage of loans at the larger banks than at the smaller banks. The same is true for loans to brokers and dealers. Agricultural loans at large money-center banks are relatively unimportant compared to such loans at smaller banks and those located in the farm belt. International lending plays a key role at large money-center banks, but plays a relatively unimportant role at smaller banks.

INVESTMENT PORTFOLIOS

Although banks employ more than half of their funds in loans, the second major use of funds is investment in U.S. Treasury bills, notes and bonds, debt instruments issued by agencies of the federal government, municipal securities, repurchase agreements, and other market instruments. These investments all offer interest-rate risk, but obligations of the federal government are free of default risk.

Obligations of municipal governments vary with respect to the risk of default. The ability to repay their debts is dependent upon the financial strength of the issuer or the relationship of source of repayment to particular sources of revenue. Although municipal securities are usually classified as low-risk securities, they are riskier than investments in Treasury securities. Most municipal securities are also less marketable than either Treasury or agency obligations. Because interest income on municipal securities is exempt from federal income taxes, interest rates on these securities are normally lower than rates on comparably rated securities of the same maturity.

Loans typically earn a higher rate of interest than marketable securities of comparable maturity. Even though banks could maximize interest income by placing most of their funds in loans, they do not. Essentially, funds are employed in securities to produce interest income, to generate possible capital gains, and to provide backstop liquidity for unexpected fund outflows or to meet unexpected demand for funds.

Prior to the advent of liability management, the investment portfolio was classified functionally into primary and secondary reserves. The primary reserves were conceptually not considered to be part of the liquidity position, but the secondary reserves represented a bank's basic liquidity reserve. The size of the secondary reserve was likely to be determined by those factors that influence the variability of loans and deposits. Secondary reserves (short- and intermediate-term securities of the bank's investment account) were always available to meet seasonal and cyclical demands for funds and deposit withdrawals.

The primary goal of bank portfolio policy is to obtain the maximum income with the minimum exposure to risk. The amount of income and the degree of risk in an investment will be directly affected by:

1. The general level of interest rates at the time of purchase and the shape of the yield curve;
2. The maturity of the investment;
3. The marketability of the investment;
4. The probability of default, that is, the credit standing of the issuer;
5. Tax considerations;
6. The pledging of qualified securities to secure public deposits; and
7. The individual situation and the type of markets or community that the bank serves.

The size of the portfolio will be determined by the amount of available funds not required to meet loan demand, the amount of securities required for pledging, and the bank's assessment as to the potential for trading profits in the portfolio. Banks are generally restricted to buying debt instruments for their security portfolio of Treasury, U.S. Agency, and state and local bonds. Banks usually do not purchase corporate bonds because the tax-equivalent yield on municipal bonds generally exceeds the yield on corporate bonds of comparable quality and maturity.

Among the key objectives of portfolio management is the matter of combining various classes of assets in order to achieve the optimum balance between the maximization of income and the maintenance of adequate liquidity and solvency. The objectives of income, liquidity, and solvency determine the pattern and distribution of assets in the portfolio. However, the advent of liabilities management in the late 1960s and early 1970s reduced the importance of the liquidity component of the investment portfolio. Rather than selling bonds from the portfolio to adjust cash flows, the bank can now raise cash by selling negotiable CDs or Eurodollars, or increasing the volume of repurchase agreements with bank customers or borrowings from other banks in the federal funds market. When demand deposits dominated the liability structure and liquidity needs were met from asset secondary reserves, the properties of short-term governments made them desirable for liquidity purposes. With the advent of purchased funds management (liability management) to cover liquidity requirements, the need for secondary reserve assets has declined.

As a large proportion of bank liabilities have become interest-rate sensitive and as rates paid on them have risen, pressure on bank net-interest margins has increased. The response to the profit pressures has been liquidation of government securities because municipals offer greater tax-equivalent yields in the intermediate- and long-term maturity sectors. (See Table 3.1.) However, changes in the tax laws have reduced bank purchases of municipal bonds.

Quality

Obligations of the U.S. government enjoy the highest credit standing, as do issues of some government agencies that are guaranteed by the U.S. government such as Government National Mortgage Association (GNMA) securities. These issues are virtually default free and are treated accordingly in bank capital adequacy formulae.

Like the obligations of corporations and other quasi-government agencies, those of the various states and their political subdivisions vary widely in credit-worthiness. Some municipal general obligations and revenue bonds have creditworthiness equal to or greater than most of the bank's best loan customers. However, some state and local obligations are guaranteed for principal and interest payments by private insurers. The credit standing of municipal and corporate obligations are rated by Moody's Investors Service and Standard & Poor's Corporation. These ratings should be recognized as guides, and not as a substitute for the knowledge and judgment of the bank portfolio manager who maintains his own credit files and makes his own careful analysis.

Closely related to credit considerations is the principle of risk diversification by geography and by industry. Although few banks hold industrial bonds, geographical distribution has significance for holdings of municipal securities. Many specialists suggest that banks avoid the acquisition of local municipal bonds for reasons other than those of community and customer relations because the loan account already represents a concentration of assets subject to adverse developments in the local economy. A leading concept of diversification that a bank needs to follow is that of not duplicating its loan account. The advantage of diversification must be balanced against the bank's knowledge of local conditions.

It is also important to note that the timing of cash flows to the investment portfolio is such that in periods of low interest rates, when loan demand is weak and core deposits strong, the investment portfolio receives maximum cash inflows. Of course, when interest rates rise, intermediate- and long-term maturity bonds show major price declines. Cash flows to the investment portfolio may be minimal when yields are most attractive because loan demand is exceptionally strong. Liquidation of short maturities may even be needed to meet this increase in loan demand. Since lending is the primary function at most banks, investments in securities are usually considered a secondary or residual use of funds. This often leads to the aforementioned timing problems in the purchase and sale of securities.

Investment Policy

Portfolio securities provide a number of functional purposes:

1. They permit impersonal flexibility in balancing a bank's overall maturity and interest sensitivity position; that is, the portfolio can serve as a balancing factor for a bank's overall asset and liability structure;
2. Short maturities often function as a liquidity source, and are sometimes labeled as "secondary reserves";
3. A major function is to implement spread management operations;
4. A trading account is a position for maintaining a broker-dealer operation in government securities, which for the most part are concentrated in large banks; and
5. Some municipal securities represent loans to local governments that are regular bank customers.

Senior management must set and review investment policies that include:

1. The extent to which the investment portfolio is intended to provide backstop liquidity or backstop revenue;
2. The amount and frequency of capital losses that the bank is willing to incur in its investment transactions;
3. The extent to which the bank should try to obtain tax-free income;
4. The amount of authority to delegate to the bank's investment specialists; and
5. The criteria by which to monitor and evaluate the performance of the specialists.

Government and Agency Portfolio

Government and agency securities have a number of properties which make them attractive for bank portfolios. For example:

1. They are classified as riskless assets for the purpose of evaluating capital adequacy by the regulatory authorities.
2. Maturity options are available from 1 week to 20 years or more.
3. Relatively large amounts can be sold or purchased through an extensive and orderly market system.
4. They are acceptable for meeting pledging requirements on public deposits and for borrowing at the discount window of the Federal Reserve.

5. Repurchase agreements (repos) and reverse repos are executed with these securities.

6. They help control risk exposure and serve a significant "window dressing" role, giving an image of a "quality" portfolio. This is based on the perception that government securities are free of default risk and represent issues of the highest quality. It would not be prudent for published statements of conditions to show government securities as a percentage of assets significantly below that of comparable banks.

7. They serve as a source of secondary reserves because of superior marketability features. The government portfolio may be regarded as the principal source of returns derived from cyclical timing strategies in the bond markets.

8. They play an important role in tax management considerations, especially in trading the portfolio.

9. In some banks, tax credits and losses may make governments more attractive than municipals strictly on an income basis.

Government maturities at most banks tend to be front-end loaded; the largest portion matures within one year, and 85 to 90 percent within five years. Maturity extension generally tends to occur on a modest scale as interest rates rise, but even then the amounts committed to extremely long maturities tend to be limited. The objective is to maximize total returns by lengthening maturities when interest rates are perceived to be high and shortening the structure when rates appear to be low. Scheduling maturities within the investment portfolio is a difficult task, which requires regular review and decision making as funds become available for investment or as opportunities to improve the income position present themselves.

As interest rates rise, CDs, borrowings, money market certificates and accounts replace cheaper sources of funds, representing an involuntary shift of the liability structure toward a much higher and more costly interest-sensitivity position. Unless some action is taken toward increasing asset interest-rate sensitivity, a negative net sensitivity position may result, and as a consequence, maturity extensions may well be precluded.

It is also important to note that during high-interest-rate periods when the yield curve is inverted, the yield derived from long maturities may be less than the marginal costs of purchased funds, including money market certificates. Most banks might tend to stay short in the government portfolio in order to avoid a negative carry on the marginal cost of funds. It could, of course, be argued that the negative carry should be temporary, assuming a subsequent cyclical decline in interest rates. However, some lack of confidence in interest rate forecasting and the uncertainties associated with the timing of the event might well inhibit major maturity extensions of the government portfolio.

Government agency obligations have usually offered a yield advantage over Treasuries for maturities longer than a year. The reasons for the yield advantage of agencies over governments are that the marketability of large units is less certain than those of Treasuries, and investors such as foreign nationals often exclude the agency universe. The U.S. government does not guarantee the debt issues of most of these agencies so that they have a modestly higher credit risk than do U.S. Treasury securities, even though many investors doubt that the government would permit one of its federally sponsored agencies to default. In the short-term maturity sector, the bond equivalent yield of discount Treasury Bills usually approximates yields on agency coupons. However, as maturities are extended, the yield spreads tend to increase. Banks tend to hold long-term agency securities in portfolio until maturity for earnings purposes because of their higher yields over comparable Treasury issues.

The amount of money committed by banks to the government portfolio tends to be subject to considerable variation as monetary conditions change. As monetary policy moves toward moderate restraint, bank holdings of governments tend to decline. Modest maturity extension tends to occur as interest rates rise. However, the amounts committed for periods beyond ten years tend to be relatively insignificant.

Municipal Securities

The term "municipal securities" encompasses a variety of tax-exempt debt obligations of states and their political subdivisions. Even though interest income is exempt from federal income taxes, a bank's capital gains from sales of its municipal securities are subject to tax. Issuers of these securities range from small fire, school, and sanitary districts to large cities, counties, and states. Most municipal securities are general obligation issues, backed by the issuer's full faith and taxing power; or revenue issues, backed by a pledge of specific revenues, such as rental income from buildings, turnpike toll revenue, and electricity or water usage fees. Subject to legal guidelines, municipalities can issue a limited amount of industrial revenue bonds. These issues are not direct obligations of the issuer, but a pledge to service this specific indebtedness of the issuing municipality which has been given by a private firm. The firm leases a municipally owned building, for example, with the proceeds of such a bond. In these cases, Moody's, Standard & Poor's, and Fitch's analyze the debt-servicing capacity of the guarantor firm. Most municipal securities have much more marketability risk than government and agency securities. This risk is lowest for large issues of top-quality municipal issuers whose bonds trade actively in nationwide markets. On the other hand, marketability risk is quite high for inactively traded, long-term bonds of small, obscure issues, whose market may be strictly local in nature.

Large banks are inclined to conduct interest arbitrage operations with purchased funds. Municipals then become one of a set of alternative investments for matching marginal yields on an after-tax basis with the marginal cost of purchased funds. When interest rates are high and are expected to decline, additional municipal commitments are appropriate in order to lock in the high interest rates and to achieve potential capital gains.

The role of the municipal investment portfolio is a combination of the following: (1) to generate the optimum after-tax yield for that portion of the core deposits not required for loans or for liquidity purposes; (2) to yield maximum after-tax spreads on purchased funds; and (3) to provide a third tier of liquidity.

In contrast to the government portfolio, which is front-end loaded, the maturity structure of most municipal bond portfolios is either longer term in nature or laddered. Banks generally regard the municipal portfolio as a quasi-permanent account that will provide a higher average yield level on an after-tax basis than any alternative in the financial markets. Municipal bond portfolios appear oriented toward obtaining long-term income rather than trading profits.

In the loan portfolio, legal lending limits represent an automatic diversification requirement, but such limits do not apply to general obligation issues of municipals. It is therefore appropriate that management establish a diversification policy that would require geographic distribution on the basis of a political and economic appraisal of the state or region and the establishment of a maximum percentage that may be given to a particular credit. Credit difficulties in cities such as New York and Cleveland have caused considerable tension in the past between commercial banks and municipal governments.

The municipal portfolio is an important source of income for most banks; in large banks the size of the tax-free portfolio often significantly exceeds the size of the government and agency portfolio. However, tax shelters from other sources, such as international activities or leasing, often reduce the need for tax-exempt municipal income. Restrictions introduced in the 1980s limit the amount of tax-free income available to banks from holding municipal bonds. Therefore, the tax position of a bank can become the determining factor in fund allocations to the municipal portfolio.

Large banks are also more inclined to conduct active spread-management operations (interest arbitrage) with purchased funds. Municipals would then become one of a set of alternative asset vehicles for matching marginal yields with marginal costs of purchased funds. The municipal portfolio of a commercial bank usually has two major components with completely different policy criteria:

1. Banks generally acquire the obligations of local government units that may use the bank depository trust, pension fund, or data processing services.
2. Banks also buy bonds on an impersonal basis where the sole criterion for purchase or sale is an objective evaluation of risk and return related to the objectives and constraints of the asset and liability committee.

Local Government Units. Assuming a valued customer relationship with a local government unit, the policy criteria for acquiring their obligations should closely resemble those used for customer loan accommodation. For example, the short-term tax anticipation notes of a local municipal customer, while technically classified as an investment security, might be properly construed as a customer loan.

The obligation to acquire local municipal debt is more ambiguous on project and serial bond issues underwritten by investment bankers. They are often acquired if yields and maturities are within policy limits. Large banks may serve as underwriters or syndicate participants for these issues, which depend on the strength or weakness of market demand for the issue and the question of whether maturity and yield targets can be satisfied. Large amounts may be acquired if external demand is weak, while only a small amount may be acquired if demand is strong.

Portfolio Configuration

Diversification. In the loan portfolio, legal lending limits related to total capitalization help lead to diversification, but such limitations do not apply to municipal units. Therefore, it is up to management to establish appropriate diversification policies. These policies usually include:

1. Establishing geographic diversification in order to avoid regional credit problems; for example, limiting exposure;
2. Avoiding portfolio clutter (an extensive number of small commitments in a given state or locality on the basis of a negative political or economic appraisal of that area) by having minimum purchase amounts for each commitment; and
3. Establishing either a maximum amount or a portfolio percentage that may be committed to any one credit.

Tax Consequences. Banks are permitted to fully deduct realized capital losses from taxable income. This means that portfolio returns can be substantially improved by taking such losses when interest rates are high and reinvesting the proceeds into alternative investments.

Since municipal coupon income is tax-exempt whereas discount return, when realized, is taxable at the full corporate rate, the maximum after-tax yield improvement for municipals can usually be obtained by selling low-coupon bonds and replacing them with high-coupon bonds. It must also be remembered that municipal securities are not as marketable as government securities and trading opportunities may be limited.

Trends. Municipal bond holdings of banks increased during the 1960s and 1970s because of:

1. Increased outstandings of municipal debt issues;
2. Improved marketability of many such issues;
3. Private insurance of many such issues;
4. Tax-exempt interest;
5. Increasing cost of bond funds; and
6. New techniques of liquidity management.

However, bank holdings of municipal bonds have declined during the 1980s because of:

1. A decline in bank earnings;
2. The growth of foreign and domestic tax credits;
3. The rising trend of interest rates;
4. Other tax and asset liability management reasons; and
5. Changes in the tax laws that limit tax-free income from bonds to banks.

The Glass-Steagall Act prevents banks from dealing in and underwriting corporate bonds and stocks as well as municipal revenue bonds, but it does not prevent them from arranging private placements of such issues. A private placement is when an issuer bypasses a public offering and directly sells new securities to one or several large institutional investors, such as insurance companies and pension funds. Compared to a public offering, a private placement often results in lower costs; for example, by avoiding underwriting fees.

Other Securities

The final investment account consists of federal funds sold and repurchase agreements (repos). These securities, which represent short-term use of funds, are among the most liquid assets held by a bank. When securities are purchased under repo, the bank is essentially lending money for a short period of time by taking title to securities and reselling the securities back to the borrower in accordance with the repo agreement. The return to the bank is the difference between the buying and selling prices of the securities.

Federal funds are essentially excess bank reserves that are lent from one bank to another. These transactions are typically for one night but they can be for longer periods of time. It is extremely important that the lending bank be aware of the credit quality of the borrowing bank (the institution with the deficiency in its reserve position).

UNDERWRITING SYNDICATES

A securities underwriter usually agrees to buy an entire new issue of marketable securities from an issuing firm or public body. The underwriter plans to sell the issue to the public at a slightly higher price. The underwriter accepts the task of publicly marketing the securities and the risk of some losses if it has to reduce the public offering price in order to sell the entire issue. While such a loss occurs occasionally, an underwriter usually earns a profit from the total underwriting revenues that it receives over time.

Some large banks have become dealers in government and agency securities, in general obligation municipal securities, or in both. At a specific time, a dealer firm makes a market in a security by standing ready to buy it at a specified bid price and sell it at a higher asked price. The difference between the dealer's bid and the asked price represents the price spread.

The dealer banks stand ready to quote bid and asked prices, maintain inventories of product, and provide product and services for correspondent banks and for trust and investment advisory accounts of wealthy individuals and organizations. They usually operate their dealer activities as separate profit centers.

SUMMARY

Most commercial banks concentrate their efforts on lending to corporations, small businesses, consumers, governments, and partnerships. In addition, most bank income is generated from lending activities. Although the type of bank loans emphasized often differ substantially among money-center, regional, and small banks, just about every bank depends upon interest income and fee income from loans for most of their profits.

A primary objective of portfolio management is to provide revenues for the bank, especially during periods of slack loan demand. Simultaneously, the portfolio may also be used to provide backstop liquidity. A bank has to explicitly evaluate the costs and benefits of its attempts to reach for higher revenues in ways that may limit its flexibility to meet a subsequent resurgence in loan demand. With the current approach and popularity of liability management, there is less need to maintain a liquid portfolio.

The total return from a bond investment portfolio can be subdivided into two parts: the interest income, which reflects explicit cash inflows received from the issuers of the bonds, and the capital gains or losses when the bonds are sold. Interest earnings on municipal bonds are exempt from federal income taxes, while capital gains and losses on the sale of municipal bonds are subject to those taxes. For example, a bank that pays taxes in the 34 percent tax bracket would earn substantially more after-tax income from an 8 percent municipal than from a 10 percent Treasury bond of the same maturity.

Banks have bond specialists who use detailed economic forecasts and advanced computer systems to help them evaluate and make major trading decisions about their bank's portfolio from riding the yield curve to arbitraging the markets. Investments constitute open-market purchases of interest-bearing debt securities, some of which serve as secondary reserves. For the most part, the acquiring bank does not anticipate establishing a permanent or continuous relationship with the issuing entity as the acquisition of securities is usually conducted impersonally.

In addition to providing a liquidity reserve, the securities that comprise the secondary reserves, such as the Treasury obligations, may also be used as: (1) collateral against borrowing from the Federal Reserve discount window; (2) a pledge against public deposits where required; and (3) primary collateral in repurchase agreements.

Income-maximizing investments that make up a bank's bond portfolio usually cover longer-term maturities, while the shorter-term maturities (which provide some income) are generally in the portfolio for "window dressing" and liquidity purposes.

In setting bond portfolio policy, management must take into account the quality of the securities to be bought, tax considerations, maturities in the portfolio, diversification, and current as well as future expectations of interest rates over all maturities and types of instruments. Banking regulation is specific germane to the securities that are eligible for a bank's investment portfolio. Since loans constitute the principal source of bank income, as well as risk exposure, banks generally purchase securities that are high rated and are deemed to be relatively low risk; that is, higher risk exposure in the loan portfolio implies a high-quality investment portfolio. With only a limited number of corporate securities in the investment portfolio, the geographic distribution of municipal security holdings are important from a risk standpoint. This is particularly crucial for smaller banks because of the localized nature of the loan portfolio. The interest rate effect upon the bank investment portfolio is of extreme importance because interest rates and bond prices move in opposite directions. For example, when interest rates are expected to decline, banks often add to their portfolios in order to obtain capital gains. If the yield curve is normal (a positive slope) there is a general tendency to buy longer-term maturities under the aforementioned conditions. On the other hand, when interest rates are expected to rise, banks often sell some of their longer-term securities or shorten up the maturity structure of their portfolio. It is important to recall that even though a Treasury security may be free of credit risk, it is still subject to interest rate risk.

Even if credit risk is not an important factor, there is always uncertainty about the level of interest rates during the period when the security is held. The longer the maturity, the greater the chance that market value will be affected by changes in the level of interest rates over the life of the investment. However, there doesn't appear to be a fixed relationship between maturity and either risk or income. Maturity is not a factor that can be measured in isolation; it must be considered in conjunction with rate levels at any point in time and with the prospects of change in rates over the holding period of the investment. It must be remembered that the prices of securities decline when rates rise and increase when interest rates fall, and that the price swings resulting from any given change in rate will increase with the length of the maturity extension.

4

The Capital and Liability Account

The liability side of the balance sheet was dominated by demand deposits until the negotiable certificate of deposit (CD) appeared in 1961. After the introduction of the CD, banks became less dependent on core demand and savings deposits to fund bank loans. Today, non-interest-bearing demand deposits and low-interest-bearing passbook deposits have declined substantially in volume relative to total deposits. This reflects a greater reliance on purchased funds and a number of relatively new consumer deposit instruments. Money market, NOW and Super-NOW accounts, and consumer CDs have become extremely popular with bank customers, while negotiable CDs and Eurodollar CDs have become the main source of corporate time deposits. These new depository products have contributed substantially to changes on the liability side of the balance sheet (see Table 4.1). Previously, banks tended to substitute long-term borrowed funds for equity capital, reflecting an attempt by bank management to stabilize the return on equity when profit margins were diminishing.

BANK CAPITAL

The role of capital in banking reflects a core of funds permanently employed in the business which afford a sense of financial strength and stability. Basically, capital stands ready to absorb adverse financial developments that could impair the viability or continuity of a bank's business. The level or degree of the presence of capital is viewed as a measure of relative financial strength. The only real determinant of capital adequacy is the aggregate consensus of the marketplace. Except for the influence of specific regulatory guidelines, the judgment of the marketplace tends to focus on relative rather than absolute values.

Table 4.1
Selected Liabilities as a Percentage of Total Assets, All Insured
Commercial Banks, 1983-1987

Item	1983	1984	1985	1986	1987
Deposit liabilities........................	77.68	77.93	77.30	76.72	76.42
In foreign offices......................	14.71	12.94	12.61	11.61	11.38
In domestic offices.....................	62.97	64.99	64.69	65.11	65.04
Demand deposits	16.53	16.47	15.63	16.03	15.40
Other checkable deposits............	4.03	4.34	4.57	5.21	6.01
Large time deposits²	12.15	12.23	11.46	10.76	10.60
Other deposits³	30.26	31.95	33.03	33.11	33.02
Gross federal funds purchased and repurchase agreements...........	7.81	7.51	7.68	8.25	8.06
Other borrowings	2.84	2.78	3.44	4.02	4.45
MEMO					
Money market liabilities⁴	37.51	35.46	35.19	34.63	34.48
Average assets (billions of dollars)........	2,245	2,401	2,559	2,753	2,882

2. Deposits of $100,000 or more.
3. Including savings, small time deposits, and money market deposit accounts.

4. Large time deposits issued by domestic offices, deposits issued by foreign offices, repurchase agreements, gross federal funds purchased, and other borrowings.

Source: Federal Reserve Bulletin, July 1988, p. 410.

A bank's capital serves as a cushion to absorb losses. The lower the capital base relative to the bank's operations, the greater the risk of insolvency. We must take into account not only the level of capital adequacy, but the earnings performance as well. Banks with a high return on good-quality assets can assume more risk through leveraging than other banks with a lesser return. Only when a bank suffers large sustained losses does the true test of capital adequacy take place. Capital is a vital component of the ongoing confidence necessary to a depository institution. Equity capital has been likened to a fire extinguishing system in a modern building. It is designed to inspire confidence. If it is used little it will be the same afterward, although the building will probably survive.

Lack of capital does not necessarily cause a bank to fail. Failures are usually associated with fraud, huge real or prospective losses on loans or securities, or the loss of liquidity which itself is typically related to the perception of prospective losses. If the equity were sufficient to absorb the prospective losses, the liquidity would probably never be threatened.

While inadequate equity does not precipitate bank failure, it is the inevitable result of a failure. It is likely that a bank will not fail if capital is adequate. Thus, capital plays a critical although passive role in maintaining the financial strength and credibility of a financial institution in the marketplace. This is because banks must rely on continuing access to funds from governments, corporations, and individuals.

Although controversies exist about what should be considered capital or how much capital a bank should have, most analysts agree that capital supports confidence in the financial stability of a bank, supports growth, and reduces moral hazard.[1]

Equity capital is the dominant form of bank capital. Stockholders' equity includes the portion of sources of funds for which there is no contractual obligation for repayment. Most equity has been accumulated through retained earnings of banks, although from time to time it has been supplemented by new issues of equity capital. For example, the percentage of net increase in equity capital from retained earnings at all commercial banks in 1986 was 52 percent, while the remaining 48 percent came from new common and preferred stock issues.

Issues of long-term debt securities by banks grew rapidly in the early 1970s, and became an important source of total capital funds for large commercial banks. Subordinated notes and debentures became popular as devices to bolster sagging overall capital ratios. Regulatory guidelines permitted banks to maintain up to one-third of their total capital in the form of debt with an original maturity in excess of seven years.

The decline that took place in equity capital ratios between the mid-1960s and mid-1970s resulted because profitability was too low to support asset growth; that is, asset growth was higher than the rate of equity retention. However, banks have raised substantial amounts of equity capital in the 1980s (see Figure 4.1). As a matter of fact, the ratio of equity capital to total assets for all banks has grown from 5.87 percent in 1982 to 6.21 percent in 1986, while the ratio of

Figure 4.1
Primary Book Capital-to-Asset Ratio Reversed Downward Trend in 1982

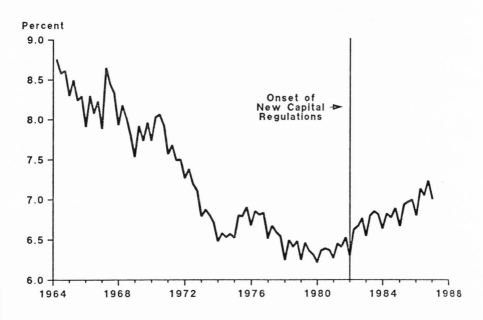

primary capital to total assets has grown from 6.47 percent to 7.07 percent during the same period (see Tables 4.2 and 4.3).

The functions of bank capital are to:

1. Protect the depositor against loss;
2. Maintain the confidence a bank must enjoy to continue in business;
3. Support the credit risk a bank assumes in its normal business lending;
4. Acquire the physical plant and basic necessities needed to offer banking services;
5. Serve as a regulatory restraint on unjustified asset expansion; and
6. Keep the bank open and operating so that time and earnings can absorb any possible losses.

Federal and most state regulations limit the maximum amount a bank can lend to any one borrower to a certain percentage of its capital. The desire for larger lending limits has inspired many banks to seek additional capital through the sale of stock or even through mergers with other institutions.

The Capital Account Balance Sheet

A capital account of the balance sheet of a bank reveals the following components:

Common Stock. The dollar figure for this line shows par value times the number of shares outstanding.

Preferred Stock. The dollar value for this line shows par value times the number of preferred shares of stock outstanding.

Capital Surplus. If banks receive funds from the sale of stock that are in excess of the par value of the stock, the difference is called a capital surplus. Banks may also transfer funds from retained earnings to the capital surplus line, which has the effect of reducing the amount that would be available for the payment of dividends. This line is sometimes designated as "paid-in surplus stock."

Retained Earnings. The dollar figure for this line represents a broad measure of the cumulative profits of a bank from all sources since the bank first opened its doors, less dividends that have been paid. Retained earnings are sometimes titled "earned surplus."

Treasury Stock. The dollar figure for this line represents stock that has been held by the public and has been purchased by the bank. It is stock held in the bank's treasury and represents issued but no longer outstanding stock. It is carried on the books at its repurchased costs.

Total Stockholder's Equity. This dollar figure is the sum of preferred stock, common stock capital surplus, retained earnings, and a deduction of any treasury stock. (See Table 4.4.)

Table 4.2
Equity Capital as a Percentage of Total Assets

Asset Size	1981:H	1982:H	1983:H	1984:H	1985:H	1986:H
Under $25 Million	9.72%	9.90%	10.15%	10.10%	10.14%	9.97%
$25-100 Million	8.36	8.39	8.38	8.30	8.37	8.37
$100-300 Million	7.57	7.56	7.42	7.39	7.47	7.47
$300MM-1 Billion	7.09	6.92	6.94	6.91	7.02	6.97
$1-5 Billion	5.77	5.85	5.85	5.97	6.12	6.48
Over $5 Billion	4.12	4.30	4.47	4.66	5.06	5.19
All Banks	5.89%	5.97%	6.03%	6.07%	6.28%	6.33%

Table 4.3
Primary Capital as a Percentage of Total Assets

Asset Size	1981:H	1982:H	1983:H	1984:H	1985:H	1986:H
Under $25 Million	10.20%	10.39%	10.63%	10.66%	10.82%	10.76%
$25-100 Million	8.89	8.91	8.90	8.86	8.99	9.10
$100-300 Million	8.15	8.14	7.96	7.96	8.08	8.19
$300MM-1 Billion	7.69	7.55	7.47	7.48	7.65	7.74
$1-5 Billion	6.42	6.52	6.40	6.55	6.71	7.17
Over $5 Billion	4.65	4.90	5.10	5.44	5.90	6.18
All Banks	6.45%	6.57%	6.60%	6.74%	6.99%	7.18%

Source: FDIC Banking and Economic Review, November/December 1986, p. 17.

Capital Requirements

Minimum capital requirements are imposed on new banks, while the "adequacy" of capital is evaluated on an ongoing basis. The issue of capital adequacy has long been a point of tension and controversy between banks and the regulatory authorities. Until 1981, there were no uniform policies on capital adequacy among the three federal bank regulators (FDIC, Comptroller of the Currency, and the Federal Reserve). Specific and unambiguous quantitative guidelines were difficult to determine, but it appeared that capital consisting of 5 to 8 percent of assets and 8 to 12 percent of risk assets (defined as all assets except cash and U.S. Government and agency securities) represented rough regulatory targets, although ad hoc negotiations on the subject of capital adequacy seemed to be the rule rather than the exception.

In 1983, federal regulators imposed minimum capital requirements on the nation's 17 largest multinational banking organizations. The capital adequacy rules required the large banks to maintain primary capital equal to at least 5 percent of their total assets and total capital equal to at least 5.5 percent of total assets. In 1981, the Federal Reserve and the Comptroller of the Currency set minimum capital standards for community and regional banks equal to 7 percent of assets for the former group and 6.5 percent of assets for the latter group. The primary capital rules applied to common stock, perpetual preferred stock, capital surplus, undivided profits, reserves for contingencies, other reserves,

Table 4.4
Components of Primary and Secondary Capital

Item		Description
PRIMARY CAPITAL MEASURE		
	Common stock	Aggregate par or stated value of outstanding common stock
	Perpetual preferred stock	Aggregate par or stated value of outstanding perpetual preferred stock. Preferred stock is a form of ownership interest in a bank or other company which entitles its holders to some preference or priority over the owners of common stock, usually with respect to dividends or asset distributions in a liquidation. Perpetual preferred stock does not have a stated maturity date and cannot be redeemed at the option of the holder. It includes those issues that are automatically converted into common stock at a stated date.
	Equity capital: Surplus	Amount received from the sale of common or perpetual preferred stock in excess of its par or stated value.
	Undivided profits	Accumulated dollar value of profits after taxes that have not been distributed to shareholders of common and preferred stock as dividends.
	Capital reserves	Contingency and other capital reserves. Reserves for contingencies include amounts set aside for possible unforeseen or indeterminate liabilities not otherwise reflected on the bank's books and not covered by insurance. Capital reserves include amounts set aside for cash dividends on common and preferred stock not yet declared and amounts allocated for retirement of limited-life preferred stock and debentures subordinated to deposits.
Plus:	Mandatory convertible instruments[1]	Debt issues that mandate conversion to common or perpetual preferred stock at some future date; they must meet the following conditions to be included in primary capital:
		1. The securities must mature (convert to common or preferred stock) in 12 years or less.
		2. The aggregate amount of mandatory convertible securities counted as primary capital may not exceed 20 percent of primary capital net of mandatory convertible securities.
		3. The issuer may redeem the securities before maturity only with the proceeds of the sale of common or perpetual preferred stock.
		4. The holder of the security cannot accelerate the payment of principal except in the event of bankruptcy, insolvency, or reorganization.

66

Table 4.4 (continued)

Item	Description
	5. The security must be subordinated in right of payment to all senior indebtedness of the issuer.
Reserves for loan and lease losses	Amount set aside to absorb anticipated losses. All charge-offs of loans and leases are charged to this capital account, and recoveries on loans and leases previously charged off are credited to this capital account.
Minority interest in consolidated subsidiaries	The sum of the equity capital of the subsidiaries in which the bank has minority interest multiplied by the percentage ownership of the bank in the subsidiaries.
Minus: Equity commitment notes	Debt obligations which the issuer must repay only from the proceeds of the sale of common or perpetual preferred stock. These notes are included in mandatory convertible instruments, but excluded from primary capital.
Intangible assets[2]	Generally these assets represent the purchase price of firms that have been acquired in excess of their book value.

SECONDARY CAPITAL MEASURE

Item	Description
Limited-life preferred stock[3]	Preferred stock with a maturity date.
Plus: Subordinated notes and debentures[3]	Debt obligations of issuer, with fixed maturity dates, that are subordinated to depositors in case of insolvency. Subordinated notes and debentures issued by depository institutions are not insured by the federal deposit insurance agencies.
Mandatory convertible instruments not eligible for primary capital[4]	See mandatory convertible instruments definition above.

[1]Only up to 20 percent of primary capital excluding mandatory convertible instruments.

[2]The FDIC and OCC subtract all intangible assets except for purchased mortgage servicing rights. The Fed subtracts only the "goodwill" portion of intangible assets.

[3]The limited-life preferred stock and subordinated notes and debentures included in secondary capital must have an original weighted average maturity of at least seven years. All three federal banking agencies limit the aggregate amount of secondary capital to less than 50 percent of the amount of a bank's primary capital.

[4]The amount that exceeds 20 percent of primary capital excluding mandatory convertible instruments; equity commitment notes excluded from primary capital.

Source: R. Alton Gilbert, Courtenay C. Stone, and Michael E. Trebing, "The New Capital Adequacy Standards," *Review* (Federal Reserve Bank of St. Louis, May 1985), pp. 14–15.

mandatory convertible instruments, allowances for possible loan and lease losses, and minority interest in equity accounts of consolidated subsidiaries. Secondary capital measures include bank subordinated notes and debentures; unsecured long-term debt issues of the bank, bank holding company, and its nonbank subsidiaries; limited life preferred stock; and mandatory convertible instruments not eligible for primary capital. The regulatory agencies limit the amount of secondary capital included in total capital to no more than 50 percent of the bank's primary capital. Regulators include subordinated long-term debt as part of capital because should the bank fail, investors in these debt instruments receive payment only after all depositors have received full payment. The subordinated debt instruments must have initial average weighted maturities of at least seven years. Each bank's secondary capital is added to its primary capital to obtain its total capital for regulatory purposes. Banks with capital-to-asset ratios that drop below required levels are subjected to increased pressures to raise more capital. In extreme cases, regulators have forced weakly capitalized banks to merge with healthy banks.

Some regulators have suggested giving a major boost to capital requirements and setting guidelines for dividend policies. The increase in capital could be in the form of subordinated debt and would provide an extra cushion of protection against the possibility of loss to depositors and the depositors' insurance fund. It is interesting to note that, at the time of this writing, on average, larger banks have lower capital-to-asset ratios than smaller banks. This was true even before the massive write-offs of Latin American debt.

When regulatory authorities set minimum standards for capital, they may have done banks a big favor. Meeting the regulatory capital requirements will oblige some banks to allocate assets in a more optimal fashion, improve the return on assets, constrain asset growth, select markets more carefully, and improve expense controls. All of these factors should lead to improved earnings and increases in return on equity.

For example, capital-rich "superregional" banks such as NCNB and PNC have begun to expand across state lines via acquisitions and limited-service banks. On the other hand, large multinational banks such as Manufacturers Hanover Corporation (MHC), which barely meet minimal capital requirements (see Table 4.5), do not have a great deal of excess capital for expansion, especially since MHC acquired CIT and boosted loan loss reserves substantially against loans to less developed countries (LDCs). MHC will have to concentrate on internal improvements to boost its return to stockholders, while the superregionals have a bit more flexibility in being able to concentrate on external expansion as well as internal improvements.

The bottom line for most of the giant-sized multinational banks that are not "capital rich" is that they will face slower asset growth than in past years and will be in the market for additional equity capital. These banks will have to select their markets and opportunities, and allocate assets with far greater care in the future. They will probably also modestly lower their dividend payout ratios in an effort to bolster internally generated capital.

Bank capital is more than a source of bank funds since the amount of capital impacts both the potential safety of the bank and its earnings per share. Relatively lower amounts of bank equity capital increase earnings per share, while at the same time increasing the risk for debt holders and depositors. The capital needs of the banking system are expected to grow rapidly for the next decade, and a lack of "adequate" capital might curtail the activities of individual banks.[2]

In 1986, federal bank regulators proposed an additional measure of capital adequacy, the supplemental adjusted capital measure. This measure took into account risk differentials among different classes of assets and recognition of the fact that some risks against which capital must protect depositors are not on the balance sheet (for example, standby letters of credit and loan commitments). The capital measures proposed by the ten nation group of central bankers in 1987 also paid considerable attention to risk-adjusted capital adequacy measures.

In December 1987, the Federal Reserve and 11 foreign central banks announced a preliminary agreement to increase the required capital base of banks worldwide. Under the accord, a bank's required capital base would rise to 8 percent of its assets by 1992, weighted by risk. At least 4 percent of the requirement would be in Tier 1 or core capital: common shareholders equity, disclosed reserves, plus perpetual noncumulative preferred stock. The higher standards would take place in two stages, with banks required to have capital equal to 7.25 percent of total risk-adjusted assets by the end of 1990.

Under these guidelines, almost every large U.S. bank would have to raise a lot of new equity capital. Though U.S. banks currently maintain minimum capital levels of 6 percent, goodwill, now included in bank capital, would be ineligible. Also, loan loss reserves would be limited to 1.25 percent of a bank's risk assets instead of the 2.5 to 4.0 percent of assets that is now in vogue at money-center banks.

The Federal Reserve will also require bank holding companies to meet the 8-percent capital ratio. They will be subject to the same two-tier requirement; but holding companies would be permitted to use both cumulative and noncumulative preferred stock to meet the Tier 1 requirement. While goodwill cannot be counted as capital by banks, goodwill on the books of bank holding companies prior to March 1988 will be eligible to be counted as Tier 2 capital. In addition, security subsidiaries of bank holding companies will be exempted from consolidated capital requirements if they meet the capital rules of securities regulators and if bank deposits are shielded by "strong firewalls" from securities activities.

Proposed Capital Guidelines

A. Capital elements
   Tier 1 (a) Ordinary paid-up share capital/common stock
          (b) Disclosed reserves and noncumulative perpetual preferred stock
   Tier 2 (a) Undisclosed reserves
          (b) Asset revaluation reserves

Table 4.5
Components of Capital

In millions	1987	1986	1985	1984	1983
			December 31,		
Shareholders' Equity:					
Nonredeemable Preferred Stock	$ 644	$ 644	$ 650	$ 650	$ 400
Common Shareholders' Equity	2,060	3,122	2,897	2,637	2,271
Total Shareholders' Equity	2,704	3,766	3,547	3,287	2,671
Reserve for Possible Credit Losses	2,652	1,008	814	631	433
Long-Term Debt Qualifying as Primary Capital[1]	759	622	502	435	100
Minority Interest	23	—	16	16	16
Total Primary Capital	6,138	5,396	4,879	4,369	3,220
Long-Term Debt Qualifying as Secondary Capital[2]	3,484	3,333	3,389	2,949	766
Total Capital	$9,622	$8,729	$8,268	$7,318	$3,986
Selected Ratios					
Primary Capital to Total Assets at Year End[3]	8.08%	7.16%	6.31%	5.72%	4.97%
Total Capital to Total Assets at Year End[3]	12.66	11.58	10.69	9.59	6.15
Common Shareholders' Equity to Total Assets at Year End	2.81	4.20	3.79	3.48	3.53

Source: 1987 Manufacturers Hanover Corporation Annual Report, p. 23.

      (c) General provisions/general loan loss reserves

      (d) Hybrid (debt/equity) capital instruments

      (e) Subordinated term debt and cumulative perferred stock

The sum of Tier 1 and Tier 2 elements will be eligible for inclusion in the capital base, subject to the following limits.

B. Limits and restrictions

    (i) The total of Tier 2 (supplementary) elements will be limited to a maximum of 100 percent of the total of Tier 1 elements;

    (ii) subordinated term debt will be limited to a maximum of 50 percent of Tier 1 elements;

    (iii) where general provisions/general loan loss reserves include amounts reflecting lower valuations of asset or latent but unidentified losses present in the balance sheet, the amount of such provisions or reserves will be limited to a maximum of 1.25 percentage points, or exceptionally and temporarily up to 2.0 percentage points, of risk assets;

    (iv) asset revaluation reserves which take the form of latent gains on unrealised securities (see below) will be subject to a discount of 55 percent.

    (v) The only consumer-type loans that escape full capital requirements are mortgages on residential property of one to four units. Claims secured by these mortgages will be in the 50-percent risk category.

C. Deductions from the capital base

From Tier 1: Goodwill

From total

   capital: (i) Investments in unconsolidated banking and financial subsidiary companies

            N.B. The presumption is that the framework would be applied on a consolidated basis to banking groups.

        (ii) Investments in the capital of other banks and financial institutions (at the discretion of national authorities).

D. Definition of capital elements

    (i) Tier 1: Includes only permanent shareholders' equity, perpetual preferred stock and disclosed reserves (created or increased by appropriations of retained earnings or other surplus, e.g., share premiums, retained profit, general reserves and legal reserves). In the case of consolidated accounts, this also includes minority interests in the equity of subsidiaries which are less than wholly owned. This basic definition of capital excludes revaluation reserves and preference shares having the characteristics specified below in (d).

    (ii) Tier 2: (a) undisclosed reserves are eligible for inclusion within supplementary elements provided these reserves are accepted by the supervisor. Such reserves consist of that part of the accumulated after-tax surplus of retained profits which banks in some countries may be permitted to maintain as an undisclosed reserve. Apart from the fact that the reserve is not identified in the published balance sheet, it should have the same high quality and character as a disclosed capital reserve; as such, it should not be encumbered by any provision or other known liability but should be freely and immediately available to meet unforeseen future losses. This definition of undisclosed reserves excludes hidden values arising from holdings of securities in the balance sheet at below current market prices (see below).

(b) Revaluation reserves arise in two ways. Firstly, in some countries, banks (and other commercial companies) are permitted to revalue fixed assets—normally their own premises, from time to time in line with the change in market values. In some of these countries the amount of such revaluations are determined by law. Revaluations of this kind are reflected on the face of the balance sheet as a revaluation reserve.

Secondly, where formal revaluations are not permitted, hidden values or "latent" revaluation reserves may be present. Of particular importance in some banking systems are hidden values relating to long-term holdings of equity securities where the difference between the historic cost book valuation and the current market price may be substantial.

Both types of revaluation reserve may be included in Tier 2 provided that the assets are prudently valued, fully reflecting the possibility of price fluctuation and forced sale. In the case of "latent" revaluation reserves a discount of 55 percent will be applied to reflect the potential volatility of this form of unrealised capital and the national tax charge on it.

(c) General provisions/general loan loss reserves: Provisions or loan loss reserves held against future, presently unidentified losses are freely available to meet losses which subsequently materialize and therefore qualify for inclusion within secondary elements. Provisions ascribed to impairment of particular assets or known liabilities should be excluded. Furthermore, where general provisions/general loan loss reserves include amounts reflecting lower valuations of assets or latent but unidentified losses already present in the balance sheet, the amount of such provisions or reserves eligible for inclusion will be limited to a maximum of 1.25 percentage points, or exceptionally and temporarily up to 2.0 percentage points.

(d) Hybrid (debt/equity) capital instruments. This heading includes a range of instruments which combine characteristics of equity capital and of debt. Their precise specifications differ from country to country, but they should meet the following requirements:

—They are unsecured, subordinated and fully paid-up;
—they are not redeemable at the initiative of the holder or without the prior consent of the supervisory authority;
—they are available to participate in losses without the bank being obliged to cease trading (unlike conventional subordinated debt);
—although the capital instrument may carry an obligation to pay interest that cannot permanently be reduced or waived (unlike dividends on ordinary shareholders' equity), it should allow service obligations to be deferred (as with preference shares) where the profitability of the bank would not support payment.

Preference shares, having these characteristics, would be eligible for inclusion in this category.

(e) Subordinated term debt: Includes conventional unsecured subordinated debt capital instruments with a fixed term to maturity and limited life redeemable preference shares. Unlike instruments included in item (d), these instruments are not normally available to participate in the losses of a bank which continues trading. For this reason these instruments will be limited to a maximum of 50 percent of Tier 1.

DEPOSITS

Demand Deposits

Demand deposits represent the largest component of the basic money supply—M1—and accounted for about 16 percent of total assets at the end of 1986. The non-interest-bearing deposits of individuals, partnerships, governments, and corporations account for most of the banking industry's demand deposits. Additional demand deposits can be found in correspondent bank balances. Banks maintain correspondent balances at other banks which are referred to as "due to" accounts. Although demand deposits are still an important source of funds to banks, the commercial banking industry no longer has a monopoly on these deposits. Non-interest-bearing accounts represented under 16 percent of bank deposits in 1987 compared to almost 74 percent in 1954.

Individuals maintain both regular and special checking accounts for use as transaction accounts. Regular checking accounts are transferable on demand and generally require small or no minimum balances. They usually provide traditional transaction services and monthly statements. Service charges are typically tied to minimum or average balances with specific charges for such things as returned items and stop payments. Special checking accounts are also usually small-balance accounts which are transferable on demand and provide periodic statements. Service charges are typically set at a charge per item. There are also bundled service accounts for individuals. They are the same as regular checking accounts except that other services provided in the bundle may include safe deposit, traveler's checks, overdrafts, and credit cards. The service charge is usually a flat fee per month, which may vary with balances. The monthly service charge is typically nominal because the cost of servicing these accounts is less than the interest the bank would have to pay to purchase the funds.

Demand deposits are subject to immediate withdrawal or transfer by a depositor. A bank devotes substantial human and physical resources to processing and managing the flow of funds in and out of demand deposits. The true net cost of services rendered depositors represents the cost of money for those deposits plus a part of personnel and operational expenses. Faced with higher costs in other markets for funds, most banks are willing to compensate the demand depositor by providing services at a charge somewhat lower than net cost. Many banks waive service charges entirely on individual accounts if sizable bank balances are kept.

Corporate demand deposit accounts provide traditional transaction services and usually require a minimum balance requirement or fee which is related to service. In addition to providing transaction services, banks also provide collection and dispersement services, electronic funds transfer, cash mobilization and management, lockboxes, zero-balance accounts, investment management, foreign exchange services, revolving credit lines, and lines of credit to back up commercial paper borrowing by corporations. A large percentage of corporate demand deposits are related to compensating balances tied to either lending arrangements or other bank services rendered. Banks are not permitted to pay interest on corporate demand deposits; each bank must compete for deposits on the basis of services rendered the corporation.

Demand deposits of correspondent banks are balances required for services provided. These services include check clearing, loan participations, investment services, general management services, or international banking services. In the case of some correspondent banks over half of their demand deposit balances are from other banks.

As interest rates have risen, all sectors of the economy, especially the corporate sector, have economized on the holdings of non-interest-yielding assets. The introduction of NOW, Super-NOW, and money market accounts and funds have attracted deposits away from demand deposit accounts. (See Table 4.6.) Nonbank competitors have also innovated interest-yielding transaction accounts in various ways and different forms. The removal of the prohibition of interest payments on demand deposits is the final remaining step in the process of deposit interest deregulation and is likely inevitable.

The short-run behavior of demand deposits has been more volatile in the 1980s than it was in the previous decade. The 1980s have been characterized by a number of financial events that have directly or indirectly affected the behavior of demand deposits, including the nationwide introduction of NOW accounts, the deregulation of interest rates on other deposits, changes in the structure of federal income taxes, numerous innovations in financial instruments and in the technology for executing transactions, improvements in cash management techniques, changes in attitudes of corporations germane to bank compensating balances, increased volatility in interest rates and financial markets, and the stock market plunge of October 1987. Evidence suggests that part of the change in demand deposits reflects an increase in their interest elasticity, prompted by the volatile and increased interest rates of the 1970s and early 1980s. These new techniques for managing cash balances helped increase the proportion of demand deposits that are held by businesses. As a matter of fact, holdings of demand deposits by businesses, which may not own NOW accounts, increased from three-fifths to about two-thirds of total demand deposits from 1980 to 1987. On the other hand, the proportion of demand deposits that are held by consumers has declined to just over one-fourth in 1987 compared to one-third in 1980. This declining consumer share is largely because of the nationwide authorization of NOW accounts and the deregulation of retail deposits.[3]

NOW and Super-NOW Accounts

The development of NOW and Super-NOW accounts, known as other checkable deposits, has resulted in a category of transaction accounts on which

Table 4.6
**Selected Liability Items as a Percentage of Consolidated Assets of
Insured Commercial Banks**

Item	A		B	
	1983	1987	1983	1987
Deposit Liabilities	87.09	88.11	78.05	78.55
In Foreign offices	–	–	3.90	2.51
In Domestic offices	87.09	88.11	74.15	76.04
Demand deposits	17.56	14.41	20.46	17.43
Other checkables	7.16	10.36	4.58	7.08
Large time deposits	10.99	10.94	14.63	12.54
Other deposits	51.55	52.44	34.47	39.00
Federal funds and repos	2.15	1.34	10.41	9.17
Other Borrowings	0.63	0.53	2.12	3.02
Money market liabilities	13.59	12.84	31.06	27.24
Loss reserves	0.55	0.83	0.65	1.02

Item	C		D	
	1983	1987	1983	1987
Deposit Liabilities	72.18	70.15	71.49	69.38
In Foreign offices	37.93	35.02	19.53	10.38
In Domestic offices	34.25	35.12	51.99	59.10
Demand deposits	11.43	12.34	16.29	16.76
Other checkables	1.19	2.03	2.70	4.59
Large time deposits	10.55	6.83	12.63	11.49
Other deposits	11.08	13.93	20.35	26.25
Federal funds and repos	7.86	6.87	11.86	13.76
Other borrowings	5.12	8.68	3.90	5.71
Money market liabilities	61.46	57.41	47.92	41.24
Loss reserves	0.59	2.11	0.74	1.54

A=Banks under $300 million in assets
B=Banks with $300 million to $5 billion in assets
C=Nine money center banks
D=Large banks other than money center banks

Source: Federal Reserve Bulletin, July 1988, pp. 415-418.

interest is paid. These accounts allow depositors to write negotiable orders of
withdrawal. These interest-bearing transaction accounts have no maturity and
must be paid by banks on demand. NOW and Super-NOW accounts accounted for
about $164 billion of deposits at insured commercial banks at the end of March
1987. NOW accounts blur the traditional boundary between interest-paying
savings accounts and non-interest-paying demand deposits. In the early 1970s,
Massachusetts and New Hampshire were the only states that permitted these
accounts. However, Congress permitted all banks and thrifts to offer NOW
accounts in 1981. Super-NOW accounts were added in January 1983. At the

time of their introduction, Super-NOW accounts had no interest-rate ceilings, while NOW accounts were limited by Regulation Q in the rates that could be paid. Super-NOW accounts offer the same features as money market accounts except that they allow unlimited transactions. These accounts are available to individuals, governmental units, and certain nonprofit organizations. As can be seen in Table 2.4, NOW accounts are subject to reserve requirements of 12 percent. With the growth of other checkable deposits, banks can no longer rely on the availability of deposit funds for which no interest is paid.

Savings Accounts

Savings accounts, once the staple of retail depository institutions and a traditional source of funds for commercial banks, have diminished in importance because of the development of numerous higher-yielding, deregulated accounts. Banks have developed Christmas and Chanukah clubs, vacation clubs, education accounts, and so forth, to help attract these core savings deposits. With the advent of money market funds and other consumer time accounts the level of passbook accounts has fallen dramatically. Technically, there is a potential 30-day waiting period for savings funds, but as a practical matter it is rarely if ever evoked. There was $161 billion in savings accounts at commercial banks in March 1987. Convenience, ease of understanding and use, liquidity, inertia, and deposit insurance have contributed to the impressive staying power of this product despite the development of higher-yielding consumer depository accounts.

Money Market Deposit Accounts

MMDAs (money market deposit accounts) with limited checking privileges were first permitted at banks on December 14, 1982. This deregulated account was not subject to any interest rate ceiling under Regulation Q or any reserve requirement. These deregulated accounts quickly became one of the fastest growing and largest deposit categories in the history of banking. At the end of March 1987, commercial banks had $371 billion in MMDAs. When first introduced, there were minimum balance requirements of $2,500; these are no longer in existence. However, there are still only six preauthorized or automatic transfers of funds permitted each month, no more than three of which may be by check or draft drawn by the depositor.

Consumer Certificates of Deposit

There are 7- to 30-day, 90-day, 180-day, 1-year, 18-month, 30-month, 42-month, 60-month and even longer-term consumer time deposits of less than $100,000 available which offer rates in excess of the passbook rate. Regulation Q interest-rate ceilings and minimum amounts required for deposits have been removed or deregulated for consumer time accounts. When first introduced, the maximum rate permitted on these accounts was tied to the Treasury bill rate at time of issue. However, these accounts have been deregulated germane to interest-rate ceilings and minimum-balance requirements. These higher-yielding time accounts have been quite popular with consumers. They were also the main source of funds when the new deregulated money market accounts were permitted.

The two accounts initially responsible for the growth in small time deposits were the 6-month money market certificate and the 2.5-year small saver certificate which were both initially pegged to a Treasury rate. The 6-month CD was introduced in June 1978, while the 2.5-year CD was introduced in January 1983. The introduction of these CDs gave banks and thrifts a weapon to fight against disintermediation. The depository institutions now had two accounts that savers could use in shifting from lower-yielding fixed-ceiling accounts into higher-yielding accounts that were tied to market rates when issued.

Time deposits became the main source of deposit growth at commercial banks in the 1979-1982 period. As savings deposits declined, growth in time deposits increased, especially time deposits with variable-rate ceilings. Large time deposits, which had become a fairly stable source of deposit funds in the early 1970s, continued to grow at about the same pace into the 1980s. Most of the growth of time deposits came from the proliferation of small time deposits. The latter category had become one of the most important sources of funds by March 1987. Time deposits differ from savings deposits because they have a predetermined maturity date and withdrawals prior to that date are subject to interest penalties. During 1986-1987, some banks introduced consumer CDs tied to the performance of the stock market.

Large Denomination Certificates of Deposit

Negotiable certificates of deposit in minimum amounts of $100,000 and with maturities of no less than 14 days are not subject to interest-rate ceilings and are often referred to as jumbo CDs. At the end of March 1987, commercial banks had $269 billion of these deposits. Such certificates represent an extremely fruitful source of funds for money-center banks as well as large regional banks. Both money-center banks and large regionals have a regular source of individual, municipal, corporate, and money-market-fund customers who supply these funds. Banks also raise CD money through brokers who receive a modest commission for obtaining these deposits in an impersonal marketplace. It is important that a bank maintain its own customer base as a source of funds, particularly in times of market tension and tight money conditions. The corporate treasurer with funds to invest will usually call a number of banks and shop the market for a favorable rate. Although most CDs have maturities of considerably under 1 year, a number of banks have initiated funding programs by offering to sell CDs with maturities of 4 to 10 years.

As a financial instrument, interest on CDs is computed on the basis of a 360-day year. CDs are usually issued at par and traded mostly on an interest-bearing basis. CDs are subject to some degree of default risk based on the credit risk of the issuing bank. Of course, deposits above $100,000 are not insured by the FDIC and have varied from about 50 basis points over Treasury bill rates for 90-day maturities to just under 200 basis points between 1978 and 1986. The level of interest rates, the perceived level of risk, the amount of funds a bank needs, and the size and maturity of the CD are among the basic determinants of the CD rate. The CD market has evolved into a multitiered market with interest rates differentiated on the basis of the strength of the borrowing bank and the liquidity of the CDs.

Money-center banks plus about 100 large regional banks account for close to 90 percent of the large denomination CDs issued. The first effective negotiable CD was developed by the First National City Bank of New York (now called Citibank) when the Discount Corporation of New York decided to provide a secondary market for jumbo CDs in 1961. The decision of other major security dealers to make a market in these CDs paved the way for the commercial bank management philosophy known as "liabilities management." Negotiable CDs have emerged as a major source of funds for commercial banks. Among money market instruments or securities, negotiable CDs are behind only Treasury bills in terms of dollar volume outstanding.

Eurodollar CDs

Banks, particularly those with branches abroad, are large buyers of funds in the Eurodollar market. Eurodollar CDs are generally issued in amounts of at least $1 million (there are some exceptions). There have never been any rate restrictions on these deposits. Although some of these funds are purchased directly from corporations and governments, the majority are purchased in the interbank marketplace. Brokers are often used when sizable liability management programs are underway. In the past there has often been a tiering of rates, which has been related to market impressions of overall credit quality of the issuing bank and the liquidity of the CD in the marketplace. Eurodollar CD rates are higher than domestic CD rates of comparable quality and maturity.

OTHER SOURCES OF FUNDS

Commercial Paper

Although treated as a nondeposit item, some bank holding companies issue large amounts of commercial paper in both the retail and the wholesale markets. Some of these funds are used by nonbanking affiliates within the holding company, while funds are often used directly by the bank. Commercial paper used by the bank is subject to a reserve requirement. The commercial paper source of funds is similar to that for domestic CDs. However, some bank holding companies sell commercial paper to retail customers in units as small as $25,000.

Brokered Deposits

Some banks have turned to brokered deposits as a source of funds. A brokered deposit refers to either a negotiable or nonnegotiable CD of a bank that is purchased by an investor through an intermediary or third party. The third party receives a fee from the issuer and acts as a broker or dealer, selling the CDs for the bank. In addition to large money-center banks that have always used brokerage assistance in funding themselves, small- and medium-sized banks raise funds through deposit brokers, providing them with national sources of funding that are often cheaper, quicker, and more flexible than local sources. These smaller banks have been able to compete successfully against larger banks because FDIC insurance coverage has given them access to investors traditionally interested only in the largest, best-known banks. Since the FDIC protects deposits up to $100,000, many depositors are no longer concerned about the financial health of their bank.[4]

The growth of the brokered deposit market during the 1980s has paralleled the increase in bank failures. There is evidence that some failed banks relied heavily upon brokered deposits. Critics have charged that banks on the brink of insolvency have a strong incentive to outbid other banks for brokered deposits and that considerable funds have been channeled to weak institutions. Some of the funds in the hands of weak banks have been allocated to high-yield, risky loans in the hope of earning enough profits to remain solvent.[5] Also, many healthy banks have complained that above-market rates paid by weak banks have coerced healthy banks into paying higher rates than normal in order to remain competitive.

Federal Funds

The federal funds market encompasses the trading of excess reserve balances by member banks and the trading of liquid funds among financial institutions. Federal funds are usually short-term loan transactions among banks. The lender has no guarantee of repayment other than the promise and reputation of the borrower. If a bank's reputation becomes tarnished, its supply of federal funds can vanish. Although most transactions are for one night, a term federal funds market has developed for periods of up to one year. Federal funds do not involve any physical securities; they involve a series of accounting entries by participants in the transactions. Both member and nonmember banks as well as thrift institutions and certain government agencies participate in the transactions.

Most banks use federal fund transactions as a cash adjustment procedure and as a tool for liability management. For example, a bank expecting 3- to 6-month CDs to decline will borrow heavily in the overnight federal funds market in an attempt to extend maturities after the anticipated rate drop occurs. Basically, when operating with a normal, upward-sloping yield curve, banks will tend to fund short-term when they expect rates to decline and tend to fund longer-term when they anticipate increases in interest rates.

Federal Reserve Discount Window

The Federal Reserve Discount Window is open to member and nonmember banks as a source of funds for adjusting reserve balances, for meeting seasonal credit needs, and for emergency credit. Some banks will occasionally borrow from the Federal Reserve when the discount rate is below the federal funds rate in order to lower their cost of funds. However, borrowing from the Federal Reserve is a privilege rather than a right, and this type of borrowing must be done discretely and without abuse.

Repurchase Agreements (Repos)

Repos are another source of funds for banks. They represent the sale of securities with a promise to repurchase the securities at a specific future date and price. A repurchase agreement is usually transacted with government or agency securities, although some repos use CDs as the underlying collateral. The difference between the sale and purchase price represents the rate of interest earned by the customer. This rate of interest is usually just under the federal funds rate and is consequently a cheaper source of funds to the bank. Repos are also considered collateralized loans by some authorities. It is important for a customer to take possession of the underlying security in a repurchase agreement in case there is a bankruptcy on the part of the participating bank or dealer. In the latter case, the security can be sold in the marketplace without serious repercussions.

Repos are not subject to reserve requirements as long as the collateral is in the form of government or agency securities. Traditional repos are wholesale instruments with a denomination of at least $100,000 and a typical size of $1,000,000 or more. Some banks have begun to offer consumers retail repurchase agreements with denominations of less than $100,000 and maturities of less than 89 days.

Purchased Funds

Purchased funds include large CDs, Eurodollar CDs, repos, federal funds, and borrowing from the Federal Reserve. These funds have several functional purposes, which include providing a source of funds to meet liquidity needs on core deposits and loan programs, providing funds to implement spread management operations and dealer operations in federal funds, and to accommodate customers.

Cost of Funds

When first introduced, MMDA, Super-NOW, and small time deposit accounts raised the cost of funds at most banks and thrifts, possibly causing a decline in the profitability of some of these institutions. This is because most of the funds deposited in those deregulated accounts came from the core depository consumer accounts of those institutions. The increased cost of funds primarily affected retail banks rather than wholesale banks because of the retail banking emphasis on consumer deposits.

On the liability side of the balance sheet, we have seen a shift away from wholesale, money market liabilities and a shift toward retail-type deposits during the 1980s. This shift helped hold down funding costs. However, as interest rates declined from 1982 to 1986, the drop in market rates quickly brought the cost of wholesale liabilities down nearly to the rate paid on interest-bearing retail depository accounts. By 1986, there was a marked narrowing between rates paid on retail deposits and those on managed liabilities (see Table 4.7). The move away from managed liabilities led to a decline in both large domestic and Eurodollar CDs during 1986. The counterbalancing increase in other checkable deposits and other deposits—the sum of MMDAs, savings, and small time deposits—grew rapidly from 1981 to 1986. The sum of other checkables, MMDAs, savings, and small time deposits grew from 26 to 38 percent of commercial bank assets from 1980 to 1986. About two-thirds of this increase matched the drop in demand deposits. The remaining increase of one-third reflected the lower share of managed liabilities.[6]

In addition to interest rate costs, there are costs associated with check clearing and the operation of branch systems to accommodate savings and time deposits. Competition for passbook savings is based on convenience factors such as location, banking hours, telephone transfers, free stamped mailing envelopes, ATM availability, and so on.

SOURCES OF DEPOSITS

Like consumer deposits, wholesale deposits that come from corporations, small businesses, governmental units, nonbank financial institutions, and other banks, consist of transaction deposits and interest-bearing time deposits. The overall account relationship of both lending and deposit services is more closely integrated in wholesale deposits than in consumer deposits. The level of deposits in a commercial account is often determined by lending arrangements in the form of compensating balances left on deposit in return for a line of credit. Other services provided by the bank in connection with commercial demand deposits include traditional checking services, collection and disbursement, electronic funds transfer systems (EFTS), payroll, investment, economic advisory, cash management, and foreign exchange services. The major source of deposits from companies is in the form of large negotiable CDs.

Table 4.7
Rates Paid for Fully Consolidated Liabilities, All Insured Commercial Banks, 1983-1987[1]

Item	1983	1984	1985	1986	1987
Interest-bearing deposits..........	9.32	9.92	8.20	6.98	5.82
Large certificates of deposit.....	8.90	10.67	8.72	7.31	6.86
Deposits in foreign offices[2]........	10.32	12.62	9.48	7.78	7.90
Other deposits...........	9.11	8.84	7.66	6.67	5.10
Gross federal funds purchased and repurchase agreements	9.69	11.22	7.97	6.77	6.51
Other liabilities for borrowed money[3]	11.88	13.92	10.62	8.01	9.65
Total	**9.46**	**10.20**	**8.29**	**7.01**	**6.11**

1. Calculated as described in the "Technical Note," FEDERAL RESERVE BULLETIN, vol. 65 (September 1979), p. 704, for years through 1984. For years after 1984, rates are derived from expense items and quarterly average balance sheet data.
2. Series break after 1983. Reporting instructions classified international banking facilities as domestic offices until the end of 1983 and as foreign offices thereafter. Income data are not sufficiently detailed to allow construction of a consistent series on the new basis for rates of return as has been done for balance sheet data in other tables in this article.

3. Including subordinated notes and debentures.

Source: Federal Reserve Bulletin, July 1988, p. 411.

Commercial banks also obtain deposit funds from federal, state, and local governmental units. The size of their accounts and the services received by state and local governments are similar to commercial accounts in terms of customer relations. Governmental deposits not covered by FDIC insurance are usually protected by pledged securities in most states. At the federal government level Treasury tax and loan accounts serve as depositories for income, social security, and unemployment taxes on behalf of the U.S. Treasury and for proceeds from the sale of U.S. Government Securities, especially savings bonds. The Treasury earns interest on funds left on deposit at banks, but also compensates the banks directly by paying fees for services rendered.

Banks are offering consumers a variety of deposit accounts characterized by deregulated rates and depository insurance of up to $100,000. Given the competitive nature of the market for upscale consumer accounts, many banks have developed integrated packages of services. Banks have been marketing bundled-service accounts for over a decade, which offer consumers a package of services such as free traveler's and cashier's checks, safe deposit boxes, credit card services, nationwide ATM services, overdraft protection, check guarantee cards, reduced rates on some consumer loans, and unlimited free checking when sizable bank balances are maintained or when a monthly or yearly fee is paid.

Since banks are paying money market rates for consumer deposits in our deregulated environment, retail accounts of the future might be provided cafeteria style with consumers paying only for services they actually choose to use. These accounts may even be structured much more like commercial accounts, with earnings credits on collected balances and charges for services used by the retail customer.[7] With banks facing increased costs with the elimination of interest rate ceilings and the availability of ATMs, other inefficiencies such as overbranching, oversized branches, branch hours, and services offered at branches will be reduced.

Keogh accounts and IRAs (individual retirement accounts) represent potential sources of long-term funds for depository institutions. Many banks have established retirement savings departments in anticipation of enormous growth in this segment of the pension market. Banks have interfaced IRAs with payroll deduction systems, provided automatic transfers from checking or savings accounts to IRAs and have arranged for transfer into IRA accounts from other institutions. Commercial banks have been the dominant factor in the IRA market. These funds are considered important because of the aggregate size of IRA accounts and because of the potential long-term nature of the deposit.

SUMMARY

Commercial banks have experienced some major changes in their sources of funds. There has been a sharp drop in demand deposits as a percentage of total liabilities in the last decade (with the exception of 1986) and a related increase in time, savings, and other checkable deposits. At one time demand deposits were the principal source of bank funds. Today, the large CDs, money market accounts, and small consumer time deposits dominate the liability side of the balance sheet. In the case of multinational, money-center banks, Eurodollar CDs play a key role in funding bank assets. Demand deposits are still an important source of funds, but they are less important than they were in the period 1950 through 1980.

While capital-to-asset ratios decreased during the 1970s and early 1980s, they began to increase in the mid-1980s, partially in response to regulatory pressures. Banks have relied more recently on raising long-term debt and equity in the capital markets rather than on retained earnings. As a matter of fact, the percentage of net increase in equity capital at all insured commercial banks from retained earnings has declined from 85 percent in 1982 to 52 percent in 1986.

NOTES

1. G. Hempel, A. Coleman, D. G. Simonson, *Bank Management: Text and Cases* (New York: John Wiley & Sons, 1983), 132-134.

2. Ibid., 154.

3. P. I. Mahoney, "The Recent Behavior of Demand Deposits," *Federal Reserve Bulletin*, April 1988, 195, 204.

4. N. A. Lash, *Banking, Laws and Regulation: An Economic Perspective* (Englewood Cliffs, N.J.: Prentice Hall Inc., 1987), 94.

5. Ibid., 94, 95.

6. *Federal Reserve Bulletin,* July 1987, 543-544.

7. F. E. Morris, "The Costs of Price Controls in Banking," *New England Economic Review,* Federal Reserve Bank of Boston (May-June 1979): 49-54.

5

Asset and Liability Management

David Leahigh

This chapter will discuss the development, applications, and pitfalls of various asset and liability management techniques used by commercial banks. While interest rates currently are less volatile than they were in the late 1970s and early 1980s, the lessons learned about managing interest-rate risk should not be filed away and forgotten; rather they should be incorporated into standard bank management practice.

Integrative asset and liability management models are relatively new in banking, having come into vogue in the mid-1970s. One reason for this late development is that many bankers really did not understand that the introduction of liability management in the 1960s put interest-rate risk on both sides of the balance sheet. The traditional problem faced by banks prior to the late 1950s was one of asset allocation. A bank had a fixed volume of funds, generated by core deposits, and it allocated those funds to various asset categories. First, the bank had to meet its legal reserve requirements on its deposits and its pledging requirements. Second, the bank would typically set up a secondary reserve to provide liquidity for the bank. Assets in this category would typically be U.S. Treasury bills, or other high-quality short-term investments. Third, the bank could then get down to the business of banking: making loans, primarily commercial loans. Finally, any leftover funds would be invested in long-term Treasury bonds and municipal bonds for income.

Bankers had essentially one problem, that of asset allocation. The size of the bank was determined by the size of the flow of demand and savings deposits into the bank. While the level of demand deposits was related to the level of loans, banks did not compete aggressively for those deposits. Thus, the major concern of bankers was credit quality. Did the loans and municipal securities have sufficiently low default risk to make them eligible for inclusion in the bank's portfolio? Interest-rate risk was confined to the asset side of the balance sheet, primarily with Treasury and municipal securities. The bulk of a bank's liabilities and demand and savings deposits, were subject to Regulation Q ceilings.

Finally, liquidity risk was also an asset-side consideration, except for the rare deposit run at a bank in the post-Depression era. At the start of the 1950s, liquidity was not a major problem for commercial banks. Additional liquidity needs that were not met by deposit inflows could be handled by selling off part of the bank's Treasury portfolio which had reached enormous proportions during World War II.

However, by the late 1950s, banks had run their investment portfolios down about as low as they felt they could go. Furthermore, deposit growth was slowing as a result of competition from savings and loans and better cash management techniques at corporations. Banks were losing good lending opportunities because of the lack of liquidity, and the traditional sources were no longer sufficient. In 1961, therefore, First National City Bank (FNCB; now Citibank) innovated the negotiable certificate of deposit. FNCB agreed to pay corporate depositors market rates for time deposits, while government securities dealers agreed to maintain an active secondary market for the CDs.

The benefits to the bank and the corporations were, and still are, obvious. FNCB obtained a new source of funds and liquidity, so that it was no longer constrained by its core deposit growth. The corporations got an additional tool for their cash management needs to compete with Treasury bills and commercial paper. If FNCB needed new cash, all it had to do was tap the major domestic corporations, which were more than willing to invest in the bank's CDs.

There are few unmixed blessings in this world, and the CD certainly is not one of them. There are risks that are now apparent, but in 1961 these were at best dimly perceived. For example, the Penn Square Bank of Oklahoma City failed in 1982, defaulting on deposits in excess of $100,000 that were not covered by FDIC insurance. Certainly from this side of the Penn Square debacle we are well aware of the credit risk investors in bank debt incur. So far, though, this seems to be a rare occurrence. A more continual concern from a bank's perspective is the interest-rate risk on the liability side of the balance sheet to which the banking industry found itself exposed. Finally, there is the liquidity risk for the borrowing banks. We can no longer measure liquidity in the traditional ways. A bank used to be liquid when it had strong primary and secondary reserves, quantifiable assets funded by core deposits on the balance sheets. Today, for many banks liquidity is the ability to borrow in short-term markets. That ability depends on the willingness of the other participants in the markets to lend to these banks. It is difficult if not impossible to measure that willingness. There may be times when banks are unable to attract or retain funds via liability management because of uncertainty about the soundness of a particular bank. A bank can lose its liquidity, as in the case of Continental Illinois in 1984 and the First Pennsylvania Bank in 1980.

The CD was not the only new tool of liability management for bankers in the early 1960s. The federal funds market reemerged after being dormant for over 30 years. Rulings by the Comptroller of the Currency that defined federal funds transactions as purchases and sales rather than loans freed those transactions from the capital restrictions on loans. Banks were therefore able to sell and buy fed funds in any amount that the market would bear.

In 1965-1966 and 1969, banks began to discover the side effects of liability management. In both instances, interest rates rose, increasing the cost of purchased money to banks. At some point, though, Regulation Q became binding on CDs. Banks were thus initially subjected to an increase in interest-rate risk and then to liquidity risk as CD depositors declined to roll over their CDs at less than market rates. These episodes prompted large banks to tap the Eurodollar markets as a way to obtain funds, yet another source of purchased money. Between June 24, 1970 and July 1, 1973, Regulation Q ceilings on negotiable CDs over $100,000 were removed, and between January 1, 1981 and April 1, 1986, Regulation Q ceilings were eliminated on virtually all retail deposits. While these moves eliminated the regulation-induced aspects of liquidity risk, they opened banks up to the full effects of interest-rate risk. Any banker who was in the business during this period doesn't need to be reminded of the swings that interest rates went through from the early 1970s to the early 1980s. For the newer members of the profession, though, let us just note that the prime rate ranged from a low of 6.25 percent in December 1976 to 21.50 percent in December 1980, and the three-month CD rate went from 4.65 percent in February 1977 to 18.65 percent in December 1980. Clearly, interest-rate risk was now a liability-side problem as well as an asset-side problem.

In response to this unprecedented rate volatility, bankers began to devise models that explicitly recognized that interest-rate risk resided on both sides of the balance sheet. Starting from simple models, bankers have moved to extremely complex paradigms capable of precise descriptions of the effects of interest-rate movements on net interest income, net worth, or both. It is to these models that we now turn our attention.

BASIC CONSIDERATIONS

Under liability management, a bank targets asset growth as given and then adjusts its sources of funds (liabilities) as needed. When a bank needs additional sources it merely buys the funds in the money markets. Bank liabilities employed are negotiable CDs, federal funds, repurchase agreements, Eurodollars, and commercial paper that has been channeled by the bank holding company to the bank. The liquidity gained by liability management enables a bank to counteract deposit outflows and to meet increases in loan demand. As long as the anticipated marginal return on new loans or investments exceeds the expected marginal cost of funds, bank income is increased by acquiring the funds through liability management.

As liability management practices became more important, it became obvious that decisions about the composition of a bank's assets and liabilities were no longer independent. On the contrary, decisions about a bank's asset and liability holdings are highly interrelated. The bank balance sheet is considered a portfolio for which financial planning is undertaken with the objective of maximizing bank profits subject to the constraints imposed by bank regulations and liquidity requirements.

With any successful asset and liability (A and L) management strategy, some basic questions must be answered right from the top. First, what is the strategy meant to accomplish? The usual goal is to manage the effects of interest rate movements on the net interest margin. The second question is, who has the authority to execute the strategy? This could be the Asset/Liability Committee (ALCO), a senior vice president, or somebody else. However, there must be an assignment of responsibility to make the program work.

On an operational level, more questions must be considered, given the objectives. How sophisticated should the program be? Models range all the way from simple, one-gap models to extremely involved duration-gap programs. Increasing levels of complexity bring with them more refinement in the measurement of interest-rate risk, but also higher costs, greater data requirements, and the need for more highly (perhaps overly) trained personnel to run the models. If the objective of the A and L strategy is to avoid massive mistakes in positioning assets and liabilities, while living with some mismatches, then a duration-gap model is probably too much for the bank in question. On the other hand, if the objective is to add two or three basis points to the bank's return on assets, then a simple one-gap model may be woefully inadequate.

In almost all the techniques of A and L management, the basic strategy is to recast the balance sheet in terms of interest-rate sensitivity and move away from the traditional arrangement based on liquidity. The question to be asked is not how liquid the instrument is, but rather when it can be repriced. This is important because, although they appear similar and may be interrelated, liquidity risk and interest-rate risk are not the same. A bank may face severe liquidity risks even with a perfectly hedged balance sheet. A scenario along these lines concerns an institution with long-term assets perfectly matched by long-term deposits, but because interest rates rise sharply, depositors elect to incur early withdrawal penalties as they take their funds out. Initially, there is no interest-rate risk here but significant liquidity risk. On the other hand, a bank may have nothing but long-term fixed-rate assets funded by overnight money. Here the bank has lots of interest-rate risk, but its liquidity risk may be nil if it can continue to borrow in the overnight markets.

ONE-PERIOD MODEL

To illustrate the basics of asset and liability management, let us look at the simple one-period gap model. The bank has a one-period horizon, say 90 days.

Assets and liabilities are now classified as rate-sensitive if they can be repriced within the one period, or as rate-nonsensitive if they cannot be repriced. In this case, rate-sensitive assets would include any Treasury instruments with less than 90 days to maturity, overnight fed funds sold, reverse repurchase agreements, and floating rate loans. Rate-sensitive liabilities are savings deposits, CDs and Eurodollars with less than 90 days to maturity, fed funds purchased, repurchase agreements, and the like. Rate-nonsensitive items would be fixed assets, long-term Treasury securities, fixed-rate loans, long-term CDs and time deposits, and so on.

It may be obvious that the most liquid assets and liabilities are not included in the discussion above. Items such as cash and due from banks and demand deposits pose an interesting question. When are they repriced? Most of these balances carry no explicit interest, so repricing does not occur directly. As interest rates change, however, the opportunity cost of holding these balances changes, so one could argue that they should be included in the rate-sensitive category. This is misleading. If we are interested in the effect that changing rates have on the bank's net interest margin, we should include in the rate-sensitive group only that portion of cash items that would be shifted into interest-bearing accounts. For example, the major component of cash and due is required reserves held by banks at the Federal Reserve. These are non-interest-bearing, and will change only as deposit levels change, not as interest rates change. As for demand deposits, to the extent that depositors such as large corporations practice cash management, deposit levels will probably be as low as permissible and therefore not overly responsive to interest rates. Many banks facilitate this process by offering sweeps, in which the bank removes any excess balances from demand deposits and invests them in interest-bearing instruments such as repurchase agreements. The amount remaining covers compensating balance requirements and basic cash needs such as payroll. Thus we have the seemingly paradoxical situation that the most liquid balance sheet items are classified as rate-nonsensitive.

After completing this procedure, the balance sheet might look something like Table 5.1.

Another basic consideration is, exactly what is it that gets repriced? One might be tempted to consider all principal as being repriced at maturity, but this could be incorrect for a large part of a bank's balance sheet. Consider a four-year amortized car loan. If the entire principal amount is classified as a four-year asset, the ALCO manager is in for a lesson in double counting. As the loan approaches maturity, cash flows are generated by the amortization. These cash flows are then reinvested; that is, repriced. When the loan finally does mature, there is only the last payment to be repriced, not the full amount. The moral of the story is that cash flows, not contract principal at maturity, are the items to be repriced.

Once the asset and liability items have been classified by repricing, there are several ways to define the gap. The first is the absolute dollar gap, $GAP:

Table 5.1
Balance Sheet

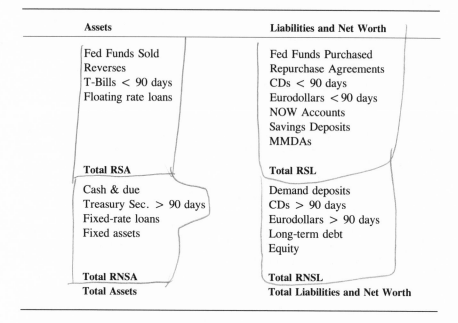

Assets	Liabilities and Net Worth
Fed Funds Sold Reverses T-Bills < 90 days Floating rate loans	Fed Funds Purchased Repurchase Agreements CDs < 90 days Eurodollars < 90 days NOW Accounts Savings Deposits MMDAs
Total RSA	**Total RSL**
Cash & due Treasury Sec. > 90 days Fixed-rate loans Fixed assets	Demand deposits CDs > 90 days Eurodollars > 90 days Long-term debt Equity
Total RNSA	**Total RNSL**
Total Assets	**Total Liabilities and Net Worth**

$$\$GAP = RSA - RSL \qquad (1)$$

where RSA = dollar volume of rate-sensitive assets and
RSL = dollar volume of rate-sensitive liabilities.

The gap can also be defined in ratio form:

$$RGAP = RSA/RSL \qquad (2)$$

Finally, the gap can also be expressed as a fraction of some balance sheet item; for example, total assets (TA) or equity (EQ):

$$TAGAP = (RSA - RSL)/TA \qquad (3)$$

$$EQGAP = (RSA - RSL)/EQ \qquad (4)$$

Each of these measures has advantages and disadvantages. Ideally, a bank should use some combination of all four. The first measure gives the ALCO manager some idea of the dollar magnitude of the transactions that would be needed to close up a gap. This may be important if a bank has limited access to various markets that might be used to eliminate a gap. For instance, a bank may find itself with a large positive dollar gap which it wants to close with CDs, but can't because the market is saturated with that bank's paper. The second measure gives the relative size of a mismatch between rate-sensitive assets and rate-sensitive liabilities, and is useful in defining the limits of risk exposure the bank is willing to take. For example, the ALCO may decide that RGAP shall be between .9 and 1.1 to keep interest-rate risk within bounds.

The third and fourth measures give the ALCO manager a good idea of how much of the bank is being bet on interest rates. The fourth measure, gap-to-equity, is probably the best measure of the risk the bank is taking. This measure, when combined with an estimate of the effect of changing rates on net interest income, is the basis for calculating how much capital is at risk for a given change in interest rates. At this point the manager should apply the first rule of gambling: never bet more than you're willing to lose. This places an upper limit on the size of the gap for any given change in interest rates. The maximum a bank should be willing to lose under the current capital adequacy requirements is the amount that would reduce its primary capital-to-asset ratio to a minimum of 5.5 percent or its total capital to asset ratio to 6.0 percent. Any loss larger than that is unacceptable to the federal regulatory agencies and therefore should be unacceptable to the ALCO manager.

This brings us to the next step in an A and L strategy: forecasting interest rates. This step is the crux of any successful A and L program, but it is extremely difficult to forecast interest rates accurately. Interest-rate forecasting models can literally range from the naive guess to sophisticated and complex econometric models. At the very least, the manager must analyze the basic economic and financial data to decide whether rates are likely to go up or down. Even this is not easy. Michael Belongia (1987) reports that of 90 predictions made by nine forecasters (10 each per forecast) and reported by the *Wall Street Journal* from December 1981 through 1986, only 38, or 42 percent, were correct as to the direction of the change. An excellent source on the behavior of interest rates is James Van Horne (1984).

Furthermore, the manager should have a range of forecasts, and have probabilities attached to each one. At the very least, the manager should have best- and worst-case, or highest-rate and lowest-rate forecasts. There must be some explicit decision about what is probable enough to plan for and what is outside the realm of likelihood. For instance, it is possible that the prime rate will again reach 21.5 percent. The relevant consideration is how likely it is that it will occur during the planning period. It may be a 1 in 1,000 chance. Managers must also decide on their tolerance for risk: what probability is low enough to ignore? Keep in mind that interest-rate forecasting is difficult; nobody is right all the time, and precious few even most of the time. However, that fact does not relieve the ALCO manager of the responsibility of making interest-rate forecasts.

Once the gap has been calculated and interest rates forecasted, the ALCO manager is able to predict the effects of expected interest-rate movements on the net interest margin. In the case of the basic-gap model, there is a simple relationship between the dollar gap and the expected net interest income:

$$E\{NII_{t+1} - NII_t\} = \$GAP \times E\{R_{t+1} - R_t\} \qquad (5)$$

where NII_t = net interest income at time t;
        R_t = interest rate at time t;
        E = expected value operator.

In this model the expected change in net interest income is a linear function of the size of the dollar gap for any given expected change in interest rates. Given a 100-basis-point change in rates, a bank with a $1 million gap over 90 days could expect a change in NII of $2,500. Combining Equation 5 with the equity gap measure gives the ALCO manager an estimate of the risk to the capital position of the bank.

RULES FOR GAP MANAGEMENT

There are some basic rules for managing gaps over a cycle, and an ALCO manager would do well to remember rule #1: don't attempt to maximize the gap at each and every point of the cycle; optimize over the entire cycle. Keeping this in mind will help the manager avoid making massive errors and being confused. Rule #2 is a corollary to #1: no gap is optimal over all points of the cycle. The gap must change as economic and financial conditions change.

The most common rules for managing the gap over an interest rate cycle are those given by John Clifford (1975) and Barrett Binder (1980):

Rising rates:	widening (positive) gap
High rates:	widest (positive) gap
Falling rates:	narrowing (or negative) gap
Low rates:	narrowest (or negative) gap

There is nothing wrong with the prescriptions for the rising and falling rate scenarios. Certainly as rates rise, the manager wants to be in an asset-sensitive position; that is, a positive gap. However, the manager also must be careful in transition phases. The old saw about the secret of a comedian's success applies here: timing is everything. Suppose interest rates are at a cyclical peak and the manager has positioned the bank with the widest possible positive gap. The manager is likely to be facing a downward-sloping yield curve, so that there is a good net interest spread, as long as rates don't shift. The problem comes in as rates do start to drop. The manager must now convert rate-sensitive assets to nonsensitive assets and nonsensitive liabilities to rate-sensitive ones in very short order to take advantage of the falling rates. There is no problem with selling marketable securities such as T-bills, and short-term floating rate funds will probably be available. However, floating-rate loans probably cannot be converted to fixed-rate without a large rate concession by the bank, and long-term fixed-rate deposits booked near the peak of interest rates will have a depressing effect on bank earnings for several periods to come.

To avoid such problems, the ALCO manager should time the largest gap to occur sometime before the top of the cycle. The manager should start to buy long-term fixed-rate assets and discourage long-term fixed-rate deposits either through below-market pricing or refusal to accept such deposits. While this narrows the gap at a time when a large positive gap is desirable, it positions the bank to take advantage of the expected turn in rates. The same line of reasoning applies at the bottom of an interest-rate cycle when the bank would like to have the largest negative gap possible, long-term fixed-rate assets, and short-term liabilities to take advantage of the positively sloped yield curve. However, as rates start to move up, the bank will need to reverse those positions quickly to avoid unnecessarily large capital losses and rising interest costs. If interest rates move too sharply, the manager may not be able to reverse positions quickly enough.

Problems with Simple Gap

This basic-gap model provides a vocabulary and some rudimentary forms of analysis but should not be taken too seriously. First, a one-period model is not realistic. Banks may well plan for 90-day or one-quarter horizons, but the one-period model could lead one to ignore the post-horizon period. While many institutions place enormous weight on quarter-to-quarter results, the most consistently successful institutions do not ignore possible events beyond the short-term planning horizon.

Second, there is a fact common to all models. If all balance sheet items are classified as either rate-sensitive or rate-nonsensitive, a positive (or negative) gap in the repricing period must be matched by a negative (or positive) gap in the time frame beyond the repricing period. This seemingly obvious and innocuous consequence of the balance sheet constraint does in fact have an important effect on one-period models: any action that changes the gap in the repricing period must also change the gap beyond the repricing interval. For instance, the purchase of 50 million dollars in 60-day Treasury bills (T-bills) must be funded with either rate-sensitive or rate-nonsensitive funds. The former will not change the rate-sensitive gap; the latter must change both.

Third, Equation 5 seems to imply that the way to avoid interest-rate risk is to have a zero gap. This completely ignores the basis risk inherent in virtually any balance sheet. For instance, suppose all RSAs are loans that will be repriced on day 90, and all RSLs are fed funds. The dollar gap is zero, but clearly there is interest-rate risk in this position: Just ask any banker who tried to buy fed funds on December 31, 1986, when the fed funds rate rose dramatically as banks tried to clean up their balance sheets, in what is commonly referred to as "window dressing."

INCREMENTAL-GAP MODEL

One of the major drawbacks of the basic one-period gap model is its lack of detail. The logical next step, therefore, is to develop a multiperiod model, one in which various repricing periods are allowed. Now, instead of asking whether or not an item can be repriced before or after a single date, one must ask ''exactly'' when that item can be repriced, and then aggregate items into discrete categories. Therefore, the first step in implementing an incremental-gap (or, less elegantly, a ''maturity bucket'') model is to determine how many intervals one wants to have and how long those intervals ought to be. For example, the ALCO manager may decide to have an overnight category for fed funds, then intervals of 30 days thereafter out to 1 year, and yearly after that out to 3 years. The framework would then look like Figure 5.1. It is possible to develop a daily-gap model, the major constraint being a bank's information system. The ALCO manager must decide if the additional detail is worth the added cost.

This model has many advantages over the simple-gap model. First, it allows the ALCO manager to identify more precisely when the bank is likely to experience some interest-rate risk. This does require a more detailed interest-rate forecast, but it will allow the manager to get a better estimate of the potential impact on earnings. Second, the refinement in time frames allows the ALCO manager to reduce the unmeasured basis risk that was inherent in the simple-gap model. Third, in many cases it makes more apparent the wide range of options the manager has for correcting unwanted gap positions. In general, these options follow the basic rules for the simple-gap model.

ALCO managers must be aware that their ability to adjust gaps depends on the markets in which they deal. They do not necessarily have perfect flexibility in adjusting their balance sheets. Though the recent movement toward ''securitization'' for various types of assets, such as auto and consumer loans, is making the balance sheet more liquid, there are many limitations managers are likely to encounter. Among these are lack of secondary markets for some items, market saturation in some kinds of bank debt, and client reluctance or refusal to be party to adjustments beneficial to the bank. This does not mean that ALCO

Figure 5.1
Incremental Gap Model

	ON	1-30	31-60	61-90	...	331-360	1-2yr	2-3yr	>3yr
A:									
L:									
Inc Gap									
Cum Gap									

managers cannot avoid interest-rate risk; it simply means they may not be able to do it on the balance sheet. Off-balance-sheet techniques will be discussed later in this chapter.

However, there are still several points to make concerning the incremental-gap model. Some of these are common to all asset and liability models, and will be discussed below. For one thing, there is no longer a simple relationship between the absolute dollar gap ($GAP) and the net interest margin. This can be easily analyzed with currently available software and computer systems. The most common conceptual problem of the incremental-gap model is the tendency to focus in too narrowly on just one gap as the only way to reduce interest-rate risk. For instance, suppose the bank has a positive gap in the 61-to-90-day position, and interest rates are expected to fall. One might read the incremental-gap model as suggesting that one should close that particular gap, possibly by issuing 90-day CDs, as the only way to avoid a reduction in net interest income. This is certainly one solution, but as we will see with a duration-gap model it isn't the only way. This myopia can lead to nonoptimal or even wrong decisions.

PITFALLS IN GAP-MANAGEMENT MODELS

While there are many advantages to gap-management models, there are several major dangers which can trap even the most cautious ALCO manager. In this section we will examine some of the most common pitfalls.

A problem common to virtually all asset and liability models is basis risk, a situation in which interest rates on assets move with less than perfect correlation with rates on liabilities. There is no practical way to eliminate basis risk completely, short of becoming a brokerage operation. It can be minimized by pricing certain assets and liabilities using some common index, such as setting rates on retail deposits based on Treasury bill rates.

Bankers must be aware that all asset and liability management techniques require continual monitoring. Even when economic and financial conditions remain relatively stable, time causes changes which in themselves are sufficient to alter the gaps. Assets and liabilities mature or move into different categories; durations change; repayments and withdrawals occur. All of these events alter the size and distribution of the gaps. A closer look at these events will reveal the effect each may have on the measurement of the gap and the amount of interest-rate risk the bank actually has.

For instance, suppose a bank using a monthly incremental-gap model has zero gaps in both the 31-to-60-day and 61-to-90-day time periods. Suppose further that the bank has a large amount of 61-day T-bills but no 61-day liabilities. Tomorrow, as those T-bills shift into the 31-to-60-day category, the bank will have a positive gap in the 31-to-60-day period and a corresponding negative gap in the 61-to-90-day period. Thus, the incremental gap model might disguise some amount of interest-rate risk, catching the unsuspecting ALCO manager unaware if interest rates do in fact fluctuate.

The opposite case is just as dangerous. If the bank finds out today that it has a negative gap in the 31-to-60-day period and a positive gap in the 61-to-90-day period, it might take action to close both gaps. If, however, the bank has 61-day bills already on the books, no action is really necessary as the gaps will narrow simply by letting time pass. The moral of these two cases is to look behind the gap report to the details.

Another problem arises from loan prepayments and early withdrawals of deposits. Either one of these events changes the distribution and size of gaps, so the ALCO manager needs to be notified of any significant activity along these lines. While prepayments and withdrawals can occur at any time, they are more likely to occur when interest rates are changing; that is, at exactly the time when interest-rate risk is of the greatest concern and the manager may have the least ability to offset such shifts. For instance, in 1986 banks experienced a large number of mortgage loan refinancings. If the loans are refinanced at the same institution, the effects are not so drastic as they would be if the loans were not replaced on the books. However, even in the case of replacement, there are some troublesome effects for the ALCO manager. First, the cash flows are probably reduced: there is a lower interest rate, and possibly a reduction in the loan balance. The amortization schedule is thus altered. The difference in amortization may in fact not be significant since the old loans would probably still have 20 years to maturity. More troublesome is the refinancing of variable-rate mortgages with fixed-rate mortgages. This significantly alters the size of the gaps if the bank has been classifying the bulk of the principal of the variable rate instruments by the earliest repricing date, for example, six months. In this case, the six-month-and-under asset positions are reduced and the principal is reallocated according to the new amortization schedule. The effects of refinancing are not as evident if the bank has been allocating the principal over the life of the loan and in essence assuming that the variable-rate instrument is a fixed-rate one so long as interest rates don't change.

Early withdrawal of deposits poses similar problems if interest rates rise. In this situation, longer-term time deposits are withdrawn and either redeposited in shorter-term deposits or removed from the bank. The first case alters the gap structure of the bank, while the second alters the gap structure and increases the bank's need for liquidity. In either case the bank will find itself in a position of having to react to changing market conditions. There is a hidden danger here, that of overreacting. Suppose interest rates rise sharply enough to cause depositors of one-year time deposits to withdraw their deposits and place the funds in money market deposit accounts (MMDAs). Suppose, further, that the bank had had zero gaps. It now has a negative gap in a short-term maturity, and a positive gap in the 12-month position. The bank then sells some one-year securities and sells off the proceeds in the fed funds market to close both gaps.

This strategy is fine as long as interest rates continue to rise, or more importantly, as long as the market expects rates to continue to rise. Once an expectation develops for rates to fall, however, the positions will reverse:

depositors will draw down the MMDAs and buy one-year certificates. The bank now has to drain its fed funds position and buy one-year securities to close the gaps. In this case, the bank might be able to ride out part of the rise by not closing the gaps completely, or by making adjustments in other gaps rather than the one-year gap. For instance, if the bank expects that the rate rise will last three months, then it might be appropriate to sell three-month bills to close up the overnight or one-month gap. The bank then has a negative gap in the three-month position, which is what it will want in three months if rates do in fact fall.

Another consideration in adjusting gaps is to realize that, unless existing assets or liabilities can be sold, their impact on earnings will remain until they mature. Adjusting a gap does not necessarily remove the negative earnings impact already present; it simply offsets it to a greater or lesser extent.

DURATION AND GAP MANAGEMENT

In the last few years, banks have started to use more sophisticated gap-management techniques. Perhaps the most important advance is the use of duration analysis in gap programs, or duration gap. The use of duration addresses several major problems in interest-rate-risk management. First, duration provides a comprehensive measure of the impact of interest rates on financial instruments. Second, it explicitly recognizes the time value of money. Third, it places the focus on cash flows and not on maturity.

One of the problems with duration is that its definition depends on the process that is presumed to generate interest rates. For instance, the simplest measure, that of Macaulay, assumes that the term structure is flat and any shifts in it are parallel to the original curve. While this leads to a very simple formula, its usefulness is theoretically limited. On the other hand, more realistic generating processes lead to much more complicated measures of duration. Furthermore, Gerald Bierwag (1987) notes that these complex models don't always outperform the Macaulay measure significantly. For our purpose here, the simple Macaulay measure will suffice to illustrate the properties of duration.

The Macaulay measure is:

$$D = \frac{\sum_{t=1}^{N} \{(CF_t) \times t/(1+R)^t\}}{\sum_{t=1}^{N} \{(CF_t)/(1+R)^t\}} \tag{6}$$

where Cf_t = cash flow at time t;
         N = maturity of the instrument;
         R = discount rate.

Duration neatly summarizes the bond theorems. The basic properties of duration are:

a. duration ≤ maturity;
b. duration is inversely related to the coupon of a bond;
c. duration is inversely related to the yield to maturity;
d. duration of par and premium bonds is directly related to the maturity of the instrument;
e. the percentage change in the price of a bond is approximately equal to the negative of the bond's duration times $(\Delta R)/(1+R)$, where R is the bond's yield to maturity:

$$\%\Delta BP = -D \times (\Delta R)/(1+R). \tag{7}$$

Duration has many applications, but the one that has gotten the most attention is that of immunization against the two effects of changing interest rates, price risk and reinvestment risk. One basic application is in the case of a life insurance company (LIC) attempting to discharge a fixed liability N years hence. The LIC could attempt to cover its position by buying bonds with a maturity of N years, a maturity matching strategy. This strategy works if rates hold steady or rise, because there would be no price risk. However if rates fall there would be reinvestment risk and the company will fall short of its target balance. A duration strategy, that is, one in which the duration of the assets equals the investment horizon, will balance reinvestment risk and price risk, and will guarantee sufficient funds to discharge the liability.

While bankers may use this technique as a form of hedge, they can also use duration to manage the interest-rate risk of the entire balance sheet. The development of duration gap is due to Alden Toevs (1983) and others. One first calculates the durations of assets and liabilities, and then, following Toevs, defines duration gap as:

$$DG = (MVRSA) \times (1-D_{RSA}) - (MVRSL) \times (1-D_{RSL}) \tag{8}$$

where   MVRSA = market value of rate-sensitive assets;
MVRSL = market value of rate-sensitive liabilities;
D_{RSA} = duration of rate-sensitive assets;
D_{RSL} = duration of rate-sensitive liabilities.

This measure has some very attractive features not found in an incremental-gap model. First, and most obvious, it is single-valued. The interest-rate sensitivity of the entire bank is summarized in this measure. Second, as with duration in general, it summarizes the magnitude and time value of cash flows. Third, it offers a very simple way to view interest-rate risk, and a wide range of policy options to close a gap. For instance, a positive-duration gap means that the bank has more cash inflows being repriced more quickly than cash outflows, and that therefore the bank will benefit if interest rates rise. Suppose the bank has a negative-duration gap. This could be because the bank has liabilities with shorter duration than its assets. The bank would then want to book net-rate-sensitive assets of amount X with a duration Y such that:

$$X = |DG|/(1-Y). \tag{9}$$

The ALCO manager now has many options, because he or she can vary both the amount and the duration of the net-rate-sensitive assets. Contrast this with the view of the incremental model which tends to focus on each individual gap in isolation from the others, and therefore removes timing as a policy option. Be aware, however, that the bank must still satisfy the balance sheet constraint, so the net-rate-sensitive assets must be funded somehow, altering the rate-nonsensitive position.

While a duration-gap model provides a theoretically superior measure of interest-rate risk, it does have some complexities. As time passes, the duration of an instrument will decline more slowly than the remaining time to maturity. This "duration drift" will cause a hedged position to become unhedged if left uncorrected. Fortunately, the size of the problem will probably be small for any relevant time frame. Duration also changes as the level of interest rates changes. A sharp move in interest rates will change the discount rate in the computation of duration, changing the duration gap. Duration will also jump in value immediately after a cash flow occurs. This is because the longer-term remaining cash flows will have larger weights and thus "tilt" or increase the value of the instrument's duration.

OFF-BALANCE-SHEET TECHNIQUES

All the techniques examined above require the alteration of balance-sheet items. This may be inconvenient, expensive, or impossible to do. However, this does not imply that a bank can't close up its interest-rate-sensitivity position. Over the last few years, there has been a proliferation of off-balance-sheet methods for handling the interest-rate risk of a balance sheet. The most popular of these are futures, options, and swaps. We will consider each in turn.

Futures

A futures contract is an exchange-traded contract that obligates the holder to take or make delivery of a specified quantity of a good of specific quality, on a certain future date, at a specified place, with the price determined today. In essence, a futures contract is a standardized forward contract. This standardization has allowed active markets for various instruments to develop, providing liquidity to market participants.

The most obvious advantage of futures is that they allow banks to hedge interest-rate risk without significantly altering the balance sheet. Some banks may have illiquid balance sheets which would be costly to adjust. Futures contracts typically require a margin that is small relative to the deliverable quantity. For instance, a $1,500 initial margin controls a $1 million contract in T-bills.

The major danger lies in this same fact. There is clearly an enormous amount of leverage involved in futures trading. Small movements in prices can cause large dollar losses; every basis point change in the T-bill contract is worth $25. Losses are charged daily to the margin accounts, which must be replenished. Thus, there is the potential for daily cash flows in using futures. This feature does restrict the usefulness of futures for asset and liability management purposes.

A second problem with futures is that there is a limited number of contracts and contract maturities available. Currently there are interest-rate-futures contracts available for 90-day Treasury bills, Treasury notes, Treasury bonds (T-bonds), municipal bonds, and Eurodollars. The most active of these, the T-bond, has ten contract dates available on a March-June-September-December basis. Trading volume declines markedly for those contracts beyond the two that are closest to their expiration dates. In all probability, a bank using futures will encounter a mismatch on dates and a mismatch on instruments, both leading to basis risk.

Third, there is the danger of a squeeze in the underlying commodity or security if sufficient numbers of traders holding long positions (that is, those who will take delivery of the commodity) hold their contracts to expiration. Such a situation developed in corn in the summer of 1983, but was defused by rules changes at the Chicago Board of Trade.

These problems do not automatically eliminate futures as a useful hedging vehicle. An ALCO manager can use futures to manage the interest-rate risk of the entire balance sheet if he takes care in setting up the program. Let us consider a very simple example. Suppose on September 1 the bank has a positive gap of $50 million in the 1-to-90 day period. If the ALCO manager expects rates to rise over the next 90 days, then the gap is correctly positioned. However, the manager may wish to hedge the bank's position against an adverse move in interest rates. There are two basic questions to ask: what is the worst thing that could happen in terms of moves in interest rates, and how can I position the bank in order to benefit from that event? In the case at hand, the worst that could happen from the point of view of the balance sheet is that rates will fall, reducing expected net interest income. In order to hedge the balance sheet, the manager should go long in interest-rate futures by buying 50 December Eurodollar or T-bill futures. If rates do fall by, say, November 30, then the bank's net interest income will be lower than expected, but the futures contracts should have gained in value. We can summarize this in Table 5.2.

In this highly simplified example, the bank experiences a reduction of $62,500 in its net interest income from its expected level (ΔNII = -50bp $\times$ $50 million $\times$ 90 days / 360 days). In the futures market, the bank made a profit of $62,500 (= 50bp $\times$ 50 contracts $\times$ 90 days / 360 days). The bank's net interest income has been effectively hedged against the unwelcome drop in interest rates. Had rates risen, the bank would have increased its net interest income but would have lost money in the futures market.

Table 5.2
Hedging

	Balance Sheet	Futures
9/1/×1	Bank has +$50 million gap in 1-90 day interval. 90-day T-bill rate = 6.00%	Bank buys 50 Dec. ×1 T-bill futures contracts at 6.25%.
11/30/×1	Bank still has +$50 million 90-day gap. 90-day T-bill rate = 5.50%	Bank sells 50 Dec. ×1 T-bill futures contracts at 5.75%.

Apart from the general problems associated with using futures, there are several real-life factors that complicate the example above. First, the bank's gap most likely will change daily, meaning the proper number of futures contracts would also have to be adjusted daily to maintain a proper hedge. This will also be true for the other off-balance-sheet instruments, options and swaps. Second, there will be two types of basis risk, one within the balance sheet (asset versus liability rates) of the type discussed previously, and one between the balance sheet (or cash markets) and the futures market. Both will make perfect hedges impossible and even make very close hedges difficult at times. Third, the timing of contracts doesn't match the call report dates. Futures contracts typically expire the third Thursday of the contract month (around the 20th day). Thus it is impossible to time futures expiration to coincide exactly with the end of a quarter. All three difficulties will probably require the ALCO manager to roll the bank's futures position over continually, in terms of both the number of contracts and the expiration dates. Fourth, accounting and regulatory considerations may restrict the types of futures trading that may be carried out.

These disadvantages may well discourage bankers from using futures as a device for hedging the interest-rate risk of the balance sheet. For those who choose to employ futures, they should do so only if they are aware of the constant attention such a strategy will require.

Options

An option is a contract that gives the holder the right to either buy a security (call option) or sell a security (put option) at a specified price, called the strike price, on or before the expiration date. The buyer of the option pays a premium for this right. The buyer of a call gains if the market price of the underlying security rises above the strike price, while the buyer of a put gains if the market price falls below the strike price. For a call, if the strike price is below the current market price, the option is "in the money"; if the strike price is above the current market price, the option is "out of the money." The definitions are reversed for puts. The option buyer risks only the amount of the premium paid. If the option expires unexercised, the buyer loses only the premium.

On the other side of the option contract is the option writer, who faces a different set of risks. A call writer agrees to sell the underlying security to the call buyer at the buyer's discretion. The writer therefore is betting that the market price will either fall or at least not rise enough to make it worth the buyer's while to exercise the option. If the option expires unexercised, the writer has the premium plus the reinvestment income from that premium. The story is essentially the same for a put writer, except that he expects prices not to fall sufficiently to make exercising the option attractive. Figure 5.2 below summarizes the positions of the major players.

Figure 5.2
Options

	Buy	Write
Call	Long	Short
Put	Short	Long

Clearly, writing options is potentially riskier than buying options. Securities may be called away or put to the options writer at any time and at any price, wiping out the value of the premium and the reinvestment income. Despite this risk, a number of financial institutions write options and futures options in order to boost noninterest income. The best illustration of the danger of this activity is the case of Guarantee Savings and Loan Association of Los Angeles in 1986. The S&L wrote $1.4 billion of put options on Treasury bonds for premium income, betting that rates would not rise. Because interest rates did rise, the options were exercised and the bonds put to Guarantee, so the S&L grew overnight from $3 billion to about $4.5 billion. It couldn't afford to sell the securities because they carried a $54 million capital loss at the current market prices. Guarantee violated the rule of not betting more than it could afford to lose.

Options have two major advantages over futures. First, an options buyer has only one cash outflow, the premium paid up front. Second, an option represents a right, not an obligation, to buy or sell the underlying security. There is still the danger, however slight, of a squeeze with options if there is a shortage of the underlying security for delivery.

Currently, the only interest-rate option that is actively traded is on Treasury bonds. Thus, interest-rate options are of limited usefulness in asset and liability management programs. However, in the last few years, options on interest-rate futures contracts have grown in popularity. There are active options trading on Treasury bond futures, Treasury note futures, and Eurodollar futures. A buyer of a futures call (or put) option has the right to take a long (or short) position in the underlying futures contract. These contracts have all the advantages of regular options, plus one more: there is never the danger of a squeeze occurring in the futures options markets. For every buyer of a futures option, there must be a futures option writer who promises to take the opposite position in the futures market.

While most of the applications of interest-rate options and options on interest-rate futures are related to individual balance sheet items, they may also be used to hedge gap positions. Again, suppose that our bank had a positive $50 million gap over the 1-to-90-day interval as of September 1. To hedge against an unwanted drop in interest rates, the bank could buy Eurodollar (E$) futures call options. If rates fall, the decrease in net interest income is offset to some extent by gains on the options position. Table 5.3 will help explain the process.

Table 5.3
Futures Options

Balance Sheet		Futures Options
9/1/×1	Bank has +$50 million gap in 90-1day interval. 90-day E$ rate = 6.50%.	Bank buys 50 Dec. ×1 9350 E$ futures call options. Premium = 10 points.
11/30/×1	Bank still has +$50 million 90-day gap. E$ rate = 6.00%.	Bank exercises options: buys 50 Dec. ×1 E$ futures at 93.50 and sells 50 Dec ×1 E$ futures at 94.00.

On the balance sheet gap the bank's expected net interest income dropped $62,500, just as in the example with futures above. The bank's net profit is $50,000 in the options, figured as follows: each point of the original premium paid is worth $25, so the bank's initial cost is 10 ×$25 × 50 = $12,500. The bank made 50 basis points in the futures market, so its profit was 50 × $25 × 50 = $62,500, for a net profit of $50,000.

Many of the comments made about the use of futures contracts apply here as well, as concern changing gap size, timing of the contract, and so on. There is, however, an important difference in practice between the two methods. The potential for both profit and loss in futures trading is unlimited. In buying options the losses are limited to the premium, while profit potential is unlimited.

Swaps

The most recent development in off-balance-sheet financing is the interest rate swap. A spin-off from currency swaps, the interest rate swaps market has grown to over $400 billion. While it is not the perfect instrument, it does have certain advantages over futures and options.

An interest rate swap is an agreement between two parties to exchange interest payments. The size of the payments is calculated on a fictitious or "notional" principal amount, which may or may not have anything to do with actual balance-sheet amounts. The typical swap involves one party willing to make interest payments based on a fixed interest rate and a second party willing to make payments based on a floating interest rate. At regular intervals, the two parties exchange or swap interest payments based on the notional principal. For example, one party may agree to make payments on $50 million notional principal at a fixed rate of 10 percent and the other party may agree to the London Interbank Offered Rate (LIBOR) plus 50 basis points (bp). Every six months the two parties exchange the interest payments. The fixed-rate payer will pay $2.5 million every six months and receive LIBOR plus 50 bp. If rates rise, the fixed-rate payer benefits; if rates fall, the floating-rate payer benefits.

The use of swaps can be beneficial in a variety of situations, both micro and macro. One of the most common, involving actual balance-sheet items, contains imperfections in the relative pricing of the debt of different companies. Two companies, one with a higher rating than the other, wish to issue debt. However, the risk differential between the two is not constant between long- and short-term credit markets. This results in a situation of comparative advantage whereby the two companies can issue the debt in which they have the relative cost advantage and, if desired, swap the debt. This results in lower costs for both firms. For a detailed analysis of swaps, see Carl Beidelman (1985).

The application of swaps to asset and liability management is essentially straightforward. Once again, our bank has a positive $50 million gap in the 1-to-90-day period as of September, 1, which it wishes to hedge. Its primary worry is that rates will fall. The bank therefore should agree to take the floating-rate side of a swap. It may agree to pay LIBOR plus 50 bp every three months, and receive payments based on a fixed rate. If rates rise, the gap is repriced at higher rates, but the swap will entail higher interest payments for the bank because LIBOR has risen. If rates fall, the bank continues to receive fixed-rate payments while making smaller floating-rate payments based on the declining LIBOR. Table 5.4 will illustrate. The bank once again has lost $62,500 from its expected net interest income, but has gained $62,500 from the swap. The calculations for the swap payments are based on simple interest paid quarterly.

There are several advantages to using swaps as opposed to futures or options for asset and liability management. First, cash flows are typically semiannual though, as in our example, quarterly payment dates are available. Compare this

Table 5.4
Swaps

	Balance Sheet	Swaps
9/1/×1	Bank has + $50 million gap in 1-90 day position. LIBOR is 6.50%.	Bank agrees to pay LIBOR + 50 basis points quarterly, and to receive 7% fixed, based on a notional principal of $50 million.
11/30/×1	Bank still has + $50 million 90-day gap. LIBOR is 6.00%.	Bank pays $812,500 based on LIBPR + 50 bp = 6.50% and receives $875,000 based on the 7% fixed.

to the daily cash flows that are possible with futures. Second, the available dates for payment are much more flexible than for either options or futures. Third, the swaps market is more liquid for longer maturities than are futures or options. The most liquid futures contracts are typically the ones closest or second closest to expiration; longer-dated futures and options markets are quite thin. Swaps contracts, on the other hand, can extend for several years. This eliminates the need to roll over contracts continually, as with options and futures. Fourth, there is no danger of a squeeze occurring, though you may have difficulty in offsetting a swap that you no longer want at an acceptable price. The only major danger in a swap is credit risk, in which one party fails to make its payment. Because interest-rate swaps involve no exchange of principal, credit risk extends only to the interest payments. From the point of view of a bank that wants to participate in swaps, the best advice is to go through a large swaps dealer and let it take the credit risk.

SUMMARY

In this chapter we have looked at the problem of managing interest-rate risk from a full-balance-sheet perspective. We have discussed the developments that led to the need for integrative asset and liability management models, and have examined three of the most common models: the one-period gap, the incremental gap, and the duration gap. Each has advantages and disadvantages; as the models become more complex, they become more accurate but require more data and expertise. However, with the computer systems now available, even the barriers to using duration-gap models at small banks are not great. As with any model, the basic problem with gap management models is defining terms in a meaningful way and realizing the limitations of the models.

6

International Banking

HISTORICAL PERSPECTIVE

The fifteenth and sixteenth centuries witnessed the growth—and demise—of family-owned and -managed merchant banking dynasties like the Medici and Fugger banks that created foreign exchange markets, financed international trade, met the financial appetite of the Papacy and national rulers, and set up new trade and industrial ventures as well as foreign subsidiaries and representative offices throughout Europe. Between the Napoleonic Wars and the late nineteenth century, international trade and investment flourished. The growth in trade and investment activity was helped by capital exports and trade finance supplied by the London and Paris financial markets. Many new banks were formed despite periodic economic crises, commodity price collapse, and financial panics, as well as an irresistible urge to invest European capital abroad. The nineteenth-century international banks were engaged in investment banking and trade financing. The Rothschild Bank, among the most successful investment banks of the period, operated in the nineteenth century as a single firm with branches in Paris, London, Frankfurt, and Vienna, each managed by a member of the family. The bank initiated the continental railroading boom, and financed a worldwide program of infrastructure and industry—factories, mines, utilities, canals, and railroads.

There was an almost relentless appetite for foreign securities. In 1893, British investors held foreign long-term publicly issued capital which was equal to about 25 percent of Britain's GNP (Gross National Product) and close to 10 percent of its net income. There were also substantial foreign investments by the French, although the proportion of French GNP invested abroad was not nearly as high as in Great Britain. Many financial institutions failed. This was partially related to the consequences of war, political conflict, violent fluctuations of commodity prices, and maladministration of less developed political systems and economies; and in part related to poor and inexperienced management that led to overconcentration of credit, mismatching of lending and borrowing currencies, and lack of analysis. Over half of the new international banks that were established between 1856 and 1865 became insolvent.

Until 1913, international banking had been dominated by the European-controlled overseas or colonial banks as a consequence of the willingness of Europeans to export their capital. London acted as the world's international banking center. The passage of the U.S. Federal Reserve Act in 1913, coupled with the outbreak of World War I, led to modest expansion of foreign branches and subsidiaries of American banks abroad. Most U.S. banks relied on their overseas correspondents to provide international banking services. The Federal Reserve Act permitted national banks to branch abroad and to accept drafts for the first time. Of the 18 banking corporations which initially came under the Federal Reserve's jurisdiction, only 3 survived beyond the early 1930s. The failures have once again been attributed to inexperienced management, aggressive expansion, eagerness for business without adequate direction or control, the 1920 foreign trade crisis, and problems of doing business in countries with political instability and vulnerability to commodity price fluctuation.

By the end of 1933, when hundred of banks around the world had permanently closed, 67 percent of the Latin American- and 46 percent of the European-issued dollar bonds were in default germane to interest payments. U.S., English, Dutch, Swiss, Swedish, and French banks and issuing houses had approached foreign states, cities, railroads, utilities, and industrial corporations with offers of loans and credits without serious study or concern about their ability to repay in the lender's currency. Despite these serious problems, American banks such as Chase, Morgan, National City Bank, and First Bank of Boston survived abroad and eventually became extremely successful international banking operations.

U.S. BANKS EXPAND ABROAD

The post-World War II period provided the impetus for U.S. banks to enter the global banking arenas as they chose to follow major U.S. corporations that set up production facilities in war-ravaged nations abroad. American banks began to expand their activities abroad in order to:

1. Service the overall expansion of U.S. international trade;
2. Service corporate customers that had become multinational in their operations, especially since the relative strength of the dollar had stimulated American corporate investment abroad;
3. Circumvent the effect of government regulations; that is, restrictive domestic regulations that placed a ceiling on select interest rates;

4. Increase their returns and rate of expansion;

5. Control their portfolio risks and variability of returns by broadly diversifying their portfolios geographically and functionally; and

6. Add additional sources of funds and additional sources of income.

Most large U.S. banks participate in the market for wholesale (corporate and government) lending and interbank deposits with a series of branches in the key money centers of the world such as London, Frankfurt, Paris, Zurich, Singapore, Tokyo, and Hong Kong, as well as representative offices, Edge Acts, and subsidiary bank activities (see the following pages for definitions of these terms and Figure 6.1). There are also "offshore" financial centers (for example, Luxembourg, Cayman Islands, the Bahamas, the Netherlands Antilles, Bahrain, Kuwait, Panama, Jersey, Guernsey, and the Isle of Man) which exist by providing a service for nonresidents while usually keeping their international business separate from their domestic business. A few U.S. money-center banks such as Citibank are also active in foreign markets in the retail (consumer) banking front in England. Most large regional banks in the United States participate in international lending with either a foreign branch, representative office, or Edge Act, or in a foreign banking consortia. However, many small banks, attracted to international banking by the lure of potential high profits, found that they did not have the skill or the size to compete profitably.

Since World War II, when U.S. corporations began their vast expansion overseas, U.S banks have moved overseas in rapid fashion in an attempt to retain their customers. At year-end 1987, more than 150 U.S. banks had close to 800 foreign branches with total assets of more than $500 billion. International deposits and earnings became important to the largest U.S. money-center banks. For example, during 1984, Bankers Trust reported that 65 percent of its total deposits were offshore, while during 1980, they generated 58 percent of their earnings from international banking activities.

Most of these foreign branches or affiliates are located in Latin America (30 percent), in Europe (20 percent), and in Asia (20 percent). U.S. banks have over 50 branches or affiliates in London. However, only about 1 percent of U.S. banks have overseas branches or affiliates. Over 80 percent of overseas branches and affiliates, and 90 percent of all overseas banking assets held by U.S. banks are held by only 20 banks. Some U.S. banks also have investment banking subsidiaries abroad. These units have been expanded because of their potential for substantial profits. In addition, U.S. banks have established Edge Act corporations in cities such as New York, Chicago, Miami, Houston, San Francisco, and Los Angeles to service their multinational customers, accept deposits related to foreign transactions, and refer potential customers to the parent bank.

More than one-half of the U.S. banks operating outside the United States do so only through single shell branches in offshore money markets such as the Cayman Islands or Nassau. Shell branches have no contact with the public;

Figure 6.1
A Multinational Banking System

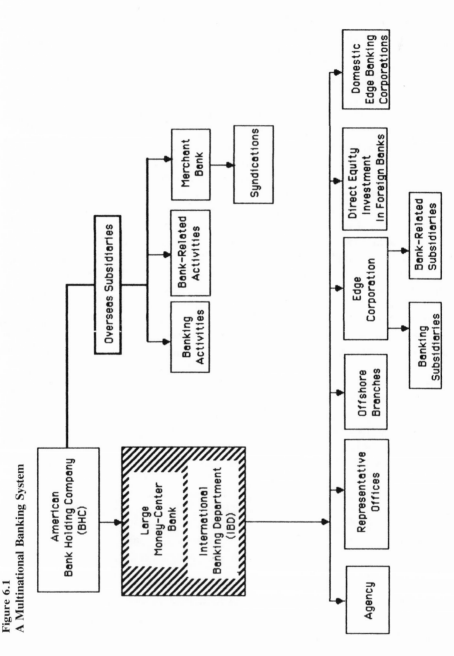

Note: In many cases the subsidiary and/or related firms can in turn operate with branches and/or subsidiaries.

location is usually selected on the basis of low operating costs and low taxes. The activities of these shell branches are directed at interbank deposits, purchases of syndicated loans and the transfer of funds throughout the worldwide banking network.

Bank Activities

For decades, large U.S. money-center banks have engaged in short-term financing for international trade using specialized financial instruments such as bills of exchange, letters of credit, and bankers' acceptances. Letters of credit cover commercial transactions and expedite the flow of goods across national boundaries. In addition to earning a fee for the bank, a bank's letter of credit for a client specifies the conditions under which the bank stands ready to make payments to a third party. Bankers' acceptances are negotiable money market instruments that are direct extensions of commercial letters of credit and provide short-term financing in international trade. By creating bankers' acceptances, an issuing bank obtains fee income for accepting a draft on behalf of nonbank customers of good standing. An issuing bank evaluates the creditworthiness of the customer on whose behalf it accepts a time draft, and establishes a limit that it will accept on behalf of each customer. In addition to internal limits, Federal Reserve member banks cannot accept unsecured drafts to any one customer in excess of 15 percent of the bank's capital stock plus surplus.

Banks also participate in Eurodollar loans (interbank deposits) to other banks. Loans to other banks are usually made for periods up to one year (some are longer) and generally provide a minimal return to the lending bank if matched by a corresponding deposit. A 5-to-25 percent basis point spread between bid and asked rates in the London interbank market provides a theoretical indication of the interest margin available on such loans. The rate paid for Eurodollars is referred to as the London interbank offered rate, usually shortened to LIBOR. In actuality, most Eurobanks (other than those associated with the world's largest banks) are not usually among those institutions that are able to buy funds at the bid side of the interbank market. Whereas little if any differentiation in the LIBOR was made prior to the Herstatt and Franklin Bank failures of 1974, the heightened sensitivity to relative creditworthiness created a situation whereby select categories (tiers) of banks were expected to pay a premium over LIBOR. (Tiering refers to the differentiation of rates among the various banks for interbank deposits.) The premiums paid were primarily a function of the presumed creditworthiness of the bank. When large American, English, Swiss, German, and French banks borrowed at the lowest rates, Japanese, Italian, consortia, and small merchant banks had to pay a premium for funds in 1974. Prior to 1974, most banks borrowed in the interbank market at roughly the same Eurodollar rate. In the period of relative calm which characterized the interbank market between 1976 and 1981, the extent of tiering declined substantially.

While it is possible to make a marginal spread by lending on a matched maturity basis to another bank in a lower tier which pays more for its money than the lending institution, this is usually not a highly profitable business from the standpoint of return on assets. In practice, interbank deposits on a matched-book basis are only a healthy profit maker to the highest quality bank in the upper tier which can purchase funds at the cheapest rate. Interbank deposits can also be profitable to those banks willing to take interest-rate risks and run an unmatched book of assets and liabilities related to final maturity. For example, bank A might pay 7 percent for a 3-month Eurodollar CD and reinvest the funds in a CD from bank B for 9 months, which might pay 7.5 percent. Given the profit constraint, the extent of interbank lending is a function of the desired level of liquidity, published balance sheet ratios, and the value of being seen by other banks on both sides of the interbank market as a lender and taker of funds. Many bankers feel that being able to offer a two-way quote to other banks reflects favorably on their professionalism and credit rating. This is particularly true of U.S. regional banks that participate in the Eurodollar market.

Although many international banking services are similar to those provided by banks on the domestic level, large money-center banks also provide the following services to multinational and foreign clients:

1. Bills of exchange;
2. Letters of credit;
3. Bankers' acceptances;
4. Export and import financing;
5. Transfer of funds;
6. Foreign exchange transactions;
7. Swaps;
8. Credit information on foreign customers;
9. Information about each nation's economy, social trends, tax laws, and regulations that affect trade and capital flows; and
10. Underwriting of securities abroad.

Multinational corporations look to their money-center banks to provide services that will:

1. Accelerate worldwide collection of funds;
2. Control the outflow of payments;
3. Provide information on the status of all bank accounts;
4. Monitor the status of letters of credit and bankers' acceptances;
5. Provide advice on how and where any excess funds can be invested; and
6. Provide guidance on foreign exchange positions.

Bills of Exchange. A bill of exchange is an unconditional order in writing addressed by one person to another, signed by the person giving it, and requiring the addressee to pay a certain sum of money to order or to bearer on demand, or at fixed or determinable time. For example, suppose that a major department store in New York has agreed to import Scottish woolens. The Scottish exporter prepares the goods for shipment and delivers them to the shipping company for delivery to the department store. The Scottish mill then executes a bill of exchange, a draft that instructs the importer to pay, say, $150,000 for the woolen goods.

The exporter takes the bill of exchange to his bank, a branch of Midland Bank, and requests that the bank send these documents to its correspondent bank in New York. When the documents are received by the American bank, the New York bank acts as a collection agent and makes a presentation to the buyer for payment of $150,000. The U.S. bank is paid a fee of between 0.1 and 0.25 percent of the amount of the bill of exchange. As soon as the department store pays the bank, all the documents are turned over to the importer, who goes to the dock to claim the woolen goods. On the other hand, if the imported goods have to be examined and approved for entry into the United States by a government agency, Midland might instruct the American bank to deliver the documents against trust receipts that stipulate that payments for the goods will be made immediately after they have passed inspection.

Bankers' Acceptances. In creating Bankers' Acceptances (BAs), an issuing bank services specific needs, and it obtains fee income, customarily a minimum of 1.5 percent per year or 1/8 of 1 percent per month, for accepting a draft on behalf of nonbank customers of good credit rating. Figure 6.2 schematically summarizes the principle participants and steps involved in creating and redeeming a BA.

For example, a U.S. importer and a foreign exporter agree on a commercial transaction that will use a letter of credit and a time draft that will become a bankers' acceptance. The U.S. importer arranges for its bank to issue a letter of credit for the pending transaction and to subsequently accept a 90-day time draft on behalf of the importer. The American bank relays this information to the foreign exporter. The foreign exporter ships the goods and then draws a time draft for the agreed-upon amount against the importer. The exporter presents this draft and supporting shipping documents to its local bank and receives prompt credit either at a discount or for a fee. The exporter's bank forwards the time draft and documentation to the American bank. After assessing that all specific conditions have been met, the importer's bank accepts the time draft by writing and signing the word "accepted" on its face. The accepting bank thus guarantees that the instrument will be paid on its due date. The accepting bank will either hold the acceptance in safe keeping until the due date, and then remit the funds or else discount the acceptance in the money market, immediately crediting the importing bank with the discounted amount. The accepting bank will follow the instructions of the importing bank on the aforementioned options. If discounted, the acceptance becomes a money market instrument because it has been guaranteed by a money-center bank. By the due date, the importer pays its

Figure 6.2
Creation of a Banker's Acceptance

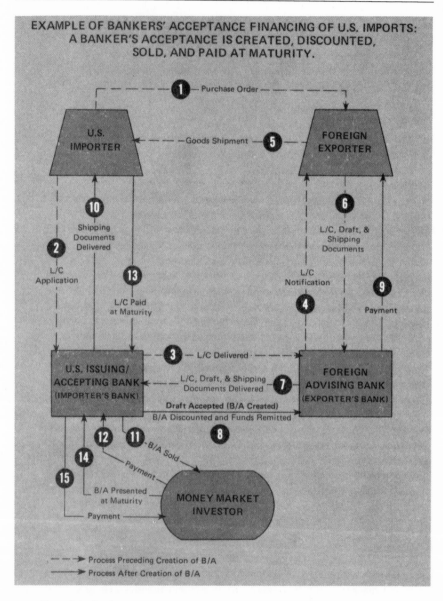

EXAMPLE OF BANKERS' ACCEPTANCE FINANCING OF U.S. IMPORTS: A BANKER'S ACCEPTANCE IS CREATED, DISCOUNTED, SOLD, AND PAID AT MATURITY.

Note: A detailed illustration of bankers' acceptance financing of U. S. exports is given in Hervey [3].

money-center bank, which redeems the acceptance. If the importer fails to pay on time, the accepting bank remains obligated to redeem the acceptance.

Letters of Credit. Analysts who worry about the safety of banks have added another source of anxiety: the letter of credit. The volume of these instruments has soared during the 1980s. At some New York City banks, the letter of credit exposure grew to approximately four times the total equity capital at the end of 1986.

Traditionally, letters of credit have been used to facilitate foreign trade. However, in the last few years, high interest rates and a jittery investment climate have led to an increase in these bank guarantees to back municipal bonds, housing agency debt, industrial revenue bonds, commercial paper, and other securities. In the case of a securities offering, a bank would typically guarantee payment of interest and principal. This tends to reassure the otherwise squeamish investors and bring about an improved credit rating. Although the issuer pays a fee for the letter of credit, the issuer usually saves a larger amount on interest costs.

Letters of credit are not listed on bank balance sheets; they do appear in the footnotes without details on what credits the letters are backing. Bankers generally like letters of credit because of their generous annual fees, which range from 0.25 percent to 3.0 percent of the amount guaranteed, depending on the risks involved. For example, assuming an average fee of 1 percent, the $15 billion in credit letters outstanding at Citibank would generate fees of $150 million. Unlike loans, credit letters do not tie up any of the capital of the bank (unless the bank must make good on their guarantee), although they do figure in the loan limits that govern a bank's commitments to any single customer. However, the regulatory authorities are anxious for banks not to increase their letter of credit exposure beyond prudent limits. It is important that banks take all their letters of credit to their credit policy committees just as they would do with a large-sized commercial loan to ensure a portfolio of good credit quality.

Note Issuance Facilities (NIFs). NIFs consist both of short-term notes that are issued as funds are needed, and of back-up credit facilities at major banks to assure fund access in case short-term note placement becomes infeasible. NIF fees fell to as low as 7.5 basis points in mid-1985 compared to 25 basis points earlier in 1985 and 37.5 basis points in 1984. The attractiveness of NIFs result from three sources.

1. NIFs provide the borrower with a medium-term revolving credit commitment at a cost near that of short-term credit. When the yield curve has an upward slope, the NIF provides a substantial cost savings.

2. NIFs make it possible to reach investors that companies could not previously tap. Access to a large pool of institutional investors is advantageous since it tends to reduce borrowing costs and improve liquidity.

3. NIFs are extremely flexible investments that can be restructured to meet a variety of special circumstances. For example, they can be designed with or without amortization schedules, and can be marketed widely or distributed to a

more select group of potential investors.[1] The structure of note issuance facilities, which combine short-term notes with a medium-term backup facility, is similar to that of commercial paper. NIFs differ from commercial paper in that notes are placed privately in the United States with institutional investors. The NIFs need not be rated by the major debt rating services. They can be used by medium-sized companies and by privately owned companies with credit support, as well as with the Fortune 500 companies. NIFs have helped American companies, multinational corporations, and sovereign credits to place short-term debt in Europe, where historically there has not been a commercial paper market. The growth of NIFs there may represent the birth of the European version of the commercial paper market.[2]

4. Under the NIF the roles of the underwriters and the actual providers of funds are separated. However, in the syndicated loan, the revolving credit facility, and the floating rate note, the underwriter and provider of funds are one.

INTERNATIONAL RISKS

As banks have expanded their international loan portfolios to include new types of loans and new borrowers via participation in syndicated loans, U.S. banks have had to reevaluate the returns, risks, and risk-control procedures associated with their international lending and interbank activities. Foreign lending risks extend beyond default and interest-rate risks to include risks of foreign exchange fluctuations, capital controls, and repudiation of debt by a sovereign nation.

Between 1970 and 1973, increased competition led banks to reduce their lending spread and to increase the average maturity of Eurodollar credits to multinational firms. Average maturities lengthened to 10 to 12 years, while the spread for prime borrowers narrowed from over 100 basis points over LIBOR to a range between 37.5 and 62.5 basis points. Following the quadrupling of oil prices by OPEC in the 1970s, worldwide concern was triggered about whether and how the financial system could recycle the new petrodollar trade surpluses of OPEC, and whether and how various oil-importing countries could finance their purchases. Initially, many banks increased their credit lines and loans to oil-importing countries and LDCs (less developed countries). However, the initial OPEC increases were followed by a number of additional price increases, many years of double-digit inflation, and record-breaking interest-rate levels and volatility, as well as revolution in Iran, and political tensions and uncertainty in other parts of the Middle East. In 1974, several banks incurred substantial losses in foreign exchange operations.

In 1974-1975, several large U.S. banks had nonaccruing loans in their international portfolios and had to restructure loans to specific LDCs such as Peru and Zaire. Since the mid-1970s, concern developed that the money-center international banks were risking potentially ruinous losses on syndicated loans to developing nations, especially in Latin America. The problems were exacerbated by the energy price increases in the 1970s, by high interest rates on floating dollar loans during the early 1980s, and by the political difficulties of imposing monetary and fiscal discipline at home.

During 1982-1983, it was clear that borrowers such as Poland, Argentina, Mexico, Brazil, and Romania could not meet interest payments and had to have their debts restructured. During 1986-1987, a number of Latin American borrowers such as Brazil, Ecuador, and Peru decided not to make payments on their outstanding loans. During the second quarter of 1987, U.S. money-center banks established huge loss reserves on their Third World loans. In order to minimize default risk in foreign lending, specialized credit personnel may be necessary to evaluate and structure loans to foreign borrowers who may provide financial statements that use different accounting conventions. Bank credit officers must evaluate a country's past, and forecast balance of payments figures, repayment schedules for external debt, international reserves, drawing rights against the IMF (International Monetary Fund), and domestic, economic, social, and political developments involved in evaluating loan requests from a foreign government or state-owned enterprise. In determining whether a credit should be approved, the international credit analyst must combine the quantitative variables from balance of payments and domestic economic analyses with subjective factors derived from sociopolitical assessments. Some loans are guaranteed or insured by public parties such as a government or its central bank, or by private parties. A lender must still evaluate the quality of the guarantee, the perceived willingness of a country's lenders to make repayment, the political trends and degrees of stability of the country's government, the resource base (minerals, oil, worker productivity, and skills), foreign exchange, and gold reserves.

Country risk analysis must also take into consideration the strategies and objectives of the political leaders, their fiscal and monetary policies, and the effects these may have on short- and long-term economic growth. In order to assess the political risk in a given situation, a bank may estimate the probabilities of civil war, a declared moratorium on all debt repayment, nationalization of industries, assumption of power by a new party, and official repudiation of official debt.[3] The bank may also wish to analyze the type of government (for example, military junta, monarchy, dictatorship), its alignment with the world's major powers, and its overall relationship with U.S. banks.

Enhanced management information is one of the keys to reduced losses in global lending. An up-to-date and comprehensive information system is needed to show the bank's cross-border exposure according to types of loans, risk rating, maturities, and current status of each outstanding obligation. The management information system affects the ability of management to police the portfolio and make decisions regarding restructuring or further commitments.[4]

In order to avoid interest-rate risk, most banks have limited the loans that they have been willing to extend at fixed rates. The bank basically protects itself either by matching the maturity structure of its sources of funds and its international loan portfolio, or by making floating-rate loans in which the lending rate is linked to the bank's fluctuating cost of funds.

When an American bank makes loans denominated in nondollar currencies, a bank must evaluate the probable future value of the nondollar loan repayments. Of course, a U.S. bank can avoid this problem by only making dollar loans to foreign lenders, by matching loans and liabilities in nondollar currencies, or by using hedging techniques to control foreign exchange risks. For example, a bank can enter a forward contract to deliver a nondollar repayment in return for a specific amount of dollars or other currencies in a medium-term nondollar loan to a customer.

In addition to the role of huge, money-center banks, there is a role for regional banks in international banking. Regional banks that have been most successful in foreign banking have been those that capitalize on a close knowledge of their own territories, especially for trade financing for regional products such as tobacco, soybeans, textiles, cotton, or heavy equipment. Regional banks that have in-house expertise to service the specialized domestic and international banking needs of regional clients have also been successful.

International banking has contributed to a greater integrated international financial system, and has permitted more diversification of bank balance sheets. However, although foreign lending offers banks geographic and credit diversification, it also exposes banks to currency risks (see Figure 6.3). Foreign banking presence in the United States has stimulated greater competition and has enhanced the international status of U.S. financial markets.

Foreign lending provides additional elements of risk when compared to domestic lending. These risks include foreign exchange risk, sovereign risk, transfer risk, and fund-availability risk.

A U.S. bank lending abroad may face foreign exchange risk on a loan not denominated in dollars unless the open currency position is hedged. There is always the possibility of political measures preventing or delaying the payment of external obligations. In dealing with sovereign risk, the bank must assess the stability of the political system and the impact that any instability could have on the repayment of the loan. Transfer risk refers to the ability of the borrower to obtain foreign exchange in order to make payments in a specified currency. There is always the possibility that a country may block or restrict convertibility of currency. Funds availability refers to longer-term loans that are funded by shorter-term Eurodollar deposits. Disruptions in the Eurodollar market could cause liquidity problems for the lending bank. Regulatory risk refers to the possibility that regulations in the bank's country of operation could be changed after a loan transaction has taken place.[5]

LOAN SYNDICATIONS

The formal-syndication loan technique arose because of the huge size of term credits required by governments and multinational firms. The credit needs were

Figure 6.3
Risk Protection Techniques of Eurobanks

Lending Risk	Source of Risk	Risk Reduction Strategy
Interest Rate Risk	Mismatched maturities coupled with unpredictable movements in interest rates	Matching assets to liabilities by pricing credits on a rollover basis
Funding Risk	Possibility that funds will not be available to particular banks on normal terms	Floating rate notes and floating rate CDs
Currency Risk	Exchange loss when currency of loan depreciates or currency of liability appreciates	Fund in same currency as loan or cover mismatched currencies with swaps
Credit Risk	Ability of an entity to repay its debts	Syndication of credit and diversification of bank's loan portfolio; corporate and government guarantees
Country Risk	Ability and willingness of borrowers within a country to meet their obligations	Syndication of credit and diversification of bank's loan portfolio
Regulatory Risk	Imposition of reserve requirements or taxes on banks	Clause in contract that forces borrowers to bear this risk

Source: Adapted from Laurie Goodman, "The Pricing of Syndicated Eurocurrency Credits," *Quarterly Review,* Federal Reserve Bank of New York, Summer 1980, p. 47.

usually beyond a single bank's lending limit to one borrower. Syndication also represents a way for banks to diversify some of the unique sovereign risks that develop in international banking. The syndication of most loans has enabled banks to spread the risk of large loans among a number of banks. Syndicated Euroloans involve formal arrangements in which competitively selected lead banks assemble a management group of other banks to underwrite the loan and to market participations in the loan to other banks. There are usually three levels of banks in a syndicate: the lead banks, the managing banks, and the participating banks. Most loans are led by one to four major banks which negotiate to obtain a mandate to obtain funds for the borrower. The lead bank or banks must then assemble a management group to underwrite the loan, although the lead bank is expected to underwrite a share at least as large as that of any other lender. A placement memorandum is prepared by the lead bank and the loan will be marketed to other banks, which are called participating banks. The memorandum describes the transaction, provides qualitative and statistical information about the borrower, and suggests that an independent credit review by the participating banks should be undertaken. After the loan is arranged, the lead bank generally serves as the agent to compute the appropriate interest rate charges, to receive service payments and disburse these to individual participants, and to keep them informed should any problems with the loan develop. If the underwriting is unsuccessful, the loan must be renegotiated or the lead bank must be willing to take a larger share into its own portfolio than originally planned.

The most common type of syndicated loan is a term loan in which the funds can be taken down by the borrower within a specified time frame. A commitment fee may have to be paid in addition to syndication fees during the period in which the loan is not drawn down. Most syndicated loans are denominated in dollars, but loans in German marks, Swiss francs, Japanese yen, and other currencies are also available.

The overseas branch of a U.S. bank can participate in Eurocurrency syndications and can compete for business of overseas-based multinational firms and for business of local firms in its market. Although banks may not syndicate corporate debt or equity in U.S. markets, their merchant banking affiliates can underwrite loans or bonds in the Eurocurrency market. This enables these affiliates to earn underwriting fees that are not tied to assets on the books of the bank. These syndicated loans are often sold within the correspondent bank network of U.S. syndicate bank managers. Since Eurodollar loans range from a minimum of about $1 million to as much as $2 billion, it is quite common for a large international bank or merchant bank to find other banks that would like to participate in a particular credit.

Euroloan pricing practices reflect the nature of the market as a pure financial intermediary, in which funds are bought and sold on a highly competitive basis. Eurobanks are specialized wholesale banks that rely on large time deposits and call deposits from banks and other interest-sensitive depositors. Therefore, the Eurobanks' cost of funds varies directly with the level of short-term rates. To protect themselves from substantial interest-rate risk when they arrange to commit funds to the borrower for term loans as long as ten years, the banks agree that interest rates will be altered every three or six months, bearing a fixed-spread relationship to LIBOR. Rollover Eurodollars bear a rate tied directly to money market and interbank cost of funds; the spreads are negotiated with the borrower prior to the initiation of the loan and either remain constant over the life of the loan or change after a set number of years. A prime borrower pays the smallest spread above this base rate, perhaps 25 to 50 basis points, depending on the duration of the loan and credit conditions within the money markets. Other borrowers would pay higher spreads above the LIBOR. Recently, spreads have ranged from 37.5 to 350 basis points over LIBOR, depending on credit quality, maturity, and general market conditions. Lending activities provide the biggest source of income that banks derive from their international operations. For some New York banks, foreign lending currently accounts for about one-fifth to one-half of total revenue.

In addition to the interest costs on a Eurocurrency loan, there are also commitment fees, front-end fees, and sometimes an annual agent's fee. Commitment fees are charged to the borrower on a percentage of the unutilized part of the credit, and average 0.5 percent annually. Front-end management fees are one-time charges of between 0.5 and 1.0 percent, and are negotiated in advance and imposed when the loan agreement is signed. The participation fees are divided among all the banks in relation to their share of the loan, while the management fees are divided between the underwriting banks and the lead bank.

Example of Syndicated Loan Charges

Annual Payment =   (LIBOR + spread) × amount of loan drawn + (commitment fee) × amount of loan undrawn + annual agent's fee

Front-End Charges =   participation fee × amount of loan + (management fee) × amount of loan + initial agent's fee

Front-end fees are a significant component of the bank's total return on a credit. Consider a $500-million, seven-year credit without a grace period. Suppose the loan is priced at 100 basis points over a 10 percent LIBOR. A 0.5 percent fee means that $2.5 million must be paid to the banks in the syndicate at the outset. This raises the effective interest cost to the borrower from 11 percent to well above 11 percent. Similarly, if banks paid an average 9.75 percent for their funds, the front-end fees will increase their margin on the loan from 125 to 131 basis points.

EUROFUNDING

Prior to the development of the Euromarkets, the primary source of funding for international lending was the deposit base of the parent bank plus funds bought in the domestic market. The Eurodollar market provides a huge pool of primary and interbank deposits for international dollar lenders, while the Eurocurrency market provides bank deposits for loans denominated in currencies other than that of the country in which the bank or branch is located. Liability management in a Eurobank attempts to (1) assure the continued availability of funds at rates close to the prevailing market, (2) keep a stable deposit base, and (3) minimize the cost of funds and the mismatch between maturities of assets and liabilities. Additionally, many banks will attempt to engage in arbitrage activities in the markets and "walk the yield curve" to seek greater profits. Arbitrage involves taking advantage of differences in yields between similar money market instruments, while walking the yield curve implies borrowing in short maturities and depositing in longer maturities, or vice versa.

Eurobanks are also not subject to reserve requirements imposed by monetary authorities or by FDIC insurance fees. Therefore, Eurodollar CDs usually offer more attractive rates than those of domestic CDs. Interbank lines of credit enable them to hold negligible clearing balances.

Interbank deposits form the chief Eurocurrency funding source for most wholesale international banks. The establishment of credit lines within the interbank market is of paramount importance. As we discussed previously, banks do occasionally face a funding risk as a result of tiering, the grouping of banks according to size or nationality that serves as a proxy variable to credit-worthiness assessments during periods of great uncertainty. The number of tiers and the differences between them have tended to increase when events focus on the possibility of bank default. On a temporary basis, some banks have effectively been cut off from the market following a bank failure.

EUROBANK ACTIVITIES

A full range of Eurobank activities and objectives might include:

1. Accepting call, short-term and fixed-date Eurocurrency deposits of up to several years in order to fund the bank's loan portfolio and for relending in the interbank market;

2. Eurocurrency lending for the bank's own portfolio on a rollover or fixed-rate basis from short dates to medium term;

3. Management of Eurocurrency rollover loans on an underwriting or best-efforts basis to be placed with a wide range of banks;

4. Exchange dealing in spot and forward currencies for the account of clients, the bank's own position, or to create deposits through the swap;

5. Origination, management, underwriting, and selling of publicly issued Euroinstruments, and maintenance of a secondary trading market in Eurobonds;

6. Arrangement of private placements of debt issues in a variety of currencies with international investors;

7. Corporate finance activities such as mergers and acquisitions, project structuring, or special project financing in sectors such as energy or transportation;

8. Portfolio management for international investors;

9. Provision of letters of credit, acceptance finance, money transfer, and collection for direct customers as well as correspondent bank customers;

10. Arrangement of lease financing or export financing;

11. Equity participations either outright or in connection with the extension of a loan;

12. Diversifying into investment banking activities to potentially earn a higher return on capital than the parent can earn in its traditional activities;

13. Standby credit lines, available to the bank under set circumstances and terms. Non–U.S. banks have a need for this kind of help should dollars become tight;

14. Term loans secured by collateral such as securities;

15. Loans for the bank's own needs (for example, construction); and

16. Interest rate and debt-for-equity swaps.

Banks use interbank lending when they cannot place funds to better advantage elsewhere, as a way to learn about other banks, as a place to engage in arbitrage of short-term deposits, and even as a long-term investment. The workings of the interbank market came under scrutiny during the debt crisis of 1982 to 1983. The interbank market proved difficult to manage as banks and their governments tried to reschedule credits and keep the borrowing countries liquid. To protect themselves, most banks established overall and daily limits of placements by bank and by country. This is quite important since the lending limits imposed on U.S. banks in their domestic activities do not affect the loans that they might make to the public and private sectors in other countries. In essence, a bank can theoretically lend any amount it wishes to a foreign government or corporation.

FOREIGN EXCHANGE SERVICES

Banks provide two major types of foreign exchange services in the form of: (1) current exchange services, and (2) forward commitment exchange services.

In a current exchange, the bank exchanges one currency for another immediately. For example, an American tourist in London may wish to exchange dollars for pounds, or vice versa. This is generally accomplished out of the bank's inventory position of either currency. Large banks that are active in foreign exchange services maintain working balances in currencies to accommodate exchanges. Alternatively, if the bank did not maintain an inventory of the currency involved, it could agree to the exchange at the current rate and then cover its position after the agreement. If this situation occurs, the bank is at risk in relative value of the currencies until its open position is covered.

A bank that provides forward-commitment exchange services is essentially agreeing to exchange currency at a later date for a specific exchange rate today. Forward delivery dates from one month to several years are quite common.

Most money-center banks are active in foreign exchange and maintain large trading staffs which adjust the bank's currency position to their cash-flow needs. The traders also take currency positions in order to speculate on market movements. These trading staffs may also be responsible for the interbank depository positions of the bank.

INTERNATIONAL INVESTMENT BANKING

Investment banking represents those activities that bring together borrowers or issuers of securities and investors through the capital markets. International investment banks originate, distribute, trade, and position securities globally, regionally, and locally.

Origination consists of all activities involving an offering to sell a debt or equity security to investors, such as the arrangement of the terms and pricing structure of the offering, and the formation of a syndicate to buy the security and resell it to investors. Distribution is primarily a sales and marketing function that is concerned with placing newly issued securities in the hands of final investors. The trading function, in which the investment banker acts either as an agent or a dealer, involves the matching of buyers and sellers of securities that are already publicly owned. In addition, another trading function involves helping corporations and other banks in the investment of their foreign exchange reserves and domestic currency holdings in money market instruments. Positioning involves the purchase of securities as an investment for the bank in response to market opportunities.

Most international investment banks are also involved in providing international portfolio management and investment research services to clients. Investment banks have also helped clients in arranging swaps, hedges, and parallel loans in different currencies. A parallel loan is an arrangement under which two institutions or corporations in different countries make loans to each other in their own currencies and countries. For example, a U.S. company might make a dollar loan to a subsidiary of a Swiss firm, while the Swiss firm simultaneously makes a Swiss franc loan to the subsidiary of the U.S. company. Each parallel loan serves as collateral for the other loan and carries an interest rate related to local credit conditions plus the cost of a long-term forward-exchange contract. The parallel loan is a clumsy and costly agreement that requires the bringing together (usually by the investment banker) of two parties with matching needs and the signing of two loan contracts and one implicit forward arrangement. The currency swap is a simple adaptation of the parallel loan that allows two parties to engage in a single agreement to exchange coupons or principal of two different kinds. For example, the fixed-rate currency swap consists of the exchange between two counterparties of fixed-rate interest in one currency in return for fixed-rate interest in another currency. On the maturity date the counterparties reexchange the principal amounts established at the outset. This swap results in the transformation of a debt raised in one currency into a fully hedged, fixed-rate liability in another currency.

An interest rate swap is even simpler than a currency swap because it usually consists of two parties exchanging coupons of fixed interest for floating rate interest in the same currency in a mutually agreed-upon principal amount. Essentially, the counterparties are able to convert an underlying variable-rate liability into a fixed-rate liability, and vice versa. Most interest-rate swap transactions take place because of cost savings that may result from differentials in the credit standings of the participants and other structural considerations, or the desire to match fixed-rate liabilities with fixed-rate assets or floating-rate liabilities with floating-rate assets. Corporations, banks, or sovereign borrowers have also made arrangements through their investment bankers for NIFs or underwriting facilities which are arranged for a few years.

The aforementioned services, along with the merger and acquisition activities, provide bankers with a potentially large source of fee income along with the usual underwriting fees earned on Eurobonds and syndicated loans. Given the rapid rate of worldwide financial innovation among investment bankers, it is likely that new sources of fee income will be generated in the years ahead.

FOREIGN BANK EXPANSION IN THE UNITED STATES

Since the late nineteenth century, several large Canadian banks have had offices in New York and several West Coast cities; during the 1920s, some European and Japanese banks opened offices in the United States, the growth of which was halted by the worldwide depression and World War II. By the 1960s, foreign banks had begun to establish offices in New York, Chicago, and San Francisco. The motivation for opening offices in the United States included:

1. Convenient access to dollar assets and deposits enabling the foreign parent bank to hedge its Eurodollar liabilities of its European offices;
2. A net source of dollar funds that the foreign parent bank can use to make dollar loans to multinational clients or to manage its system-wide liquidity;
3. Expansion of its in-house participation in foreign exchange transactions; short-term financing of international trade between American subsidiaries of foreign-based firms, and American firms whose overseas affiliates are serviced by the foreign bank;
4. Develop U.S. offices that provide retail banking services (originally to American ethnic minorities by Japanese banks in California) as evidenced by takeovers and penetration of large banks in California and New York by large British banks; and
5. Develop a major position in U.S. banking in order to provide broader geographical diversification for their stockholders.

Until 1978 there was limited federal supervision of foreign bank expansion in the United States. If the foreign banks chose to expand directly via additional offices in the United States, the foreign bank had only to receive approval from the relevant state banking commission. The International Banking Act of 1978 provides a more comprehensive federal policy for foreign bank expansion in the United States.

The important role of the dollar in international finance in the decades of the 1960s and 1970s made a dollar-based operation advantageous for foreign banks doing international business. Foreign banks set up operations in the United States to compete in domestic money markets, to gain access to another dollar outlet, and to expand the corporate relationship established in their home country. The foreign banks were able to provide global and around-the-clock services to their clientele. They also wanted to set up foreign exchange operations in New York, finance trade with the home country, and generate U.S. investment in the home country. Most of the growth in the operations of foreign banks in the United States has taken place since the mid-1970s. Whereby most of the U.S. expansion abroad took place earlier and has been in wholesale banking, the foreign expansion in the U.S. banking market has been split between wholesale and retail banking. While most foreign banks in the United States operate solely in the wholesale market, some foreign banks, particularly banks from England, Canada, Japan, and Israel, maintain retail (consumer-oriented) operations in urban areas.

Foreign banks operate in this country through agencies, branches, subsidiaries, representative offices, investment companies, and Edge Act corporations.

Correspondent Banking. Most major banks maintain a two-way channel of "correspondence" through cable and mail, specifying activities to be undertaken and fees to be charged. The services provided via this channel are concerned generally with the collection and payment of foreign funds stemming from trade transactions that include acceptance drafts and provision of credit information, and honoring letters of credit. Correspondent banks keep deposit balances with each other. The advantage of correspondent banking is the provision of services, whatever the correspondent's country, by knowledgable, indigenous bankers who are acquainted with their country's customers and regulations. The main disadvantage is the inability of a customer to make deposits, borrow, or withdraw funds from the home bank's own offices.

Representative Office. The representative office is a low-cost way to maintain a presence in selected locations, while providing limited services to corporate clients and directing business to the parent bank's head office or full-service branch in the United States. The office can neither make loans or accept deposits directly. The office serves as a listening post or an "ambassador of goodwill," and its existence does not pose a threat to correspondent relationships established previously. This is essentially an information and liaison office for the parent bank.

Agencies. Agencies are banking offices that can lend and transfer funds but cannot accept deposits from domestic residents. However, they may accept credit balances that are incidental to their customers' banking transactions. An agency faces no legal lending limit to any one borrower and has access to the U.S. money markets. Agencies perform many functions related to international finance, including trade financing, issuance of letters of credit, and foreign exchange operations.

Shell Branches. These branches are located primarily in the Bahamas or the Cayman Islands, and are characterized by the absence of an operational staff because the main office of the bank performs the work. The shell branches are used as booking offices to gain access to the Eurocurrency market and to take advantage of favorable tax treatment and reserve-free locations from which to issue foreign loans. These branches do not provide full-service operations.

Branches. A branch of a foreign bank is a full-service bank that is permitted to accept foreign and domestic deposits and to make foreign and domestic loans. Although books are kept separately, branches hold none of their assets or liabilities. They do gather credit information and economic and business intelligence. Many large banks have a foreign branch network of international banks, and are active in world money and capital markets. Branches function as an integral part of the parent bank; they are an extension of the bank rather than a separate entity. A branch does not require separate capitalization. The branch has the same status as the parent bank in the international market. The organizational form is flexible, and service can be integrated with the parent bank.

Subsidiaries. Subsidiaries have their own capitalization and charter. They are usually state-chartered financial institutions that engage in banking or bank-related activities subject to the Bank Holding Company Act and Federal Reserve supervision. A subsidiary bank can accept deposits, make loans up to the legal lending limit, provide trust services, obtain FDIC deposit insurance, and choose to be a member or nonmember of the Federal Reserve System.

Edge Act Corporations. The International Banking Act of 1978 permits a foreign bank to organize or acquire control of an Edge corporation. An Edge corporation can accept demand and time deposits that are incidental to international or foreign transactions. As a matter of fact, Edge corporations can transact only international or foreign business. Edge corporations can establish international banking offices with limited capital commitment in the United States. This allows domestic banks to set up interstate locations, although activities are limited to international business.

Foreign Affiliates. This form of banking operation generally involves the acquisition of an equity interest in a foreign bank. The advantage of this form of banking stems from the fact that the institution is not "foreign" in the host country. The activities undertaken by affiliated banks are the same as those undertaken by indigenous banks.

Joint Banking Ventures and Consortia. They represent associations of two or more banks seeking to pool efforts toward a particular task or project. Consortium banks are joint ventures separately owned and incorporated by two or more parent banks of different nationalities. The consortium banks service the clients of the parent organizations and also seek new business. They generally provide full-service banking-related investment and underwriting services, as well as consulting services for banking entities. The consortium allows large banks to pool operations in a separately owned banking operation, loan risks, and different expertise. The domestic bank has less control than it would have over a fully owned subsidiary.

International Banking Facilities (IBFs). In 1982, U.S. banks were authorized to establish international banking facilities as adjuncts to the regular banking facilities of U.S. banks, Edge corporations, or U.S. offices of a foreign bank. It was hoped that the establishment of these facilities would make it possible for U.S. banks to recapture a portion of the Eurocurrency market lost to foreign banks because of Regulations D and Q. IBFs are restricted from issuing negotiable CDs, bankers' acceptances, or transaction accounts, but they can accept deposits of at least $100,000, which are exempt from reserve requirements from non-U.S. residents and other IBFs. These funds must be used to make international loans. The business is limited to wholesale services, and allows a bank to use a domestic office to book Eurocurrency transactions without employing a shell branch. No formal application is necessary to form a facility.

As U.S. banks have increased their international activities, foreign banks have become more active and visible in the United States. Foreign bank assets in the United States have grown from about $7 billion in 1965 to more than $600 billion at the end of 1987. Over 225 foreign banks with over 860 offices are located in this country with concentrations in New York (371), Chicago (74), Los Angeles (107), San Francisco (69), and Houston (60). Just as U.S. banks followed American companies abroad, foreign banks have followed their customers into the United States. Foreign banks have also initiated or expanded U.S. operations to improve their access to U.S. money and capital markets and obtain new sources of dollar deposits. They also wanted to participate in the growth of the U.S. economy and avoid their home country's restrictions and regulatory constraints.

U.S. subsidiaries of overseas commercial banks have made approximately 20 percent of the total commercial and industrial loans in the United States. Among New York banks, foreign banks held close to 35 percent of commercial and industrial loans in mid-1987. In contrast, foreign banks held only 4 percent of U.S. business loans in 1973. Among foreign banks, Japanese banks had the largest share of business loans in the U.S. market, at 34 percent. Banks from the United Kingdom held 18 percent, while Canadian banks held 10 percent. The next largest share of business loans held by foreign banks can be found among banks from Hong Kong, with 7 percent, and France, with just over 5 percent.

The share of all domestic banking assets controlled by foreigners grew from less than 3 percent in 1970 to almost 20 percent in 1987. These assets include a much higher percentage of interbank and international assets than do those of other domestic banking offices so that market shares can be misleading. For example, the foreign banks' penetration of the domestic consumer market is small, while the share of domestic commercial lending is quite large. A number of large acquisitions of U.S. banks by foreign banks helped contribute to the rapid growth of assets of foreign offices of U.S. banks.

The different leverage positions between foreign and U.S. banks made it difficult for U.S. banks to compete in the lending business because this higher leverage permitted foreign banks to price loans lower than their U.S. counterparts. Foreign banks were also willing to offer loans at lower rates than their domestic counterparts in order to gain market entry and share. As a matter of fact, the growth in assets of non-U.S. banks has been far more rapid than that of comparative U.S. banks. This is due in part to the lower pricing of loans and the willingness of foreign banks to accept a lower return on assets. Foreign banks are often government-owned, or have implied government guarantees or subsidies, along with their willingness to operate with more leverage.

U.S. banks are subject to constraints on the amount of leverage they can employ. Such constraints are imposed by regulatory limits, a negative view by stock market analysts on excessive leverage, and a higher cost of funds encountered by highly leveraged banks. A high level of equity capital and low leverage are considered to be consistent with prudence, safety, and image in the U.S. market.

Until enactment of the International Banking Act of 1978, a foreign banking organization had more latitude than an American bank. For example, foreign banks were able to operate at a competitive advantage over U.S. banks because of their lower reserve requirements. Although a foreign bank could control a subsidiary bank in only one state, a foreign bank could also operate agencies and branches in other states. In this way some foreign banking organizations developed interstate networks of full-service offices. This opportunity was not and still is not available to U.S.-owned banks. Without a subsidiary in the U.S., a foreign bank could obtain state licenses to operate offices in one or more states and also have nonbanking subsidiaries which engage in activities forbidden to U.S. banks. The International Banking Act of 1978 extended the nonbanking provisions of the Bank Holding Company Act to the American operations of all foreign banking organizations, but contained a grandfather clause that allowed the foreign organizations to retain nonbanking activities, such as investment banking, that were in operation prior to July 27, 1978.

INTERNATIONAL BANKING CRISIS

Since 1982, newspaper headlines have called attention to the debt problem of the less developed countries (LDCs). Initially, most analysts believed that debt-servicing problems would be temporary, and that creditworthiness and more normal growth of most countries would be restored in a period of several years at most. (See Table 6.1.) However, events have demonstrated that the initial assessment was overly optimistic.[6]

The international banking crisis is a widespread failure of debtors in developing countries to pay their foreign debts on time. This has aroused anxiety that large commercial bank creditors might fail because the major borrowers in difficulty, such as Argentina, Brazil, and Mexico have defaulted on their loans outstanding to U.S. money-center banks that are well in excess of their total capitalization. The debt crisis has a number of causes: imprudent economic management and borrowing by the debtor countries, as well as imprudent lending by commercial banks. Many countries are having difficulties servicing their debts because of depressed exports, high interest rates, and only modest worldwide economic growth.[7]

Prior to 1986, actual loss ratios on international loans were more favorable than those on domestic loans. As a matter of fact, international lending had been an extremely profitable activity for many of the world's largest money-center banks. However, after the refusal of Brazil and some other Latin borrowers to meet debt payments during 1986-1987, the major banks established loan loss reserves of over $17 billion for their Third World debt. The buildup of reserves, which results in a dollar-for-dollar reduction in banks' shareholder equity, has reduced the equity position in most money-center banks. For example, as a result of the increase in loan-loss reserves, total shareholders' equity as a percentage of total assets declined to between 3 and 4 percent for most large New York banks during the second quarter of 1987. The pairing of shareholder equity implies that lending practices should become more conservative and

Table 6.1
Latin American Debt

Country	Total Foreign Debt (% of Exports)		Total Foreign Debt ($ billions)		Gov't Debt Owed to U.S. Banks* ($billions)
	1982	1987	12/1982	12/1986	
Argentina	405	554	45.4	5.6	5.64
Brazil	339	471	85.3	110.3	14.00
Chile	333	370	18.0	21.5	3.95
Mexico	299	366	87.6	100.3	14.53
Peru	269	551	12.2	16.2	0.90
Venezuela	84	278	37.2	34.1	5.56

* 1986

dividend payments should be stingier. The erosion in equity should lead to slower asset growth and fewer acquisitions by the money-center banks. This has come at a time when traditional domestic lending spreads are thin and when money-center banks need to invest in new strategies to compete with foreign banks, fast growing regional banks, investment banking firms, and other financial service companies. In addition, if equity becomes sufficiently small, then at a certain point public confidence may become eroded, and the cost of bank borrowing may increase. There is also likely to be a flood of banks seeking to raise equity capital in the absence of a turnaround in the Third World debt situations. It is also possible that the slippage in capital could add momentum to proposals to broaden bank ownership to include well-capitalized industrial companies.

The moving of money from the bank's net worth accounts to its loan loss reserves is merely an accounting entry. The actions acknowledge a reality that occurred several years ago—losses on loans.

Three important trends have emerged since the onset of the LDC loan crisis in 1982. First, banks have curtailed net new international lending. Second, exposure to troubled LDCs has fallen, but not by as much as exposure to other foreign borrowers. Third, concentration of exposure to troubled borrowers is shifting increasingly towards the largest money-center banks. For example, the nine major U.S. banks held 63 percent of total loans outstanding to troubled LDC borrowers in early 1988 compared to a low of 56 percent in 1982. In contrast, all other U.S. banks have reduced their share of total bank exposure to troubled LDCs. In addition, U.S. bank regulators have endorsed proposals that would require banks with large exposures to troubled LDCs to hold higher amounts of capital relative to assets than would other banks.

Proposed Solutions

Prior to the huge buildup of bank loan-loss reserves in 1987, rescheduling and reduction in interest rates had been a practical way for bankers to salvage their loans and avoid a write-off against their capital and surplus accounts. Rescheduling and the loan-exposure problem had become a great embarrassment when it was revealed in the mid-1980s that LDC debt had reached a level of close to 275 percent of the primary capital of the nine largest U.S. money-center banks.

Although a broad solution to the international debt crisis has not been reached, officials of the indebted nations and their creditors have reached some solutions on a limited basis. The heart of the problem is that most of the LDCs do not have—and are unlikely to have—enough dollars to make their interest payments let alone pay back principal for many years. In most cases, Latin American nations are not generating trade surpluses large enough to service their debts and still leave them money to grow. In addition to rescheduling the effective interest maturity of the debt and making interest-rate concessions, banks have increased secondary-market sales of these loans and debt-for-equity and debt-for-commodity swaps. For example, banks will sell an LDC loan to a third party, usually a multinational corporation or another bank, at a large discount. The corporation often exchanges the loans at the country's central bank for local currency in an amount equal to the debt's original face value, which it then invests in local industry. The debt is extinguished from the bank's books and new investment may come into the country. These debt-for-equity swaps may also encourage privatization of companies that are burdensome to a government. The aforementioned buildup of reserves means that banks can sell their loans at a discount without incurring further losses in earnings. Also, in debt-for-equity swaps, investment bankers (including money-center banks) have begun to earn sizable fees by pairing banks wishing to sell debt with corporations looking to buy that debt for an equity exchange.

Another plan to deal with LDC loans is to swap debt for commodities. For example, First Interstate Bank's trading company subsidiary has proposed to export Peruvian asparagus, shrimp, and textiles, keeping part of the proceeds as debt payment. Thus, the country's export industries are stimulated and hard currency is preserved. A third plan involving Japanese banks is to set up a factoring company that restructures and collects Latin debt that it bought from banks at a discount. Although banks must book losses equal to the discount, they get tax deductions which are otherwise unavailable, and can remove the loans from their balance sheets.

Nancy J. Needham, president of the Institute for Corporation and Government Strategy, suggested that banks must become equity participants in the debtor nations' enterprises. Converting much of the outstanding debt into equity will stop the current hemorrhage of cash and let borrowers use capital to produce saleable goods and services. The balance sheets of banks would be damaged less than if the loans were in default or declared dubious. The risk profile of the balance sheets and their ability to make further loans would be essentially unchanged. Also, equity in potentially successful businesses is preferable to defaulted loans. International financial structures would remain intact and the borrowers' internal turmoil would be eased.

One way to convert debt would be to establish stock arrangements similar to close-end trusts. For example, there are over 500 state-owned enterprises in Brazil which could become partially owned by foreign banks. Bankers could become board members, provide advice and assistance, and help find export markets. The government could pool a variety of its stocks and lending banks would own a diversified group of common stocks, or countries could establish holding companies to own stock in state enterprises, and banks could have holding company shares. In the ideal sense, it is desirable that debt-to-equity swaps involve more than a liquefaction of the initial loan at a discount. From the viewpoint of the debtor country, the debt-to-equity conversion should constitute a net addition to the foreign direct-investment inflows. From the bank's viewpoint, it is desirable that the bank be in a position to partake in the potential profits that the equity investment affords to the holders. Merely selling a loan at a discount to a potential investor (as is the case in many instances) does not fulfill that objective.[8]

Reform proposals can be distinguished according to whether they propose extending the effective maturity of the debt or changing the nature of claims on the LDCs, whether they offer genuine debt relief, and what sort of conditions or external constraints are placed on domestic policymakers.[9] There are some worldwide macroeconomic preconditions that must be met if the debt problems of the LDCs are to be resolved. For example, if the LDCs cannot expand their export earnings at a rate sufficient to permit a gradual reduction of the debt-service ratio over time, there can be no satisfactory resolution to the current problems. This also means that the developed country markets must remain open to the exports of the LDCs.

Debt-servicing obligations can present two problems for a country. There is the necessity to earn (save) the foreign exchange for debt-service and, especially when the debt is public, there is a public finance problem of either raising taxes or lowering expenditures. While lowering some forms of expenditures and reducing inefficiencies in the public sector can and should be part of the longer-term realignment of incentives, it is often difficult politically to increase taxes or cut government expenditures. In addition, some countries are caught in a low-growth, high-debt-service trap.[10]

The initial burden of the debt crisis was borne largely by the debtor countries. Subsequently, however, bank shareholders have paid the price of lower price-earnings ratios, increased loan-loss reserves, and reduced earnings per share.

According to H. Robert Heller, of the Board of Governors of the Federal Reserve Bank, international debt will remain an important concern in the years ahead, and it is in the best interests of the creditor banks and the debt countries to cooperate in overcoming the current difficulties. Banks will have to continue to make temporary sacrifices if they want to see the long-term quality of their assets improve. On the other hand, some banks may see their own strategic interests better served by equity investment rather than a continuation of debt holdings.[11]

The debtor countries can enhance the long-term strategic interests of the banks by opening up their financial markets and granting new franchises. It will also be important for the countries to focus on improved export performance rather than import curtailment. At the same time, it would be appropriate for industrial countries with strong current account positions to lead the world toward a more open and growth-oriented economic and financial system that will not only benefit the developing countries in need of export markets but will also provide the industrial countries with a wider and cheaper variety of products.

In addition, the World Bank and the International Monetary Fund (IMF) should continue to play the key roles envisioned in their respective charters as providers of balance-of-payments and development finance. These institutions must also serve as a forum for the international policy discussions on appropriate adjustment measures being implemented by surplus and deficit countries alike.

The Reagan Administration has been holding out for full payments of interest on the bank debt owned by Latin America. According to some political observers, this strategy has left Latin America in financial and economic stagnation and could threaten the new democracies in Argentina, Brazil, and Peru. Even with a decline in interest rates in the five-year period since the outbreak of the debt crisis, the ratio of debt to exports was higher in 1987 than in 1982, despite years of austerity. Poverty has increased and public services have deteriorated. Much of these Latin American taxes and export earnings have gone toward servicing the foreign debt. Most Latin American governments are forced to print money to cover their internal expenses; this has fueled inflation in these countries. These mammoth inflation rates help contribute to economic stagnation, capital flight, and political despair.

Since in July 1987 secondary market prices for Latin American debt ranged from 10 percent of par value for Bolivian debt to 67 percent for Venezuelan and Chilean debt, real debt relief might be offered to Latin American nations through the IMF and World Bank, allowing these countries to pay interest on, perhaps, the secondary market value of the loans or at the level that has not been reserved against by banks. This debt relief would give the new democracies the will, incentive, and political standing to go forward with true reform programs. The Latin American governments could tell their people that the reforms and sacrifices are truly for their own benefit, and not for the foreign banks. For debtor countries willing to pursue rigorous adjustment programs under IMF and

World Bank supervision, the World Bank might purchase the bank debt with marketable bonds rather than cash. The debt burden would be reduced to a level that the country could reasonably be expected to service.

Can the banks afford the losses? The answer is that they probably can, since most banks have already reserved against between 25 and 50 percent of their Latin American debt, and the stock market reacted positively to the setting up of the Latin American loan-loss reserves. Risks to taxpayers in the creditor countries could arise only to the extent that the debtor countries could not service even the greatly reduced debt burden. In that case, the World Bank would require new funding to make up the difference. Some of the risks could be lessened by the World Bank charging a spread between the purchase price from the banks and the relief price to the debtor, or by the debtor pledging gold reserves as partial collateral.

There is also the strong possibility that loan-loss reserves could be increased, even though most major banks have already built their reserves to at least 25 percent of their loans to developing countries. Since the initial Citicorp increase in loan loss reserves in the second quarter of 1986, secondary market prices of LDC debt have begun to decline (see Table 6.2). The reason for the decline is that supply has increased without a commensurate increase in demand. In the future, there may be increased market pressure to increase loan loss reserves even more.

The fundamental premise of former Treasury secretary James Baker's plan was that it is far better for the debtor countries themselves—and for the international financial system—to keep debt management on a track that points back to reestablishment of normal access to capital markets. The Baker Plan envisions coordinated resumption of capital flows to the debtor countries in return for policy reform. In addition to continued lending by the commercial banks, the Export-Import Bank, World Bank and regional banks should also increase their lending to Latin American nations. Essentially, the Baker Plan calls for economic changes in 15 major debtor countries in return for loans from the World Bank and commercial banks.

The basic idea of the Baker Plan was a good one, but it lacked government support and participation. On the other hand, the Mexican Government, the U.S. Treasury, and J. P. Morgan offered another plan in December 1987 under which Mexico attempted to auction as much as $10 billion of 20-year new collateralized bonds to creditor banks that were willing to tender their debt for less than face value during 1988. The new bonds paid a higher rate of interest than existing Mexican government debt and were backed by zero-coupon U.S. Treasury bonds which Mexico purchased from the U.S. Treasury. However, this plan was accepted by a handful of foreign banks, but only a limited number of money-center banks in the United States. Many U.S. money-center banks did not have sufficient capital to absorb the loan losses so they did not tender their loans back to the Mexican government.

For Western nations and Japan, the developing world's stagnation and debt

Table 6.2
Latin American Debt and Its Price in the Secondary Market

Country	Market Price of Loans as % of Face Value			
	11/86	3/87	7/87	11/87
Argentina	66	63	47	35
Brazil	76	69	55	40
Chile	68	68	67	52
Mexico	57	58	53	50
Peru	na	17	11	5
Venezuela	74	na	67	50

burden has been a drag on economic growth. The developed countries, especially the United States, have watched valuable export markets in Latin America shrivel. This has affected the U.S. balance of trade negatively, since Latin America represented a large traditional importer of U.S. goods.

LDCs have found it extremely difficult to borrow additional funds from either commercial banks, governments, or the IMF. Also, there has been a flow of local money out of LDCs since 1982. In 1983 alone, local investors who lacked confidence in their own countries sent an estimated total of $19 billion abroad from ten of the largest debtor nations. That slowed to about $5.4 billion in 1985 and to a trickle in 1986. In addition, banks that are under government pressure to expand their international lending are quarreling among themselves about who should make new loans. Governments and agencies are a dwindling source of finance for the so-called "Baker 15" countries; although they lent the "Baker 15" debtors about $13.8 billion a year in 1983 and 1984, they lent them only $6.6 billion in 1986.

SUMMARY

The segment of international banking activities comprises payment- and transaction-oriented services such as the execution of international payments, foreign exchange services, letters of credit, trade finance, traveler's checks, and credit cards. A second segment involves the financing of balance-of-payment imbalances and the financing of medium- and long-term financing of projects. A third segment involves syndicated Eurocurrency credits, which made it possible for many banks to participate in these lending activities and spread the associated risk among the group of banks that participated in the syndications. The large money-center banks also benefited from the income derived from the management and syndication fees. The broad tendency in the financial markets toward the securitization of lending is carrying over to the international markets. It is likely that international loan syndications will eventually be replaced by the securitization technique. However, in order to gain access to the international security markets, the credit quality of the borrower must be unquestionable. Therefore, it is in the interest of both the debtor country and the creditor banks to enhance the creditworthiness of the debtor nations, so that the security markets can eventually be used to offer the developing nations a broader access to world financial resources.

International banking operates under the following different types of organizational structures: correspondent banking, representative offices, agencies, shell branches, subsidiaries, foreign affiliates, joint banking ventures, consortia, international banking facilities, and merchant and investment banking.

The LDC debt crisis has weakened the balance sheets and income statements of the leading money-center banks. It has led to a curtailment in international lending and a slowdown in the growth of assets of U.S. multinational banks. Although no solutions that are satisfactory to both the lender and borrowers have been found, banks have begun to participate in both debt-for-equity and debt-for-commodity swaps, as well as the sale of LDC loans at a discount to third parties. Prices on the small but significant private market for Third World debt dropped as much as 40 percent since most banks boosted their loan-loss reserves in the second and fourth quarters of 1987.

Assets of foreign offices of U.S. banks grew from less than $5 billion in 1960 to more than $500 billion at the end of 1987. The pace of international lending and the expansion of foreign offices by U.S. banks has slowed since the mid-1980s, partly because of the problems of many heavily indebted LDCs. On the other hand, the asset growth of U.S. banking offices of foreign banks and foreign nonbank investors shows no sign of slowing. From less than $30 billion in 1970, these assets have climbed to more than $600 billion by the end of 1987. The share of all domestic banking assets controlled by foreigners grew accordingly from less than 3 percent in 1970 to almost 20 percent in 1987. These assets include a much higher percentage of interbank and international assets than do those of other domestic banking offices so that   market shares can be misleading. For example, the penetration of the domestic consumer market by foreign banks is smaller, while the share of domestic commercial lending is considerably larger.[12]

NOTES

1. J. E. Le Grand and P. C. Kells, "Focus on Industry," *Journal of Accountancy* (November 1985): 136-139.

2. Ibid., 146.

3. E. N. Compton, *The New World of Commercial Banking* (Lexington, Mass.: Lexington Books, 1987), 174-175.

4. Ibid., 175.

5. E. P. Johnson and R. D. Johnson, *Commercial Bank Management* (New York: Dryden Press, 1985), 579-580.

6. A. O. Krueger, "Debt Capital Flows and LDC Growth," *American Economic Review,* vol. 77, no. 2 (May 1987): 165.

7. S. Fischer, "Sharing the Burden of the International Debt Crisis," *American Economic Review,* vol. 77, no. 2 (May 1987): 165.

8. H. R. Heller, "The Debt Crisis and the Future of International Bank Lending," *American Economic Review,* vol. 77, no. 2 (May 1987): 172-173.

9. Fischer, "Sharing the Burden," 167.

10. Krueger, "Debt Capital Flows," 163.

11. Heller, "The Debt Crisis," 175.

12. J. R. Houpt, "International Banking Trends for U.S. Banks and Banking Markets." *Federal Reserve Bulletin,* vol. 74 (May 1988): 289.

7

Savings and Loans

ORIGIN AND PURPOSE

Today's savings and loans are the successors to the building societies that had been established in Europe to collect the deposits of individuals and to offer residential mortgage loans. Savings and loans, originally called building and loan associations, first appeared in 1831 in the United States when the Oxford Provident Building Association was founded in Philadelphia. They were established to encourage thrift and to finance home construction and purchase. Their current statement of condition still reflects this business focus as mortgage loans outstanding accounted for 54.6 percent of all insured association assets at the end of 1987 (see Table 7.1).

Building and loan associations occupied a tiny niche in the financial world until the 1920s, when they enjoyed a rapid rate of growth, becoming the second largest of the financial intermediaries after commercial banks, as measured by total assets. Many of the institutions were set up by real estate professionals, insurance agents, lawyers, and contractors with the intention of using these associations as sources of income for their own businesses.[1] The control of savings and loans by real estate concerns was and still is a dominant feature of the thrift industry.[2]

Savings and loans were also organized by groups of individuals who wished to buy their own homes but did not have enough savings to finance the purchase. At the time, neither banks nor insurance companies, the major financial intermediaries of that period, lent money for residential mortgages. The members of the groups essentially pooled their savings and lent them back to a few members to finance their home purchases.

For years the savings and loan industry benefited from Regulation Q (which

Table 7.1
Condensed Statement of Condition of FSLIC-Insured Savings Institutions as of December 31, 1987*

Item	Amount (Millions)	Percentage of Total
ASSETS:		
Mortgage Loans	$ 683,289	54.6%
Insured Mortgages and Mortgage-backed Securities	198,578	15.9
Mobile Home Loans	7,381	0.6
Home Improvement Loans	4,503	0.4
Loans on Deposits	3,496	0.3
Education Loans	4,385	0.4
Other Consumer Loans	36,581	2.9
Cash and Government Securities	66,892	5.3
Other Investments	102,697	8.2
Investment in Service Corporations	22,753	1.8
Building and Equipment	15,672	1.3
Real Estate Owned	24,567	2.0
Real Estate Held for Development	8,410	0.7
All Other Assets	72,378	5.8
Total Assets	$1,251,582	100.0%
LIABILITIES AND NET WORTH:		
Savings Deposits:		
Accounts of $100,000 or Less	$ 808,222	64.6%
Accounts of More than $100,000	124,445	9.9
Federal Home Loan Bank Advances	116,309	9.3
Other Borrowed Money	133,289	10.6
All Other Liabilities	21,848	1.7
Net Worth	47,469	3.8
Total Liabilities and Net Worth	$1,251,582	100.0%

Note: Components may not add to totals due to rounding.
*Preliminary.

Source: 88 Savings Institutions Sourcebook, United States League of Savings Institutions, Chicago, Ill., p. 56.

expired in 1986) and a 25-basis-point differential on passbook rates over commercial banks (which expired with the passage of the Garn-St. Germain Act in 1982). This enabled thrifts to have a competitive advantage and to attract relatively inexpensive deposits which they lent primarily in the long-term fixed-rate mortgage market at a positive spread over their cost of funds.

THE RECENT ROLE OF THE FHLBB AND THE FSLIC

Savings and loans may be federally or state-chartered, stock holder-owned or mutuals. Virtually all of them are members of the Federal Home Loan Bank System (FHLBS), which operates for savings associations in a manner similar to the Federal Reserve System for commercial banks. Regional FHLBs make loans to their members for extended periods of time and offer depository insurance of up to $100,000 per account through a subsidiary of the FHLB called the Federal Savings and Loan Insurance Company (FSLIC). The FHLB Board regulates savings and loans by chartering and examining them, as well as approving applications for branches and mergers. Although branching is dependent upon individual state laws, it is more liberal for the savings associations than for commercial banks. In recent years, branching across state lines has not been uncommon. As a matter of fact, between 1982 and 1987, many savings and loans were merged with FSLIC assistance to create financially stronger institutions. In some cases an ailing thrift institution was merged into or acquired by a healthy commercial bank.

Some of these mergers also took place across state lines. The Garn-St. Germain Act permits savings associations to acquire and maintain financially troubled thrifts in other states. Many associations have begun to operate on a nationwide basis. For example, Nationwide Savings has offices in over a dozen states. Also, Garn-St. Germain permits commercial banks to acquire troubled associations. For example, Citicorp has purchased associations in California, Florida, Illinois, Nevada, and Maryland. The New York-based holding company has changed the names of the acquired thrifts to Citicorp Savings. In addition, many involuntary mergers or conversions occurred to protect the integrity of the FSLIC reserves and to minimize the long-run average cost to the industry of providing deposit insurance.

In order to save the limited reserves of the FSLIC and to encourage mergers of weak thrifts into healthier ones, the supervisory agencies allowed certain cosmetic changes to the balance sheet and income statement of merged savings associations. Initially, the FHLBB allowed the surviving thrift to make the following adjustments to the consolidated balance sheet. First, assets and liabilities were permitted to be "marked to market"; that is, the difference between book and market values will eventually be recovered because assets are redeemed at book rather than market value upon maturity. The assets are "written up" over the period remaining until maturity; in other words, they reflect their eventual redemption at book value. This procedure generates income over time.

The other change in the consolidated balance sheet is the recording of "goodwill" (the excess of the purchase price of an acquired thrift, after assets and liabilities have been marked to market) after a merger. The surviving firm initially records goodwill as an asset on its books; the thrift writes it off gradually as an expense over a long period. The FHLBB began allowing a 40-year maximum in 1981; the previous maximum was only 10 years. If net assets are permitted to be added to income over a relatively short time frame, with goodwill diminishing income over a much longer period of time, the result will be favorable to net profits in the early years following a merger.[3]

The FHLBB also allowed savings associations to take into account appreciation in market value of buildings and land (appraised equity capital), as well as adjusting certain liabilities (including loans in process and unearned discounts) to raise the ratio of net worth to liabilities. The FHLBB also permitted net worth certificate additions by the Federal Deposit Insurance Corporation (FDIC) and FSLIC to be counted as capital. These agencies injected funds into weak but salvageable depository institutions with net worth less than 3 percent of assets but greater than 0.5 percent of assets. The FSLIC's interest-bearing notes can be carried by thrifts as assets with the net worth certificate issued by the weakened savings associations shown as capital additions rather than as debt. These net worth certificate additions plus the appraised equity capital charges expired in 1985 along with the favorable treatment of goodwill mentioned earlier.

In August 1986, the FHLBB issued extensive amendments to its net worth regulation for FSLIC-insured institutions. Over time, the regulation will require S&Ls to build their capital ratios from 3 to 6 percent of liabilities. The items that may count toward net worth include most liability reserve accounts, common and preferred stock, retained earnings, undivided profits, appraised equity capital, equity securities, mutual capital certificates, and subordinated debt securities issued in conformity with strict regulations, income capital certificates, and net worth certificates.

The FSLIC deposit insurance fund is threatened by problem thrifts. As a matter of fact, Congress had to come to the rescue of the FSLIC during 1987 by giving the FSLIC the authority to issue $10.8 billion in bonds over a 3-year period. However, as losses at hundreds of the nation's insolvent S&Ls continue at a rate of close to $9 billion a year, many industry executives and government officials acknowledge that the 1987 legislation that permitted the FSLIC to borrow $10.8 billion through 1990 is far from sufficient. Bank Board officials estimated that the FSLIC net worth at the end of 1987 was a negative $11.6 billion. This figure was based on estimated losses at 204 insolvent S&Ls that totaled $15.3 billion versus $3.7 billion in FSLIC assets. Bank Board officials also acknowledged that if generally accepted accounting principals, or GAAP, were used to measure S&Ls' financial conditions, the number of institutions that should be closed but that the FSLIC would allow to continue to operate would grow to 510, and the losses would total $21.8 billion. If those losses were placed on the balance sheet of the insurance fund, it would push the FSLIC into the red by $18.1 billion.

During 1987, a third of the nation's 3,147 S&Ls lost money, giving the industry a record net loss of $6.8 billion. The unprofitable institutions lost a total of $13.4 billion, which overwhelmed the $6.6 billion in profits posted by the rest of the industry. The losses were concentrated in Texas and the surrounding region. The regional concentration of losses is in contrast to the situation in 1981, when record high interest rates caused losses nationwide. The net loss for 1987 exceeded by 50 percent the $4.6 billion that savings associations lost in 1981. These enormous losses and the lack of sufficient reserves have handicapped FSLIC rescue operations of insolvent thrifts.

The ideas being considered to rescue the FSLIC range from merging the FSLIC with the healthier FDIC, to tapping into the money generated each year by the Federal Home Loan Mortgage Corporation, to requiring the Federal Reserve to pay interest on the $43 billion of reserves that banks and thrifts are required to keep at the Federal Reserve Bank. Another approach is to ask Congress for a direct appropriation of about $25 billion to bail out the FSLIC. Most industry and government officials acknowledge that Congress is likely to try more indirect approaches before considering a direct approach by the

Treasury. However, most observers predict that in the end there will be little choice other than to approve a taxpayer bailout of the FSLIC.

While both the FSLIC and the FDIC impose annual premiums equal to one-twelfth of 1 percent of an institution's domestic deposits, the FSLIC also imposes a special premium on its members equal to one-eighth of 1 percent of their deposits. Officials of healthy thrifts have warned that if this special assessment continues much longer, they will leave the FHLB system and join the FDIC.

About a third of the nation's S&Ls could qualify for leaving the system as of August 1988 and that, if the special assessment is not phased out, the cost of staying in the FSLIC could be three times the penalties imposed on those institutions that decide to leave. In response to these problems and in order to keep the strong S&Ls in the FSLIC, the FHLBB has proposed a reduction in deposit premiums for well capitalized thrifts.

STOCKS VERSUS MUTUALS: FEDERAL VERSUS STATE CHARTER

Savings and loans had total assets of $1,262 billion at the end of 1987. There were approximately 2,648 insured and 313 noninsured savings and loans in the United States at the end of 1987, well below the peak of 4,098 insured and 2,222 noninsured savings associations in 1960. The significant reduction in the number of associations is the result of liquidations, mergers, consolidations, and conversions to savings banks. While the number of savings and loans has been declining, the number of branch offices has been increasing. Of the total, about 67 percent had a mutual form of ownership, while approximately 33 percent were privately held stock associations. These private stock associations hold close to 45 percent of all association assets. There has been a recent trend to convert from mutuals to stock associations. As of this writing, more than 750 institutions have converted from mutual to stock ownership.

Associations chartered by the federal government and insured by the FSLIC totaled 1,288 or about 40 percent of the total at the end of 1987, while state-chartered associations totaled 1,796, with 1,480 of them insured by the FSLIC (see Table 7.2). Federally chartered associations held 55 percent of industry assets, while state-chartered associations held the other 45 percent. Close to one-third of the FSLIC-insured state-chartered associations were capital stock associations which held about 60 percent of industry assets. They tended to be concentrated in California, Texas, and Florida. The asset size distribution of the S&L industry is quite skewed, with the 37 largest institutions holding just under 33 percent of industry assets, while the 1,583 smallest associations hold less than 6.6 percent of the industry total. As a matter of fact, more than 60 percent of savings association assets are held by less than 7 percent of the thrifts (see Table 7.3). Additionally, seven states (California, Florida, Illinois, Pennsylvania,

Table 7.2
Number and Assets of All Savings Associations, by Charter

Year-end	Federally Chartered†	State-chartered			Grand Total
		Total	FSLIC-insured	Noninsured‡	
1960	1,873	4,447	2,225	2,222	6,320
1965	2,011	4,174	2,497	1,677	6,185
1970	2,067	3,602	2,298	1,304	5,669
1971	2,049	3,425	2,222	1,203	5,474
1972	2,044	3,254	2,147	1,107	5,298
1973	2,040	3,130	2,123	1,007	5,170
1974	2,060	2,963	2,081	882	5,023
1975	2,048	2,883	2,030	853	4,931
1976	2,019	2,802	2,025	777	4,821
1977	2,012	2,749	2,053	696	4,761
1978	2,000	2,725	2,053	672	4,725
1979	1,989	2,695	2,050	645	4,684
1980	1,985	2,628	2,017	611	4,613
1981	1,907	2,385	1,872	513	4,292
1982	1,727	2,098	1,616	482	3,825
1983	1,553	1,949	1,487	462	3,502
1984	1,463	1,930	1,475	455	3,393
1985	1,419	1,778	1,488	290	3,197
1986	1,345	1,733	1,466	267	3,078
1987*	1,288	1,673	1,360	313	2,961
Millions of Dollars					
1960	$ 38,511	$ 32,965	$ 28,919	$ 4,046	$ 71,476
1965	66,715	62,865	57,861	5,004	129,580
1970	96,259	79,924	74,386	5,538	176,183
1971	114,229	91,794	85,755	6,039	206,023
1972	135,925	107,202	100,424	6,778	243,127
1973	152,240	119,665	112,557	7,108	271,905
1974	167,671	127,874	120,552	7,322	295,545
1975	195,410	142,823	134,849	7,974	338,233
1976	225,763	166,144	157,409	8,735	391,907
1977	261,920	197,321	188,078	9,243	459,241
1978	298,195	225,347	215,115	10,232	523,542
1979	323,058	255,904	245,049	10,855	578,962
1980	348,461	281,368	270,004	11,364	629,829
1981	407,351	256,816	243,717	13,099	664,167
1982	483,898	223,748	208,765	14,983	707,646
1983	499,254	274,163	254,946	19,217	773,417
1984	528,104	375,384	351,851	23,533	903,488
1985	552,465	396,316	385,633	10,683	948,781
1986	541,292	422,024	412,259	9,765	963,316
1987*	541,927	435,813	425,359	10,454	977,740

*Preliminary.
†All federally chartered associations are insured by the Federal Savings and Loan Insurance Corporation.
‡Includes the assets of institutions insured by state insuring agencies.
Sources: Federal Home Loan Bank Board; United States League of Savings Institutions.

Table 7.3
Distribution of FSLIC-Insured Savings Institutions by Asset Size

Asset Size (Millions)	Number of Institutions	Percentage of Total	Assets (Millions)	Percentage of Total
Under $25	341	10.8%	$ 5,422	0.4%
$ 25 and under $ 50	540	17.2	19,976	1.6
$ 50 and under $ 100	702	22.3	50,001	4.0
$ 100 and under $ 250	806	25.6	126,951	10.1
$ 250 and under $ 500	340	10.8	116,229	9.3
$ 500 and under $1,000	186	5.9	131,150	10.5
$1,000 and under $5,000	195	6.2	394,107	31.5
$5,000 and over.	37	1.2	407,745	32.6
Total	3,147	100.0%	$1,251,582	100.0%

Note: Components may not add to totals due to rounding.
Sources: Federal Home Loan Bank Board; United States League of Savings Institutions.

New Jersey, Texas, and Ohio) account for 66 percent of all savings and loan assets. The uneven distribution of savings and loan assets among the states is caused by factors such as state population size and income, the degree of urbanization, historical institutional entrenchment in some states, and competition from other types of financial institutions. The largest savings and loans are considerably smaller than the largest commercial banks. For example, the largest thrift has only about 15 percent of the assets of Citicorp, the largest bank holding company.

The concentration in mortgage lending has not changed much over time because of favorable tax treatment given to savings and loans who hold 82 percent of their assets in "qualifying assets" such as home mortgages and Treasury securities. The government offers thrift institutions a tax break on interest earned from home mortgages held in portfolio. Thrifts are permitted to deduct a high percentage of their income as bad-debt reserves for tax purposes. The higher the percentage of mortgages held in their portfolios, the lower the effective maximum tax rate. This tax advantage raises the net after-tax return on mortgages, encouraging thrifts to concentrate their efforts on mortgage lending. If a thrift were to take full advantage of this government subsidy, the maximum tax rate for a savings and loan association would be less than the maximum tax rate for most other corporations.

New housing-related instruments have entered savings association operations and are reflected in the balance sheet in the form of mortgage-backed securities and insured mortgages; these accounted for 15.9 percent of assets in 1987. Although an institution receives a lower yield on a mortgage-backed security than it would if it held the underlying loans directly, there are several advantages to holding mortgage assets in the form of a security. The key benefit is that the thrift may use these assets as collateral for borrowing purposes. A second benefit is in their liquidity; mortgage-backed securities are more easily sold in the secondary market than are mortgage loans. It is also important to note that even though mortgages written by savings and loans have an original maturity of close to 28 years, most mortgage loans remain on the books for only about 8 years. The average maturity of mortgages varies directly with the level of mortgage rates and the job transfer rate. When mortgage rates rise, debtors tend to hold on to their mortgages, while they tend to pay off their mortgages and refinance at lower rates when mortgage rates fall.

THE PROBLEM OF DISINTERMEDIATION AND MISMATCHED MATURITIES

Disintermediation, the age-old problem that haunted thrift institutions whenever interest rates rose to high levels, may no longer be a problem. Disintermediation is the withdrawal of deposits from financial intermediaries followed by their direct investment in higher-yielding financial instruments. Disintermediation was a serious factor in 1969, 1974, and 1981, as thrifts lost considerable deposits because of regulated interest rate ceilings on deposits under Regulation Q. Savings and loans did not make many mortgage loans because of a shortage of available funds related to the outflow of funds under Regulation Q in the aforementioned years.

Disintermediation was particularly prevalent among large depositors, for whom close substitutes were readily available in the money market. Initial attempts to reduce disruptive disintermediation focused on the removal of interest-rate ceilings for large negotiable or marketable certificates of deposit (1973), or tied to market rates for six-month certificates of at least $10,000 (1978), and longer-term deposits for smaller denominations. As market rates of interest almost tripled between 1976 and 1981, more exemptions from Regulation Q were introduced as it became apparent that stopgap attempts to delay disintermediation discriminated against the smaller saver.

These new deposit forms, which paid variable market rates of interest, raised the cost of funds to the thrifts and caused a shifting of funds out of inexpensive passbook accounts into higher-yielding time deposit accounts. The Depository Institutions Deregulation and Monetary Control Act of 1980 and the Garn-St. Germain Act of 1982 essentially deregulated the financial services industry. They gave thrifts added powers that could help change the nature and essence of the savings and loan industry. The Garn-St. Germain Act also permitted thrifts to have deregulated money market accounts and Super-NOW accounts while expanding their asset powers significantly. Deregulated accounts offered savings associations the opportunity to price accounts with different maturities according to their funding needs, local market competition, and the general level of market interest rates.

Many savings and loans in the United States encountered serious problems of profitability and survival between 1981 and 1984. During the period of 1981 to 1982, the thrift industry lost $9 billion in capital, representing 27 percent of the industry's total capital base. At the peak of the interest rate debacle in 1981, 80 percent of thrifts operated in the red. Essentially there was a maturity mismatch between assets and liabilities, which has always haunted these institutions during periods of rising interest rates. Savings associations tend to have short-term sources of funds that are interest-rate sensitive and long-term fixed-rate assets. The root of the earnings problem for thrifts in the early 1980s was related to the fact that regulatory agencies started deregulating savings rates several years before savings associations were permitted to make adjustable-rate mortgages (ARMs). The deregulation of assets which followed also resulted in some asset problems, but many of the problems which developed occurred after a lag of several years.

The 1980s have seen the failure of the largest number of savings and loans since the Great Depression of the 1930s. Between January 1, 1980 and December 31, 1984, there were 193 official and an additional 318 supervisory failures. An official failure is one that is publicly listed by the FHLBB as closed or merged with FSLIC assistance. A supervisory failure represents a savings and loan that ceased independent operation as a consequence of supervisory actions. Generally, supervisory failures are not publicly announced.[4]

The deregulatory actions of the early 1980s included the lifting of interest-rate ceilings on time and savings deposits, federal permission for thrifts to offer ARMs as well as consumer and commercial loans, and state permission for thrifts to engage in direct investments such as ownership of land held for development, housing, and other building projects, as well as equity investments in service corporations. A major question is whether the failures resulted from deregulation.[5]

The principal conclusion in a study by G. Benston (1975) is that most of the failures in the late 1970s and early 1980s were caused by the effect of interest-rate increases on fixed-rate mortgages which were funded by short duration liabilities.[6] For the most part, the data indicate that thrift failures appear related to interest payments that exceeded interest income. Foreclosed mortgages played a small role. Brokered deposits may have played a role, although the relationship is not consistent. Extremely high rates of growth are associated with the failure of some thrifts, while expanded portfolios of nonmortgage commercial loans and consumer loans do not appear related to failures. Deregulated assets do not appear responsible for failure through 1984. However, after 1984, it does appear that the asset quality of thrifts began to deteriorate in the agricultural and energy belts and that there were some bad mortgage and construction loans made for multifamily and commercial real estate in these segments of the country, as well as in some overbuilt urban areas. These bad loans appear to have led to the failure of some thrifts in 1985 and 1986. A House of Representatives study released in September 1986 identified faulty and fraudulent appraisals of real estate properties as a primary contributor to the collapse or weakening of hundred of financial institutions. The collateral securing real estate loans that were not generating enough cash flow to make payments to the bank exceeded the real market value of the property.

Asset deregulation allowed thrifts to enter new lines of business away from traditional home-mortgage lending. The shift in investments was to types of lending that were inherently more risky, and that in many cases outstripped management capability to underwrite loans and direct equity investment into new lines of business in geographically dispersed areas.

A large proportion of savings association liabilities are held in the form of deregulated money market accounts and consumer time deposits tied to money market yields (see Table 7.4). When interest rates rise, S&Ls have to pay more to get new money and maintain their interest-sensitive liabilities, while the yields on their fixed-rate mortgage and bond portfolios fail to rise correspondingly. Most savings and loan deposits are relatively short-term in nature and must be "rolled over" during the life of the long-term fixed-rate mortgages that remain on the books. This has proved troublesome at times; also, the rise in interest rates resulted in reduced market values for the fixed-rate mortgage loans held by thrifts. Since the majority of the assets in a typical savings and loan are in long-term fixed-rate mortgages, one can see the basic source of the problem.

Liquidity of the deposits in savings and loans is supported by holdings of cash and government securities, by borrowings from the FHLB, and by other factors such as the regular inflow of amortization of mortgage loans. It is remarkable that savings institutions with short-term liabilities would fund long-term investments in fixed-rate housing instruments after being whipsawed on rates so many times in the past. If savings institutions continue to maintain unmatched books of assets and liability maturities unmitigated by hedging in the futures market, there will be an even greater list of failing institutions the next time that rates increase substantially. Variable-rate mortgages are being made in increasing volume, but thrift institutions must do more than run a matched book of assets and liabilities germane to maturities. Savings and loans are struggling to wean the public away from fixed-rate mortgage loans and are beginning to concentrate more on shorter-lived consumer and corporate loans as well as adjustable-rate mortgages. When initially put on the books, consumer loans have an average maturity of two to three years, and usually carry a higher interest rate than the short-term cost of funds to a thrift.

Table 7.4
Savings Deposits at FSLIC-Insured Institutions by Type of Account, Year-End 1987 (Dollar Amounts in Millions)

Type of Account	Amount	Percentage
Passbook	$ 87,251	9.4%
NOW and Super NOW	56,705	6.1
Money Market	118,182	12.7
Fixed Maturity	546,084	58.6
Subtotal	$808,222	86.7%
More than $100,000 Certificate	124,445	13.3
Total Savings	$932,666	100.0%

Note: Components may not add to totals due to rounding.
Source: Federal Home Loan Bank Board.

The aforementioned deregulatory acts permit thrifts to issue credit cards and extend credit on them, to exercise trust powers for a fee, and to invest up to 30 percent of their assets in consumer loans and 10 percent in corporate loans. Along these lines, a large number of thrifts have informally banded together by pledging to pool some assets to meet commercial banks head on on their traditional commercial-lending turf. For example, there is a consortium of 40 savings and loans called the Financial American Network and another syndicate of 15 large savings associations called Savers Capital that seek to make commercial and industrial loans. In general, the legislation attempted to make thrift insitutions less specialized and less subject to the vagaries of financial market conditions. Increases in consumer lending by thrift institutions to the full 30-percent ceiling permitted under the Garn–St. Germain bill are unlikely under the current tax laws. Savings and loans must still have 82 percent of their assets invested in eligible mortgages and other assets in order to qualify fully for the 40 percent bad-debt-reserve tax deduction. Unless this tax restriction is liberalized, it should serve as a barrier against large shifts away from mortgage lending. Nevertheless, it appears likely that the mortgage-lending ratio at thrift institutions will decline somewhat. The unknown is whether the effect on this decline will exceed or be less than the increase in thrift institutions' total resources from deregulation and their increased ability to compete with other financial institutions. Thus, even though the Depository Institutions Deregulation and Monetary Control Act (DIDMCA) and Garn-St. Germain diminish the difference between different types of financial institutions, they do not put an end to specialized institutions any more than the supermarket put an end to convenience food stores.[7]

Fortunately, the FHLBB reported that residential mortgages held by the nation's thrifts had a higher market value at year-end 1985 than book value for the first time since 1979. Additionally, declining interest rates were responsible for the return of most thrift mortgage-loan portfolios to a positive spread over their cost of funds. The improvement, however, will have a negligible effect on roughly 20 percent of all thrifts at or near insolvency and will not ease the pressures on the FSLIC, whose deposit and insurance fund is threatened by problem thrifts. The great majority of these thrifts have poor asset quality and are only marginally affected by declining interest rates.

CHANGING COMPETITION AND STRUCTURE

Increased competition among institutions has produced significant changes in the services and operation these institutions offer. For example, competition has resulted in new savings instruments offering money-market rates of return, credit and debit cards, broader lending powers, leasing of consumer products, travelers checks, money orders, safe deposit boxes, payroll deduction plans, trust department services, telephone and electronic funds transfer, and services such as third-party payment mechanisms. Actually, competition is moving savings institutions closer to operations that are similar to commercial banks, while still retaining their traditional role as depositories for savings and as the dominant private source of funds for residential mortgages.

In a historic widening of the powers of savings and loan associations, the FHLBB authorized them to offer their customers investment and brokerage services. The board had previously approved a plan by a consortium of four associations to form a jointly held subsidiary called the Savings Association Financial Corporation that would offer brokerage services and investment advice to the public from offices set up in the lobbies of the participating institutions. Associations participating in the so-called Invest network would execute orders to buy or sell stocks and other securities through representatives registered with the National Association of Securities Dealers. Ownership of Invest was broadened to 35 savings and loan associations. Over 300 additional savings and loans use the service. Additionally, savings and loans have been granted trust-management powers. The move is part of a nationwide trend to provide one-stop shopping for financial services. Another complementary proposal from the FHLBB is one that would pave the way for thrift institutions to sponsor mutual funds and even sell real estate through special service corporations.

Real estate certificates of deposit (CDs) are a relatively new offering by thrift institutions. The money that is deposited in a real estate CD is generally invested by a savings and loan in local commercial real estate. The thrift institution guarantees a minimum interest rate that is about half a point less than the yield on a regular CD of the same maturity—usually five to seven years. However, if the investment works out well, the yield on the CD can rise to 12, 13, 14, or even 15 percent over the life of the CD as rents are raised and properties are sold for capital gain. These CDs are insured up to $100,000 by the FSLIC, which means that even if the real estate deal sours or if the savings and loan fails, the depositor will still receive the principal and the interest payments.

Historically, the earnings of savings and loan associations have been sensitive to fluctuations in interest rates. Before the deregulation of deposit liabilities, thrift institutions suffered deposit outflows, reduced liquidity, and lower earnings whenever market interest rates increased above the Regulation Q ceiling-rates on deposits. As deregulation progressed, new types of accounts were authorized with rates that were either indexed to market interest rates or not limited at all. These new instruments helped savings and loans attract and retain deposits. The bulk of these new deposits are priced at market interest rates, while the existing small-time deposits have already adjusted to market levels, and passbook savings account levels have gradually declined. While the deregulation of most small-time deposits increased the reliance of savings and loans on liabilities with rates related to market interest rates, it also gave those thrifts the opportunity to price accounts and to attract funds of desired maturities.

As previously mentioned, there has historically been a fundamental imbalance in the asset and liability structure of savings and loan associations. For the most part, savings and loans continue to fund large holdings of fixed-rate long-term mortgages with shorter-term liabilities, even though savings and loans have been given new and expanded powers in the areas of commercial and consumer lending and the authority to issue adjustable rate mortgages. However, the current profitability of the savings and loan industry is a result of the lower average level of market interest rates more than of structural changes in the balance sheets of these institutions. By necessity or choice, most savings and loans have retained the structure and activities that have been traditional in their industry. The savings and loans are primarily mortgage lenders with these loans funded by liabilities with effective maturities much shorter than those of their assets.

Although some savings and loans may specialize in ARMs or in specific types of mortgage lending, the industry as a whole appears to be changing slowly. Nonmortgage loans have increased only marginally over the last few years and account for under 5 percent of total assets. The lack of expertise and substantial start-up costs associated with instituting new lending programs may have deterred some savings and loans. Other thrifts, faced with strong demand for mortgages, have preferred to concentrate on traditional mortgage lending. It is interesting to observe that the ten largest holders of leases and commercial and industrial loans accounted for 71 and 26 percent, respectively, of these assets at FSLIC-insured institutions. On the other hand, the ten largest holders of consumer loans held less than 18 percent of such loans. As of November 1985, the nation's commercial banks had total commercial and industrial loans outstanding of $429.8 billion, compared to $12.9 billion in similar outstanding loans at FSLIC-insured institutions. Additionally, it is expected that changes in income tax laws will act as a catalyst in increasing the demand for home equity loans. These loans, which enable homeowners to use the untapped equity in their homes as security to borrow for any purpose, now offer tax savings over traditional forms of consumer borrowing.

While the addition of ARMs, and consumer and nonmortgage loans are among the strategies used by savings associations to restructure their asset portfolios away from fixed-rate mortgages and to increase the interest-rate sensitivity of their assets, some savings institutions have pursued a strategy of rapid growth to dilute the effects of older mortgages on their portfolios. While rapid growth of the mortgage portfolio helped generate substantial origination fee income and shorten the period of time required to diminish the effects of older assets on the average returns on their portfolios, there are problems with this strategy. Rapidly growing institutions usually cannot rely on core-deposit growth to finance their asset acquisitions. They turn to managed liabilities and brokered deposits that increase their interest-rate exposure and cost of funds. The rapid acquisition of assets may also result in lowered credit standards, possibly leading to increased future losses from defaults in the loan portfolio.

ASSET AND LIABILITY MANAGEMENT

Asset and liability management (ALM) is concerned with accurately measuring the risk exposure of the institution and how various financial strategies affect risk exposure. It is concerned with projecting expected profitability under various interest-rate scenarios and financial strategies, as well as providing management with a profit and risk assessment.

The basic problem to be addressed by ALM is the traditional habit of savings and loans to borrow short-term at essentially variable rates and to lend long-term at fixed rates. Under these conditions there is a basic maturity mismatch of short-term deposits and long-term loans. The critical point is that thrifts usually bet that interest rates will remain stable or decline whenever they borrow at short-term variable rates and lend at long-term fixed rates. There are numerous solutions to the problem. The thrift can attempt to borrow long-term deposits, advances, and debt issues, or it can lend short-term by making more adjustable-rate mortgages, consumer loans, and business loans. Alternatively, the thrift can bridge the asset and liability gap by hedging in the interest-rate futures and options markets and through interest-rate swaps. Also, thrifts can generate conventional fixed-rate mortgages and sell them in the secondary market, earning origination and servicing fees. As savings and loans shorten the interval over which they can reprice their assets—for example, by holding a larger proportion of ARMs—gross operating income should become more variable as the yields on such loans adjust with market interest rates. The spread between gross operating income and interest expense should become more stable, reducing the sensitivity of operating earnings to changes in market interest rates.

Solving the imbalance problem by moving in the direction of a matched book of maturities on both sides of the balance sheet will not work if it eliminates the yield spread. On the other hand, maintaining equal durations on both sides of the balance sheet is prudent without being overly restrictive. The major problems with duration matching arise from the shape and variability of the yield curve and the influence of option-type exposures. Portfolios with different maturities but the same durations move together only when yields on different maturities change by the same amount. Usually short-term rates are more volatile than long-term rates. A stretched portfolio is less volatile than a cluster with the same duration. Since the extent of the difference is variable, duration matching works only as an approximation.

Financial futures are often used to hedge against interest-rate swings. The object of such an "asset hedge" is to guarantee that if interest rates increase and if acquired fixed-rate mortgages decline in value, the thrift can buy back the contracts at a lower price; that is, paper profits on future hedges would compensate for much of the loss caused by increasing interest rates on the value of newly acquired mortgages. When the contracts expire, the thrift would realize any gains or losses, amortizing them over the life of the mortgages. This has the effect of transforming fixed-rate assets into variable-rate assets.

While the asset hedge allows mortgage rates to float along with interest rates, its counterpart on the liability side of the balance sheet enables savings associations to fix borrowing costs for up to two years. The advantage of liability hedges is to control the costs of borrowing and to minimize the effect of rising interest rates on the cost of funds to the institution. If a savings and loan does not hedge against rising rates on the cost of funds, it may be risking its survival on declining interest rates. It should be noted that hedging in the futures market is neither easy nor sure, and should not be undertaken until it is carefully studied and understood.

An Example of Hedging

Suppose that a thrift makes a mandatory commitment to a developer to fund FHA mortgages at a predetermined rate and also intends to pool the loans and sell them in the secondary market within six months. If mortgage rates rise, the loans will have to be sold at a loss. Therefore, the thrift can sell futures as shown in Table 7.5 to offset this exposure. Table 7.5 demonstrates how 15 contracts (instead of 10) at $100,000 face value were used to hedge $1 million in mortgages. The hedge ratio was calculated to maintain dollar equivalency.

Traditionally, savings and loans primarily held long-term fixed-rate mortgages in their portfolios that were funded with short-term deposits. The mismatch was never a problem during periods of stable or declining interest rates. However, problems developed when interest rates rose, raising the cost of short-term deposits above the yield on the fixed-rate mortgage portfolio. Most savings institutions have reduced, but have not eliminated their exposure to interest rate risk by restructuring their balance sheets. In addition, some savings associations have further reduced their exposure to interest rate risk by using interest rate swaps, financial futures, and options on financial futures to hedge against changes in interest rates. Although a savings association that institutes a hedging program reduces its exposure to interest rate risk, it is still exposed to

Table 7.5
Mortgage Operations-Hedging against Rising Rates

June 1: The S&L makes commitments for $1 million mortgage pool based on current GNMA 16% on cash price of 98-28.	June 1: The S&L sells 15 March 1982 GNMA future contracts at 54-26
Jan 1 : The S&L sells $1 million of GNMA 16% to investors at 93-28	Jan 1: The S&L buys 15 March 1982 contracts at 54-26
Loss : $50,000 (5% of $1 million)	Gain : $40,156.25 (107/32 x 32.25 x 15)

Source: N. H. Rothstein and I. M. Little, "The Market Participants and Their Motivations," in their *Handbook of the Financial Futures* (New York: McGraw-Hill, 1984), pp. 75-76.

the many other risks to which all thrifts are exposed, such as liquidity risk, credit risk, and the risk that the slope of the yield curve will change.

Adjustable-Rate Mortgages (ARMs)

Most thrifts offer ARMs in an effort to have variable-rate assets that will adjust with changes in the cost of funds. It is important for thrifts to make sure that the first-year rate set on an ARM is high enough to make a profit not only in the initial year but also in future years. Many thrifts have set an extremely low first-year "teaser rate" in order to induce home buyers to take an adjustable-rate rather than a fixed-rate mortgage. These mortgages usually have a 500-basis-point interest-rate "cap" on the lifetime of the loan, with a 200-basis-point "cap" in any one year.

The "teaser" rates present two great risks to the lending institution. One risk is a credit risk, while the second is a spread or profitability risk. In the first case, if borrowers were qualified for loans based on payments calculated at the discounted or "teaser" rate, lenders may encounter increased delinquencies or defaults when the instruments are repriced to market rates at the end of the discount period. For example, the home buyer might find that the mortgage rate is 500 basis points higher after three years and may not be able to meet the monthly payments. Also, increased interest-rate risk may be a problem even with appropriately priced ARMs if there is a sharp, sustained increase in market rates of interest. Suppose that market interest rates rise by 400 basis points in one year. Unfortunately, the thrift can only raise interest rates on ARMs already in portfolio by 200 basis points because of the interest rate "cap." Thus, the thrift could have a negative interest rate on the adjustable rate mortgage loan for a few years if the "teaser" rate is priced too low at the outset.

Most ARMs are usually priced between 150 and 250 basis points above the one-, two-, or three-year Treasury constant after the initial teaser-rate period. This affords some protection against rising interest rates. However, a financial institution is better protected from interest rate risk when the rates on its outstanding mortgages change in perfect synchronization with its own cost of funds, and not with any other rate.

ARM closings at savings and loans as a proportion of all mortgage loans closed, fell from 54 percent in 1985 to 38 percent in 1986 before rising above 50 percent in 1987. At the end of 1986, ARMs accounted for more than 43 percent of the savings and loan industry's mortgage portfolio. One of the reasons for the shift toward fixed rate mortgages was that the spread between fixed rates and ARMs declined from 150 basis points in 1985 to 100 basis points in 1986. Another reason for the increase in the percentage of fixed rate mortgages during 1986 was that these mortgages were available at under 10 percent for much of the year. However, in 1987 the spread between fixed rate mortgages and ARMs increased to about 250 basis points. This shifted borrowings in favor of ARMs.

Secondary Market Activities

The history of the savings and loan industry has been one of rigid specialization and strict statutory controls on many aspects of operations. The current regulatory climate provides thrift institutions with the power to engage in just about any activity that is permitted to a bank holding company. Rather than just holding mortgage loans in portfolio, thrifts have begun to sell loans into the secondary market, earning some origination and mortgage servicing fees.

In addition to originating mortgages, many thrifts participate actively in the secondary mortgage market. Although savings and loans still purchase more mortgage loans than they sell in the secondary market, their mortgage-lending operations have been undergoing gradual changes in recent years since their usual role as holders of fixed-rate mortgage debt has become less attractive. Therefore, some thrift institutions are beginning to act like mortgage bankers, originating mortgages and selling them in the secondary market. Front-end origination fees of between 1 and 4 percent are typically earned on these transactions (see Table 7.6).

The Federal National Mortgage Association, the Government National Mortgage Association, the Federal Home Loan Mortgage Corporation, Salomon Brothers, First Boston Corporation, Goldman Sachs, and other investment bankers form the basis of the secondary market for home mortgages. The purpose of the secondary market is to increase the liquidity of mortgages by providing a mechanism for the buying and selling of home mortgages. The secondary market allows thrifts to adjust their mortgage portfolio by buying or selling mortgages to suit their liquidity and income needs.

Swaps

During the 1980s savings associations participated in two different types of swaps—mortgage participation certificate swaps and interest rate swaps. As interest rates increased in the early 1980s, weakened thrifts often found it difficult to redeploy their assets to take advantage of new opportunities and higher rates. If thrifts had sold their fixed-rate mortgages to raise cash, they would have been sold at a loss, reduced their earnings, and eroded their net worth. A way to obtain cash was to sell mortgage-backed bonds. Unfortunately, collateralized bonds were hard to sell unless the savings association posted mortgages worth 150 percent of the value of the bonds as collateral to insure the bonds against default.

The Federal Home Loan Mortgage Corporation (FHLMC) and the Federal National Mortgage Association (FNMA) began to issue swap agreements to thrifts. Swap agreements required that savings and loans pledge all income and principal payments on a pool of mortgages to FNMA or FHLMC. In turn, FNMA and FHLMC would issue a "participation certificate" to the savings and loan that guaranteed to pass through all payments of principal and interest on the

Table 7.6
Purchases and Sales of Mortgage Loans, by Lender (Millions of Dollars)

Year	Savings Associ- ations†	Savings Banks	Commer- cial Banks	Mort- gage Com- panies	Federal Credit Agencies	Mort- gage Pools	All Others	Total
				Purchases				
1970	$ 3,694	$1,809	$ 818	$ 60	$ 5,687	$ 2,726	$ 1,612	$ 16,406
1971	7,508	2,433	1,312	415	4,243	4,554	1,203	21,668
1972	10,550	3,222	1,236	1,462	5,553	5,882	1,400	29,305
1973	7,019	2,517	1,176	1,396	8,371	5,007	2,081	27,567
1974	5,865	1,521	1,112	899	10,151	7,485	1,906	28,939
1975	8,471	1,751	431	820	12,526	12,829	1,776	38,604
1976	13,088	2,581	1,022	2,239	10,738	17,855	1,164	48,687
1977	14,791	3,409	2,216	4,236	11,363	26,015	1,974	64,004
1978	11,188	3,244	2,046	4,004	21,884	26,733	4,768	72,867
1979	12,235	2,891	2,410	5,856	17,864	33,423	7,076	81,755
1980	13,189	1,212	4,902	3,445	16,333	29,355	9,708	78,144
1981	10,596	371	4,150	4,708	14,221	24,110	7,961	66,117
1982	23,724	1,531	3,270	4,953	20,021	59,329	5,793	118,621
1983	44,966	2,748	5,107	13,174	26,923	88,122	8,816	189,856
1984	64,623	3,175	8,133	11,205	26,785	68,218	8,037	190,176
1985	64,992	2,934	11,953	20,944	32,953	114,294	9,604	257,674
1986	71,255	3,385	42,779	55,230	39,530	260,435	25,280	497,894
1987*	64,608	3,454	58,192	50,088	25,181	230,566	30,214	462,303
				Sales				
1970	$ 996	$ 283	$ 1,965	$ 12,509	$ 2,587	$ 331	$ 262	$ 18,933
1971	2,013	270	2,262	15,777	2,464	438	675	23,899
1972	3,582	341	2,727	17,831	4,791	323	1,052	30,647
1973	3,416	266	2,723	17,727	5,180	656	427	30,395
1974	3,527	376	2,430	16,164	3,794	1,132	139	27,562
1975	5,234	269	3,386	16,324	8,694	871	512	35,290
1976	8,641	548	4,792	19,144	12,842	850	248	47,065
1977	14,124	284	6,844	33,457	10,092	1,916	757	67,474
1978	15,775	352	7,638	42,602	13,270	2,505	673	82,815
1979	18,667	577	7,733	51,325	9,957	1,279	615	90,153
1980	16,140	782	8,403	36,987	10,463	4,059	295	77,129
1981	12,832	484	5,458	30,492	11,683	3,829	464	65,242
1982	54,446	2,218	8,298	30,893	12,697	4,321	415	113,268
1983	54,194	3,211	15,419	70,362	13,674	5,410	1,140	163,410
1984	64,097	3,374	13,610	56,571	12,244	6,044	2,768	158,708
1985	103,217	6,001	19,173	78,009	7,960	5,535	4,367	224,262
1986	164,585	12,998	40,074	181,155	15,943	1,422	2,280	418,457
1987*	123,579	12,868	52,558	166,478	7,240	278	2,330	365,331

*Preliminary.
†Includes federal savings banks insured by the FSLIC.
Source: Department of Housing and Urban Development.

mortgages less a fee, to the holder. The thrift would then have almost the same amount of mortgage principal and interest payments as before. Since they were backed by a government agency the participation certificates could be sold easily in the capital markets if the thrift needed cash. Participation certificates, unlike private mortgage-backed bonds, did not need to be overcollateralized and could be sold without recording a loss. These swaps let S&Ls raise cash without booking losses on their low-valued mortgages.

The interest-rate swap involves an exchange of interest payments received on underlying assets. Typically, a fixed-rate interest payment stream from a mortgage will be exchanged for a variable rate payment stream. Such swaps let institutions match the cash flow of their assets and liabilities more easily and enable institutions to reduce their interest rate risk.

For example, an S&L may find it easier to obtain funds by issuing short-term deposit accounts to consumers. At the same time, that S&L may have a portfolio of fixed-rate mortgages. The thrift will have a maturity mismatch with the average maturity of its assets greater than the average maturity of its liabilities. Typically, the S&L may try to eliminate this mismatch by swapping interest rate obligations with a commercial bank. Suppose a bank is able to obtain a large amount of 7-year IRA deposits or 7-year capital note issues on which interest payments are guaranteed at a fixed rate. Since commercial banks usually acquire short-term assets, some banks can also benefit from an interest rate swap. If the S&L and the commercial bank decide to swap interest payments on $100 million, the bank might agree to make a payment at the prime rate minus ½ percent of $100 million of liabilities and agree to receive in return a fixed-rate payment of 10 percent for 7 years. The S&L receives an interest payment equal to the prime rate minus ½ percent on $100 million and agrees to make a payment of 10 percent per year on $100 million for 7 years. Since the S&L should be able to pay depositors about 2 percent less than the prime rate, the incoming variable-rate interest payment will enable the thrift to cover the costs of its deposit accounts, and still make a profit. The S&L will pay out most of the interest it receives on its fixed-rate payment of 10 percent that is more than sufficient to cover the interest obligations and the costs associated with either the intermediate-term IRA account or capital note issue. Also, by agreeing to pay out less than the prime rate and by lending at the prime rate plus, the commercial bank will generate revenues in excess of its cost of funds on at least $100 million of short-term assets. Thus, even if interest rates fall to 7 percent, the bank can still profit from its prime rate lending, even though it has agreed to pay 9 percent to depositors of long-term funds (see Figure 7.1).

ASSETS, LIABILITIES, INCOME, AND EXPENSES

The average asset maturity for a savings institution is much longer than for the average commercial bank. In addition, commercial banks have more diversified portfolios than thrifts. Savings and loans remain the largest originators and

Figure 7.1
An Interest Rate Swap

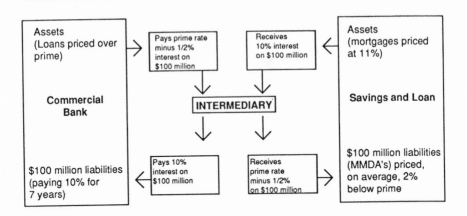

holders of conventional mortgages in the country. At the end of 1987, savings and loans held 27.9 percent of the outstanding residential mortgages, compared to 14 percent for commercial banks and just over 5 percent for savings banks. Most of the loans originated by thrifts are in conventional mortgages rather than in lower-yielding FHA-insured or VA-guaranteed mortgage loans. Savings and loan mortgage-lending has been primarily in single-family homes. As a matter of fact, mortgage loans account for almost 54.6 percent of the total assets of FSLIC-insured savings institutions, while mortgage-backed securities and insured mortgages account for 13.5 percent. The investment portfolio accounts for an additional 16 percent of total assets, while nonmortgage consumer loans represent about 4.0 percent of assets and commercial loans comprise 2 percent of assets (see Table 7.1).

Savings and loans had the bulk of their gross operating income from interest earned on mortgage loans and mortgage-backed securities (72.6 percent), while loan fees and discounts accounted for under 5 percent and investments for about 11 percent during 1987 (see Table 7.7). On the expense side, interest paid on deposits and borrowed money equaled about 68.3 percent of total operating income, while salaries, wages, and fringe benefits accounted for 9 percent of expenses. The ratio of operating expense to operating income has undergone a major decline over the years because of increases in operating efficiency. Interest expense is a bigger portion of total operating expenses for savings and loans than for commercial banks, because thrifts have almost no noninterest-bearing deposits. Their noninterest operating expenses, such as salaries, wages, and occupancy expenses, are relatively low compared to commercial banks. Thrifts have begun to streamline operations in order to cut noninterest costs, since interest costs cannot be cut by much if a thrift is to remain competitive with other depositories.

Table 7.7
Total Operating Income of FSLIC-Insured Savings Institutions
(Percentage Distribution)

Year	Interest on Mortgage Loans†	Interest on Invest-ments	Loan Fees and Discounts	All Other
1960	83.3%	5.1%	11.6%	
1965	86.8	5.4	3.5%	4.3%
1970	84.3	7.7	3.7	4.3
1971	82.6	8.8	4.9	3.7
1972	83.4	7.9	5.3	3.4
1973	83.5	8.3	4.4	3.8
1974	82.3	9.1	3.6	5.0
1975	81.6	8.6	4.1	5.7
1976	80.5	7.6	4.7	7.2
1977	80.8	6.8	5.0	7.4
1978	80.5	7.5	4.4	7.6
1979	78.8	9.1	3.7	8.4
1980	80.7	10.0	3.2	6.1
1981	79.2	11.6	2.7	6.5
1982	77.5	11.4	3.9	7.2
1983	74.9	11.3	5.9	7.9
1984	73.2	11.9	5.2	9.7
1985	73.3	10.6	4.7	11.4
1986	72.4	9.9	5.1	12.6
1987*	72.6	10.8	4.6	12.0

*Preliminary.
†Beginning in 1980, includes mortgage-backed securities.
Sources: Federal Home Loan Bank Board; U.S. League of Savings Institutions.

Thrifts are an example of a margin business. These institutions have only limited control on the rates they can earn on mortgages and the loan-origination fees that can be charged. Although the cost of money in depository accounts is unregulated, the savings industry is highly competitive since most customers are rate-conscious. Savings and loans pay 25 to 80 basis points more for these time deposits than do commercial banks. If thrifts must pay a great deal above market interest rates to attract and retain funds, their longer-term earnings prospects will be impaired. Thrifts do have control over the volume of and type of loans and investments, as well as the maturity and interest-rate sensitivity. Changes in savings and loan earnings are largely a function of changes in spreads, loan volume, and fee income earned. Earnings are also cyclical in nature.

Operating income of savings and loans as a percentage of average assets was 8.96 percent in 1987, compared to operating expenses as a percentage of average assets at 2.02 percent. Although the average return on assets was only 0.01 percent in 1986, it was considerably higher than the negative 0.73 and 0.65 percent return on assets in 1981 and 1982, respectively. Return on equity (net after-tax income divided by average net worth) was 0.20 percent in 1986, 9.14 percent in 1985, and −15.44 percent and −16.13 percent in 1981 and 1982, respectively. (See Table 7.8.)

Table 7.8
Selected Significant Ratios of Federally Insured
Savings Institutions

	FSLIC-insured Savings Institutions				FDIC-insured Savings Banks			
Year	Asset Utiliza-tion[1]	Profit Margin[2]	Return on Equity[3]	Return on Average Assets[4]	Asset Utiliza-tion[1]	Profit Margin[2]	Return on Equity[3]	Return on Average Assets[4]
1960	5.55%	15.55%	12.35%	0.86%	4.25%	11.50%	5.76%	0.49%
1965	5.72	11.63	9.83	0.67	4.93	9.33	5.83	0.46
1970	6.60	8.56	8.02	0.57	5.87	4.31	3.37	0.25
1971	6.93	10.24	10.51	0.71	6.15	7.59	6.56	0.47
1972	7.02	11.01	12.14	0.77	6.38	9.05	8.41	0.58
1973	7.34	10.31	12.15	0.76	6.68	7.88	7.64	0.53
1974	7.63	7.03	8.63	0.54	6.87	4.89	4.85	0.33
1975	7.73	6.06	7.82	0.47	7.06	5.08	5.30	0.36
1976	8.01	7.87	11.10	0.63	7.29	6.09	6.81	0.44
1977	8.23	9.32	13.94	0.77	7.43	7.23	8.39	0.54
1978	8.50	9.57	14.84	0.82	7.75	7.58	9.09	0.59
1979	9.08	7.37	12.06	0.67	8.24	5.42	6.79	0.45
1980	9.60	1.38	2.44	0.13	8.67	− 1.58	− 2.56	−0.17
1981	10.48	− 6.96	−15.44	−0.73	9.47	− 9.91	−16.21	−0.94
1982	11.27	− 5.64	−16.13	−0.65	9.72	− 8.21	−15.77	−0.80
1983	11.20	2.34	6.77	0.27	9.76	− 1.07	− 2.16	−0.10
1984	11.66	1.05	3.15	0.13	10.35	0.68	1.56	0.07
1985	11.49	3.27	9.14	0.39	10.61	7.11	14.49	0.75
1986	10.68	0.08	0:20	0.01	10.15	10.55	16.21	1.07
1987*	9.44	− 6.00	−13.10	−0.56	n.a.	n.a.	n.a.	n.a.

n.a. = not available.
Note: Beginning in 1982, average assets exclude certain contra-asset balances that had been reported as liabilities.
*Preliminary.
[1]Total income divided by average assets (net of loans in process or contra-assets).
[2]Net after-tax income divided by total income.
[3]Net after-tax income divided by average net worth.
[4]Net after-tax income divided by average assets (net of loans in process or contra-assets).
Sources: Federal Deposit Insurance Corporation; Federal Home Loan Bank Board; United States League of Savings Institutions.

On the liability side of the balance sheet, although passbook, NOW and Super-NOW accounts supplied about 15.5 percent of deposits, money market accounts supplied close to 12.7 percent of deposits in 1987. The largest deposit categories were consumer CDs of minimum 2.5-year maturity (10.8 percent), 92- to 182-day CDs (13.2 percent), jumbo CDs (13.3 percent), and six-month to one-year CDs (12.4 percent). The composition of deposit categories is generally a function of interest-rate spreads between alternative accounts, as well as interest rates available in the marketplace (see Table 7.4). Although not a depository account, Federal Home Loan Bank advances account for close to 9.3 percent of total liabilities and approximately 12 percent of savings deposits.

CONVERSION FROM MUTUAL TO STOCK

Between 1983 and 1986, some of the largest federally chartered savings and loans and savings banks changed from the mutual form of organization to the stock form. Between March 1983 and July 1986, about 300 thrifts switched from mutual to stock ownership, generating $5 billion in new capital. The reasons for the changes were the desire for a new means of infusing capital, the facilitation of mergers and acquisitions, the raising of additional funds for housing, the provision of stock options and profit-sharing plans for management, and the forestalling of supervisory action by increasing equity capital. In many instances these thrifts had inadequate net-worth-to-deposit ratios to meet regulatory standards. Stock companies can increase their capital by increasing retained earnings, by selling stock or debt, or by having a parent holding company sell debt or equity securities that can be passed through to the thrift in the form of debt or equity capital.

The FHLBB set up guidelines to prevent the windfall distribution of stock to account holders of converting mutuals because these stock distributions could serve as an incentive for investors to shift their funds from one mutual to another. Such deposit withdrawals would threaten the financial stability of mutuals.

BROKERED DEPOSITS

Brokered deposits are large deposits of potentially highly liquid money placed in banks and thrifts by third-party intermediaries for a brokerage fee. For example, brokered deposits at savings and loans reached 3 percent of total deposits in mid-1983. Federal regulators contend that brokered money tempts thrifts to hype their growth and take large loan risks without bothering to fortify underlying net worth. As a matter of fact, during 1981-1982, brokered deposits were a significant factor in 35 mergers of troubled savings associations, which relied on third-party money for as much as 70 percent of deposits. Regulators fear that a broker providing a depository institution with "hot money" could potentially hold an institution hostage by threatening to withdraw large deposits at inappropriate moments unless increased fees are paid to the broker for those deposits.

At the time of this writing, the FDIC and FSLIC have ruled that troubled banks and thrifts could not accept deposits from brokers without their approval. The two agencies are also expected to limit insurance coverage in funds placed in banks or thrifts by a third party that collects a fee. The counter argument is that the small investors in out-of-the-way places can get more competitive rates on their deposits, while small banks can have access to the national money markets. Also, brokerage firms claim that they tend to stay away from troubled institutions in an effort to protect their clients' money. Most brokerage firms combine personal visits with management and an analysis of financial information to study the credit risks involved.

FUTURE OF SAVINGS AND LOANS

It is anticipated that thrifts will become more dependent on money and capital markets as a source of funds now that Regulation Q has been phased out. This could lead to a higher cost of funds and a dominance of variable-rate mortgages offered to the public in order to avoid the interest-rate risk of owning fixed-rate mortgages. The thrift industry will become more diversified in terms of the mix of both assets and liabilities, and will have to become more profit-oriented and liquidity-conscious if they are to survive. Broader loan and investment powers are likely to be an effective solution for many of the thrift industry's problems in the long run. As previously mentioned, some thrifts have increased their investment in ARMs, while others have increased their investments in nonmortgage loans in an effort to restructure their portfolios away from fixed-rate mortgage loans. Some thrifts have begun to use futures contracts and interest-rate swaps in an attempt to reduce their interest-rate risk as they restructure. Other thrifts have increased their investments in service corporations in a further attempt to diversify their assets and supplement their earnings. These service-company investments have allowed many institutions to participate in activities, such as direct real-estate investment, that they are not authorized to undertake themselves. Returns on investments in service corporations appear to have varied widely, as these holdings have not benefited all savings and loans. To the extent that the activities of these corporations are concentrated in direct real estate investment, holdings in them may entail higher risks than mortgage lending, or may in effect involve the acquisition of long-term assets.

Many of these institutions will in all likelihood operate on a multistate basis. It is hoped that economies of scale will result from increased size. Out-of-state loan production offices or branches on a regional or national basis will be utilized by the largest and strongest of these institutions.

Some experts foresee a thrift industry with:

1. Some thrifts evolving into one-stop family financial centers or supermarkets;
2. Other thrifts offering more specialized real estate services that may emphasize lending to industrial and commercial organizations in the form of short-term construction, acquisition, and development loans;
3. Yet other thrifts emulating mortgage bankers with their focus on secondary activities such as the buying, selling, and servicing of mortgages;
4. The largest thrifts forming thrift-controlled financial conglomerates that might include, for example, insurance companies, brokerage firms, and mortgage banking companies; and
5. Many savings and loans emulating commercial banks, offering transaction deposits and making a wide variety of short-term commercial and consumer loans.

This restructuring of assets should enhance the ability of these companies to cope with changing interest rates.[8]

Some experts feel that there will no longer be a need for thrift institutions that specialize in home-mortgage lending because of increased competition within the home-mortgage lending field. Insurance companies and brokers have begun to play a much more active role in this segment of the business. Also, with the advent of ARMs, commercial banks have begun to play a more active role in the mortgage markets.

In summary, thrifts may wish to consider the following actions in regard to increasing profits and maintaining stability without having to borrow short at variable rates and lend long in the mortgage market at fixed rates:

1. Increasing the percentage of adjustable-rate mortgages, consumer loans, and business loans in the portfolio;

2. Reducing the maturity imbalance that exists between asset and liability portfolios by reinvesting liabilities in shorter-maturity assets, lengthening the duration of liabilities, or both;

3. Offering variable, long-term coupon-rate deposits to complement variable-rate mortgages. Such a deposit would give thrifts greater flexibility over the degree of interest-rate risk that they may wish to assume and would provide them with an easier way of minimizing this risk while still remaining active in mortgage lending;[9]

4. Offering new savings instruments where interest is paid out only at maturity; for example, a zero-coupon instrument;

5. Hedging interest-rate risks with financial futures or options;

6. Trading financial options on organized exchanges;

7. Operating debt collection services;

8. Offering real-estate brokerage services and discount brokerage services;

9. Utilizing service corporations to generate fee income from equity interests in real-estate joint ventures; and

10. Generating increased volumes on mortgages, and selling these mortgages in the secondary markets; this will lead to a large increase in fee income.

SUMMARY

The economic climate of the 1980s has generated substantial changes in the structure of the savings and loan industry. These institutions suffered widespread losses in 1981 and 1982 as market interest rates increased to extremely high levels; with the lower average levels of interest rates prevailing in 1983 and 1984, the industry as a whole became marginally profitable. Profits as a whole increased further within the industry during 1985 even though the number of troubled institutions remained at high levels. The large losses of the early 1980s depleted capital positions, and many savings associations failed or were merged out of existence. Even though most savings and loans survived the losses of the early 1980s, these losses have left a legacy of problem institutions with which regulators are still dealing. As a matter of fact, it was necessary to pass legislation to rescue the beleaguered FSLIC, which was on the brink of insolvency because of heavy losses within the thrift industry.

Long-term fixed-rate mortgages dominate the asset portfolios of most savings and loans, and exacerbate the earnings problems of these institutions when market interest rates increase. This is because the value of these assets declines and the return on a fixed-rate mortgage portfolio responds to such changes only as new funds from prepaid and maturing loans are invested in market-yielding assets.

The most important determinant of the future of the savings industry is the level and shape of the yield curve. When interest rates are high, the industry will be an ailing one. When interest rates are relatively low with a positively sloped yield curve, thrift profits can be substantial.

FSLIC deposit insurance has been a valuable, intangible asset to thrifts, but it has actually encouraged additional interest-rate-risk exposure because deposit premiums are insensitive to the interest-rate-risk exposure of an individual savings and loan. A technique to prevent the abuse of deposit insurance and to encourage the reduction of interest-rate-risk exposure would involve tying the level of deposit premiums to the magnitude of the duration mismatch. While adjustable-rate mortgage lending, consumer lending, and commercial lending have increased modestly at savings and loans, most thrifts have restructured their portfolios only modestly, and remain vulnerable to the threat of increased interest rates. Even though disintermediation is no longer a problem, many savings and loans have depleted much of their net worth, and remain close to being declared insolvent by the regulatory authorities.

Many associations of the future will be larger, more diversified, and more involved in national capital markets. Other thrifts will offer more specialized real estate services or emulate investment bankers. Some thrifts will become similar to commercial banks, while others will evolve into one-stop family financial centers or supermarkets. Some state chartered savings and loans in Texas, California, and other states with lenient laws hold a wide variety of other assets including real estate development, fast-food outlets, food chains, funeral homes, and bond and equity interests in all types of companies. On the other hand, most S&Ls do not speculate or engage in investments far removed from mortgage lending. A reason for this is that tax laws allow savings associations to exclude a large allowance for bad debts from their taxable income if they hold a sufficient percentage of their assets in real estate-related loans and other qualifying investments.

Since savings and loans dominate the home mortgage market they have a distinct advantage in marketing home equity loans over other lending institutions. With the 1986 tax reform bill affirming the fact that interest on home mortgage loans was tax deductible, while interest on loans not secured by residential properties was usually not tax deductible, home equity loans should become the primary consumer credit source of the future.

NOTES

1. W. J. Woerheide, *The Savings and Loan Industry: Current Problems and Possible Solutions*, (Westport, Conn.: Quorum Books, 1984), 1.

2. Ibid.

3. W. B. Harrison, *Money, Financial Institutions, and the Economy* (Plano, Tex.: Business Publications, Inc., 1985), 35.

4. G. J. Benston, *An Analysis of the Causes of Savings and Loan Failures,* Monograph Series 1985-45 (New York: Salomon Brothers Center for the Study of Financial Institutions, Graduate School of Business, New York University) 9, 12.

5. Ibid., 9.

6. Ibid., 171.

7. G. G. Kaufman, "Impact of Deregulation on the Mortgage Market," Staff Memorandum, Federal Reserve Bank of Chicago, February 1981, 1-15.

8. A. Gart, *The Insider's Guide to the Financial Services Revolution* (New York: Mc Graw-Hill, 1984), 75-76.

9. Kaufman, "Impact of Deregulation," 16.

8

Savings Banks

HISTORICAL PERSPECTIVE

The first mutual savings banks were established in Scotland in 1810. By 1819, there were over 300 savings banks in Great Britain. Earlier, institutions known as "penny" banks had sprung up in England; these institutions received weekly deposits of coins from individuals, invested those deposits, and paid dividends periodically.

Mutual savings banks were originally established by wealthy individuals to encourage savings among the poorer working classes by providing accessible and safe savings facilities, while building and loan associations were originally established to pool funds in order to make it possible for some members to borrow for the purpose of building or buying homes. In contrast to the savings and loans, where the emphasis was on providing funds for housing, the emphasis of savings banks was on long-term investment for the benefit of the small depositor.

The Philadelphia Savings Fund Society (PSFS), founded in 1816, is usually designated as the first savings bank in the United States, although the Provident Institution for Savings in Boston and the Bank of Savings in New York City also have a claim to the honor. The names of many savings banks remind us that these institutions once catered to particular segments of the population, for example, the Emigrant Savings Bank and the Seaman's Savings Bank (New York), and the Workman's Savings Bank (Boston). The introduction of savings banks in this country virtually coincided with the development of investment trusts, trust companies, mutual life insurance companies, and building and loan companies. With the industrial revolution underway and population and income growing, wage earners needed a place to deposit their funds since commercial banks would not accept savings deposits.

Although there are savings banks with more than 4,000 offices located throughout the country, most of these institutions are located in Connecticut, New Hampshire, Ohio, New Jersey, Pennsylvania, Massachusetts, and New York (see Tables 8.1 and 8.2). As a matter of fact, total deposits at savings banks in Massachusetts, New Hampshire, Maine, and Connecticut have exceeded regular consumer savings and deposits at the commercial banks in those states. Less than 15 percent of savings banks are found outside the northeastern section of the country. Although the greatest number of savings banks are located in Massachusetts, the largest concentration of savings bank assets is in New York. The industry is extremely important in the particular markets in which it is most active. Savings banks rank third in total savings deposits held, and fourth in total mortgage loans held. At the end of 1987, total assets had reached $544 billion. Just over half of the assets belong to FDIC-insured institutions, while just under half belong to FSLIC-insured savings banks. This latter category of savings banks consists primarily of institutions that converted from FSLIC-insured savings and loans.

GROWTH: SAVINGS BANKS VERSUS SAVINGS AND LOANS

The reason that savings and loans grew more rapidly than mutual savings banks from the mid-1930s through the mid-1980s can be found in the following facts:[1]

1. There is a direct and highly significant relationship between local changes in personal income and the growth of individual institutions. The large majority of savings banks are located in the northeast and north-central parts of the country, areas that experienced below-average population and income growth in the postwar period.

2. Mutual savings banks are also heavily concentrated in large urban centers where population has been declining and where the average per capita income has been rising less rapidly than in most suburban and other nonurban regions.

3. Savings and loan associations, having been favored by more liberal branching privileges, are more widely dispersed not only throughout the nation but also in areas of more rapid population growth. In part, the limited geographic expansion reflected the unavailability of federal charters (available since 1978).

4. The growth of mutual savings banks was affected by commercial bank competition, as their location forced them to compete more directly with large and aggressive commercial banks.

5. The net worth accounts have grown slowly (until the mid-1980s), limiting mutual-savings-bank expansion of assets.

REGULATION

Most mutual savings banks are state-chartered and are required to have insurance with the FDIC or FSLIC, or to have state deposit insurance, such as is

Table 8.1

Number and Assets of All Savings Institutions, by State, December 31, 1987*

State	All Savings Associations		All Savings Banks		All Savings Institutions	
	Number of Associations	Total Assets (Millions)	Number of Banks	Total Assets (Millions)	Number of Institutions	Total Assets (Millions)
Alabama	27	$ 5,229	9	$ 3,740	36	$ 8,969
Alaska	3	315	3	481	6	796
Arizona	10	13,544	2	10,552	12	24,096
Arkansas	29	5,035	8	1,761	37	6,796
California	192	294,181	15	52,179	207	346,360
Colorado	30	10,155	6	4,595	36	14,750
Connecticut	23	10,442	65	33,026	88	43,468
Delaware	2	134	4	1,792	6	1,926
District of Columbia	4	3,199	2	1,227	6	4,426
Florida	128	78,253	29	5,523	157	83,776
Georgia	53	10,621	16	7,598	69	18,219
Guam	2	95	0	0	2	95
Hawaii	4	3,801	2	1,711	6	5,512
Idaho	6	845	1	84	7	929
Illinois	236	56,956	28	11,932	264	68,888
Indiana	74	6,337	43	7,722	117	14,059
Iowa	44	7,291	10	2,179	54	9,470
Kansas	52	20,050	3	443	55	20,493
Kentucky	56	4,504	11	2,990	67	7,494
Louisiana	80	14,280	18	1,958	98	16,238
Maine	11	1,193	24	5,998	35	7,191
Maryland	63	11,884	35	10,442	98	22,326
Massachusetts	109	10,835	250	52,876	359	63,711
Michigan	30	17,543	21	19,655	51	37,198
Minnesota	28	11,719	8	4,595	36	16,314
Mississippi	32	2,787	12	3,005	44	5,792
Missouri	77	23,384	5	610	82	23,994
Montana	8	788	3	432	11	1,220
Nebraska	18	9,953	6	1,415	24	11,368
Nevada	4	4,575	1	48	5	4,623
New Hampshire	8	1,423	31	7,257	39	8,680
New Jersey	149	38,228	25	29,376	174	67,604
New Mexico	17	4,908	8	1,126	25	6,034
New York	63	18,864	104	142,113	167	160,977
North Carolina	131	19,126	6	1,072	137	20,198
North Dakota	3	319	3	3,912	6	4,231
Ohio	213	43,974	18	14,806	231	58,780
Oklahoma	45	9,422	8	783	53	10,205
Oregon	13	6,703	4	3,040	17	9,743
Pennsylvania	214	38,418	21	26,322	235	64,740
Puerto Rico	0	0	10	6,233	10	6,233
Rhode Island	3	143	7	8,131	10	8,274
South Carolina	38	8,259	11	2,618	49	10,877
South Dakota	8	794	4	616	12	1,410
Tennessee	46	8,843	17	2,418	63	11,261
Texas	267	98,461	12	1,616	279	100,077
Utah	12	4,792	1	2,295	13	7,087
Vermont	3	103	6	1,806	9	1,909
Virginia	51	15,717	15	9,917	66	25,634
Washington	34	10,490	14	15,957	48	26,447
West Virginia	14	1,093	4	918	18	2,011
Wisconsin	74	16,274	3	291	77	16,565
Wyoming	10	953	1	255	11	1,208
Entire U.S.	2,961	$977,740	984	$544,499	3,945	$1,522,239

Note: Components do not add to totals because of differences in reporting dates and accounting systems.
*Preliminary.

Source: 88 Sourcebook United States League of Savings Institutions, Chicago, Ill.

Table 8.2
Number and Assets of All Savings Banks, by Insurance Status

| Year-end | Total Insured | | | | Grand Total |
	Total†	By FDIC	By FSLIC	By State Funds	
1960	502	325	. . .	185	515
1965	501	330	. . .	179	506
1970	493	329	. . .	172	494
1971	489	327	. . .	170	490
1972	485	326	. . .	167	486
1973	481	322	. . .	167	482
1974	479	320	. . .	167	480
1975	475	329	. . .	166	476
1976	473	331	. . .	166	473
1977	467	323	. . .	166	467
1978	465	325	. . .	163	465
1979	463	324	. . .	163	463
1980	463	323	3	162	463
1981	448	331	6	159	448
1982	424	315	6	155	424
1983	534	294	143	146	534
1984	602	291	229	130	602
1985	696	392	302	2	696
1986	882	472	410	0	882
1987*	984	485	499	0	984
	Millions of Dollars				
1960	n.a.	$ 35,092	. . .	n.a.	$ 40,571
1965	n.a.	50,500	. . .	n.a.	58,232
1970	n.a.	68,740	. . .	n.a.	78,995
1971	n.a.	77,892	. . .	n.a.	89,581
1972	n.a.	87,650	. . .	n.a.	100,593
1973	n.a.	93,013	. . .	n.a.	106,650
1974	n.a.	95,589	. . .	n.a.	109,550
1975	n.a.	107,281	. . .	n.a.	121,056
1976	n.a.	120,840	. . .	n.a.	134,812
1977	n.a.	132,201	. . .	n.a.	147,287
1978	n.a.	142,353	. . .	n.a.	158,174
1979	n.a.	147,112	. . .	n.a.	163,405
1980	n.a.	152,566	n.a.	n.a.	171,564
1981	n.a.	155,859	n.a.	n.a.	175,728
1982	n.a.	155,307	$ 6,859	n.a.	174,197
1983	n.a.	170,718	64,969	n.a.	244,501
1984	n.a.	178,902	98,559	n.a.	302,457
1985	n.a.	205,279	131,868	n.a.	348,644
1986	$447,446	236,884	210,562	n.a.	447,446
1987*	544,499	260,203	284,296	n.a.	544,499

n.a. = not available.
*Preliminary.
†Data on insured savings banks do not add to total because some institutions are both FDIC-insured and state-insured.
Sources: Federal Deposit Insurance Corporation; Federal Home Loan Bank Board; National Council of Savings Institutions.

Source: 88 Sourcebook.

available in Massachusetts and Connecticut (see Table 8.2). Most savings banks exhibit the mutual or cooperative form of ownership, in which depositors ostensibly elect the governing body (actually this is done by management proxy-holders). The savings bank is not technically owned by its depositors, but its surplus, in the event of dissolution, would be divided among depositors after payment of liabilities. The management of mutual associations may have more operating latitude than the management of stock organizations because it does not have to be concerned about the impact of its decisions on the price of the institution's stock. Perhaps this explains in part why mutuals have been inno-vators in the area of electronic funds transfer and payment mechanisms such as NOW accounts.

Mutual savings banks are unique among depository institutions in that there is no separate federal regulatory agency having jurisdiction over them. They have been able to join either the Federal Reserve System or the Federal Home Loan Bank (FHLB) if they choose, and to take full advantage of credit availability on short-term notice from one or both of these sources. With the passage of the Monetary Reform Act of 1980, a federal charter is available with FHLB super-vision; new FHLB members have access to the Federal Reserve Discount Window regardless of their supervisory agency. Until 1978, savings banks were eligible only for state charters, and until 1982 they were required to be mutuals. Until 1982, they purchased deposit insurance only from the FDIC.

NEW POWERS

The Garn–St. Germain Act has given savings banks powers similar to those granted to savings and loans. Savings banks have been given the flexibility to engage in a wide spectrum of financial activities. The variety of financial services includes mortgage lending, commercial and consumer lending, life insurance, brokerage services, and trust management. However, only a small number of thrifts have the strength in management or assets to exploit these emerging opportunities. A few thrifts have moved into these activities and now even operate as interstate and multistate depository institutions.

Although savings banks can now lend up to 10 percent of their assets in the form of commercial and industrial loans, and 30 percent of their assets in the form of consumer loans, most savings banks have proceeded slowly into these markets. Some individual thrift institutions have formed syndicates among them-selves to move into commercial lending. Most savings institutions do not have the expertise required to make commercial loans, and have found experienced loan officers difficult to hire due to growing competition and salary premiums. Also, most savings institutions are not quite prepared to offer business customers sophisticated cash management services, and they lack experience in international transactions. While most savings banks have viewed commercial lending with trepidation, the Dime Savings Bank and PSFS have rather aggressively pursued small- and medium- as well as large-sized businesses as loan customers. On the other hand, most savings banks have expanded their efforts to make consumer loans. However, they average less than 5 percent of industry assets. The average commercial bank holds at least 10 percent of its assets in consumer loans, with many smaller commercial banks having much larger concentrations.

ASSETS AND LIABILITIES

Although the liabilities of savings banks are quite similar to those of savings and loan associations, the savings banks have a more diversified portfolio of assets. Mortgages comprise a greater proportion of investments at savings banks than at commercial banks, but less than the proportion held by savings and loans. Savings banks are among the largest providers of residential mortgages in the country; about 52 percent of the assets at FDIC-insured savings banks consist of mortgage loans, compared to 56 percent at FSLIC-insured savings banks. They also hold large quantities of mortgages on property other than one- to four-family residences. In part, this reflects the fact that many savings banks are located in the northeastern section of the country, in urban areas that are heavily populated by apartment dwellers. Savings banks typically use conventional financing for loans made close to home, but they have purchased large quantities of government-guaranteed mortgage loans outside their traditional home-market areas.

FDIC-insured institutions have a higher proportion of assets invested in cash and securities than do FSLIC-insured institutions. Savings banks have for many years had broader authority to invest in securities than did savings and loan associations. Corporate and other bonds account for about 8 percent of assets and mortgage-backed securities account for 11.4 percent of assets, while investments in U.S. Government securities account for about 6 percent of assets at FDIC-insured savings banks. Loans to individuals account for just under 5 percent of assets, while investments in other assets such as municipal bonds, commercial paper, repurchase agreements, and federal funds account for another 5 percent. Unlike other depositories, savings banks are permitted equity holdings in some states. (See Table 8.3.)

A majority of savings banks' security investments are long-term in nature, while their liquid asset holdings are considerably less than 5 percent of their total assets. The rather quick amortization of consumer loans and monthly mortgage payments of both principal and interest from the mortgage loan portfolio provide savings banks with a regular source of funds. The industry does not face the full corporate income-tax rate that commercial banks do, so they normally purchase few tax-exempt notes and bonds.

Historically, passbook savings have been the primary source of funds. This resulted from their dependence on small savers. Savers became more sophisticated in the 1970s as interest rates rose and as alternative investments, such as money market funds, became popular with the small investor. Mutual

Table 8.3

Selected Financial Institutions: Selected Assets and Liabilities

Millions of Dollars, End of Period

Account	1985	1986	1987 Feb.	Mar.	Apr.	May	June	July	Aug.	Sept.	Oct.	Nov.ʳ	Dec.
						Savings and loan associations							
1 Assets	948,781	963,316	936,858	939,721	944,229	952,671	949,069	949,223ʳ	955,105ʳ	956,517ʳ	973,816ʳ	978,319	977,978
2 Mortgage-backed securities	97,303	123,257	128,856	129,274	134,746	141,023	142,241	140,897	144,146ʳ	146,209ʳ	150,275ʳ	152,932	154,383
3 Cash and investment securities¹	126,712	142,700	135,885	138,746	136,370	138,303	138,125	138,520	137,207ʳ	131,729	139,648ʳ	138,234	135,710
4 Other	103,768ʳ	110,445ʳ	100,339ʳ	101,031ʳ	102,566ʳ	103,250ʳ	103,861ʳ	103,915ʳ	105,120ʳ	104,445ʳ	105,580ʳ	106,143	106,208
5 Liabilities and net worth	948,781	963,316	936,858	939,721	944,229	952,671	949,069	949,223ʳ	955,105ʳ	956,517ʳ	973,816ʳ	978,319	977,978
6 Savings capital	750,071	741,081	722,226	722,548	716,798	718,633	715,662	716,385ʳ	717,257ʳ	721,407ʳ	727,333ʳ	731,061	737,347
7 Borrowed money	138,798	159,742	152,176	158,192	165,883	171,279	175,394	174,358ʳ	178,643ʳ	180,382ʳ	190,644ʳ	191,020	191,037
8 FHLBB	73,888	80,194	75,671	76,469	77,857	78,583	79,188	78,888	79,546	80,848	83,303	84,266	87,697
9 Other	64,910	79,548	76,505	81,723	88,026	92,696	96,206	95,470ʳ	99,097ʳ	99,534ʳ	107,341ʳ	106,754	103,340
10 Other	19,045	20,071	21,878	18,958	20,869	22,628	19,584	20,684ʳ	21,956ʳ	19,174ʳ	21,036ʳ	21,287	16,760
11 Net worth²	41,064	42,423	40,579	40,023	40,678	40,127	38,428	37,796ʳ	37,249ʳ	35,554ʳ	34,803ʳ	34,951	32,833
						FSLIC-insured federal savings banks							
12 Assets	131,868	210,562	235,763	241,418	246,277	253,006	264,105ʳ	268,781ʳ	272,316ʳ	272,837ʳ	276,556ʳ	279,223	284,296
13 Mortgages	72,355	113,638	136,505	138,882	140,854	144,581	150,421	152,881	154,054ʳ	154,655ʳ	156,459ʳ	158,885	161,909
14 Mortgage-backed securities	15,676	29,766	34,634	36,088	37,500	39,371	40,969	42,714ʳ	43,532ʳ	44,421ʳ	45,132	45,251	45,877
15 Other	11,723	19,034	16,060	16,605	17,034	17,200	17,923ʳ	17,523ʳ	17,793ʳ	17,572ʳ	17,410ʳ	17,353	17,303
16 Liabilities and net worth	131,868	210,562	235,763	241,418	246,277	253,006	264,105ʳ	268,781ʳ	272,316ʳ	272,837ʳ	276,556ʳ	279,223	284,296
17 Savings capital	103,462	157,872	177,355	178,672	180,637	182,802	189,998	193,890	194,853	195,213	197,298ʳ	199,114	203,231
18 Borrowed money	19,323	37,329	39,777	43,919	46,125	49,896	53,255	53,652	55,660	56,549ʳ	57,551	58,277	60,695
19 FHLBB	10,510	19,897	20,226	21,104	21,718	22,788	24,486	24,981	25,546	26,287	27,350	27,947	29,617
20 Other	8,813	17,432	19,551	22,815	24,407	27,108	28,769	28,671	30,114	30,262ʳ	30,201	30,330	31,078
21 Other	2,732	4,263	5,484	5,264	5,547	6,044	5,987	6,144ʳ	6,455ʳ	5,632ʳ	6,304ʳ	6,363	5,290
22 Net worth	6,351	11,098	13,151	13,564	13,978	14,272	14,871	15,100ʳ	15,172ʳ	15,445ʳ	15,417ʳ	15,483	15,098
						Savings banks							
23 Assets	216,776	236,866	238,074	240,739	243,454	245,906	244,760	246,833	249,888	251,472	255,989	260,600	256,623
Loans													
24 Mortgage	110,448	118,323	119,737	121,178	122,769	124,936	128,217	129,624	130,721	133,298	135,317	137,044	136,742
25 Other	30,876	35,167	37,207	38,012	37,136	37,313	35,200	35,591	36,793	36,134	36,471	37,189	33,380
Securities													
26 U.S. government	13,111	14,209	13,525	13,631	13,743	13,650	13,549	13,498	13,720	13,122	13,817	15,694	13,430
27 Mortgage-backed securities	19,481	25,836	26,893	27,463	28,700	28,739	27,785	28,252	28,913	29,655	30,202	31,144	32,498
28 State and local government	2,323	2,185	2,168	2,041	2,063	2,053	2,059	2,050	2,038	2,023	2,034	2,046	2,004
29 Corporate and other	21,199	20,459	19,770	19,598	19,768	19,956	18,803	18,821	18,573	18,431	18,062	17,583	18,472
30 Cash	6,225	6,894	5,143	5,703	5,308	5,176	4,939	4,806	4,823	4,484	5,529	5,063	5,909
31 Other assets	13,113	13,793	13,631	13,713	13,967	14,083	14,208	14,191	14,307	14,325	14,557	14,837	14,188
32 Liabilities	216,776	236,866	238,074	240,739	243,454	245,906	244,760	246,833	249,888	251,472	255,989	260,600	256,623
33 Deposits	185,972	192,194	192,559	193,693	193,347	194,742	193,274	194,549	195,895	196,824	199,336	202,030	199,162
34 Regular³	181,921	186,345	187,597	188,432	187,791	189,048	187,669	188,783	190,335	191,376	193,777	196,724	193,778
35 Ordinary savings	33,018	37,717	39,370	40,558	41,326	41,967	42,178	41,928	41,767	41,773	42,045	42,493	41,299
36 Time	103,311	100,809	100,922	100,896	100,308	100,607	100,604	102,603	105,133	107,063	109,486	112,231	111,193
37 Other	4,051	5,849	4,962	5,261	5,556	5,694	5,605	5,766	5,560	5,448	5,559	5,306	5,384
38 Other liabilities	17,414	25,274	25,663	27,003	29,105	30,436	30,515	31,655	32,467	32,827	34,226	36,167	35,165
39 General reserve accounts	12,823	18,105	18,486	18,830	19,423	19,603	19,549	19,718	20,471	20,407	20,365	21,133	20,349

Source: Federal Reserve Bulletin, December 1987, A26.

savings banks were forced to compete for deposits by offering a number of alternative investments at higher yields. Certificates of deposit at regulated rates were offered in the late 1970s, and a highly successful "small savers certificate," a virtually unregulated 30-month instrument, was offered in 1981. A 6-month money market certificate whose rate ceiling varied with market rates was also extremely popular. With the introduction of money market accounts in December 1982 and the Super-NOW account in January 1983, there was a continuation of the structural shift away from low-yielding passbook rates into higher-yielding deposit forms.

In contrast to the case of commercial banks and savings and loans, small retail-type deposits are the primary source of funding for savings banks. In 1985, for example, money market liabilities (large time deposits, repurchase agreements, federal funds purchased, and other borrowings) offset 25 percent of total assets at domestic offices of insured commercial banks and 58 percent at savings and loans. During the same period, the proportion of money-market liabilities compared to total assets at savings banks was less than 12 percent.

EARNINGS, KEY RATIOS, AND FAILURES

Mutual savings banks must meet capital requirements set by the chartering state, the FSLIC, or the FDIC. The capital funds of a mutual savings bank are analogous to the net worth of a stock company, and include undivided profits, surplus, and reserve accounts which include subordinated debentures. As the amount of capital at savings banks has increased less rapidly than deposits since 1951, the percent of capital and reserves to deposits declined substantially through the end of 1984. For example, this ratio declined from .06 in 1981 for FDIC-insured savings banks to .052 in 1984. Commensurate with a return to profitability, the ratio rose to .065 in 1985 and an estimated .094 in 1986. In the case of FSLIC-insured savings banks, the net-worth-to-savings-capital ratio improved from .054 in 1984 to .07 in 1986.

With a lack of earnings in the early 1980s, there was a substantial decline in reserves relative to deposits and other liabilities through 1983. Losses at savings banks were substantial. Because of inadequate reserves, a number of savings banks were forced to merge or close their doors. The FDIC arranged many assisted mergers of mutual savings banks in danger of failure. Net worth at many savings banks was severely eroded by late 1982 when a net-worth certificate program and voluntary assisted merger plan were introduced. However, most savings banks returned to profitability in 1984 or 1985, when interest rates on short- and intermediate-term deposits began to decline and when new mortgages placed on the books helped to increase substantially the average yield of the mortgage portfolio. Also, considerable fee income was generated from new mortgages put on the books and sold in the secondary market. Although many mortgages that were originated during the period of high interest rates were refinanced during 1985 and 1986, and although rates on new loans declined, the low-yield fixed-rate loans from the 1960s and early 1970s matured or were paid down substantially, allowing banks to reinvest these funds at higher rates.

Essentially, most of the losses of savings banks in the early 1980s could be attributed to the high deposit and borrowing costs, and inadequate return on investment. The cost of funds exceeded the return on a primarily fixed-rate mortgage portfolio, putting a squeeze on net interest margins. The earnings squeeze had been exacerbated by a shift of depositor funds from relatively low-yielding savings deposits into higher-yielding money market and time deposits when interest rates increased. By year-end 1981, the average cost of funds at mutual savings banks had climbed above 10 percent, double what it had been prior to the introduction of the six-month certificate in 1978. During the same year, the yield on the mortgage portfolio approximated 9 percent. The average return on assets had fallen to −0.12 percent in 1981.[2] Also, the cost of funds tended to shift with more speed than did returns from the portfolio, which was dominated by long-term fixed-rate mortgage loans. In addition to the afore-mentioned problems of savings banks in the 1981-1983 period, four additional problems became apparent between 1984 and 1987: poor or nonexistent under-writing procedures, problem participation loans, lack of management systems, and fraud.

By 1985, the industry generated a net income of $1.448 billion. This was approximately equal to the losses suffered by the industry in 1981 and 1982. (See Table 8.4.) Official industry earnings for 1986 were not available at the time of this writing but the figure was expected to be higher than in any of the preceding years of the 1980s. It is known that interest on mortgage loans accounted for more than one-half of operating income for savings banks in 1986, while interest on investments accounted for about one-third of savings bank income. Return on assets (ROA) at savings banks has been quite volatile. ROA has been at 0.38, 0.45, 0.55, 0.58, 0.46, −0.12, −1.2, −0.79, −0.8, 0.01, 0.71, and an estimated 1.0 percent between 1975 and 1986 (see Table 8.4 and Figure 8.1).

It is interesting to note that commercial bank profitability was much more

Table 8.4
Return on Assets and Income

	1975	1977	1979	1981	1983	1985	1986
FDIC-insured Savings Banks	00.38	00.55	00.46	(0.83)	(0.08)	00.71	1.00E
FDIC-insured Commercial Banks	00.69	00.71	00.80	00.76	00.67	00.71	00.65

Net Income ($Millions)

	1975	1977	1979	1981	1983	1985	1986
FDIC-insured Savings Banks				(1,448)	(170)	1,448	N.A.
FDIC-insured Commercial Banks				14,720	14,933	18,057	17,900

Source: FDIC Banking and Economic Review, January/Febuary 1987 and March/April 1987

FDIC Statistics on Banking 1985

Figure 8.1
Return on Assets at Commercial Banks and Thrifts, 1975-1985

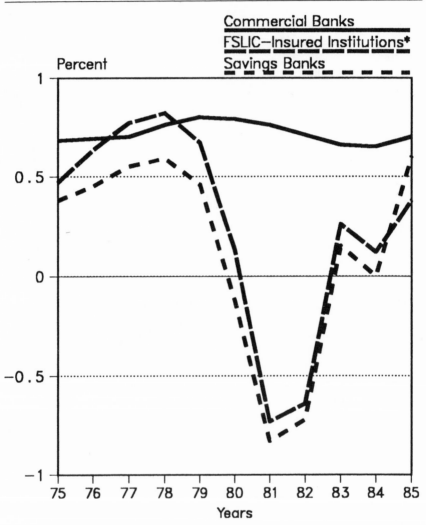

* FSLIC—Insured Savings and Loans and Savings Banks

Sources: Federal Deposit Insurance Corporation,
         Federal Home Loan Bank Board,
         National Council of Savings Institutions.

stable during this period than were savings bank earnings and return on assets. Changes in the regulatory and economic environment of depositories have not affected the net interest margin of all depository institutions equally. Institutions with asset maturities substantially longer than liability maturities always have earnings difficulty if market interest rates increase rapidly, which raises liability costs while asset returns remain relatively unchanged. While savings banks found themselves in that unenviable position by late 1980, commercial banks, with much shorter asset maturities and a greater percentage of variable rate assets, did not.[3]

Broader asset powers and an emphasis on adjustable-rate mortgages (ARMs) should help the savings banks avoid the interest rate traps of the past. For most of 1985 and 1986, ARMs were about 50 percent of new mortgage loans. Savings banks will now be able to determine their own area of lending expertise and identify the markets in which they want to participate. This will be a break from the past, when their markets were determined by legislation. Management should be able to influence income and expenses in ways that were unimaginable a decade ago.

NOTES

1. A. Teck, *Mutual Savings Banks and Savings and Loan Associations: Aspects of Growth,* New York: Columbia University Press, 1968, 1-21.

2. Alane K. Moyisch, "Cost of Funds and Profitability at Savings Banks," *Banking and Economic Review,* vol. 5, no. 1 (January/February 1987): 7-8.

3. Ibid.

9

Credit Unions

HISTORICAL PERSPECTIVE

The idea of credit unions originated in Great Britain and Germany in the nineteenth century. They were organized to allow people to pool their resources and make loans to one another, and to promote thriftiness. Credit unions tried to help the "little man" who did not have access to other financial institutions.

Historians report that Edward Filene (of the family associated with the Boston department store) fathered credit unions in the United States, having learned about credit unions from an employee of the British government. The first North American credit union appeared in Canada. The first credit union in the United States was formed in 1909 at St. Mary's Parish in Manchester, New Hampshire. That institution still exists, and today is known as St. Mary's Bank. Like savings banks and savings and loans, credit unions were formed to encourage savings and to make relatively inexpensive loans available to members. Unlike the thrifts, credit unions are nonprofit cooperative associations. This means that they are exempt from paying income taxes. They are formed by people with a common bond, such as religious or fraternal organizations, employment, or residence. Members of a credit union elect a board of directors to manage it and a credit committee to approve loans.

Historically, the number of credit unions increased at a slow pace until 1934 when the Federal Credit Union Act permitted federally chartered credit unions to organize in all states. Before 1934, credit unions were chartered only under state law and some states did not permit them. The early credit unions emerged because they filled an unmet need in American cities as commercial banks at that time did not provide consumer credit or accept deposits of small savers. The early goals of the credit unions were to encourage savings among their members through education, to provide a safe and convenient location to save, to offer financial advice and counseling, and to lend on reasonable terms to their members.

In recent years, credit unions have been among the fastest growing financial intermediaries in the United States, serving close to 54 million members. In 1986, there were 16,910 credit unions, compared to 3,132 insured savings and loans and approximately 855 savings banks. Of the total number of credit unions, about 9,746 were federally chartered, while the remaining 7,164 were chartered under the laws of various states. It is interesting to note that there were almost 24,000 credit unions in 1971 but the number began to decline in the 1970s and 1980s due to consolidation and failures. Despite their large number, credit unions held assets of just over $166 billion compared to just under $1 trillion for S&Ls and about $444 billion for savings banks in 1986 (see Table 9.1). Credit unions, usually associated with firms of over 500 employees, have begun to invite smaller groups of workers into their membership in order to maintain their growth.

Table 9.1
U.S. Credit Union Totals ($ Millions)

	# of Credit Unions	# of Members	Savings (Shares & Deposits)	Loans Outstanding	Reserves	Assets
1986p	16,910	54,066,729	$152,693	$96,397	$6,816	$166,063
1985	17,581	51,721,709	125,512	85,139	5,330	137,168
1984	18,375	49,268,223	102,568	75,442	4,646	112,960
1983	19,095	47,507,019	89,693	60,517	3,951	98,327
1982	19,897	46,693,623	74,847	51,488	3,560	82,680
1981	20,786	45,313,237	64,649	50,371	3,339	72,295
1980	21,467	44,047,759	61,748	48,707	3,118	68,996
1979	21,983	41,355,370	55,878	51,230	2,943	64,193
1978	22,204	40,813,117	52,728	49,436	2,751	61,022
1977	22,383	36,851,813	45,997	41,214	2,544	53,043
1976	22,582	33,700,390	38,565	33,926	2,267	44,303
1975	22,678	31,321,234	32,800	28,105	2,015	37,554
1970	23,688	22,776,676	15,484	14,100	1,125	17,951
1965	22,219	16,753,106	9,249	8,095	669	10,552
1960	20,456	12,037,533	4,975	4,377	272	5,653
1955	16,201	8,153,641	2,447	1,934	110	2,743
1950	10,591	4,610,278	850	680	52	1,005
1945	8,683	2,842,989	369	127	24	435
1940	9,023	2,826,612	222	190	NA	253
1935	3,372	641,797	38	36	NA	50
% change 1985-1986	-3.8%	4.5	19.4	11.0	27.9	21.1
% change 1976-1986	-25.1	60.4	288.5	178.6	200.7	274.8

p-preliminary

Source: Credit Union Report, 1986, p. 2.

REGULATION

Credit unions, like other thrifts and commercial banks, have a dual chartering system. Federal credit unions are chartered by the National Credit Union Administration (NCUA), which is an independent agency. State-chartered credit unions in many states are chartered and supervised by a special office within the state banking department. Only four states, Wyoming, Delaware, Alaska, and South Dakota, have no specific supervision for state-chartered credit unions. The NCUA provides share insurance of up to $100,000 per member account, periodic examination of member unions, and consultation on the management of the credit union. All federally chartered credit unions are regulated by the NCUA, which is completely financed by funds received from its own member organizations for services provided and by depository insurance. Some state-chartered credit unions are members of NCUA, while others are insured by state-operated programs and by private bond and insurance programs. Nearly 99 percent of all credit-union savings were insured under federal or state programs at the end of 1986. Supervisory responsibilities of NCUA are exercised through the National Credit Union Board, which consists of three people appointed by the president of the United States.

Credit union shares are insured through the National Credit Union Share Insurance Fund, which was established in 1970. Credit unions can borrow funds from the Federal Intermediate Credit Bank on an as-needed basis. Federal and state credit unions are also permitted to borrow funds from commercial banks, although the ability of state-chartered credit unions to borrow in this manner is a function of individual state regulation.

Congress passed legislation in 1978 authorizing the creation of a Central Liquidity Facility (CLF) within the NCUA which would act as a lender of last resort for emergency credit needs. The CLF provides credit unions with funds for stabilization and to meet other liquidity needs. The CLF was privately capitalized by member corporate credit unions. Finally, credit unions and other institutions were granted access to the Federal Reserve Discount Window in 1980.

The credit unions' chief trade association at the national level is the Credit Union National Association (CUNA), which was established in 1934 and to which 90 percent of the U.S. credit unions belong. CUNA, through offices in Madison, Wisconsin, is the major voice of the industry germane to national and international issues, and represents the industry before government and legislative bodies. It also supplies a substantial amount of educational material to members and to the public, conducts research and pursues public relations campaigns in support of the credit union movement.

INTERESTING STATISTICS AND CHARACTERISTICS

Most credit unions are relatively small, with 39 percent having assets under $1 million and 31 percent having assets under $5 million at year-end 1986. (See

Table 9.2.) They employ about 101,300 full-time and 25,900 part-time employees, as well as over 223,000 volunteers. Also, many credit unions operate in rent-free space donated by the sponsoring organization. Some credit unions also receive volunteer labor and free accounting and legal services. These subsidies are more extensive in small occupational credit unions. Large credit unions tend to be more like other financial intermediaries in that they receive fewer subsidies, pay larger salaries, and hire professional management.

Table 9.2
Distribution of Credit Unions by Asset Size

$0-200,000	11.6%
200,001-500,000	14.2
500,001-1,000,000	13.2
1,000,001-2,000,000	14.4
2,000,001-5,000,000	18.2
5,000,001-10,000,000	10.4
10,000,001-20,000,000	8.1
20,000,001-50,000,000	5.9
50,000,001-100,000,000	2.3
100,000,001 & over	1.7
	100.0%

Source: Credit Union Report, 1986, p. 5.

At year-end 1986, the ratio of loans outstanding to savings averaged close to 63 percent, with smaller credit unions have bigger ratios than larger institutions. The ratio of operating expenses to income averaged 29 percent in 1986, with smaller credit unions once again having much bigger ratios than larger institutions. It is also interesting to note that the average consumer loan made in 1986 was $2,410, while the annual growth in loans in 1986 over 1985 averaged 14.2 percent (see Table 9.3).

Credit unions differ from other financial intermediaries in that they are non-profit associations, operated for the benefit of their members. They enjoy a regular inflow of funds because of the widespread use of payroll deduction plans. Payroll deduction plans usually do not terminate during employment tenure, have generally lower operating costs, increase savings flows, reduce delinquency rates, and provide an effective way to obtain fast and accurate information on changes in borrower earnings or employment status.

Credit union earnings have increased since 1980. Like savings institutions, before deregulation credit unions were less diversified than commercial banks. Credit-union assets were also of considerably shorter maturity than those of

Table 9.3
Operating Ratios by Asset Size $ Millions

	0-$2	$2-5	$.5-1.0	$1-2	$2-5	$5-10	$10-20	$20-50	$50-100	$100+	Total
Loans Outstanding/Savings	72.2%	76.2%	76.0%	72.8%	67.9%	64.1%	62.4%	61.9%	63.3%	61.4%	62.9%
Capital/Assets	13.8	12.3	10.7	9.2	8.1	7.5	7.0	6.5	6.2	5.9	6.6
Operating Expense/Income	44.6	41.8	38.9	36.7	33.8	32.2	30.9	30.4	29.2	25.2	29.0
Share Drafts/Savings	0.1	0.3	0.6	1.3	3.1	5.7	7.4	9.8	10.8	10.8	9.1
Certificates/Savings	1.5	3.2	5.4	7.6	9.5	11.6	13.2	14.8	16.1	14.1	13.7
Loans Outstanding/Assets	61.5	66.0	67.1	65.4	61.8	58.8	57.5	57.3	58.7	56.5	57.9
Savings/Assets	85.2	86.6	88.2	89.8	91.0	91.7	92.1	92.6	92.7	92.0	92.0
Savings/Members*	$468	$831	$1,126	$1,429	$1,844	$2,231	$2,573	$2,767	$3,164	$3,871	$2,830
Loans Outstanding/Members*	$338	$633	$856	$1,041	$1,252	$1,430	$1,606	$1,712	$2,002	$2,379	$1,781
Avg. Consumer Loan Made in 1986*	$1,171	$1,723	$1,940	$2,264	$2,629	$2,534	$2,559	$2,619	$2,632	$2,183	$2,410
Investments/Assets	30.6%	28.4	28.5	31.0	34.5	37.2	37.8	37.6	36.4	38.6	37.3
Members/Potential Members	18	26	32	28	28	30	27	29	28	32	29
Annual Savings Growth	5.4	11.0	16.5	21.3	23.4	23.9	24.2	23.1	21.2	22.9	22.7
Annual Loan Growth	1.4	3.7	7.3	10.3	10.8	11.5	12.6	14.3	14.8	16.2	14.2
Annual Asset Growth	5.0	10.0	15.1	19.8	22.1	22.7	23.2	22.4	20.5	22.4	22.0

*In Dollars

Source: Credit Union Report, 1986, p. 5.

thrifts. However, high interest rates drove up deposit costs and dampened loan demand at credit unions during the 1981-1982 recession; occupationally based credit unions were hit hard by unemployment, and experienced savings outflows and increased loan delinquencies. Fortunately, by 1984 profits began to improve and loans increased. More than any other depository institution, credit unions obtain their operating income primarily from interest on loans and investments. There is limited fee income except at the largest credit unons. In 1985-1986, credit unions outperformed thrifts and banks as measured by return of assets.

The granting of charters generally requires at least 100 potential members. The number of credit union charters is closely linked to population size and growth. The populous states of Texas, New York, California, and Pennsylvania have accounted for a disproportionate number of credit union charters.

In 1986, 77 percent of the more than 54 million credit union members were organized around a common occupational bond, 6.1 percent by residence, 16.9 percent by association, 22.1 percent by government, and 12.2 percent by education services. The Navy and the Pentagon had the largest federally chartered credit unions.

A CUNA-sponsored survey found that credit union members are somewhat younger, more affluent, and more concentrated in professional and managerial occupations than nonmembers. Members use a broad range of financial services, often patronizing credit unions, commercial banks, and savings associations at the same time. Credit union members were more likely to have two wage earners in the household than nonmembers, to be better educated, to own their own home, and to have spent five years or more in their current jobs.

The distribution of credit unions by asset size shows a large number of small institutions holding a small portion of the total assets, while a small number of large credit unions hold a disproportionate share of the total. Substantial size and customer-penetration differences exist among credit unions according to the type of common bond. Loans to credit union members compose a lesser proportion of total assets for large institutions than for smaller ones, while larger institutions also have lower capital ratios.

The balance sheets of credit unions contain reserve accounts, which are portions of retained earnings designated to serve as cushions against which future loan and investment losses can be charged. Earnings retained in excess of those officially designated as reserves are called individual earnings, and are similar to undivided profits in commercial banks. The total of undivided earnings is equal to the capital or net worth of the credit unions. In 1986, capital for credit unions as a whole was just over 7 percent of assets. This exceeded the ratio of net worth to assets for most other depositors with the exception of small commercial banks.

ADVANTAGES AND DISADVANTAGES OF CREDIT UNIONS

The small size of some credit unions causes them to incur cost disadvantages compared to larger depository institutions. Their smallness makes it difficult for many of them to afford the specialized skills and managers needed to adapt to the rapidly changing technology of the financial services world. The overall required spread or profit margin for small credit unions is higher than that required by banks because credit unions tend to make small loans and accept small deposits, which are costly to service. On the other hand, credit unions have overcome some of the disadvantages of their small size by taking advantage of payroll deduction plans by sponsoring employers, volunteer help, employer subsidies such as free or low-cost office space, and favorable regulation by the NCUA. Through the NCUA, most credit unions have been given access to the new technology and financial services. As a result, many credit unions have become full-service financial institutions for consumers.

The total assets of credit unions are relatively low when compared to the assets of banks or savings and loan associations. There are a number of explanations for this. First, the credit union philosophy of the "common bond" restricts the membership population for individual credit unions.

Second, because of this common-bond approach, the number of credit unions is theoretically limited by the number of organizations with which a credit union could be affiliated. From a practical standpoint, credit unions are limited to the portion of these organizations that have an employee base which could support a credit union. Third, because of their cooperative nature, credit unions are limited in scope. Their expressed purpose is to benefit their shareholders; thus, they do not accept funds from nonmembers on a regular basis, nor do they lend to nonmembers.

Fourth, since many smaller credit unions do not provide a full range of services, many shareholders deal with other financial institutions as well as with their credit union. However, deregulation is increasing the number of services offered by credit unions and expanding their membership base, which enables them to compete more effectively for deposits.

The fifth reason is that, since credit unions are small, local organizations operated by the shareholders, directors are often not experienced and knowledgeable financiers. Also, the shareholders are more concerned about the safety of their savings than about the maximization of returns. For these reasons, assets are usually managed conservatively. No attempt is generally made to optimize returns by providing funds for a specific investment purpose through borrowing.

A major difference between credit unions and other financial intermediaries is that their focus is on service to members; profit is a by-product. Credit unions have certain advantages over other depository institutions: (1) they generally pay higher rates on savings and charge lower rates on loans; (2) they are usually on the premises of their customer base; and (3) they leverage the value supplied by volunteer labor and employer-contributed free office space.

SOURCES AND USES OF FUNDS

Although the majority of shares are still in the form of savings deposits, NOW accounts, money market fund accounts and market rate certificate accounts have become quite popular. Credit union savings accounts pay a modestly higher average interest rate than banks and thrifts. They also offer "share-draft accounts," which operate like interest-bearing checking accounts. These accounts do not require a minimum balance and usually do not have fees. Borrowings, notes, reserves, and undivided earnings account for the remainder of liabilities and equity.

Credit union assets are highly concentrated in consumer installment loans. They typically offer lower borrowing rates than other consumer lenders because they are exempt from federal income taxes; their operations are often subsidized by their employers, and they used to have lower reserve requirements than competing institutions. Automobile loans and personal loans to cover household and medical expenses, vacations, education, tax payments, and debt consolidations dominate the consumer-installment-loan category.

Credit unions have lost a significant part of their share of the overall consumer loan market at a time when this market is becoming increasingly attractive to other financial institutions, while finance companies have achieved major gains (see Tables 9.4 and 9.5). However, credit unions are still the third largest provider of consumer credit. The credit union delinquency rate is about three times the delinquency rate at commercial banks, but the default rate for credit union loans is usually lower than that for other consumer lenders. The loan-loss rate for all federal credit unions was about 0.35 of the dollar amount of total loans outstanding, while loan-loss rates for commercial banks and finance companies have approximated 0.45 and 2.14 percent, respectively. Credit unions appear more willing to renegotiate a loan and convince the delinquent borrower to repay than to write off the loan. Credit unions can make home mortgage loans, mobile home loans, home improvement loans, credit card loans, investment in U.S. government and agency securities, and deposits at financial institutions. The proportion of credit unions offering credit cards was 15.0 percent in 1986, while the proportion offering financial planning was 16.2 percent. Federal credit unions were granted the right to make mortgage loans in 1977 with terms up to 30 years; however, they are only allowed to issue mortgages on one- to four-unit structures.

The Garn–St. Germain Act of 1982 granted federally chartered credit unions much broader real-estate lending authority, expanding their ability to make larger and longer-term mortgages. Refinancing loans and mortgage credit not secured by first liens were permitted. Although the volume of mortgage credit outstanding is presently modest, credit union participation in the mortgage market is expected to expand significantly over the next decade. Now that there is a more active secondary market for mortgages, it is likely that credit unions will become more active in originating and selling single-family mortgages in the secondary market. In addition, 17.7 percent of credit unions offered home equity loans in 1986, compared to only 11 percent in 1984.

True to their cooperative principles, all credit unions are mutuals. Deposits are classified as shares in the organization, and interest paid on deposits is

Table 9.4
Share of Installment Credit Outstanding by Selected Lenders $ Millions

	December, 1986		December, 1985			
	Outstanding	Market Share	Outstanding	Market Share	Change 1985-1986	
Commercial Banks	$ 264,829	45.3%	$ 245,055	46.2%	$ 19,774	8.1%
Finance Companies	136,581	23.3	113,398	21.4	23,183	20.4
Credit Unions*	77,485	13.2	71,730	13.5	5,755	8.0
Savings Institutions**	58,391	10.0	52,720	9.9	5,671	10.8
Retailers***	44,679	7.6	42,776	8.1	1,903	4.4
Gasoline Companies	3,271	0.6	4,304	0.9	-1,033	-24.0
Total	**$585,236**	**100.0%**	**$529,983**	**100.0%**	**$55,253**	**10.4%**

* not seasonally adjusted

*CUNA adjusts Federal Reserve credit union totals to more accurately reflect credit union lending.
**Includes S&Ls, MSBs, and federal reserve savings banks.
***Includes auto dealers and excludes 30-day charge credit held by travel and entertainment companies.

Table 9.5
Share of Auto Loans Outstanding by Selected Lenders $ Millions

	December, 1986		December, 1985			
	Outstanding	Market Share	Outstanding	Market Share*	Change 1985-1986	
Finance Companies	$ 93,274	38.1%	$ 70,091	33.7%	$ 23,183	33.1%
Commercial Banks	100,711	41.1	93,003	44.7	7,708	8.3
Credit Unions	39,027	15.9	35,635	17.1	3,392	9.5
Savings Institutions	12,043	4.9	9,328	4.5	2,715	29.1
Total	**$245,055**	**100.0%**	**$208,057**	**100.0%**	**$36,998**	**17.8%**

*Recent revisions of this data by the Federal Reserve mean market share figures are different from those reported in the 1985 CU Report.

classified as dividends. Income earned from borrowers is returned to savers after expenses and required allocations to reserves. Member-owners receive earnings from the net income of their credit union in proportion to the amount of deposits (shares) they hold in the union.

The largest source of credit union income represents interest paid on loans and income from investments such as government securities and deposits at other financial institutions. After share costs, employee compensation is the largest expense. Wages, salaries, and fringe benefits account for about 40 percent of total expenses. Other important expense items include interest on borrowed money, borrowers' protection insurance, office operation expense, and professional and outside services. The resulting net income is the source for shareholder dividends. In addition to paying dividends, many credit unions refund a portion of the interest paid on borrowings as a means of competing with other lending institutions and as a direct benefit to credit union owners. It is interesting to note that interest paid on deposits is not technically an expense item for a credit union, since the depositor is not actually an owner and does receive a portion of the association's net income after expenses.

THE FUTURE OF CREDIT UNIONS

The future evolution of credit unions into more diversified intermediaries is likely because of their favorable tax status, convenient locations, and fine reputation for serving their customers. The greatest threat to this favorable future is that the small size of credit unions will put them at a competitive disadvantage against bigger and more efficient institutions. However, credit union managers are expected to launch major membership drives by pushing loans and credit and debit cards, and by redrafting their charters to broaden the customer base. Credit unions have offered new services such as share drafts, variable-rate mortgages, consumer credit lines, equity mortgage loans, money market accounts, ATMs (automated teller machines), credit and debit cards, and savings certificates to help them compete within the financial services industry. Credit unions and thrifts are now in areas of banking that the commercial banks formerly had to themselves. This is a cause of concern to some bankers, who believe that credit unions may get the upper hand in such areas because of their tax-exempt status and their low operating costs. Credit unions offer good value in personal loans and savings accounts. They often require less stringent qualifications and provide faster service on loans than do many banks or savings and loans. In many cases the loans are cheaper and their savings rates are more attractive.

Along with the other financial institutions, credit unions are being deregulated. Deregulation may be a mixed blessing for the credit unions. It could present a high risk of insolvency for credit unions with inexperienced management, although this risk is offset by the limited scope of credit unions and by their general concern for the safety of funds in the shareholders' accounts. If, as most do, managers err on the side of safety, they will sacrifice shareholders' returns in exchange for minimizing the risk of failure. Failure to deal adequately with deregulation and a volatile economic environment have led to contraction within the industry during the 1980s.

Over 150 credit unions lost $106.3 million in uninsured deposits in the failure of the Penn Square Bank in Oklahoma City in 1982. These credit unions purchased certificates of deposit with an attractive yield—as much as 1.5

percentage points higher than available elsewhere—and often well in excess of the $100,000 FDIC coverage limit. The managers felt that their money was with a safe bank since it was apparently tightly regulated and had recently been audited by a reputable accounting firm. In this case, attempts to maximize yield resulted in losses. The recession of the early 1980s weakened some credit unions tied to such industries as steel and automobiles, and regulators allowed some of them to merge with unions serving unrelated industries. Since most credit unions are small and members must have a common bond, financial problems of these institutions rarely evoke concern about their spilling over to other institutions.

Credit unions have normally been economically viable, with substantial profit spreads and minimal loan losses. Prior to deregulation, they charged about 12 percent for loans and paid 8 percent for deposits. In the postderegulation period, credit unions have adjusted and attempted to protect themselves against prevailing fluctuations in the cost of funds by offering both variable-rate deposit accounts and variable-rate loans. While 3,400 credit unions were closed by merger or liquidation during this period, the survivors are more firmly capitalized than they were prior to deregulation.

Even though financial services are expanding at the larger credit unions, many credit unions do not provide first mortgages, and virtually none of them hold trust accounts or make commercial loans. Moreover, many credit unions do not have the depth of management and depth of services of banks or thrifts.

10

Investment Companies

HISTORICAL PERSPECTIVE

William I helped lay the groundwork for today's mutual funds by establishing the "Societé Generale des Pays-Bas pour favoriser l'industrie nationale" in Belgium close to 150 years ago. However, the Foreign and Colonial Government Trust was formed in London in 1868 to provide "the investor with moderate means the same advantages as the large capitalists, in diminishing the risk of investing in Foreign and Colonial Government Stocks." Essentially, the concept of the investment company came to the United States from Britain.[1]

Commensurate with the growth of the United States economy in the nineteenth and early twentieth centuries, investment companies were established in the United States in Philadelphia, Boston, and New York by brokers, bankers, investment counsels, and others who saw the need of making diversification and financial management available to investors of moderate means. The first mutual fund in this country was organized in 1924 in Boston, while as early as 1823, a New England insurance company had features that resembled those of an investment company.[2]

Following the Depression, in 1936, the Securities and Exchange Commission (SEC) commenced a study of investment companies under a congressional mandate. This culminated in the Investment Company Act of 1940. The act was to provide statutory safeguards for the investor as well as a framework within which the mutual fund industry could grow. The Investment Company Amendments Act of 1970 imposed a "fiduciary duty" upon the investment advisor and established new standards for management fees and mutual fund sales charges. Mutual fund organizations are currently among the most strictly regulated entities under the federal securities laws. These laws require complete disclosures to the SEC, state regulators, and fund shareholders, and include continuous regulation of fund operations.

Provided that the mutual fund qualifies under Subchapter G of the Federal Internal Revenue Code of 1954, the fund pays no federal income tax on dividends, interest, and capital gains distributed to shareholders. Shareholders are treated substantially as if they held the securities directly in the funds portfolio. Shareholders must report any payments received from a mutual fund on their own tax returns.

TYPES OF INVESTMENT COMPANIES

Investment companies are a device for indirect investment in common stock, bonds, or money market instruments. There are two types of investment companies: open-end, commonly known as mutual funds, and closed-end (see Table 10.1). Mutual funds are sold continuously and are redeemable at any time at or near net asset value; they are the only type of financial institutions whose funds are raised primarily by the sale of their own stock. A mutual fund is a financial service organization that receives money from shareholders, earns returns on it, tries to make it grow, and agrees to pay the shareholder cash on demand for the current asset value of the investment. Closed-end investment companies acquire funds from time to time by making public offerings of their securities. Unlike mutual funds, closed-end companies issue only a limited number of shares and do not redeem them (buy them back). Closed-end shares are traded in the securities markets, with supply and demand determining the price. They often sell at large discounts from their net asset value. There has tended to be a significant variation over the years in the magnitude of the discount. The reason for the discount is not known with certainty, but is believed to be the result of taxation of capital gains.

The purchase of closed-end mutual funds by investors involves three costs. First, there is the brokerage commission involved in purchasing or selling the shares on the open market. Second, there is a management fee of from 1 to 2 percent of the net asset value to operate the fund. Third, when the investment company sells or buys securities, it passes on to the investor the brokerage commissions it has to pay.

In the 1960s, close to 90 percent of the mutual funds were involved in load products—products for which a sales charge or commission is added on top of the net asset value of the fund. However, by 1987, 98 percent of mutual fund sales (including money market funds) were on a no-load basis; that is, they are sold without a sales commission. Another salient development has been product line proliferation. The mutual fund industry has introduced a wide variety of funds— "families of funds"—satisfying different investor needs. In addition to the popular common stock and bond funds, mutual funds have added tax-exempt funds, option funds, international funds, money market funds, junk bonds, long-

Table 10.1
Open-End Investment Companies

Millions of dollars

Item	1986	1987ʳ	1987							1988
			June	July	Aug.	Sept.	Oct.	Nov.	Dec.ʳ	Jan.
INVESTMENT COMPANIES[1]										
1 Sales of own shares[2]	411,751	381,260	28,637	27,970	26,455	24,834	25,990	21,927	26,494	30,343
2 Redemptions of own shares[3]	239,394	314,252	23,693	22,807	22,561	28,323	34,597	20,400	28,099	22,324
3 Net sales	172,357	67,008	4,944	5,763	3,894	−3,489	−8,607	1,507	−1,605	8,019
4 Assets[4]	424,156	453,842	516,866	531,022	539,171	521,007	456,422	446,479	453,842	468,998
5 Cash position[5]	30,716	38,006	41,467	41,587	40,802	42,397	40,929	41,432	38,006	40,157
6 Other	393,440	415,836	475,099	489,435	498,369	478,610	415,493	405,047	415,836	428,841

1. Excluding money market funds.
2. Includes reinvestment of investment income dividends. Excludes reinvestment of capital gains distributions and share issue of conversions from one fund to another in the same group.
3. Excludes share redemption resulting from conversions from one fund to another in the same group.
4. Market value at end of period, less current liabilities.

5. Also includes all U.S. government securities and other short-term debt securities.

NOTE. Investment Company Institute data based on reports of members, which comprise substantially all open–end investment companies registered with the Securities and Exchange Commission. Data reflect newly formed companies after their initial offering of securities.

term corporate bonds, intermediate term bonds, short-term notes and bonds, government and agency bonds, and pass-through funds.[3]

Although mutual fund shares are usually thought of as financial products for individuals, primarily small investors, institutions had invested $272 billion by the end of 1987. Although the bulk of these funds ($150 billion) were in money market and short-term municipal bond funds, close to $122 billion was invested in equity, bond, and income funds. Institutional assets represented close to 48 percent of total money-market-fund assets at the end of 1987; they held close to 27 percent of equity, bond, and income funds and close to one-third of total mutual fund assets (including money market funds). The institutional market consists primarily of fiduciaries (bank trusts and individuals serving as trustees, guardians and administrators), retirement plans, and business corporations.

There were 2,324 funds at the end of 1987, a dramatic increase over the 426 funds that were available in 1975. (See Figure 10.1.) Total assets have also sky-rocketed over this period, having grown from $46 billion in 1975 to $770 billion in 1987. In 1975, equity funds accounted for 70 percent of mutual fund assets, bond-income funds accounted for 26 percent, and money market funds accounted for 7 percent of assets. In 1987, equity funds accounted for 23 percent of assets, bond and income funds accounted for 36 percent, money market funds accounted for 33 percent, and short-term municipal bond funds accounted for 9 percent of total mutual fund assets. (See Figure 10.2.)

FUND CLASSIFICATION

A large number of mutual funds have been created to provide investors with the opportunity to purchase portfolios with fairly narrow investment objectives. It is possible to classify mutual funds by investment policy and type of investment. For the most popular funds, see Figure 10.3 and Table 10.2.

Figure 10.1
Number of Mutual Funds

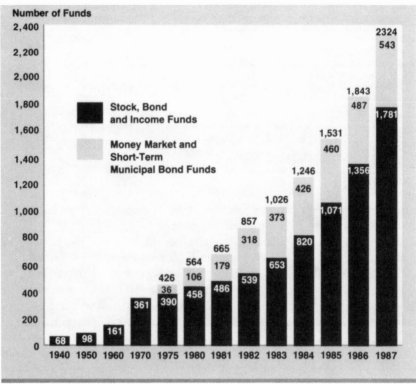

Source: *1988 Mutual Fund Fact Book*, p. 13.

Diversified Common Stock Funds

Most of the assets of diversified common stock funds are invested in good-quality common stock with the balance in money market instruments. Although current income is important, the primary objective is long-term capital growth. With the exception of money market funds, diversified common stock funds are the most popular type of mutual fund.

Growth Stock Funds

The primary objective of growth stock funds is the growth of capital, but the portfolio is more aggressive than that of the diversified common stock funds. These funds typically look for small or thinly capitalized companies that are

Figure 10.2
Percent Distribution of Total Net Assets by Type of Fund

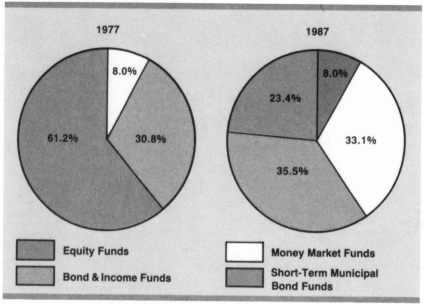

Source: *1988 Mutual Fund Fact Book,* p. 12.

often in high-technology industries. Many of these so-called "go-go funds" feature high portfolio turnover and borrow money for leverage to improve their performance. In markets where stocks are doing well, their performance can often be superb, but in bear markets, their performance is often poor.

Income Funds

Income funds seek a high level of current income for their shareholders. Most income funds purchase bonds, preferred stocks, and high-yielding common stocks in order to provide a higher-than-average income return. Another group of mutual funds that has increased in popularity are the high-yield or income funds. These funds tend to buy lower-grade securities (generally rated Baa or lower) that offer yields between 200 and 400 basis points higher than those of investment-grade securities (A rated or better). These are often called "junk bond" funds. The average default rate on junk bonds has averaged about 2 percent per year, while the yield on these bonds tends to range from 250 to 600 basis points above Treasury securities with comparable maturities. The default rate tends to increase considerably during recessions.

Table 10.2
Mutual Fund Assets Classified by Investment Objective (Billions of Dollars)

| | Yearend | | |
Investment Objective	1986	1987	Percent Change
Aggressive Growth	$ 25.0	$ 27.3	+ 9.2%
Growth	43.6	48.0	+ 10.1
Growth & Income	55.9	64.0	+ 14.5
Precious Metals	2.0	4.1	+ 105.0
International	7.2	7.0	− 2.8
Global Equity	8.3	10.4	+ 25.3
Flexible Portfolio	1.5	4.3	+ 186.7
Balanced	7.5	9.0	+ 20.0
Income-Equity	12.6	14.7	+ 16.7
Income-Mixed	10.3	11.4	+ 10.7
Income-Bond	11.4	12.6	+ 10.5
Option/Income	7.0	5.1	− 27.1
U.S. Government Income	82.4	88.9	+ 7.9
Ginnie Mae	39.6	34.2	− 13.6
Global Bond	0.5	2.1	+ 320.0
Corporate Bond	9.1	9.5	+ 4.4
High-Yield Bond	24.6	24.2	− 1.6
Long-Term Municipal Bond	49.9	49.2	− 1.4
Long-Term State Municipal Bond	25.8	27.8	+ 7.8
*Total Long-Term Funds	$424.2	$453.8	+ 7.0%

Source: 1988 Mutual Fund Fact Book, p. 29.

There are also tax-exempt municipal bonds which provide a diversified portfolio of tax-free general obligation and revenue bonds. The primary objective of these funds is current, tax-free income. Many of these funds are insured for both principal and interest payments.

Prior to 1987, tax-exempt funds dominated the mutual-fund bond business. However, since 1984, taxable bond funds have flourished. High-yield and other corporate bond funds, as well as those involving options, have increased substantially. Funds specializing in U.S. Treasury issues and in Ginnie Mae securities have been especially popular.

Bond funds owe some of their popularity to a new form of disintermediation. The old form of disintermediation of the late 1960s and 1970s was related to Regulation Q interest-rate ceilings and rising interest rates that redirected money away from depository institutions. The 1984-1986 version of disintermediation was triggered by falling money-market rates rather than by increasing interest rates. This can be attributed to the fact that consumers are both desirous of and accustomed to earning high yields. CD rates at banks have been between 250 and 600 basis points less than rates available at bond mutual funds. During 1984-1986, consumers have invested heavily in these fixed-rate mutual funds.[5]

Figure 10.3
Number of Mutual Funds Classified by Investment Objective

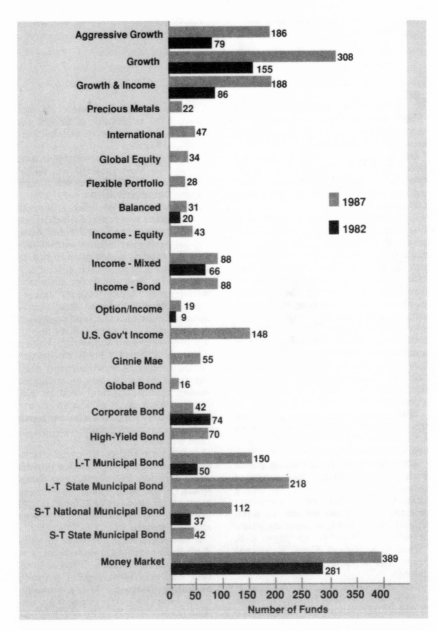

Source: 1988 Mutual Fund Book, p. 20.

Balanced Funds

Balanced funds typically have the following investment objectives: (1) to conserve the investors' initial principal, (2) to pay current income, and (3) long-term growth of both principal and income.

The portfolios are balanced among bonds, common stocks, and preferred stocks, in proportions that are often explicitly specified in the prospectus. The objective is to preserve principal, to generate income, and then to obtain capital gains. During rising markets, fund performance is usually not as good as among the more aggressive funds. However, balanced funds tend to outperform their more aggressive counterparts during bear markets.

Specialty Funds

Specialty funds are like other mutual funds except that they concentrate on investments in a single industry, in a group of related industries, in industries within a specified geographic region, or even in nonsecurity assets such as real estate.

Foreign Stock Funds

With the volatility of foreign exchange rates, the weakness of the dollar during 1985-1988, and differences in rates of inflation and real gross national product (GNP) growth among nations of the world, some investors expected investments abroad to offer a grater total return than investments in the United States. There were additional investors who wanted to diversify their holdings by investing in foreign equities. These factors led to the increased popularity of foreign-equity mutual funds that offered a diversified portfolio of foreign stocks and currencies.

Hedge Funds

Hedge funds appeal to speculative investors because the funds use the most aggressive techniques, including high leverage, short sales, and the purchase of put and call options to achieve maximum growth of capital. Most hedge funds are borrowed funds and place few restrictions on the types of securities held in portfolios. The original hedge funds attempted to reduce market risks by selling short on certain securities at the same time that they were long on others. With this strategy, the funds hoped to reduce the effects of wide fluctuations in the general market.

Option and Income Funds

The investment objective of option and income funds is to seek a high, current return by investing primarily in dividend-paying common stocks on which call options are traded on national securities exchanges. Current return consists of dividends, premiums from writing call options, net short-term gains from sales of portfolio securities on exercised options or otherwise, and any profits from closing purchase transactions.

Dual Purpose Funds

A dual purpose fund is a closed-end investment company which has two classes of shares: income shares, which receive 100 percent of the net investment income, and capital shares, which receive 100 percent of the capital appreciation.

Money Market Funds

Money market funds (MMFs) are typically no-load funds that invest exclusively in money market instruments, providing current income, relative safety of principal, liquidity, and check-writing and bill-paying privileges. Money-market-fund investments include Treasury bills, certificates of deposit (CDs), commercial paper, Eurodollar CDs, bankers' acceptances, time deposits, and repurchase agreements. (See Table 10.3.) Most money market funds that are part of a family of mutual funds allow free conversion privileges to other types of funds managed by the same investment group. There are both taxable and tax-exempt money market funds. The first money market fund was established in 1971.

After years of relatively slow growth, MMFs grew rapidly from $3.9 billion in total assets in 1977 to $232.3 billion on December 1, 1982. Competition from financial institutions' newly authorized money market depository accounts (MMDAs) and Super-NOW accounts, authorized with the passage of the Garn–St. Germain Act in December 1982, terminated the rapid growth of MMFs. MMF asset holdings fell by $60 billion in less than six months. When depository institutions cut their initially high payout rates on their MMDAs, the MMFs were able to grow once again, finally surpassing their 1982 peak level of assets in 1987.

In response to the introduction of MMDAs by banks and thrifts, MMFs stressed their memberships in families of mutual funds, which allowed depositors to switch accounts between stock, bond, money market, and other specialized funds. In addition, some funds began to specialize in short-term tax-exempt commercial paper, bills, and notes.

Index Funds

The purpose of index funds is almost diametrically opposed to the traditional purpose of a mutual fund. Index funds "buy the market" by tracking one of the stock market indices such as the Dow-Jones Industrial Average or the Standard

Table 10.3
Money Market Funds Asset Composition
Money Market Year-End, 1982-1987
(In Millions of Dollars)

	1982	1983	1984	1985	1986	1987
Total Net Assets	$206,607.5	$162,549.5	$209,731.9R	$207,535.3	$228,345.8	$254,676.4
U.S. Treasury Bills	37,935.9	20,484.0	20,197.9	20,391.5	20,428.6	4,944.0
Other Treasury Securities	4,706.0	2,354.6	5,214.7	4,271.9	7,602.9	9,358.6
Other U.S. Securities	11,972.0	13,375.2	16,974.3	18,043.1	15,120.3	26,998.9
Repurchase Agreements	16,222.1	13,028.5	22,769.8	26,068.6	32,160.1	39,290.6
Commercial Bank CDs(1)	35,479.4	18,931.3	18,362.5	13,256.3	13,427.2	24,216.9
Other Domestic CDs(2)	5,310.9	5,107.4	5,270.7	3,578.5	5,684.3	9,333.7
Eurodollar CDs(3)	23,758.8	21,911.1	21,213.5	19,027.0	22,168.4	21,611.7
Commercial Paper	50,327.1	46,752.6	78,408.1	87,555.4	94,882.0	100,534.4
Bankers' Acceptances	18,776.1	19,586.2	19,564.2	11,578.3	10,405.7	10,771.2
Cash Reserves	278.3	(274.5)	(1,244.5)	154.8	(24.9)	(326.7)
Other	1,840.9	1,293.1	3,000.7	3,609.9	6,491.2	7,943.1
Average Maturity(4)	37	37	43	37	40	31
Number of Funds	281	307	329	348	360	389

(1) Commercial bank CDs are those issued by American banks located in the U.S.
(2) Other Domestic CDs include those issued by S&Ls and American branches of foreign banks.
(3) Eurodollar CDs are those issued by foreign branches of domestic banks and some issued by Canadian banks; this category includes some one day paper.
(4) Maturity of each individual security in the portfolio at end of month weighted by its value.

Comparable data for long-term funds can be found on pages 82–85.

Source: 1988 Mutual Fund Fact Book, p. 90.

and Poor's (S&P) 500 index. The objective is to reduce portfolio turnover and the cost of unprofitable security analysis, letting the investor determine his own leverage and market timing positions. Index funds should perform in tandem with the market as a whole.

Commodity Funds

Commodity funds are usually organized as limited partnerships to afford the small investor the advantages of diversification, which minimizes the risk associated with extreme price movements by any one commodity. Also, in an inflationary environment, well-selected commodities can provide an effective inflation hedge and provide the speculative investor with an opportunity for considerable gains. There can also be huge leverage involved in commodity trading. Some commodity funds are managed using fundamental analysis attempting to anticipate price movements based on expectations of supply and demand for specific commodities. On the other hand, most funds use technical trading systems that attempt to identify trends in commodity prices.

Unit Trusts

A unit trust is a variation on the closed-end investment company and holds a fixed portfolio of securities such as government, corporate, or tax-exempt bonds. A unit trust is a passive investment in which the assets are essentially frozen until maturity without any trading. The trust collects interest on its portfolio and on the repayment of principal when the bonds mature. The trust is self-liquidating because as funds are received, they are distributed to shareholders and not reinvested. In addition, the originating broker will often make a market in the trust shares until the trust is dissolved.

Retirement Market

The retirement market is an extremely important one for mutual funds. For example, mutual funds have achieved substantial earnings in attracting employee pension and profit-sharing accounts which totaled $29.2 billion at the end of 1986. Keogh plans of mutual funds totaled $10.1 billion and accounted for just under a third of the total market at the end of 1987, while IRA plans totaled $72.2 billion and accounted for 21.6 percent of the total market in 1987 ($31.6 billion and 14.2 percent of the total market at the end of 1985). In each of the aforementioned plans, equity funds dominated the investments, with money market funds in second place. The IRA market holds vast potential for mutual funds since only about 25 percent of households hold any type of IRA accounts. This leaves about 60 million households as potential IRA investors, compared to under 30 million households already participating in IRA plans.

Most mutual funds offer shareholders plans for the reinvestment of investment income, dividends, and capital gain distributions. They also offer contractual plans whereby an investor agrees to invest a fixed amount on a regular basis for a specified time frame. Many funds offer a service whereby shareholders may receive payments from their investment at regular intervals. In addition, most funds offer exchange privileges among and within a family of mutual funds. This enables shareholders to transfer an investment from one type of fund to another within the same fund group as their needs or objectives change. The mutual funds' custodian bank holds in custody and safekeeping the securities and other assets of the fund, and usually acts as the transfer and dividend-distributing agent.

DISTRIBUTION OF MUTUAL FUNDS

Mutual funds typically contract with an investment advisor for investment advice and other management services, and with a principal underwriter for the distribution of the fund's shares. The investment advisor usually receives a fee based on the total value of the assets under management. The underwriter sells and distributes the securities issued by the fund to the investing public through brokers and dealers, or through the underwriter's own salespeople, or both. The principal underwriter either acts as agent for the fund or purchases the securities issued by the fund for resale, for which the underwriter typically receives a fee in the form of a portion of the sales commission, which is included in the selling price of the mutual fund shares. The underwriter usually has exclusive national distribution rights that may be characterized as dealer to investor, underwriter to investor, or fund to investor. Most open-end funds market their shares through brokerage houses and broker-dealers who specialize in selling mutual fund shares. A fund using this method to distribute its shares gives these dealers contract distribution rights and grants them distribution terms, which essentially means that they buy shares at the net asset value and sell them at a retail markup over the net asset value. These funds are known as load funds. From this load fund, the mutual-fund broker-dealers derive their profit and pay their representatives a commission.

In the dealer-to-investor sales approach, the underwriter carries on a wholesale function in distributing the mutual fund shares to retailers—securities brokers and dealers. The underwriters support the retail sales effort by sales promotions, advertising, and personal contact. The dealer contacts the public directly in attempting to sell the mutual fund shares. The underwriter-to-investor approach is one in which the underwriting organization handles the retail function by employing sales representatives to sell to the investing public. In the fund-to-investor distribution system, mutual funds deal directly with investors without the use of field salespersons. Advertising and direct mail are the key methods used to obtain investors. In the latter case, these shares are usually sold to the public without a sales charge. (See Table 10.4.)

Table 10.4
Sales of Mutual Funds by Investment Objective within Method of Sales, 1984-1987
(In Millions of Dollars)

Sales Force

	1984	1985	1986	1987
Aggressive Growth	$ 1,463.9	$ 1,517.5	$ 2,380.5	$ 4,077.6
Growth	3,505.1	4,751.2	7,697.4	10,508.8
Growth & Income	2,749.9	4,730.3	12,044.4	12,856.3
Precious Metals	81.0	223.5	204.6	1,277.5
International	149.7	198.8	1,048.5	1,988.8
Global Equity	969.1	1,088.3	3,088.5	3,076.4
Flexible Portfolio	85.4	138.1	344.5	2,610.9
Balanced	141.5	629.5	2,567.1	2,132.8
Income-Equity	338.9	1,104.6	2,640.6	3,175.3
Income-Mixed	1,611.6	3,197.6	5,335.9	4,723.4
Income-Bond	584.3	1,202.7	3,628.7	3,767.7
Option/Income	1,795.2	2,708.7	3,041.0	1,710.3
U.S. Government Income	5,849.6	35,654.5	51,624.5	42,050.7
Ginnie Mae	2,690.7	11,765.1	24,930.1	9,710.8
Global Bond	5.9	25.7	407.6	775.3
Corporate Bond	728.0	1,384.8	3,808.4	2,875.6
High-Yield Bond	2,061.8	4,665.3	10,541.5	7,012.8
Long-Term Municipal Bond	3,764.6	6,753.9	15,441.4	10,371.1
Long-Term State Municipal Bond	1,617.0	4,686.0	10,802.4	7,313.3
Total	**$ 30,193.2**	**$ 86,426.1**	**$161,577.6**	**$132,015.4**

Direct Marketing

	1984	1985	1986	1987
Aggressive Growth	$ 2,717.4	$ 5,125.3	$ 7,267.9	$ 7,285.9
Growth	1,550.8	2,050.2	3,624.6	5,723.8
Growth & Income	3,166.8	3,594.2	5,552.4	8,473.5
Precious Metals	166.5	385.3	452.0	1,900.5
International	450.7	562.3	3,121.4	2,192.6
Global Equity	0.0	0.3	22.6	50.3
Flexible Portfolio	9.0	30.2	142.6	232.4
Balanced	84.9	259.3	759.4	1,061.2
Income-Equity	661.6	1,179.5	2,829.5	3,584.2
Income-Mixed	457.7	733.1	1,345.9	1,112.1
Income-Bond	422.8	847.7	1,518.0	1,387.7
Option/Income	50.4	64.0	61.8	300.5
U.S. Government Income	87.6	884.8	2,554.6	1,702.4
Ginnie Mae	171.4	1,281.7	3,660.0	3,301.7
Global Bond	0.0	0.0	31.6	343.4
Corporate Bond	137.9	152.9	368.0	579.7
High-Yield Bond	320.1	1,051.1	2,993.7	2,610.1
Long-Term Municipal Bond	3,567.8	5,875.7	9,218.7	7,620.0
Long-Term State Municipal Bond	907.5	2,108.3	4,417.0	3,605.5
Total	**$ 14,930.9**	**$ 26,185.9**	**$ 49,941.7**	**$ 53,067.5**

Source: 1988 Mutual Fund Fact Book, p. 72.

MANAGEMENT FEES AND EXPENSE RATES

Generally, an investment company enters into a contract with a management or advisory company to perform research, review credits, and meet the investment objective of the fund. The standard advisory fee is equal to one-half of 1 percent of the fund's assets. However, the fee per dollar of asset is determined on a sliding scale, which declines as the fund size grows. Funds incur other expenses such as the cost of services offered to investors, which might include custodial transfer and registration services, employee salaries, and other selling and operating costs. Total annual expenses, including the management fee, for large investment companies average somewhat less than 1 percent of the value of assets. Some funds require their management company to cover all costs over a specified amount, effectively limiting total expenses.

The individual investor should pay careful attention to the fee structure of a mutual fund. In the typical load fund, there is an 8.5 percent fee on each new investment in a fund, although this usually declines a bit as investments exceed $10,000 or $25,00. Some loads are only 4 to 7 percent, while low load funds charge 1 to 3 percent. Even a few no-load funds levy an annual charge of up to 1.25 percent of the funds' net assets to cover advertising and sales commission. These are known as 12b-1 plans, named after a rule of the SEC that permits mutual funds to use assets to help cover costs for marketing, advertising, and so forth. A fund administrator can say such charges will be levied but need not specify the amount. Unlike a front-end load fee, which is charged when the shares are purchased, the 12b-1 fee can be a continuous annual fee. It is entirely possible that over a number of years, investors in no-load funds that assess this charge could pay more than they would have paid in loading fees. There are also back-end loads or redemption fees at some funds, which charge from 1 to 5 percent when investors cash in their shares, and funds with "contingent deferred sales charges" of up to 6 percent of the initial investment if investors withdraw their assets before a specific date.

Mutual funds also charge other fees, which include investment advisory fees and fees for preparing and distributing prospectuses, financial reports, and proxy statements, as well as fees for directors. The accumulation of these fees or operating expenses is often expressed as a percentage of the net-asset value, and is called the expense ratio. These ratios tend to vary from 0.5 to 4.0 percent. Investors should be extremely conscious of these costs in choosing a mutual fund, because almost every study has found that on the average, load and no-load funds have comparable performances. As a matter of fact, *A Study of Mutual Funds* (1962), conducted for the SEC by Irwin Friend, Francis H. Brown, Edward Herman, and Douglas Vickers, found that the performance of mutual funds between 1952 and 1958 was not significantly different from that of an unmanaged portfolio of similar assets. About half of the funds outperformed the S&P 500 index, while the other half underperformed. When the loading charges were later included in another study, the return earned by investors tended to be less than would be achieved through a random selection of securities. These results do not imply that the managements of mutual funds are incompetent, but they do give strong support for the efficient market hypothesis. The market is said to be efficient because it quickly incorporates any new change, information, or event affecting the value of the security, i.e., at any given time, the price of a stock represents its best valuation since all factors affecting it would have been taken into consideration.

Operating expenses for funds vary by type of fund and size of fund. For example, median operating expenses vary from 0.68 percent for large equity funds to 1.04 percent for smaller funds. Similarly, median operating expenses for taxable bonds vary from 0.76 percent for large funds to 0.99 percent for small funds.

THE SMALL INVESTOR

Investment companies are not a panacea for the small investor, but do provide the uninitiated investor with little knowledge of the risk and reward aspects of portfolio management with safety through diversification, professional management, and strict and effective regulation. Although the cost of buying and selling shares is high for many funds, investment companies tend to offer a great deal of flexibility in meeting individual investment objectives. Mutual funds are usually able to obtain lower brokerage commissions than an individual small investor, and offer investors liquidity in the form of ready marketability or an ability to redeem shares with the fund itself.

In choosing a mutual fund, the individual must match investment objectives with those of the fund. Investors should consider the age and size of the fund, its past performance, its current portfolio holdings, the performance of the portfolio in the last bear market, the expenses of the fund and its costs of operation, and the potential for hidden tax liabilities.

Choosing a mutual fund is not easy. The prospectus of the fund will provide the investor with a statement of the fund's goals, its current portfolio, its recent performance, services offered, and fees charged. There are publications such as *Forbes, Barron's, Money Magazine,* and *Business Week* that have either special mutual fund editions or regular coverage of most funds. In addition, Weisenberger Services, Inc., publishes a summary of investment company performance. The securities held in each fund are published annually in *Moody's Investment Company Manual.* There is also a money-market fund report that is published weekly by Donaghue.

The difficult task of trying to unearth costs buried in prospectuses by mutual funds was ended by the SEC in mid-1988. The regulatory body now requires easy-to-read tables detailing fund charges to appear near the front of all new or updated prospectuses. In addition to the annual operating expenses, the full disclosure table in prospectuses will also ferret out previously hidden load charges such as the perpetual sales load levied by some funds on reinvestment of dividend distributions. Also, all yields featured in fund advertisements must be accompanied by the fund's one-, five-, and ten-year average annual total return. These new regulations should allow potential investors to compare fund performance more accurately and easily. It will prevent fund sponsors from artificially boosting their advertised yields by counting as income short-term capital gains from options trading.

HIDDEN CAPITAL GAINS AND LOSSES

Investment companies are a conduit through which income and capital gains are passed to stockholders. The investor ultimately must pay any capital gains taxes if the mutual fund shares are sold at a profit or if the mutual fund realizes capital gains on its portfolio. Also, if the mutual fund earns income, the investor pays the appropriate income tax on those earnings.[6]

The individual mutual fund can have the potential for considerable tax liability built into its portfolio. It is possible that this liability may fall on investors who do not experience the gains. This potential tax liability is the result of profits that have not been realized by the fund. There is no taxation until the mutual fund sells the appreciated assets and realizes the capital gain. For example, it is possible for an investor to be responsible for the tax without experiencing the capital gain. Suppose the shares are purchased at the current net asset value of $10 for a cost basis of $10. Suppose that shortly thereafter, the fund realizes a $3-per-share profit that it had accumulated over the last year, and distributes the capital gain. The investors who purchased the shares prior to the capital gain for, let us say $7 per share, have earned a profit and must pay any appropriate capital gains tax. The person who just bought the shares for $10 also receives a capital gains distribution, and must also pay the capital gains tax. Even though the investor paid $10 per share, that investor is the holder of record for the distribution, and must pay the tax. Also, after the capital gains distribution, the net asset value declines to $7 per share. It is important for a potential investor to study the unrealized capital gains of any mutual fund prior to making an investment. Of course, the new investor can then sell the shares at $7, establishing a capital loss. Such a sale offsets the distribution, and thus avoids any tax obligation. The original investment and the redemption may involve transaction costs for the investor.[7]

While the existence of unrealized capital gains implies the potential for future tax liabilities, the existence of unrealized capital losses offers the potential for tax-free gains. Suppose that a fund has dropped in net asset value from $12 to $8 as a result of a declining market. If an individual purchases shares at the current price of $8, and if the value of the portfolio rises, it is possible that the investor will not have a tax liability on this gain. Suppose the portfolio's net asset value rises back to $12, at which time the mutual fund sells the securities. Since the cost basis to the fund of the old securities is $12, the fund has no capital gain.

The investor has seen the net asset value increase from $8 to $12 without any tax liability having been created by the investment company.[8]

FUTURE OF MUTUAL FUNDS

The experience of direct-marketing no-load funds has given fund sponsors a new sophistication in how to approach advertising and how to support broker-dealers more effectively. Large pension and profit-sharing plans have shown an interest in mutual funds, as have some institutional investors. In addition, whenever the yield on money market funds exceeds that of repurchase agreements, institutional money tends to flow into these liquid money-market mutual funds. However, the biggest near-term opportunity for the mutual fund industry lies with the neophyte investors—the savers who have had their first dip into mutual funds through the money market funds or through an IRA and are perhaps ready to consider alternative vehicles as a hedge against possibly declining interest rates.

Changes in the regulatory environment, inflation rates, investment preferences, and attitudes of the brokerage community, as well as other factors, have significantly changed the mutual fund industry in the last decade. The industry has come alive again after a discouraging five years following the bear market in stocks in 1973-1974. The industry introduced families of new no-load mutual funds, including the highly popular money market funds and tax-free long-term and short-term funds. The mutual fund industry has experienced enormous change germane to image, asset mix, breadth of product line, growth rate, primary method of distribution, types of shareholders, and marketing requirements. The traditional mutual fund industry, which consisted of stock and bond funds, began in the 1940s and peaked in assets at $57 billion in 1972. By year-end 1987, stock, bond, and income funds had assets close to $454 billion distributed among 1,781 mutual funds with an additional $316 billion distributed in 543 money-market mutual funds. Much of the growth came from the revival in mutual funds investments in common stocks, government income funds, and municipal bond funds.

It is interesting to note that there were 36.9 million industry shareholder accounts in equity, bond, and income funds in 1987, while there were 17.7 million shareholder accounts in money market funds and short-term municipal bond funds. At year-end 1987, tax-exempt money market funds held in excess of $61.3 billion in assets. In the period since their introduction, they have grown from relative obscurity to an asset position equal to that of aggressive growth funds, which have been in existence for a long time. These liquid funds were popular for investors in the highest tax brackets, since yields in these funds range from 55 to 70 percent of the yields offered in taxable money-market funds. Institutions hold close to 26 percent of the assets held in short-term municipal-bond funds.

Mutual funds have grown rapidly during the 1980s commensurate with the positive performance of both the stock and bond markets between summer 1982 and fall 1987. Mutual funds have also benefited from demographic changes in the United States as well as favorable tax laws which encouraged the setting up of IRA, Keogh, and other retirement, pension, profit sharing, or tax-deferred plans.

The performance of mutual funds has been the subject of many studies. These studies suggest that mutual fund managers do no better than would be expected, given the riskiness of portfolios. It was also generally found that investor returns in mutual funds tend to be less than the average for the securities in which they invest.

NOTES

1. Investment Company Institute, *Mutual Fund Fact Book* (Washington, D.C.: Investment Company Institute, 1980), 10.

2. Ibid., 16.

3. A. Gart, *An Insider's Guide to the Financial Services Revolution* (New York, McGraw-Hill, 1984), 122.

4. R. J. Doyle, Jr., "Investment Companies and the Small Investor," *Investments*, No. 5328, Study guide, The American College (Bryn Mawr, Pa., 1984), R11.7-R.11.

5. R. M. Giordano, "Financial Market Perspectives," *Economic Research*, Goldman Sachs (May 7, 1986): 2-3.

6. F. J. Fabozzi and A. A. Groppeli, "Investment Companies," in *Handbook of Financial Markets*, edited by F. J. Fabozzi and F. G. Zarb (Homewood, Ill.: Dow-Jones Irwin, 1981), 526.

7. H. B. Mayo, *Investments* (Chicago: Dryden Press, 1988), 520.

8. Ibid., 520-521.

11

Pension Plans

A pension plan is a fund established and maintained by an individual, employer, or union to provide for the payment of definitely determinable benefits to people during their retirement. There must be a written plan that specifies who participates, benefits, and administers the pension's funds. Pension plans have benefit provisions based on earning levels, contributions, and duration of employment. An organization called a pension fund administers the program, and manages assets purchased with the contributions of employers and employees. Investment selection and maintenance is performed by a fund manager, either an insurance company or a trustee. The issues of vesting, disclosure, and fiduciary responsibility have important social ramifications.

A dual retirement system has evolved in the United States. We have both a social security system (Old Age, Survivors, and Disability Insurance System) of the federal government, and the large and diverse retirement systems operated by unions, fraternal orders, and governmental and private employers. Pension funds, as the name indicates, administer savings that are set aside primarily for old age and retirement. Public and private pension funds had assets of $12 billion in 1950, assets of $170 billion in 1970, and assets of $1105 billion in 1986 (see Table 11.2), as the growth of such funds after World War II was rapid and continuous. Their rapid growth was fueled by demographic trends, inflation, the wage controls of World War II, employee desire for guaranteed retirement income, and the tax advantages of retirement savings in this form. As a matter of fact, private pension-fund growth continued at an average annual rate in excess of 13 percent between 1970 and mid-1980s.

Savings by individuals is in part dependent upon adequate funds for retirement. Historically, people provided for their own retirement income from a stock of financial assets held directly. However, over the last two decades,

Table 11.1
Number of Persons Covered by Major Pension and Retirement Programs in the United States (000 omitted)

	Private Plans		Government-Administered Plans			
Year	With Life Insurance Companies	Other Private Plans	Railroad Retirement	Federal Civilian Employees†	State and Local Employees	OASI‡
1940	695	3,565	1,349	745	1,552	22,900
1945	1,470	5,240	1,846	2,928	2,008	41,070
1950	2,755	7,500	1,881	1,872	2,894	61,506
1955	4,105	12,290	1,876	2,333	3,927	74,887
1960	5,475	17,540	1,654	2,703	5,160	91,496
1965	7,040	21,060	1,661	3,114	6,780	103,827
1966	7,835	21,710	1,666	3,322	7,210	107,438
1967	8,700	22,330	1,641	3,499	7,594	110,746
1968	9,155	22,910	1,625	3,565	8,012	113,804
1969	9,920	24,410	1,620	3,627	8,303	116,904
1970	10,580	25,520	1,633	3,624	8,591	120,014
1971	10,880	26,580	1,578	3,596	9,079	122,735
1972	11,545	27,400	1,575	3,739	9,563	125,549
1973	12,485	28,700	1,582	4,040	9,850	129,045
1974	13,335	29,240	1,588	4,057	10,635	132,583
1975	15,190	30,300*	1,564	4,171	11,230	135,744
1976	16,965	N.A.	1,572	4,210	12,290	138,633
1977	19,205	N.A.	1,567	4,292	13,124	141,596
1978	21,615	N.A.	1,580	4,380	13,400*	144,260
1979	23,460	N.A.	1,567	4,398	13,680*	147,178
1980	26,080	N.A.	1,533	4,460	13,950*	153,634
1981	27,825	N.A.	1,483	4,566	14,230*	157,569
1982	30,375	N.A.	1,404	4,610	14,504	160,611
1983	32,425	N.A.	1,383	4,683	14,464	161,836
1984	35,510	N.A.	1,362	4,791	14,788	161,986
1985	40,010	N.A.	1,309	4,887	15,235	162,881
1986	45,830	N.A.	1,268	4,938	15,426	164,438

Notes: It is not possible to obtain a total for number of persons covered by pension plans by adding together the figures shown by year. Each series has been derived separately and there are differences in amount of duplication within each series and among the various series and also differences in definition of "coverage" among the series.

Private plans with life insurance companies include persons covered by Keogh plans, tax-sheltered annuities and, after 1974, IRA plans.

Data for "Other Private Plans," compiled by the Social Security Administration, exclude plans for the self-employed, those having vested benefits but not presently employed at the firm where benefits were accrued, and also exclude an estimated number who have vested benefits from employment other than from their current employment.

These data represent va ·us dates during the year, since the fiscal years of the plans are not necessarily the same. Trends from year to yeu. within each series are not affected. The number of persons covered include survivors or dependents of deceased workers and beneficiaries as well as retired workers. Retirement arrangements for members of the armed forces, and provisions for veterans' pensions, are not included.

N.A.—Not available.

*Estimated.

†Includes members of the U.S. Civil Service Retirement System, the Tennessee Valley Authority Retirement System, the Foreign Service Retirement System, and the Retirement Plan for Employees of the Federal Reserve System.

‡Includes living workers insured for retirement and/or survivors benefits, including the self-employed, plus dependents of retired workers and survivors of deceased workers who are receiving periodic benefits.

Source: Compiled by the American Council of Life Insurance. From the *Life Insurance Fact Book Update*, p. 23.

company and governmental retirement plans have become important. For example, in 1987, close to 55 million persons were participants in pension and retirement programs other than social security, compared to approximately 8 million in 1940 (see Table 11.1).

FEDERAL GOVERNMENT PENSION PLANS

Social Security is the broadest pension program in the United States, providing potential coverage to over 162 million people employed in the private sector and state and local government. The Social Security program, a pay-as-you-go system, is the most important federal pension, and was designed initially to establish a floor under retirement income for many individuals. Many private pension plans are designed to mesh with Social Security, providing a supplement to meet some desired level of retirement income. Social Security payments are adjusted for inflation, but most private payment plans do not promise the same adjustment. Social Security is financed through employer-employee contributed FICA taxes. In addition to retirement benefits, the system supplies benefits to the disabled and to families in which the main source of family support has died.

Social Security faces financial problems after the year 2000, as the number of contributors declines relative to the number of benefit recipients, and as the level of promised benefits continues to rise with increases in inflation. For the immediate future, the Social Security fund appears to be adequately financed. As a matter of fact, the growing proportion of retired persons could threaten the solvency of many pension funds. When the Social Security Act was passed following the Depression, there were 11 working adults for each retired person. The present ratio is just under 3 to 1; this ratio should shrink to 2 to 1 by 1995. The federal government also operates retirement funds for 4.9 million federal civilian service employees and a few million military employees, as well as smaller separate funds for employees of the foreign service, the Tennessee Valley Authority, and the federal judiciary and Federal Reserve systems. State and local government retirement systems covered 15.5 million persons at the end of 1987.

The railroad retirement system, the only retirement system administered by the federal government for a single private industry, covered 1.2 million persons at year-end 1987. This system has funding difficulties that are similar to the more publicized problems of the social security system in that the plan has a decreasing number of active participants and an increasing number of people obtaining benefits.

CHARACTERISTICS OF PENSION FUND INVESTMENTS

The investment management of a pension fund has salient characteristics that are favorable to the achievement of fine investment results.[1] These include:

1. Absence of tax considerations at the fund level;
2. Absence of distinctions between capital (principal) and income;
3. Limited liquidity needs; and
4. A long-term view of investment strategy.

Income taxes are deferred until retirement, and are often lower after retirement than during the working years. Participants usually pay less total tax, and may always defer income taxes under a qualifying pension plan.

The type of securities bought vary with the nature of funds and also with circumstances, but the dollar amounts are large and the influence of pension funds is pervasive. Some private pension funds consist mostly of the stock of the company sponsoring them, as in the case of Sears. Some favored the bond of their sponsoring company, as did the pension funds of AT&T, while some public pension funds have often been limited to governmental obligations. At one time, government pension funds were considerably larger in asset size than private funding, but now the opposite is true.

The long-term nature of pension-plan liabilities suggests that a great deal of liquidity is not required. Pension funds must have some liquid assets for benefit payments. The bulk of the assets are long-term investments. Pension plans pay no income taxes as long as they satisfy specific IRS rules.

ASSETS

Combined assets of public and private pension plans (over $1 trillion in 1987) place pension plans among the largest types of financial institutions, exceeded only by commercial banks. Pension plans are sponsored by private companies and associations, insurance companies, and state, local, and federal governments. Pension plans are an important factor in the economy, and represent an important source of funds for the money and capital markets. As a matter of fact, in combination, the pension funds hold controlling interest in the common stock of many large corporations.

Private pension plans have become important financial intermediaries, funneling the deferred wages of workers into investments. Pension funds sell contractual agreements that provide benefits to participants upon retirement. Most pension plans offer benefit provisions that are directly related to an employee's level of earning, contributions, and length of employment. Pension plans place current savings in a portfolio of stocks, bonds, money market instruments, real estate, and other assets in the expectation of building a bigger pool of funds in the future. The composition of these investment portfolios depends on whether plan assets are held in a trust fund or by insurers. The assets of plans funded through insurance companies tend to be in bonds and mortgages, while the assets of pension trusts tend to be in common stocks. The assets of pension funds have become so large that some analysts have suggested they are becoming dominant owners of American business because of their heavy purchases of corporate stock.

Close to 30 percent of the funds of state and local government pension funds are invested in corporate and foreign bonds, while equities accounted for 32 percent of assets. Government and agency issues constitute about 30 percent of such assets. The remainder of the assets are distributed among mortgages, trade credit, money market instruments, and municipal bonds. Because of strict regulations, public plans hold a larger proportion of cash and liquid government securities than do private plans. They also place moderate amounts of funds in municipal securities—usually IOUs issued by their own governmental unit.

It is much more common for employees of public pension funds than for employees of private pension funds to provide a share of the ongoing contributions to these retirement benefits. Also, the investment policies of public pension funds have been more strictly regulated and are less risk-oriented on average than those of private pension plans. For example, private pension plans hold a greater proportion of their assets in common stock than do public pension plans.

Private pension plans have more than 70 percent of their assets invested in corporate equities. They also have close to 20 percent of their assets invested in corporate and foreign bonds. Treasury and agency securities account for close to 18 percent of the holdings, while mortgages account for only a tiny portion of the investment portfolio (see Table 11.2).

International diversification on a modest scale has been widely adopted by corporate pension funds. Developmental drilling for oil and gas, and investments in paintings, collectibles, rare coins and stamps, and in gold, silver, and other precious metals have become popular during periods of inflationary pressures. Of late, there has been a growing tendency to invest more funds into mortgages and equity participation in commercial real estate, particularly commercial office building and shopping centers; through this trend, American pension funds appear to be following in the footsteps of their European counterparts. European pension funds have invested 10 to 25 percent of their assets into real estate compared to a much lower percentage in this country. Many experts expect U.S. pension funds to follow suit and to have 10 percent of their assets invested in real estate by 1990. Investment management companies, bank trust departments, and insurance companies wage a continuous battle to maintain and increase assets under management. (See Table 11.3 for the largest tax-exempt money managers.)

In soliciting new pension fund business, investment management companies tend to stress investment performance. Return on investment is critical, given that the funds are invested for the long-term. The cost of a pension plan for the sponsoring company can be dramatically affected by the yield on its pension fund. For example, a rule of thumb is that an increase of ½ of 1 percent in the yield on a pension fund could reduce benefit costs by approximately 12 percent. Occasionally, pension funds receive pressure to avoid investing in certain companies, regions, or countries, such as the Republic of South Africa.

During the early 1960s, equity purchases by public pension plans and life

Table 11.2
Pension Fund Assets at Year-End 1986 (Billions of Dollars)

ASSETS	PUBLIC	PRIVATE
U.S. Treasury Issues	94.8	61.8
U.S. Agency Issues	48.6	50.3
Corporate Equities	150.2	456.4
Corporate and Foreign Bonds	140.6	128.3
Mortgages	15.6	7.4
Demand and Time Deposits	18.9	64.1
Tax-Exempt Obligations	0.8	-
Money Market Fund Shares	-	12.5
Mutual Fund Shares	-	25.0
Open Market Paper	-	52.5
Miscellaneous Assets	-	-223.0
Total	469.5	635.0

Source: Flow of Funds Accounts

Financial Assets and Liabilities Year-End, 1963-1986, Board of Governors of the Federal reserve System, Washington, D.C. 20551, September 1987,p.25.

insurance companies were minimal. Before the end of that decade, life insurance companies were allowed to manage pension fund monies as separate accounts— accounts separate from their life insurance activities and, therefore, not subject to the strict investment regulations in that business. As life insurance companies expanded into this business, their purchases of equities grew. Equities grew as a proportion of total portfolio holdings because it was recognized that a significant part of pension liabilities would eventually be affected by inflation. Investment managers sought an investment asset whose nominal total returns might keep pace with inflation. At that time, equities were thought to offer the best hedge

Table 11.3
Top Tax-Exempt Asset Managers

Prudential Asset Management
Bankers' Trust
J. P. Morgan
Metropolitan Life
Aetna Life and Casualty
Wells Fargo
Travellers Companies
Alliance Capital Management
Manufacturers Hanover
CIGNA
Jennison Associates Capital
Citicorp Investment Management
John Hancock Financial
Chase Investors Management
Equitable Capital Management
Equitable Real Estate

against low and moderate levels of inflation. Second, equities had a history from 1926 to 1976 of providing a better return than debt-oriented issues. Third, since pension funds anticipated a prolonged period of asset growth with limited need to liquidate asset holdings to meet short-run overflows, pension funds could be less concerned with any year-to-year variability in market asset values. This longer-run outlook put pension funds in a better position to deal with equity risks.

TYPES OF PLANS

A pension plan may take various forms and attributes. First, the plan may be public, private, or individual. Public plans are established for workers of the federal, state, or municipal governments, while private plans are those instituted by corporations. Individual plans, known as Keoghs and individual retirement accounts (IRAs), were originally designed for the self-employed or for people not covered by another plan. Today, under the Economic Recovery Act of 1981, any wage earner is eligible to set up an IRA.

Second, a pension plan may be classified as either unfunded or funded. A funded plan is one in which the employer deposits contributions into a trust fund, specifically designated for pensions. Funded pension plans formally establish charges against current income to meet pension liabilities as they accrue in order to minimize risk that benefits will not be available upon retirement. An unfunded plan has the employer paying benefits out of current income. Underfunding means that employee/employer contributions are not large enough actuarially to cover the benefits promised to be paid when the employee retires or the plan terminates.

Third, a funded pension may be insured or uninsured. An insured plan operates under a service arrangement with a life insurance company, which holds responsibility for collecting receipts, paying benefits, and/or administering the assets of the pension plan. An uninsured plan is one in which the employer places the contributions in a trust fund to be managed by a fiduciary, in the expectation of generating income sufficient to meet future obligations. Noninsured plans are twice as large as insured plans. Finally, pension plans are either noncontributory or contributory; an employee shares in the contributions in a contributory plan.

The nature of the retirement income commitment affects the firm's financial position and cost structure. For example, a profit-sharing plan involves a cost contingent on profitability; however, the avoidance of a fixed charge can turn out to be an expensive method of providing benefits. A defined-contribution plan appears to limit liability to negotiated pension benefits, while the defined-benefit plan involves a specific commitment. A defined-benefit plan usually promises to pay a stream of retirement income payments to employees as a function of final wage levels and years of service. The benefit is treated as a given, while the contributions are variable. The defined-contribution plan consists of a specific sum contributed annually by the employer which is invested in the employee's name. The employer accepts no responsibility for the investment returns that are realized on the funds invested. Although the annual pension contribution is fixed by the pension plans, the pension benefit is variable. Essentially, in a defined-benefit plan the employer takes the investment risk. In a defined contribution plan, the employee takes the investment risk.

Sponsoring companies have established pension plans into which they make regular contributions in order to provide for these future liabilities. While employees and the sponsoring companies often share in providing some of the retirement contributions, many companies do not require any contribution from their employees. The precise contribution formula is often complex, but the contributions to the fund are tax deductible for the corporation, as are the investment returns within the fund. An employee pays income taxes on the benefits received only after their distribution following retirement.

Defined benefits are desirable to employees for reasons of financial security. While a profit-sharing plan can be extremely beneficial to employees when a firm is highly profitable, there is no guarantee of a company contribution unless a certain level of company profitability is achieved. Many employees in highly cyclical and low-profit industries do not like the contingent nature of the company contribution to this type of plan.

Private, noninsured pension funds account for approximately 36 percent of total pension fund assets, private insured pension funds account for just under 20 percent, and state- and local-government employee retirement funds account for 26 percent of the total, while federal government employee retirement funds represent close to 19 percent of the total. Approximately 25 percent of the employee benefit and retirement funds are estimated to be internally managed, while the rest are managed by bank trust departments, private investment counselors, or by other sources such as unions. Many insurance companies offer guaranteed investment contracts (GICs). Some minimum rate of return is guaranteed by the issues for a specified period in the future. The GIC is presumed to have a fixed value for accounting and actuarial purposes. Typically, the funds are invested in a broadly diversified portfolio of corporate bonds and private placements. Although GICs are designed to reduce uncertainty in pension-fund earnings, they are not risk-free, as the "guarantee" is only as sound as the financial condition of the life insurer. It is interesting to note that those funds managing significant portions of assets internally reported that the performance of internal managers exceeded the returns achieved by external professional managers. Internal management was also said to be accompanied by significant cost savings.

PENSION FUND GROWTH

There have been many reasons for the outstanding growth of pension funds in the past 30 years:

1. Inflation and the wage controls of World War II;
2. All contributions under qualified plans are tax-deductible for the employer;
3. There is a need for supplementary retirement in addition to Social Security;
4. Pensions are legitimate collective bargaining issues and in a highly competitive job market, pension and profit-sharing plans become an important part of a company's fringe benefit package; and
5. They have given older employees incentive for early retirement.

Today, pension funds cover approximately 50 percent of the work force. Prior to the industrial revolution, pension plans in the United States were almost nonexistent, especially since America was a land of farmers and self-employed businessmen. With the advent of technology and big business, pensions became more common. The first private pension plan was begun in 1875 by the American Express Company, then a railroad company. The railroad industry was the pioneer in the field of pension benefits. By 1905, 35 percent (488,000) of all railroad workers were covered by a pension plan. Companies such as Carnegie Steel (now U.S. Steel) formulated their first plan in 1901; it is still in place today.

By 1929, there were some 397 penson plans, of which 77 percent were noncontributory (noncontributory plans are now eligible as a tax deduction). The typical plan had no vesting rights, and required the employees to be 65 years of age and have 20 years of continuous service. The benefits ranged from 1 to 2 percent of average salary multiplied by the years of service. Most of the plans (60 percent) were financed by trust funds. At this time, potential retirees were concerned that employers could cancel a plan at any time. The early plans were financially vulnerable, and most had been bankrupted by the Great Depression, while benefits under others were cut drastically. The railroads best exemplified the crisis. After laying off 800,000 workers, 25 percent of the remaining 1,000,000 were over age 65 and going into retirement. However, the railroads were one of the hardest hit industries and therefore there were no funds to pay the benefits. The Depression plunged the elderly into poverty and undermined confidence in private provisions for old age. This environment created public demand for institutionalized retirement savings, which was partially met by the enactment of the Railroad Retirement and Social Security Acts of 1935. Since Social Security benefits were initially quite small, heightened interest in private pension benefits as a supplement to Social Security was the natural outgrowth of the desire for guaranteed retirement income.

By clarifying the conditions under which corporations could deduct contributions to private plans from taxable income, the 1942 amendments to the IRS code made pensions an attractive investment for employers. These amendments were introduced at a time when employers faced strict control on the wages they could offer and were, therefore, eager to increase benefits to attract workers in the tight civilian labor force. The favorable tax accorded employer contributions not only encouraged the growth of private pension plans, but also influenced their structure. Allowing a deduction for employer contributions without treating these contributions as income to the employee has encouraged the growth of plans that are financed primarily by employers. The postwar years began an era of unprecedented growth in the pension industry. In the early 1950s, the auto, mine, and steel workers' unions secured pensions through collective bargaining. By 1962, 75 percent of all state and municipal workers were covered by pension plans and, by 1970, 3.6 million federal workers were covered by plans (excluding military personnel). Today, there are roughly 450,000 private pension plans, as well as 6,600 state and municipal plans, and 38 federal plans; these vary greatly in structure, financing, breadth of coverage and benefit provisions.

Pensions, like everything else today, have been subject to more than their fair share of regulations. Until 1943, there was only one, simple rule governing pensions: All contributions by the employer were tax-deductible, and all benefits resulting from employer contributions were taxable to the employee when the benefit was received. Following the Depression, it became apparent that some guidelines were needed. In 1942, a new tax code was passed, which set rules that pensions had to meet in order to qualify as tax-deductible. Specifically, they were:

1. The plan must be for the exclusive benefit of the employee;
2. Retirement income must be distributed to eligible employees;

3. The employer cannot withdraw funds without proving that all liabilities can be met; and

4. Plan coverage must be nondiscriminatory.

Although this covered many of the problems, many loopholes still remained. The code was amended in 1962 by the Termination-Vesting Provision. Until then, it was possible for an employer to set up a fund, pay benefits to key retired employees, and then terminate the plan. This amendment required all plans seeking tax-deductibility status to guarantee the right of the employee to contributions made prior to the plans' termination. Other laws also affected pensions and their operations. The Taft-Hartley Act (1948) guaranteed the rights of employees to bargain collectively for wages, compensation, and so forth. A court ruling in 1949 determined that pensions were included in the term "wages." On the other hand, unions were forbidden to be the sole administrator for a pension fund to which an employer contributes. The Welfare and Pension Plan Act of 1958 required all qualified plans to file statements of financial position and operations with the Secretary of Labor. This law was repealed and replaced with the Employee Retirement Income Security Act of 1974 (ERISA).

During the 1960s, numerous studies were conducted pertaining to pension plans. They called for standards regarding vesting, funding, plan termination, and fiduciary responsibility, and led to ERISA. The salient points under ERISA were that the rights of employees in pension plans must be vested by one of three ways:

1. Full vesting after 10 years;

2. Graduated vesting to be complete after 15 years; or

3. Rule of 45: if the employee had five years of service and the sum of his or her age and service years was 45, then he or she was 50 percent vested; five years later he or she would be fully vested.

An employee is said to be vested the day he or she gains the right to employee benefit credits in the pension system that are designed for future retirement income, even if he or she leaves the employer before retirement. Without vesting, retirement benefits may be lost if an employee is laid off prior to retirement. There are different types of vesting. In immediate full vesting, benefits are vested as soon as they are earned, whereas in deferred full vesting, an employee must meet certain age and service requirements before full vesting.

ERISA established the Pension Benefit Guarantee Corporation (PBGC), a self-financing government corporation within the Department of Labor. PBGC was formed to guarantee the payment of up to 85 percent of vested pension benefits in case of pension-fund bankruptcy, and to insure any funds seeking such coverage. The PBGC obtains most of its funds from insurance premiums charged to participating private plans. If a plan is terminated, the PBGC takes control of the funds' assets and uses them to pay as large a portion of the benefits as possible. The sponsoring company of a terminated plan may be held liable for unfunded benefits based on a formula established by Congress in the Single Employer Pension Plan Amendment Act. Firms are now liable for any deficiencies in funding, and fiduciaries can be held responsible if a fund has financial problems. Although ERISA was written to protect employees, in the three years that followed its passage, 30 percent of all pension funds (mostly small funds) terminated, since they could not meet the new funding standards. During the mid-1980s, the PBGC must insure all private defined benefit plans, so it may be affected by poor pension funds management. Also, companies with financial problems and unfunded liabilities in excess of a specific percentage of net worth can turn their obligation over to the PBGC. Two of the biggest such funds were that of Wheeling-Pittsburgh Steel Corporation, which filed for bankruptcy in 1985 and that of LTV which filed for bankruptcy in 1986.

After the market crash in October 1987, the PBGC's net worth was estimated at a negative $4 billion (that is, it was insolvent because of the financial difficulties of several large firms that sought to transfer to the PBGC their unfunded liabilities). Most pension experts believe that the federal government would not let the agency fail to meet its obligations to plans it had taken over. In the hope of increasing the assets of the PBGC, a law was passed in 1986 that more than tripled the required per-participant insurance premium that sponsors must pay. (See Table 11.4.)

The postwar emphasis on the use of fringe benefits in attracting good personnel and on tax factors favoring the receipt of funds in this form gave private pension funds a strong boost. Not only did the number of pension funds increase, but the trustees of these funds came under greater pressure to increase their rate of return. Sometimes funds shifted from lower-yielding bonds into better-paying bonds; others shifted from debt to equity positions, while public retirement funds, some of which had been investing only in municipal bonds or federal government obligations, became buyers of corporate bonds. In recent years, many pension funds have begun to invest more funds in tangible assets, while others have increased their investment in short-term money market instruments. Guaranteed investment contracts have also increased in popularity, with 1986 assets at a level of approximately $10 billion compared to a 1980 level of $5.1 billion.

Pension funds play an extremely important role in the capital markets of the United States. In a way, pension funds have an exposure similar to that of life insurance companies in that future payments to retirees can be forecast with relatively high accuracy. The unlikelihood of withdrawals of pension reserves permits pension funds to engage in a long-term investment program and purchase securities with a long average maturity. As a matter of fact, aggregate inflows into pension funds from the contributions of employers and employees are contractual in nature and are not difficult to predict. Also, pension fund outflows in the form of retirement benefits are highly predictable and can be anticipated in advance.

Table 11.4
The Financial Status of the PBGC (in Millions of Dollars)

Program Experience During 1985 and 1986

	1985	1986
Premium Income	82	201
Investment and Other Income	129	262
Benefits Paid	170	261
Number of Participants Receiving Benefits	74,800	90,750
Number of Underfunded Plans Terminated	77	103
Annual Addition to the Accumulated Program Deficit	863	2,501

Cumulative Program Experience, 1974-1986

Number of Underfunded Plans Terminated	1,345
Number of Participants Owed Current or Future Benefits	355,000
Assets	3,600
Liabilities	7,400
Accumulated Program Deficit	3,800

SOURCE: Congressional Budget Office using data from Pension Benefit Guaranty Corporation, *Annual Report*, 1986.

THE PROBLEMS OF OVERFUNDING AND UNDERFUNDING

An insurance company administers the pension fund under an insured plan, while a trust department of a bank or other trustee administers noninsured plans. A pension plan is fully funded when all past service credits have been financed and the earnings of the plan's investments are paying the costs of all current service credits. A fully funded pension plan has assets large enough to cover all claims of all participants should the plan be terminated. If a pension fund is overfunded, the value of its assets is larger than that of its estimated obligations, and the fund accumulates an excess of assets over liabilities. When a fund is underfunded, the pension fund has a negative net worth; that is, assets are less than the value of estimated obligations. The adequacy of contributions also depends upon actuarial assumptions.

Inflation is a problem facing many unfunded pension plans, since unfunded pension plan liabilities grow as workers demand higher wages and pension benefits to help them keep up with cost-of-living increases. Unfunded pension liabilities are often substantial in both private and public funds. Many states and local governments do not have sufficient taxing power to fund those liabilities, while some companies do not have the earning power to fund their pension plan obligations.

There are a number of solutions to the underfunding problem. They include mandatory insurance for vested pension rights and minimum funding standards. Before 1974, firms were not legally liable for the payment of unfunded vested pension benefits. ERISA established minimum funding standards for all private pension plans. The act requires full funding and sets maximum time limits in which to make up underfunding deficiencies. Private pension plans are required to purchase insurance protection for vested individual retirement benefits to a current limit of $1,687 per month from the PBGC. Arguments against this mandatory insurance requirement are that:

1. The insurance costs could reduce the amount of benefits that can be funded by a company;
2. Pension plans might be induced to invest in excessively risky assets; and
3. Costs could become excessive if companies promised benefits in excess of their capacity to finance them.

Pension-plan funding leads to the accumulation of assets dedicated to the payment of administrative expenses and plan benefits. Productive investment of these assets reduces the direct cost of a defined benefit plan and raises the benefits that can be paid under a defined contribution plan. For example, if the assets of a fully funded plan will earn a total rate of return of 6 percent, about 70 percent of the plan's benefits will be paid out of investment earnings. Only 30 percent will be met out of contributions to the plan.[4]

In 1982-1983, the biggest worry about corporate pension plans was unfunded liabilities; that is, companies did not have enough funds invested to cover their potential payouts to retirees. In 1984-1987, the problem was reversed, as many pension plans were overfunded. The reasons for this were:[5]

1. Recessionary layoffs left many companies with more accumulated pension money than needed;
2. High interest rates gave them a higher interest rate than expected; and

3. The rally in stock and bond prices during the latter half of 1982 through 1986 enriched many pension plans in excess of actual expectation.

Many companies have discovered that they now have more assets in pension funds than they need to pay off their anticipated obligations. This is both a bonanza and a risk. The potential bonanza is that a company can siphon off millions in excess pension assets for other corporate purposes by terminating their current pension programs and then setting up new, less generous plans. Companies can use surplus cash to finance mergers, expand operations, or simply improve the bottom line. Many firms with overfunded pension plans have reduced corporate contributions to pension funds. This has helped to improve overall corporate profitability. On the other hand, the risk is that the excess cash could invite a takeover by a greedy investor. Since 1981, more than 500 firms have terminated their pension plans, recapturing close to $5 billion. An additional 200 firms have notices of intent to terminate pending with the federal government's Pension Benefit Guarantee Corporation, with close to $2.8 billion in excess pension funding.[6] The Tax Reform Act of 1986 discourages termination, however, by imposing a 10 percent excise tax on recaptured excess pension fund assets.

RETIREMENT PLANS

The Self-Employed Individuals' Tax Retirement Act of 1962, commonly called the Keogh Act, permits self-employed individuals to establish for themselves voluntary retirement plans with certain benefits. Self-employed individuals may make tax deferrable contributions of up to $30,000 or 15 percent of earned income (whichever is less) into a qualified retirement plan. In addition, all workers may set aside a tax-deferrable contribution of $2,000 or 100 percent of an individual's compensation (whichever is less) to put into an individual retirement account (IRA). For individuals who are working and are married to nonworking spouses, the limit is increased to a maximum of $2,250 if spousal IRAs are maintained. If both husband and wife work, each may set up their own IRA. An IRA must be a domestic trust (or custodial account) created or organized by a written instrument for the exclusive benefit of an individual or his or her beneficiaries. The trustee (or custodian) must be a bank, savings and loan, insurance company, federally insured credit union, or other person who can demonstrate to the IRS the ability to properly administer the trust (or custodial account) in accordance with the law. Limitations and penalties exist for transferring and withdrawing funds prior to retirement. Under specified conditions an individual can make a tax-free rollover of assets from an IRA, annuity, or bond to another retirement account, annuity, or bond.

The initial marketing battle for IRA accounts has been fierce, as whoever captures the funds initially has a good chance of keeping them until the individual retires. They have substantial future self-generating benefits to those institutions that acquire them initially, as there is a tendency toward institutional loyalty and simplified bookkeeping. Depository institutions have offered short- and intermediate-term investments with both fixed and variable rates, while non-depository institutions have offered money market funds, zero-coupon bonds, ordinary corporate bonds, stocks, real estate investments, and a variety of money market instruments. Insurance companies have offered guaranteed yields on long-term contracts which are a bit below rates available by direct investment in the money and capital markets or in some depository institutions, but will guarantee their rates for a longer period of time than banks.

At the end of 1987, commercial banks and thrifts were the largest factors in the IRA market, each with $77 billion in deposits (23.1 percent), while mutual funds managed $72.2 billion (21.6 percent), life insurance companies held $26.0 billion (7.8 percent), credit unions held $22.6 billion (6.8 percent), and brokerage firms held $58.9 billion (17.6 percent) in self-directed accounts. (See Tables 11.5 and 11.6.)

Table 11.5
Estimated Value of IRA Plans (Value in Billions of Dollars/Percent Market Share)

	12/83		12/85		12/87	
Commercial Banks	$26.5	29.0%	$51.5	25.8%	$77.0	23.1%
Thrifts	31.7	34.7	56.4	28.2	77.1	23.1
Life Insurance Companies	9.0	9.9	16.9	8.5	26.0	7.8
Credit Unions	5.0	5.5	13.9	7.0	22.6	6.8
Mutual Funds	10.7	11.7	31.6	15.8	72.2	21.6
Self Directed	8.4	9.2	29.4	14.7	58.9	17.6
Total IRA Dollar Value	**$91.3**		**$199.7**		**$333.8**	

Source: 1988 Mutual Fund Fact Book, p. 40.

Since the beginning of 1982, the flow of savings into IRAs has been huge. This flow reflects the easing of rules governing IRAs, which expanded the number of eligible participants from about 63 million to 111 million people and increased the maximum contributions per worker. By year-end 1987, the total value of IRA accounts had exceeded $333 billion. this compares favorably to year-end 1981, when total IRA assets amounted to $26.1 billion. In addition to Keogh (HF10) Plans and IRAs, which are tax-deferred annuities, there are tax-sheltered annuities available to employees of academic and nonprofit organizations.

Table 11.6
Age at Which You Establish Your IRA

	50	45	40	35	30
If you contribute yearly:	$ 2,000	$ 2,000	$ 2,000	$ 2,000	$ 2,000
At age 65 you will have contributed:	32,000	42,000	52,000	62,000	72,000
Interest on your Contributions:	42,831	88,858	165,950	293,000	497,926
Your total retirement fund at age 65 (which you may choose to take in a lump sum):	74,831	130,558	217,950	355,000	569,926
Your annual retirement income at age 65 (if you choose payments over a ten-year period):	10,853	17,935	31,609	51,486	82,656
Total payments over ten years:	$108,530	189,350	316,090	514,860	826,560

NOTE: All figures are computed on the basis of a time deposit annual interest rate of 9.00% compounded daily to yield 9.416% annually, and are rounded to the nearest dollar. Contributions are assumed to be make at the beginning of the year, including the year in which the depositor attains age 65. Payment is assumed to start at the end of the year in which the depositor attains age 65.

401(K) Plans

At the end of 1984, approximately 14 million workers were involved in 401(K) plans. (See Table 11.7.) The attraction of these plans comes largely from their tax breaks and the way some employers are "sweetening the pot" to induce participation. Under 401(K), part of an individual's income is set aside in a special account such as a portfolio of stocks or bonds, money market instruments, or savings through a guaranteed-income fund that promises a fixed return each year. The amount that is set aside each year in the plan is not included when computing the wages subject to federal income tax. As far as the IRS is concerned, the individual has reduced his or her pay by the amount of the deposit. Also, there is no yearly tax on investment earnings that accumulate, and taxes are not due until the funds are withdrawn. In a way, these plans are similar to IRA plans. However, they have added benefits. In an IRA plan, a worker can

Table 11.7
Comparison With and Without 401(K) Plan

How a worker who saves 10 percent of a $40,00-a-year salary would fare with a
401(K) plan and without one.-

	With 401(K) Plan	Without 401(K) Plan
Base Pay	$40,000	$40,000
Savings Set Aside Before Taxes	4,000	None
Taxable Pay	$36,000	$40,000
U.S. Income and Social Security Taxes	$ 8,159	$ 9,279
Savings Set Aside after taxes	None	$ 4,000
Take-home pay	$27,841	$26,721

Extra take-home pay under 401(k) $1,120

Larger Retirement Savings	Total After 10 Years	
	Inside Plan	Outside Plan
$4,000 a year invested in an 11% C D compounded daily	$77,708	$64,361

Extra Amount under tax-sheltered plan $13,347

Funds in a tax-sheltered retirement plan become taxable when withdrawn.

save up to $2,000 a year ($2,250 if a nonworking spouse is covered). On the
other hand, a 401(K) plan allows a maximum yearly investment of $7,000 per
year, but no more than up to 25 percent of the "reduced salary." (See Table
11.8.) It is also possible to withdraw funds from this plan under "liberal
hardship" conditions without penalty, and to qualify for ten-year averaging if
the balance is paid out in a lump sum.[7]

Table 11.8
Comparison of 401(K) versus IRA

Comparison	401(K)	vs.	IRA
Investment of Pretax Funds	Yes		Yes
Employer Matching Contribution	Yes		No
Tax-Deferred Compounding	Yes		Yes
Maximum Yearly Contribution			
(including employer contribution)	$7,000		$2,250
Withdrawal before age 59 1/2	For hardship		Only with 10% penalty
Borrowing Priviledges	Yes		No
Eligible for 10-year averaging	Yes		No

While the 1986 Tax Reform Act lowered the maximum annual contribution to $7,000 from $30,000, it also contained a cost of living provision, so that the maximum contribution would increase each year to keep pace with inflation. For 1988, the first year the provision was in effect, the limit rose to $7,313.

FUTURE GROWTH

Pension funds have grown rapidly in the last two decades, and have changed from a relatively small force in the financial services industry prior to World War II to one of the dominant factors in the capital markets, particularly the equity market. However, this rapid growth is not expected to continue because of demographic factors. There is expected to be a significant increase in the ratio of beneficiaries to contributors with few workers relative to retired persons. Also, since pension plans are quite expensive to employers and since profit pressures abound throughout the economy, employers have begun to resist increases in pension benefits. One of the biggest threats facing private pension plans is increased Social Security taxes. Since these taxes are mandatory, many businesses and individuals will not be able to afford both a government-operated retirement system and a private plan. Another negative factor is the rapidly increasing cost of government regulation, which has imposed costly reporting requirements on pension plans. Consequently, some of the smaller private pension plans will cease to exist or will not grow beyond their present size in terms of contributions.

After years of phenomenal growth, the $1.2 trillion pension fund industry growth rate has declined dramatically. Plan sponsors have been withdrawing surplus assets and the pendulum has shifted in favor of sponsors rather than beneficiaries. The number of defined benefit plans has also dropped. The tax-free status of certain aspects of pension funds has also come under the scrutiny of individuals eager to decrease the federal budget deficit through cutting untapped revenues.

Since pension plans have been established by most large employers, the future expansion of private pension coverage will depend largely on the extent to which programs are started by smaller employers, future salary increases of those already covered by plans, and investment performance. Since small employers must compete with the large firms for qualified employees, it may be increasingly necessary for small firms to provide pension benefits despite the expense.

NOTES

1. Roger F. Murray, "Pension and Profit Sharing Plans," in *Financial Handbook*, 5th edition, ed. E. I. Altman (New York: John Wiley & Sons, 1981), 34.13.

2. A. H. Munnell, *The Economics of Private Pensions* (Washington, D.C.: Brookings Institution, 1982).

3. B. Gup, *Financial Intermediaries* (Boston, Mass.: Houghton Mifflin Company, 1980): 334-335.

4. Dan McGill, *Fundamentals of Private Pensions,* 5th edition (Homewood, Illinois: R. D. Irwin, 1984).

5. J. Pelham, "Pension Plans: Problems of Plenty," *Dun's Business Monthly* (January 1984): 39.

6. W. English, "As Corporate Raids on Pensions Pick Up Steam," *U.S. News and World Report,* July 29, 1985, 65.

7. L. Wiener, "For Both Young and Old, A New Retirement Plan," *U.S. News and World Report*, August 5, 1985, 57-58.

12

Finance Companies

HISTORICAL OVERVIEW

During the colonial period, the first extensive use of credit in the United States was to support farmers who could not pay off their debts until their crops were harvested and sold. Merchants also sold goods on credit in the form of payments made over time. During the 1700s and the early part of the 1800s, the principal nonbank agencies that extended credit were merchants, doctors, and pawnbrokers.

The industrial revolution brought about changes in credit demands and institutions: it made more goods available to consumers and created a class of wage earners. The credit needs of these industrial workers differed from those of farmers. Organized cash lending to consumers in the United States probably began in cities of the Middle West, following the end of the Civil War.

The concept of installment credit evolved as workers demanded credit to raise their standard of living. The sale of durable goods on installment goes back to the early years of the nineteenth century, when furniture was sold by some cabinet makers on that basis. In the latter part of that century, sewing machines, pianos, and sets of books were also frequently sold on installment plans. Small loan companies were formed to satisfy these credit needs. These loan companies primarily made personal loans secured by personal property and wage assignments. Loan sharks, in turn, charged exorbitant rates, lending money to those who could not obtain credit from the small loan companies or other sources.

After World War I, sales finance companies, commercial banks, and department stores entered the consumer credit field. The big growth of sales financing came with the development of the automobile industry. However, commercial banks did not engage in sales financing on a large scale until the 1940s. The basic philosophy under which commercial banks were operating held that they should restrict themselves to short-term business loans that were self-liquidating.

In 1951, the now-defunct Franklin National Bank of New York issued the first credit card. This was the forerunner of Visa, Mastercard, and a plethora of credit cards issued by oil companies, retail stores, and banks. The availability of consumer durables for the home and automobiles dramatically expanded the demand for consumer credit. Sales finance companies, which buy consumer installment contracts from retail dealers, expanded from this demand. They provide these dealers with an alternative to bank financing. In addition to standard accounts-receivable financing or factoring, the finance company may offer private-label credit-card financing to a merchant.

Consumer finance companies came into prominence with the adoption of the so-called small loan law by most states. This law was sponsored by the Russell Sage Foundation in an effort to combat the loan-shark evil, under which rates of 1,000 percent a year often prevailed. Financial institutions which grant consumer credit engage chiefly in making personal loans and loans for the purchase of durable goods. Most of the loans are on an installment basis, calling for regular payments related to principal and interest. The purposes for which these loans are made include education, vacations, debt consolidation, recreation vehicles, appliances, and cars. Consumer credit, like real estate credit, increased dramatically after World War II.

Initially, the growth in noninstallment loans—distributed equally among single payment loans, charge accounts, and service credit—was less rapid than in installment credit, but the growth and cost of automobiles and the popularity of bank charge cards shifted the borrowing pattern. The share of installment credit supplied by commercial banks has risen rapidly. Only credit unions have grown more quickly since 1950; however, their share of consumer credit is considerably smaller than that of other depository institutions or finance companies.

Until well into the 1960s, finance companies were generally highly specialized and could be distinguished as consumer finance companies, sales finance companies, or commercial finance companies. By the late 1970s, most large- and medium-sized finance companies had become more diversified germane to lending and sources of funds.

Federal Reserve economists define a finance company as

any company (. . . excluding banks, credit unions, savings and loan associations . . . and mutual savings banks) the largest of whose assets is in one or more of the following kinds of responsibilities[:] . . . sales, finance receivables, personal cash loans to individuals and families, short- and intermediate-term business credit, [and] junior liens on real estate.[1]

Two things characterize firms that are traditionally considered finance companies: (1) their lending practices are regulated almost entirely at the state level, and (2) their fund sources are not deposits.

TYPES OF FINANCE COMPANIES

Finance companies lend to businesses and consumers for a wide variety of purposes, including the purchase of inventories, automobiles, business equipment, vacation, mobile homes, home repairs, home appliances, and accounts receivable financing. Finance companies can be catgegorized as mortgage, consumer loan (called industrial or Morris Plan banks in some states), commercial finance, and sales finance companies, or they can be classified according to ownership. Captive finance companies are usually owned by a parent firm and usually finance the products or services of the parent, or both. They were established to support company sales and to guarantee the availability of credit during periods of credit restraint. Examples of captive finance companies are John Deere Credit, Sears Roebuck Acceptance Corporation, Ford Motor Credit, and General Motors Acceptance Corporation (GMAC). Auto and truck companies place large quantities of their loans with GMAC, which is profitable in its own right. It supports dealer operations and is convenient for customers. Wholly owned finance companies generally finance the products or services (or both) of firms other than their parent, while independent finance companies such as Beneficial and Household Finance finance activities on a completely autonomous basis. Some captives have discovered that single-line financing is less profitable than diversified financing, so they have provided wholesale financing for a wide range of companies as well as retail financing for consumers.

Consumer Finance Companies

When the cost of funds increased between 1980 and 1982, finance companies such as Household International, Beneficial, and Avco Financial were forced to pare the number of their money-lending shops as their profit spreads narrowed. The fundamental problem of the consumer finance companies had been both the competition from the banks and credit unions and a narrowing profit spread, as the cost of funds pressed up toward state usury ceilings. To counter profit-sensitivity to changes in short-term borrowing costs, some finance companies began offering variable-rate loans to consumers and businesses. Some finance companies have advanced against second mortgages. Mortgage lending offers collateral, high yields, and large-sized loans which reduce dollars of overhead per dollar lent out.

Since the major purpose of cash loans made by finance companies is to tide consumers over during a period of financial emergency, finance company rates tend to be higher than bank rates. With the passage of the Truth in Lending Act in 1986, rate quotations were required to provide the borrower with the actual percentage rate on the loan. At most finance companies, average finance rates on personal loans have remained above bank rates (except when captive finance companies were offering discounts on loans to induce purchase of company

durable goods). At the same time, the maturity and average amount of such loans
have been increasing since the mid-1970s.

Nationwide or regional branch networks are what have made consumer
finance companies attractive to bank holding companies. Bank holding
companies have been active buyers of finance companies over the last ten years,
partially with an eye toward the eventual passage of nationwide branch banking
and in part as a geographic and economic diversification consideration (see
Table 12.1). At the end of 1987, over one-fourth of the nation's 100 biggest
finance companies were owned by bank and thrift holding companies. The simple
placement of a drive-in window and teller cages would permit the acceptance of
deposits and facilities to carry on every phase of retail banking.

Table 12.1
**Top Ten Domestic Commercial Bank-related Finance Companies in the
United States by Size of Capital Funds December 31, 1985
or Nearest Fiscal Year-End**

		Total Capital Funds ($ Millions)
1.	General Motors Acceptance Corp., Detroit, MI........	$ 6,562.9
2.	Ford Motor Credit Co., Dearborn, MI.................	3,269.9
3.	Chrysler Financial Corp., Troy, MI..................	2,790.5
4.	General Electric Credit Corp., Stamford, CT.........	2,252.7
5.	Sears Roebuck Acceptance Corp., Wilmington, DE......	2,199.5
6.	C.I.T. Financial Corp., Livingston, NJ..............	1,591.9
7.	Associates Corp. of North America, Dallas, TX.......	1,372.5
8.	Household Financial Services, Prospect Heights, IL..	1,371.2
9.	ITT Financial Corp., St. Louis, MO..................	1,277.3
10.	Avco Financial Services, Inc., Newport Beach, CA....	1,166.7

Unlike durable goods loans, for which the borrower pledges a car or an
appliance, personal signature loans are usually not secured by collateral. Rates
vary from a low of close to two percent on subsidized loans from auto companies
with excess inventories, to 36 percent on small, unsecured signature loans.
Much of the credit extended by the consumer finance companies is to households
that are unable to obtain credit elsewhere. These loans often have high origination costs as well as a high risk of default. Because a large proportion of the
clientele are low-income and less-educated individuals, these finance companies
are regulated by the states with respect to the size of loans and the level of
interest rates that they may charge, as well as the terms and conditions of
collection. The maximum permissible interest rates are usually considerably
higher than the rates charged by banks. However, most consumers seem more
concerned with the level of monthly payments than with the interest rate on the
loan. As a matter of fact, rising auto prices have led to an extension of the auto

installment loans from two to four or five years in order to keep monthly payments at acceptable levels for consumers.

There are less than 1,800 independent consumer finance companies which operate just under 25,000 offices throughout the United States. These offices range from national firms such as Household Finance with over 2,500 offices, to tiny, one-office firms. The finance company industry consists of many relatively small firms and a few extremely large ones. In mid-1985, about 74 percent of the industry had under $5 million in total loans outstanding, while fewer than 5 percent of the finance companies had assets in excess of $500 million. However, firms in the latter category controlled 88 percent of finance company assets.

Industrial or Morris-Plan Banks

Another type of institution in the consumer installment loan industry is the industrial bank. The first industrial banking company was established in the United States in 1901 when David Stein, a Latvian immigrant, founded the Merchants and Mechanics Savings and Loan Association at Newport News, Virginia. This bank was patterned after the consumer banks and savings associations that had been developed in Europe to make loans to workers. Arthur J. Morris set up the Fidelity Savings and Trust Company at Norfolk, Virginia. This bank proposed to lend money to people employed in industry; this is the reason for the term "industrial" bank or loan company. In 1911, Mr. Morris copyrighted the name "Morris Plan" and began to promote such units in cities throughout the United States. He had set up over 70 companies by 1917. Today, industrial banking firms continue to emphasize consumer installment loans, real-estate second-mortgage loans, and loans for home repair and modernization, as well as the purchase of retail installment contracts.

Factoring

In the soft goods industry, a great deal of financing is often accomplished by factoring, whereby the factor actually purchases the receivables and assumes the effort and collection. Factoring can be characterized by the outright sale of accounts receivable, credit services, notification, and nonrecourse other than merchandise disputes. A factor might charge 1 percent of sales for credit checking, setting of credit lines, collections, and ledgering of accounts. When a company borrows from a factor, the company pays at least 2 to 3 points over the prime rate. Factoring differs from secured lending in that the accounts receivable secures the loan, but there is no credit servicing or notification. However, there is recourse, should there be a default.

In the case of default, the dealer must repay a contract purchased on a full-recourse basis. On nonrecourse loan payments, the finance company assumes all cash and collection costs. In the case of a repurchase agreement, the merchandise is repossessed by the dealer and sold for the unpaid balance. Most of the loan losses suffered by finance companies have been a result of fraud.

Commercial Finance Companies

Finance companies constitute another important source of funds for business corporations. Commercial finance companies are primarily asset-based lenders. They acquire funds from capital suppliers by selling common stock, notes, and bonds, as well as commercial paper. Much of the lending is for the purpose of financing inventories such as cars, equipment, and accounts receivable.

The type of credit extended by a finance company closely resembles commercial bank lending except for one major exception. They make relatively high-risk, high-yielding loans to business. The spreads on these loans are much lower today than they were a decade ago because of greater competition as well as higher rate levels in general.

Sales Finance Companies

Sales finance companies finance the sale of consumer goods, chiefly automobiles and appliances, on the installment plan. Lending is of two types, wholesale and retail. Wholesale financing consists of advancing funds to dealers, usually on the dealer's promissory note. The notes are usually secured by warehouse or trust receipts covering, for example, the cars that are being financed. In addition to holding the promissory note of the buyer, the finance company is protected by documents allowing the article purchased, such as a car, to be attached in case of default in payment, as well as by insurance companies covering fire, theft, and accident. Sales finance companies are major supporters of retailers with floor-plan loans.

Additionally, retailers write loans at the point of sale, but the down payment, charges, terms, and maturity are specified by the sales finance company. The finance company buys the loan from the retailer on three bases: (1) Full recourse; (2) Nonrecourse; or (3) Repurchase.

Large business-finance companies have entered the rapidly growing leasing field. The finance company purchases the equipment upon agreement with a customer, and leases it to the customer at a prearranged rental fee for a prearranged number of years. These arrangements are most popular in the railroad and airline industries.

SOURCE OF FUNDS

Finance companies are usually heavy users of debt in financing their operations. Equity capital, surplus, and undivided profits represent about 12 percent of the total sources of funds. Most finance companies operate with a leveraged capital structure, including several classes of senior and subordinated debt. They often employ large amounts of short- and intermediate-term debt. It is not uncommon for more than half of the borrowed funds to be in the form of short-term funds. To support most of their lending activities, finance companies are major issuers of commercial paper, often fully or partially backed by commercial-bank lines of credit. A rather large amount of the total commercial paper outstanding is issued by finance companies. As a matter of fact, close to one-third of the funds of finance companies are raised through commercial paper. In 1985, only 78 finance companies accounted for 93 percent of the industry's commercial paper. Since only large, nationally known firms raise money in the commercial paper market, commercial paper is usually inaccessible to the small firms that make up most of the industry. These small finance companies tend to rely heavily on commercial bank financing.

At times, certain finance companies may experience difficulty or extremely high costs in obtaining funds. Those finance companies that have not properly matched the maturities and the fixed-rate versus floating-rate portions of their receivables with their debt liabilities can face severe earnings problems when upward pressures on interest rates emanate from the money and capital markets. Profits were squeezed or losses occurred for many firms during 1974-1975 and at the beginning of the 1980s. Those companies that held primarily fixed-rate receivables and short-term variable-rate liabilities suffered most during the aforementioned periods.

Large finance companies have more access to the bond markets than do small firms, so large firms rely more on long-term borrowings. Also, large finance companies are more heavily involved in leasing and mortgage lending, activities contributing to longer asset portfolio maturities. Longer-term funds are more attractive to large firms than to small finance companies whose assets are usually concentrated in short-term consumer loans. Since small finance companies have limited access to the debt markets, small finance companies rely on equity for close to half of their financing. (See Table 12.2.)

TYPE OF CREDIT

The Federal Reserve defines consumer credit as loans to individuals for households, family, and personal expenditures (sans mortgage housing loans). It further classifies consumer credit as installment or noninstallment credit. Noninstallment credit is defined as consumer credit that is to be repaid in one payment. It includes service credit, single payment loans, and nonrevolving credit. Installment credit consists of all consumer credit that is to be repaid in more than one payment. In April 1987, there was $582 billion in consumer installment credit outstanding, compared to just over $100 billion in noninstallment credit.

The five major types of installment credit are auto, mobile home, home improvement, revolving credit, and a nebulous category called "other," that includes boat and airplane loans. The major institutions holding consumer credit are commercial banks, finance companies, credit unions, retailers, savings and loan associations, gasoline companies, and savings banks (see Table 12.3).

Table 12.2
Percentage Distributions of Total Liabilities, Capital, and Surplus at Sample Companies

	1977	1978	1979	1980	1981	1982	1983	1984	1985	1986
Bank Loans	4.1%	4.0%	5.1%	2.9%	5.5%	4.7%	3.7%	2.5%	2.8%	2.5%
Commercial Paper	29.2%	28.3%	30.0%	29.9%	30.9%	26.1%	27.2%	32.0%	35.6%	37.4%
Other Short-term Debt	5.9%	6.0%	6.3%	7.0%	8.1%	6.3%	6.6%	3.2%	3.3%	1.8%
Deposit Liabilities & Thrift Certificates	0.7%	0.6%	0.9%	1.0%	1.0%	1.3%	1.9%	1.9%	1.3%	1.0%
Long-term Indebtedness	29.3%	28.8%	27.6%	31.9%	27.2%	33.2%	31.8%	32.6%	31.2%	34.8%
Subordinated Debentures	6.8%	6.3%	6.1%	6.0%	5.4%	5.2%	4.4%	4.0%	3.4%	3.0%
All Other Liabilities	12.4%	14.4%	12.3%	9.3%	10.6%	11.0%	14.1%	13.7%	13.0%	10.6%
SUBTOTAL - Liabilities	88.3%	88.4%	88.4%	87.9%	88.8%	87.8%	89.7%	89.9%	90.7%	91.0%
Capital, Surplus, & Undivided Profits	11.7%	11.6%	11.6%	12.1%	11.2%	12.2%	10.3%	10.1%	9.3%	9.0%
TOTAL LIABILITIES & CAPITAL	100.0%	100.0%	100.0%	100.0%	100.0%	100.0%	100.0%	100.0%	100.0%	100.0%

Source: Finance Companies 1977-1986, *American Financial Services Association Research Report and Second Mortgage Lending Report,* p. 28.

Table 12.3

Consumer Installment Credit[1]   Total Outstanding, and Net Change, Seasonally Adjusted (Millions of Dollars)

Holder, and type of credit	1986	1987'	1987								1988
			May	June	July	Aug.	Sept.	Oct.	Nov.	Dec.'	Jan.
Amounts outstanding (end of period)											
1 Total	577,784	612,101	583,276	587,821	591,175	596,182	602,607	605,488	608,122	612,101	617,522
By major holder											
2 Commercial banks	261,604	274,966	263,463	264,396	265,085	265,893	269,155	270,836	272,274	274,966	277,846
3 Finance companies[2]	136,494	143,788	136,398	138,038	138,745	140,689	142,648	143,118	142,767	143,788	144,228
4 Credit unions	77,857	84,387	79,476	80,585	81,492	82,486	83,340	83,639	84,419	84,387	84,867
5 Retailers[3]	40,586	40,647	40,318	40,287	40,364	40,391	40,482	40,678	40,559	40,647	41,009
6 Savings institutions	58,037	64,788	60,045	60,983	61,910	63,080	63,279	63,525	64,502	64,788	65,982
7 Gasoline companies	3,205	3,525	3,576	3,532	3,580	3,643	3,703	3,691	3,600	3,525	3,590
By major type of credit											
8 Automobile	245,055	261,448	247,578	250,130	250,980	254,013	257,470	258,710	259,134	261,448	262,993
9 Commercial banks	100,709	106,508	102,189	102,810	102,829	103,382	104,662	105,382	106,036	106,508	107,692
10 Credit unions	39,029	42,302	39,841	40,396	40,851	41,349	41,777	41,927	42,318	42,302	42,543
11 Finance companies	93,274	99,195	93,089	94,270	94,455	96,193	97,900	98,219	97,395	99,195	99,066
12 Savings institutions	12,043	13,444	12,459	12,654	12,846	13,089	13,130	13,182	13,384	13,444	13,692
13 Revolving	134,938	145,925	136,869	137,401	138,741	139,837	141,704	143,142	143,620	145,925	147,926
14 Commercial banks	85,652	95,270	87,133	87,590	88,685	89,535	91,226	92,459	92,992	95,270	96,702
15 Retailers	36,240	36,213	36,009	35,971	36,021	36,022	36,087	36,264	36,148	36,213	36,547
16 Gasoline companies	3,205	3,525	3,576	3,532	3,580	3,643	3,703	3,691	3,600	3,525	3,590
17 Savings institutions	7,713	8,610	7,980	8,105	8,228	8,383	8,410	8,443	8,572	8,610	8,768
18 Credit unions	2,128	2,306	2,172	2,202	2,227	2,254	2,278	2,286	2,307	2,306	2,319
19 Mobile home	25,710	25,608	25,542	25,685	25,860	25,695	25,699	25,677	25,731	25,608	25,750
20 Commercial banks	8,812	8,353	8,615	8,609	8,626	8,518	8,538	8,453	8,407	8,353	8,282
21 Finance companies	9,028	8,470	8,785	8,807	8,839	8,623	8,580	8,610	8,578	8,470	8,521
22 Savings institutions	7,870	8,785	8,142	8,269	8,395	8,554	8,581	8,614	8,746	8,785	8,947
23 Other	172,081	179,120	173,287	174,605	175,594	176,637	177,733	177,959	179,637	179,120	180,853
24 Commercial banks	66,431	64,835	65,527	65,387	64,945	64,458	64,728	64,542	64,840	64,835	65,170
25 Finance companies	34,192	36,123	34,524	34,962	35,452	35,874	36,168	36,289	36,794	36,123	36,641
26 Credit unions	36,700	39,778	37,463	37,986	38,413	38,882	39,285	39,426	39,794	39,778	40,005
27 Retailers	4,346	4,433	4,310	4,315	4,343	4,369	4,395	4,415	4,411	4,433	4,462
28 Savings institutions	30,412	33,949	31,463	31,955	32,441	33,054	33,158	33,287	33,799	33,949	34,575
Net change (during period)											
29 Total	54,979	34,317	-319	4,545	3,354	5,007	6,425	2,881	2,634	3,979	5,421
By major holder											
30 Commercial banks	19,520	13,362	30	933	689	808	3,262	1,681	1,438	2,692	2,880
31 Finance companies[2]	23,424	7,294	-693	1,640	707	1,944	1,959	470	-351	1,021	440
32 Credit unions	5,738	6,530	221	1,109	907	994	854	299	780	-32	480
33 Retailers	1,722	61	-149	-31	77	27	91	196	-119	88	362
34 Savings institutions	5,604	6,751	219	938	927	1,170	199	246	977	286	1,194
35 Gasoline companies	-1,030	320	54	-44	48	63	60	-12	-91	-75	65
By major type of credit											
36 Automobile	36,998	16,393	-85	2,552	850	3,033	3,457	1,240	424	2,314	1,545
37 Commercial banks	7,706	5,799	408	621	19	553	1,280	720	654	472	1,184
38 Credit unions	3,394	3,273	111	555	455	498	428	150	391	-16	241
39 Finance companies	23,183	5,921	-649	1,181	185	1,738	1,707	319	-824	1,800	-129
40 Savings institutions	2,715	1,401	45	195	192	243	41	52	202	60	248
41 Revolving	12,917	10,987	163	532	1,340	1,096	1,867	1,438	478	2,305	2,001
42 Commercial banks	9,786	9,618	204	457	1,095	850	1,691	1,233	533	2,278	1,432
43 Retailers	1,545	-27	-130	-38	50	1	65	177	-116	65	334
44 Gasoline companies	-1,030	320	54	-44	48	63	60	-12	-91	-75	65
45 Savings institutions	2,008	897	29	125	123	155	27	33	129	38	158
46 Credit unions	608	178	6	30	25	27	24	8	21	-1	13
47 Mobile home	222	-102	-84	143	175	-165	4	-22	54	-123	142
48 Commercial banks	-726	-459	-83	-6	17	-108	20	-85	-46	-54	-71
49 Finance companies	-363	-558	-31	22	32	-216	-43	30	-32	-108	51
50 Savings institutions	1,311	915	30	127	126	159	27	33	132	39	162
51 Other	4,842	7,039	-313	1,318	989	1,043	1,096	226	1,678	-517	1,733
52 Commercial banks	2,754	-1,596	-499	-140	-442	-487	270	-186	298	-5	335
53 Finance companies	604	1,931	-13	438	490	422	294	121	505	-671	518
54 Credit unions	1,736	3,078	104	523	427	469	403	141	368	-16	227
55 Retailers	177	87	-18	5	28	26	26	20	-4	22	29
56 Savings institutions	-429	3,537	114	492	486	613	104	129	512	150	626

1. The Board's series cover most short- and intermediate-term credit extended to individuals that is scheduled to be repaid (or has the option of repayment) in two or more installments.
2. More detail for finance companies is available in the G.20 statistical release.
3. Excludes 30-day charge credit held by travel and entertainment companies.

Source: Federal Reserve Bulletin, May 1988, A40.

Business versus Consumer Loans

At the end of 1987, close to 52 percent of finance companies' lending was with business, while 38 percent was made up of consumer loans and 10 percent of real estate loans (see Table 12.4). Of the credit supplied to business, just over 28 percent was used to finance retail purchases, just under 28 percent was used to finance dealer inventories, just over 20 percent was in the form of leasing, and other important loan categories were for commercial accounts receivable, factoring, and other business borrowers. Commercial loans made by finance companies are usually asset-based. These secured assets of the borrower may be plant, equipment, inventory, or accounts receivable. Accounts receivable financing is often used by apparel, textile, electronics, metals, and food-processing companies.

Finance companies have traditionally held large amounts of consumer credit. However, their business receivables have grown substantially and now exceed their consumer loans. One reason for the shift toward business credit is that finance company consumer lending operations have become heavily regulated, while business lending has not. Another reason is that with the below market rates offered by captive automobile finance companies, margins on these loans have declined substantially. A third reason is that finance companies began to lend more heavily in real estate, leveraged buyouts, and leasing.

NEW DIRECTIONS IN ASSET MANAGEMENT

Finance companies have expanded the scope and direction of their operations during the 1980s. One of the fastest growing areas of finance-company lending has been the leveraged buyout. An example of the leveraged buyout is a deal in which entrepreneurs become owners by putting up very little money. Nearly 100 percent of the company's purchase price is borrowed. Operating earnings pay off debt; the collateral is the company itself. Essentially, when an acquisition is sought and financial resources are restricted, a lender such as GECC might structure a tailored leveraged buyout that uses the collateral of the company being purchased to generate the necessary funding amount.[2]

In addition to expanding their activities in the primary residential market, finance companies began to participate in the secondary mortgage markets by selling the mortgages that they originated. As a matter of fact, GMAC purchased the mortgage lending and servicing units as well as the mortgage banking units of a large regional bank. An additional development in secondary market activities for finance companies has been the securitization of automobile loans.

Finance companies are also issuing credit cards to consumers. Lending via credit card is a cheaper alternative than operating bricks-and-mortar branch networks. Also, credit-card issuers have found that the loss rate on credit card loans is less than that on personal cash loans, because borrowers do not want to lose the convenience and prestige associated with a credit card. Finance companies have also begun to participate with commercial banks in asset-based lending. In

Table 12.4
Domestic Finance Companies: Assets and Liabilities
(Billions of Dollars, End of Period)

Account	1983	1984	1985	1986 Q2	1986 Q3	1986 Q4	1987 Q1	1987 Q2	1987 Q3	1987 Q4
Assets										
1 Consumer	83.3	89.9	113.4	125.1	137.1	136.5	133.9	138.0	144.4	143.8
2 Business	113.4	137.8	158.3	167.7	161.0	174.8	182.8	189.0	188.7	202.6
3 Real estate	20.5	23.8	28.9	30.8	32.1	33.7	35.1	36.9	38.3	40.3
4 Total	217.3	251.5	300.6	323.6	330.2	345.0	351.8	363.9	371.5	386.8
Less:										
5 Reserves for unearned income	30.3	33.8	39.2	40.7	42.4	41.4	40.4	41.2	42.8	45.3
6 Reserves for losses	3.7	4.2	4.9	5.1	5.4	5.8	5.9	6.2	6.6	6.8
7 Accounts receivable, net	183.2	213.5	256.5	277.8	282.4	297.8	305.5	316.5	322.1	334.7
8 All other	34.4	35.7	45.3	48.8	59.9	57.9	59.0	57.7	65.0	58.2
9 Total assets	217.6	249.2	301.9	326.6	342.3	355.6	364.5	374.2	387.1	392.9
Liabilities										
10 Bank loans	18.3	20.0	20.6	19.2	20.2	22.2	17.3	17.2	16.2	16.5
11 Commercial paper	60.5	73.1	99.2	108.4	112.8	117.8	119.1	120.4	123.5	126.5
Debt										
12 Other short-term	11.1	12.9	12.5	15.4	16.0	17.2	21.6	24.4	26.9	27.0
13 Long-term	67.7	77.2	93.1	105.2	109.8	115.6	118.4	121.5	128.0	130.1
14 All other liabilities	31.2	34.5	40.9	40.1	44.1	43.4	46.3	48.3	48.7	50.1
15 Capital, surplus, and undivided profits	28.9	31.5	35.7	38.4	39.4	39.4	41.8	42.3	43.8	42.6
16 Total liabilities and capital	217.6	249.2	301.9	326.6	342.3	355.6	364.5	374.2	387.1	392.9

NOTE. Components may not add to totals because of rounding.

Source: Federal Reserve Bulletin, December 1987, A37.

most cases, the asset-based loan has been generated by the finance company and a participation in the loan has been sold to a bank in exchange for cash. The finance company originating the loan would usually monitor the receivables and inventory of firms to whom credit has been extended; that is, the finance companies remained active in tracking the performance of the assets pledged as collateral.[3]

PROFITABILITY OF FINANCE COMPANIES

Finance companies tend to hold relatively low levels of cash and securities. This is because liquidity planning for finance companies is easier than it is for depository institutions, since their funds are not subject to unanticipated withdrawal by investors. Also, maturity dates on long-term debt, bank notes, and commercial paper are known in advance. Despite these facts, cash-flow planning cannot be ignored because loan demand cannot be completely anticipated and maturities of liabilities must be rolled over. Default risk and interest sensitivity tend to be just as important as cash-flow planning. Since finance companies often lend to consumers with few financial resources and no previous financial relationship with the lender, the credit or default risk becomes the salient issue. Careful personal credit analysis is an essential element of finance-company management. Credit-scoring models have been developed to help screen loan applications. Poor asset quality—especially the default-risk exposure of receivables— is of great importance to management. Poor asset quality can depress earnings through loans charged off, but it can also affect their ability to raise funds in the money and capital markets. Finance company management must establish systems to monitor the payment of individual loans and set up policies for collecting on delinquent receivables.[4]

Since 1981, return on assets and return on net worth have improved for finance companies. This is because interest costs as a percentage of assets declined more than gross income as a percentage of assets. Finance company managers controlled the spread quite well between 1982 and 1985 when interest rates were declining. This is in part related to the fact that finance-company borrowing rates declined more rapidly than finance-company lending rates.

During 1975-1985, large finance companies had higher returns on assets and on net worth on a pretax basis than did commercial banks, although on an after-tax basis, banks had higher returns on net worth (see Table 12.5). The superior performance of finance companies over banks can be attributed to better spread management and to the larger portion of high-yielding consumer loans in finance company portfolios.[5]

SUMMARY

In response to deregulation of the financial markets, independent finance companies have changed to resemble banks. Large independent finance com-

Table 12.5
Selected Income and Expense Items as Percentage of Year-End Assets at Sample Companies

	1977	1978	1979	1980	1981	1982	1983	1984	1985	1986
GROSS DOMESTIC INCOME*	11.4%	12.0%	13.1%	15.0%	15.4%	16.0%	14.3%	14.2%	13.2%	13.0%
Salaries and Wages	1.7%	1.6%	1.6%	1.7%	1.6%	1.5%	1.4%	1.3%	1.1%	1.1%
Advertising and Publicity	0.1%	0.1%	0.1%	0.1%	0.1%	0.1%	0.1%	0.1%	0.1%	0.1%
Losses and Additions to Loss Reserve	0.8%	0.8%	1.0%	1.3%	0.9%	0.9%	0.7%	0.7%	0.8%	1.2%
Other Operating Expenses	2.0%	2.0%	1.9%	2.2%	1.9%	2.1%	2.2%	2.5%	2.7%	2.7%
TOTAL OPERATING EXPENSES	4.6%	4.5%	4.6%	5.3%	4.5%	4.6%	4.5%	4.6%	4.6%	5.0%
Cost of Borrowed Funds	4.7%	5.4%	6.8%	8.0%	9.4%	8.9%	6.8%	7.2%	6.3%	6.0%
Income Taxes	0.8%	0.7%	0.5%	0.5%	0.5%	0.9%	1.2%	0.9%	0.9%	0.6%
NET DOMESTIC INCOME*	1.3%	1.3%	1.2%	1.2%	1.0%	1.5%	1.9%	1.6%	1.4%	1.3%
Income from Foreign Receivables	na	na	na	na	na	na	na	na	0.1%	0.1%
Income from Nonconsolidated Subsidiaries	na	na	na	na	na	na	na	na	.0%	0.1%
TOTAL NET INCOME	1.3%	1.3%	1.2%	1.2%	1.0%	1.5%	1.9%	1.6%	1.5%	1.5%
Net Income as a Percent of Year-end Equity	11.2%	11.3%	10.6%	9.6%	8.6%	12.3%	18.2%	15.4%	16.2%	16.2%
Number of Companies	34	34	34	34	34	33	31	30	30	29
Number of Offices	13,040	13,442	14,399	13,654	11,357	10,129	9,860	9,769	9,923	9,762

* Includes some income from foreign receivables and nonconsolidated subsidiaries prior to 1984.

Source: Finance Companies 1977-1986, *American Financial Services Association Research Report and Second Mortgage Lending Report,* p. 34.

panies have used their national network of offices to their best advantage in delivering consumer financial services in a national market by offering credit cards, ATMs, safe deposit boxes, savings accounts, mortgage loans, tax preparation, and financial planning services.[6]

Finance companies can no longer remain the "lender of last resort." Because of higher operating expenses and a higher cost of funds than the banks with whom they compete, finance companies will have to avoid product markets where margins are slim and where financial products are viewed as commodities. In fact, finance companies will have to break with their past by either diversifying away from traditional finance operations, emulating commercial banks, or staying one step ahead of the competition. Finance companies have begun to take measures to tighten control of operating expenses by shrinking the number of offices in operation and by reducing the number of employees per branch.[7]

The number of finance companies operating in the United States was close to 3,000 in 1989, compared to more than 6,000 in 1960. The decline in the number of finance companies reflected rising cost and credit pressures, the broadening of the market, liquidations, mergers, absorptions, failures, and intensified competition from other financial institutions. Many of the smaller finance companies have been sold out to larger firms, conglomerates, or bank holding companies. The economics of the business has encouraged finance companies to strive for greater efficiency and larger size. Despite their declining number, finance companies have experienced rapid asset growth and have proven to be strong competitors in the market for business and consumer credit.

The consumer market share of finance companies increased from 1985 to 1987, largely as a result of a big increase in auto credit outstanding. The auto financing companies spent much of that period offering extremely low interest rates on loan contracts as an incentive to purchase certain new car models. These car loans were later securitized and sold in the secondary market. In addition to increases in automobile financing, finance companies have expanded into residential mortgage lending, mortgage banking, loans for leveraged buyouts, asset-based lending in cooperation with commercial banks, and the issuance of credit cards. Diversification of services and innovation in new service offerings took place at a record pace in the 1980s.

NOTES

1. E. M. Hurley, "Survey of Finance companies, 1980," *Federal Reserve Bulletin* 67 (May 1981): 402-403.

2. M. J. Gardner and D. Mills, *Managing Financial Institutions* (Hinsdale, Ill.: Dryden Press, 1988), 614.

3. Ibid., 629-631.

4. Federal Reserve Bank of New York, *Recent Trends in Commercial Bank Profitability* (New York: 1986), 277-281.

5. Ibid.

6. A. C. Sullivan, "Making Money in Finance Companies," in *The Financial Services Handbook*, ed. by E. M. Friars and R. N. Gogel (New York: Wiley-Interscience, 1987), 179, 190-191.

7. Ibid.

13

Life Insurance Companies

HISTORY

Life insurance companies hold long and distinguished spots in American history, offering their risk protection services in the United States for over 225 years. The Presbyterian Ministers Fund holds the distinction of being the oldest life insurance company in the world. It was incorporated in Philadelphia in 1759 with the Corporation for Relief of Poor and Distressed Presbyterians and of the Poor and Distressed Widows and Children of the Presbyterian Church. This life insurance company was formed prior to the independence of the United States from Great Britain and more than two decades before the establishment of the first commercial bank in the United States, which was formed in 1782. At the end of 1986 there were close to 2,321 life insurance companies, with combined assets of about $937 billion. There are approximately 400 million life insurance policies in force in the United States, which generated premiums of $194 billion in 1986. Close to 2 million persons are employed in the insurance business, with approximately 40 percent of them serving in agency brokerage operations.

The primary business of insurance companies is the elimination of certain financial risks for businesses and individuals. The events that have been insured against may represent risks for individuals, but they are a predictable expense for the population as a whole. The insurance company serves by converting the individual's risk or benefit to a regular individual or business expense. The premiums that the insurance companies charge those who choose to be insured and the income received from investments are usually sufficient to pay the benefits to those who suffer losses.[1]

In addition to the insurance function, insurance companies also serve a function as a financial intermediary. Insurance companies invest policy premiums and surplus in the money and capital markets, and provide loanable funds for a wide range of borrowers. They also manage large sums of money in the form of employee benefits, pension retirement, and profit-sharing plans.

REGULATION

Insurance is considered interstate commerce and is, therefore, subject to federal regulation. In practice, however, as a result of Public Law 15, regulation has been left to the individual states. Each state creates its own laws and regulates companies selling insurance within its boundaries, often causing national insurance companies to face 50 different sets of regulations. Specific rules vary from state to state, but the areas of finance, licensing of insurers, solvency, examination, investment policy, premium rate reserves, agent competency, and contract provisions are regulated in all states. Federal regulation is limited to matters such as antitrust and fraud. Insurers are regulated by the states in which they are incorporated, but are also subject to extraterritorial regulations by other states where they conduct business. Each state may enact its own insurance legislation, although there has been a trend toward uniform legislation among states. The National Association of Insurance Commissioners, composed of representatives from all states, has encouraged the present trend toward uniformity in state insurance laws.

The preparation of financial statements for insurance companies follows Statutory Accounting Principles. These principles differ from the general accepted accounting principles (GAAP) used by other corporations and businesses. The deviations from the GAAP are usually related to requirements imposed by insurance regulatory authorities at the state level. Statutory Accounting Principles are an adaptation to the special characteristics of the insurance businesses, and involve a mix of accrual and cash accounting. They demand a much more conservative methodology than GAAP.[2]

Insurance accounting procedures apply special rules for the valuation of assets that are readily convertible into cash. Nonadmitted assets include cars, furniture and fixtures, premiums due in over 90 days, and other assets of an insurance firm, and do not appear on the balance sheet. In addition, statutory accounting carries stocks at market value and bonds at their amortized value, while the GAAP system reflects investments at market or cost, whichever is lower. Unrealized capital gains and losses are recognized under the statutory system, but not under GAAP.[3]

TYPES OF INSURANCE

Life insurance companies, the fourth largest financial intermediary, offer public products involving both insurance protection in the case of death and a means of saving for over 80 percent of all families in the United States. There are close to 2,000 property and casualty insurance companies that provide most businesses and families with automobile insurance, as well as homeowner's, fire, theft, liability, and workers' compensation insurance.

There are four basic types of insurance: property, liability, life, and health. In practice, insurers tend to sell either property-casualty and liability insurance or life insurance, with health insurance being sold by both property and life insurers. Through the use of holding company arrangements, multiple-line underwriting began to take place. For example, the parent holding company may be a life and health insurer with a property and liability insurance subsidiary, or vice versa.

Life insurance is designed to provide, on the death of the insured, cash benefits to third parties called beneficiaries, although the beneficiaries are not necessarily parties to the contract. The basic contracts are term, whole life (cash value available), and endowment. These may be sold on an individual or group basis, with the latter type of contract forming the basis for a common employee benefit.

The concept of life insurance took hold at the time of the Civil War. One innovation that fueled this growth was the introduction of small policies peddled door to door with weekly payments collected. Another innovation was the incorporation of systematic saving through tontine plans. Subscribers formed a pool of money which, together with interest, went to the final surviving member.

Health insurance has been written in the United States since before the Civil War, with the early policies providing protection against loss of income related to accidents and certain diseases. Modern health insurance started in the 1930s with the beginning of associations similar to Blue Cross. More than nine out of ten persons have some form of private health insurance coverage, a remarkable increase from the ratio of five out of ten in 1950. Since the 1930s, life insurance companies have become increasingly important in providing health insurance as a form of prepayment for and protection against hospital and medical costs. New forms of protection, particularly major medical plans, long-term disability coverage, and dental insurance, have grown rapidly.

During the past decade, group health insurance has emerged as a growth business, especially for the multi-line insurance organizations. Although the companies had difficulties in the late 1960s in adjusting to Medicare, the group health-insurance business has become profitable because it has become a business of fees rather than underwriting risk. Most large group business is written on an experience-related or cost-plus basis. Consequently, except for some inevitable year-to-year volatility, premium and profit growth have outpaced inflation, aided by above-average growth in medical care expenditure and increasingly comprehensive coverage such as unlimited major medical and dental insurance.

Medicare, Medicaid, health maintenance organizations (HMOs), and other forms of private, prepaid insurance have contributed to the growth in demand for medical services. HMOs are essentially prepaid group-medical-practice systems that provide comprehensive services to subscribers for a premium paid in advance.

The two types of health insurance are disability benefits, which provide partial replacement for income lost because of sickness, and accidental and medical expense benefits that reimburse the insured for the costs of medical care and hospital bills. Although most health insurance is purchased as part of a group employee or association benefit, many people still purchase individual health insurance from commercial insurers, Blue Cross and Blue Shield, independent and group practice plans, and health maintenance organizations (HMOs). HMOs can be sponsored by employers, government, insurance companies, and private groups, and provide a barrage of health-care services that emphasize preventive medicine for a specified group at a fixed price. The federal government has encouraged the development of HMOs in the hope that they will reduce the cost of health care. The Kaiser Health Care Plan in California is the best-known and one of the oldest HMOs. It is now open to the public, even though it was originally designed for employees of Kaiser Corporation.

Blue Cross and Blue Shield are not insurers, but are nonprofit, prepaid hospital- and medical-expense associations. Both of these associations make payments directly to the hospitals and doctors for services rendered. Hospitals and doctors established these health care plans in order to guarantee that they would be paid for medical services performed. In some parts of the country, these associations are considered charitable institutions and receive certain tax exemptions. They are generally governed by boards of directors that represent the doctors, hospitals, and general public of a particular region.

NATURE OF OWNERSHIP

From the standpoint of ownership organizations, over 90 percent of the insurance companies are either stock companies or mutuals. Stock insurance companies are organized as profit-making business concerns, with investors expecting a return in the form of dividends and capital gains. About one-third of property-casualty companies are stock companies, accounting for close to three-fourths of the value of written premiums. Stock property-casualty insurers range from small insurers writing only one line of business to giant insurers writing most lines of insurance coverage. Even though most life insurance companies are stock companies, the largest ones are mutuals. In 1986, there were 2,133 shareholder-owned stock companies and 131 life insurance mutuals. The mutuals hold 53 percent of life insurance industry assets and accounted for 41.4 percent of life insurance in force in 1986. Aetna, Cigna, and Travellers are the three largest stock insurance companies in the United States. Prudential, Metropolitan, and Equitable are the largest mutuals in the country, and they specialize in life insurance. There are three other forms of insurance company ownerships: (1) government, (2) reciprocals, and (3) Lloyd's organizations.

Government insurance refers to insurance written by federal and state agencies. The government insures crops, and mortgage deposits at banks, thrifts, and credit unions. It also has a variety of social insurance programs.

More than 50 percent of the insurance premiums in the United States are collected by federal and state government insurers. The government provides social insurance to particular sectors of the economy. Social insurance is based on the concept that there are many people who face financial and other risks that they cannot deal with themselves. If these risks are considered sufficiently important and widespread, the government translates them into national objectives.

There are a number of Public Guarantee Insurance Programs, which include:

1. FDIC, FSLIC, and NCUA insurance of deposits up to $100,000 in each account against losses resulting from bank, savings and loan, or credit union failure respectively;

2. SIPC (Securities Investor Protection Corporation) protects investors who have accounts with stock-brokerage firms from losses due to failure, up to a loss of $500,000;

3. PBGC (Pension Benefits Guarantee Corporation) guarantees employees covered by private pension plan their vested benefits up to a specified amount should the plan be terminated;

4. The Railroad Retirement System and Supplemental Security Income for the blind, disabled, and aged; and

5. Government insurance against crop failure, war damage, fire, riots, floods, and crime, and for mortgage loan coverage.

The use of individuals as insurers is the basic concept at Lloyd's organizations. Individuals accepting risks through the Lloyd's concept do so on their own responsibility and assume liability extending to nonbusiness assets. Organizations of the New York State Insurance Exchange operate in a manner similar to a Lloyd's association. The exchange provides an international marketplace for the insurance reinsurance of large and unusual risks.

Reciprocals are unincorporated associations that exchange insurance risks. These associations involve individuals writing insurance as individuals, not jointly. Each subscriber agrees to insure individually all the other subscribers in the exchange, and in turn is insured by each of the other subscribers. There is a "reciprocal exchange" of insurance promises. Reciprocals are similar to mutuals because each member of the association is both an insurer and insured, but they differ from mutuals in that the chief administrator (the attorney-in-fact) receives a fee for services rendered. The members of the reciprocal actually insure each other. Less than sixty of these exchanges exist in the United States in the property and casualty insurance field, and they account for only a small percentage of the premiums written. They write no life insurance, and many specialize in only one line: usually auto insurance.

Although life insurance premium receipts are still dominated by ordinary life insurance, group life insurance has been growing rapidly. Annuities and health insurance premiums have also experienced rapid growth, especially in group lines.

Life insurance policies are often classified by the method of sales. Ordinary life is usually sold through agents to individuals, while group life is made available through work, professional, or other association.

Group life insurance accounted for about 42 percent of all life insurance in force in the United States and at the end of 1986 (see Table 13.1). Group life insurance provides coverage under a master policy for employees and union, social, or trade associations as well as professional organization members. Life and other types of insurance are considered by many employees to be an essential fringe benefit, and part of the basic wage package. Group life has become increasingly popular because it costs less to provide one policy covering a lot of people than to provide many individual policies. Employees are thus able to provide (or employees are able to buy) more life insurance for each dollar of life insurance premium than on an individual basis. Also, most group policies do not require a physical examination to obtain life insurance.

TYPES OF POLICIES

Whole Life

Whole life insurance is sometimes called "ordinary life," "straight life," or "permanent life," and accounts for about half of all life insurance in force in the United States. It gives permanent protection and cash value for a level annual premium. Upon death or at a specified age (frequently 65), the face-value amount of the policy is payable either as a death benefit to the beneficiary, or to the policyholder if still alive. The level premium is larger than the term premium for an equal amount of life insurance in the early years. As cash values accumulate, the insured has the option of borrowing against the cash value in the form of a policy loan at attractive rates of between 5 and 8 percent, depending upon the issue date of the policy. The insured also has the option of stopping the payment of premiums and using the accumulated cash value to buy a reduced amount of paid-up insurance or term insurance.

Some industrial life policies are whole life policies, but most are small term insurance contracts with, for instance, $5,000 rather than $100,000 in death benefits. The premiums, which may vary from a dime to five dollars, are collected by an insurance company representative as frequently as weekly at the policyholder's home. Industrial life carried by U.S. companies represents under 1 percent of the amount of all outstanding life insurance policies.

Endowment

Endowment insurance policies are savings plans supplemented by insurance protection. Most endowment policies are written for periods of between 10 and 30 years, and have premiums that are generally higher than those of a whole life policy issued at the same age, because the insurer must develop an accumulation

Table 13.1

Life Insurance in Force in the United States (000,000 omitted)

Year	Ordinary No.	Ordinary Amount	Group Cert.	Group Amount	Industrial No.	Industrial Amount	Credit No.†	Credit Amount	Total No.	Total Amount
1900	3	$ 6,124	—	—	11	$ 1,449	—	—	14	$ 7,573
1905	5	9,585	—	—	17	2,278	—	—	22	11,863
1910	6	11,783	—	—	23	3,125	—	—	29	14,908
1915	9	16,650	*	$ 100	32	4,279	—	—	41	21,029
1920	16	32,018	2	1,570	48	6,948	*	$ 4	66	40,540
1925	23	52,892	3	4,247	71	12,318	*	18	97	69,475
1930	32	78,576	6	9,801	86	17,963	*	73	124	106,413
1935	33	70,684	6	10,208	81	17,471	1	101	121	98,464
1940	37	79,346	9	14,938	85	20,866	3	380	134	115,530
1945	48	101,550	12	22,172	101	27,675	2	365	163	151,762
1946	53	112,818	13	27,206	104	29,313	3	729	173	170,066
1947	56	122,393	16	32,026	106	30,406	5	1,210	183	186,035
1948	58	131,158	16	37,068	106	31,253	6	1,729	186	201,208
1949	61	138,862	17	40,207	107	32,087	8	2,516	193	213,672
1950	64	149,116	19	47,793	108	33,415	11	3,844	202	234,168
1951	67	159,109	21	54,398	109	34,870	12	4,763	209	253,140
1952	70	170,875	24	62,913	111	36,448	14	6,355	219	276,591
1953	73	185,007	26	72,913	112	37,781	18	8,558	229	304,259
1954	76	198,599	29	86,410	111	38,664	21	10,046	237	333,719
1955	80	216,812	32	101,345	112	39,682	28	14,493	252	372,332
1956	83	238,348	35	117,399	110	40,109	32	16,774	260	412,630
1957	87	264,949	37	133,905	108	40,139	34	19,366	266	458,359
1958	89	288,607	39	144,772	104	39,646	35	20,536	267	493,561
1959	93	317,158	41	160,163	102	39,809	38	24,998	274	542,128
1960	95	341,881	44	175,903	100	39,563	43	29,101	282	586,448
1961	97	366,141	46	192,794	98	39,451	45	31,107	286	629,493
1962	99	391,048	49	209,950	95	39,638	47	35,341	290	675,977
1963	102	420,808	51	229,477	93	39,672	52	40,666	298	730,623
1964	104	457,868	55	253,620	92	39,833	58	46,487	309	797,808
1965	107	499,638	61	308,078	89	39,818	63	53,020	320	900,554
1966	109	541,022	65	345,945	88	39,663	69	58,059	331	984,689
1967	113	584,570	69	394,501	84	39,215	70	61,535	336	1,079,821
1968	116	633,392	73	442,778	81	38,827	75	68,357	345	1,183,354
1969	118	682,453	76	488,864	79	38,614	78	74,598	351	1,284,529
1970	120	734,730	80	551,357	77	38,644	78	77,392	355	1,402,123
1971	123	792,318	82	589,883	76	39,202	76	81,931	357	1,503,334
1972	126	853,911	85	640,689	76	39,975	78	93,410	365	1,627,985
1973	128	928,192	88	708,322	75	40,632	78	101,154	369	1,778,300
1974	131	1,009,038	94	827,018	71	39,441	84	109,623	380	1,985,120
1975	134	1,083,421	96	904,695	70	39,423	80	112,032	380	2,139,571
1976	137	1,177,672	100	1,002,647	67	39,175	78	123,569	382	2,343,063
1977	139	1,289,321	106	1,115,047	66	39,045	79	139,402	390	2,582,815
1978	142	1,425,095	111	1,243,994	64	38,080	84	163,081	401	2,870,250
1979	146	1,585,878	115	1,419,418	62	37,794	84	179,250	407	3,222,340
1980	148	1,760,474	118	1,579,355	58	35,994	78	165,215	402	3,541,038
1981	149	1,978,080	123	1,888,612	55	34,547	73	162,356	400	4,063,595
1982	146	2,216,388	124	2,066,361	52	32,766	67	161,144	389	4,476,659
1983	146	2,544,275	127	2,219,573	50	31,354	64	170,659	387	4,965,861
1984	145	2,887,574	127	2,392,358	47	30,104	66	189,951	385	5,499,987
1985	142	3,247,289	130	2,561,595	44	28,250	70	215,973	386	6,053,107
1986	143	3,658,203	135	2,801,049	42	27,168	71	233,859	391	6,720,279

Note: "Credit" is limited to life insurance on loans of 10 years' or less duration. "Ordinary" and "Group" include credit life insurance on loans of more than 10 years' duration. Totals for "In the United States" represent all life insurance (net of reinsurance) on residents of the United States, whether issued by U.S. or foreign companies. Beginning with 1959, the data include Alaska and Hawaii.

*Fewer than 500,000.   †Includes group credit certificates.

Sources: Spectator Year Book and American Council of Life Insurance. Presented in *1987 Life Insurance Fact Book Update*, p. 10.

equal to the face value by the end of the contract period, which is shorter than for whole life. The policy provides for the payment of its face amount to the beneficiary upon death, or to the insured at the end of the endowment period if the insured is alive. Once the face amount is paid, the policy expires. This form of policy is no longer popular, but it was once used to accumulate funds for education and retirement purposes. Endowment policies represented just under 1 percent of the policies purchased in the United States during the first half of the 1980s. They lost much of their appeal in the late 1980s because of their low return compared to alternative investments.

Term

Term policies come in four varieties: (1) regular, (2) renewable, (3) decreasing term insurance, and (4) convertible term. Regular term may be purchased for one year, five years, or longer. Renewable term insurance guarantees the right to continue the policy annually beyond the expiration date. Premiums tend to rise each year or at renewal time, as the risk of death increases with age. With decreasing term insurance, payments remain fixed, and the amount of death benefit decreases each year.

Decreasing term insurance provides large amounts of protection in the early years of coverage, with the amount declining every year until it stabilizes at some small, predetermined level. It is popular with policy holders who may have low income but high insurance obligations. This type of insurance coverage is also popular for homeowner's mortgage coverage as the decline in insurance policy value can be made to parallel the decline in the outstanding mortgage value of the home.

Term insurance provides insurance protection for a fixed period of time without any saving features. The insurance expires at maturity if the insured dies. Since term insurance premiums are calculated to meet expected benefit payments over a short period of time, only a limited accumulation of assets and reserves is needed. Term insurance is much less expensive than whole life. The price of term insurance per $1,000 of policy coverage has dropped about 50 percent in the last decade because of intense competition, higher investment yields, and increased length of life.

Convertible term insurance is an option that gives the insured the right to convert the term insurance contract into a whole life policy. The conversion requires no evidence of insurability. However, the premium increases to the level required for the new policy at the insured's attained age.

Another form of term insurance is credit life. It is usually sold through a lender to cover the payment of a specific loan in case the borrower dies prematurely. While dwarfed in importance by individual and group policies, credit life insurance has been increasing rapidly. One-year renewable term insurance has also grown in popularity recently because of its relatively low price. (See Table 13.2.)

Table 13.2
Analysis of Ordinary Life Insurance Purchases in the United States

	% of Policies		% of Amount	
	1976	1986	1976	1986
SEX OF INSURED				
Male Insureds Under 15	8	7	3	3
Female Insureds Under 15	7	6	2	2
Male Adults	57	52	78	69
Female Adults	28	35	17	26
Total	100	100	100	100
AGE OF INSURED				
Under 15	15	13	4	5
15-24	29	16	22	10
25-34	31	30	41	36
35-44	14	22	20	30
45-54	8	11	10	13
55 and over	3	8	3	6
Total	100	100	100	100
INCOME OF INSURED*				
Under $5,000	3	†	1	†
$5,000-$7,499	15	2	7	1
$7,500-$9,999	19	5	11	2
$10,000-$24,999	53	47	54	30
$25,000-$49,999	7	34	18	37
$50,000-$99,999	2	9	7	19
$100,000 or more	1	3	2	11
Total	100	100	100	100
SIZE OF POLICY				
Under $2,000	5	2	†	†
$2,000-$4,999	13	4	2	†
$5,000-$9,999	18	8	5	1
$10,000-$24,999	38	19	27	4
$25,000-$49,999	17	18	27	9
$50,000-$99,999	6	25	17	24
$100,000 or more	3	24	22	62
Total	100	100	100	100
TYPE OF POLICY				
Straight Life	33	31	25	15
Limited Payment Life	16	7	7	1
Endowment and Retirement Income	8	†	5	†
Modified Life	6	3	4	2
Level, Decreasing and Modified Term	16	20	33	35
Family Plan	2	†	2	†
with Additional Term	1	—	2	—
Regular Policy with F/P Rider	5	5	5	4
and Additional Term	2	1	2	1
Universal Life	—	20	—	25
with Rider	—	5	—	8
Variable Life	—	1	—	1
with Rider	—	†	—	†
Variable-Universal	—	2	—	3
with Rider	—	†	—	†
Combination	11	5	15	5
Progressive and Other	†	†	†	†
Total	100	100	100	100

Note: Figures exclude credit life insurance.

*Ages 0-14 and persons reporting less than $3,000 income are excluded.

Source: Life Insurance Marketing and Research Association. Presented in *1987 Life Insurance Fact Book Update,* p. 8.

Variable Life

Under a variable-life plan, benefits are related to the market value of an investment portfolio, which might consist of a money market fund, a bond fund, a mixed fund, or a portfolio of equity securities held in a separate account. There is a minimum death benefit guaranteed, and the death benefit is adjusted for investment performance of the cash accumulation. In addition, the contracts usually carry the options for full and partial surrenders as well as policy loans.

There are several varieties, including variable life, adjustable life, and variable-premium life. Adjustable life permits the policyholder to shift to term insurance or to permanent (whole life) insurance based upon the customer's financial situation and preferences, change benefits, premium payments, or policy maturity dates consistent with contract specifications. On the other hand, variable-premium policies permit variation in premium rates that are based upon the earnings of the life insurance company. Policies that offer a death benefit that varies with investment performance must be sold with a prospectus.

Universal Life

Universal life is designed to overcome the drawbacks of whole life (low rate of return, high commission charge, insufficient disclosure) and term insurance (high premiums in later years, no cash buildup, eventual policy expiration). Under universal life, premiums are paid into a cash accumulation fund. Each month, the insurance company deducts from the fund the amount needed to pay for renewable term insurance. What remains, after underwriter fees, is invested in short- and medium-term government and corporate securities, and earns a return that is advertised to be near those paid by money market funds.

Conceived and introduced by E. F. Hutton Life Insurance Company in 1978, universal life accounted for only 2 percent of new, annualized, ordinary life insurance purchases in 1981, 10 percent of the industry total in 1982, over 20 percent of the market in 1983, and 36 percent in 1986 (see Table 13.2). Universal life offers market interest rates, but no participation in the equity market. The policyholder's premiums flow into a general savings fund that yields a tax-deferred interest rate. Enough money is withdrawn from the fund to pay the insurance premiums. The policy has an added flexibility that enables the investor to add extra money to the savings fund or increase insurance coverage. Essentially, the policyholder may at any time alter the amount of premium paid, the coverage provided, and the savings fund. The policyholder can also withdraw cash from the policy without treating the withdrawal as a loan. A drawback is that fees and the cost of insurance, particularly in a new policy, can use up a large portion of the premium payment, leaving little in the savings fund to earn a return. The return usually exceeds that earned from conventional, whole life policies.

Cash values, under the universal life concept, can accumulate using a number of different interest-rate approaches. Two examples are the indexed-rate basis and the portfolio-rate basis. Under an indexed-rate assumption, the interest accruing to the cash accumulation is declared at regular, frequent intervals, usually monthly, and is tied to some current economic indicator such as the current Treasury bill discount rate. The cash accumulation in the policy can be earning several different rates of interest concurrently at any point in time. The portfolio rate is calculated by the insurance company based on the total investment return on its entire portfolio, both short- and long-term.

Flexible-premium variable life insurance, another relatively new form of life insurance, is a hybrid combining the features of both universal and variable life. With such a policy, an owner can obtain more or less coverage within the same policy at different times in his or her life. In addition, the policy's cash value may change periodically, in keeping with the investment experience of the funds in the account managed by the insurance company. Flexible-premium variable life insurance, like universal life, allows policyholders to raise or lower their premiums—and thereby their coverage—within a single contract. The policy provides that the death benefit and the cash value vary in accordance with the performance of a separate policyholder account. Premiums in the account are segregated by the insurer and invested in a portfolio of stocks, bonds, or money market funds. It is also possible to miss premium payments, make prepayments, or use a portion of the cash value to pay premiums.

Annuities

The annuity has been called the ''upside-down application of the life insurance principle'' because of the notion that the purpose of life insurance is the scientific creation of an estate, whereas the purpose of the annuity is the scientific liquidation of an estate. The estate is created at death with a life insurance contract, while the estate is fully liquidated by death under an annuity contract. In exchange for the premium, the life insurance purchaser expects the insurance company to pay the beneficiary a specified sum upon death, while the purchaser of an annuity expects the insurance company to pay a fixed periodic sum to the annuitant as long as he or she lives.

Annuities may be purchased with either a single premium or through a series of installment premiums. Under the single-premium life annuity contract, the insurance company promises to pay a given amount each period, normally monthly, to the annuitant during his lifetime in exchange for a single premium, which immediately becomes the property of the company. No part of the premium is returnable in the event of the annuitant's death.

If annuities were classified on the basis of the time at which the benefits stopped, there would be four classifications of annuities. The first two are the life annuity with no refund and no further equity in the contract after death, and the guaranteed minimum annuity, which guarantees a minimum number of payments such as 120 or 240 (if the annuitant dies prematurely, the payments are continued to the beneficiary for the remainder of the minimum period). The third classification, the annuity certain, is a contract that provides the annuitant a given income for a specified number of years, independent of his or her life or death (upon the termination of these years, the payments cease). In the fourth classification, temporary life annuities are similar to the annuity certain except that payments cease upon death of the annuitant. For example, a 15-year temporary life annuity will provide monthly payments for 15 years or until the prior death of the annuitant.

There are immediate-payment annuities, deferred-payment annuities, and tax-deferred annuities. It is the last category that has experienced significant growth during the 1980s. The single-premium deferred annuities feature the tax-deferred buildup of funds at current market rates. In 1982, all issuers sold approximately $9 billion in single-premium deferred annuities. However, the bankruptcy of two providers that previously had accounted for the bulk of the deferred annuities market caused investors to shy away from these investments in late 1983; sales have once again gained momentum as companies with solid reputations have entered the annuities market. (See Table 13.3.)

Table 13.3
Ordinary Life Insurance Premium Receipts
U.S. Life Insurance Companies (000,000 omitted)

	1982	1983	1984	1985	1986
LIFE INSURANCE PREMIUMS					
Ordinary	$ 38,371	$ 37,978	$ 38,625	$ 46,096	$ 51,618
Group	9,433	9,560	9,702	11,041	11,826
Industrial	1,484	1,066	1,108	905	787
Credit	1,512	1,661	1,839	2,085	1,982
Total Life Insurance Premiums	50,800	50,265	51,274	60,127	66,213
ANNUITY CONSIDERATIONS					
Individual	15,196	14,003	15,706	20,891	26,117
Group	19,448	16,541	27,153	33,008	57,595*
Total Annuity Considerations	34,644	30,544	42,859	53,899	83,712
HEALTH INSURANCE PREMIUMS					
Individual	7,168	7,926	8,626	9,143	10,379
Group	26,930	29,131	30,704	31,023	32,130
Credit	862	1,144	1,341	1,671	1,644
Total Health Insurance Premiums	34,960	38,201	40,671	41,837	44,153
Total Premium Receipts	$120,404	$119,010	$134,804	$155,863	$194,078

Note: Credit life insurance is limited to insurance on loans of 10 years' or less duration.

*Unusually large increase in group annuity considerations due to an NAIC-mandated change in statutory reporting methods.

Source: American Council of Life Insurance. Premium information on a slightly different basis was collected for the years 1957-1968 by the Life Insurance Marketing and Research Association. Presented in the *1987 Life Insurance Fact Book Update*, p. 28.

ESTIMATING THE AMOUNT OF LIFE INSURANCE TO BUY

What is the optimal amount and type of life insurance to have? The answer to this question depends upon age, health, income, tax bracket, alternative investment, dependents, job security, goals and needs, and other factors. The answer will vary from individual to individual, and it is unlikely that any two insurance professionals will give the same advice.

In purchasing life insurance, consumers must evaluate the trade-offs among (1) their need for low-cost premature death insurance; (2) their wish to accumulate a savings fund; and (3) their need for permanent protection with level cost.

For example, in most cases a single person without any dependents really does not need any life insurance beyond what is provided by his or her employer as a free fringe benefit. On the other hand, a 30-year-old male with a nonworking wife and two children has a definite need for life insurance protection. If resources are limited and the need for low-cost death insurance is dominant, either regular or decreasing term with renewal or conversion options (or with both options) is probably appropriate to fit the needs of young couples with small children. However, as family income and permanent protection needs increase over time, families may wish to consider universal or variable life policies. Even purchases of whole life might be considered by wealthy individuals because of the advantages associated with the accumulation of cash value tax-free. There is also an insurance strategy that suggests buying term insurance and investing the difference. Under this plan, one would buy lower-premium renewable term, or 20- or 30-year term insurance to protect against premature death over a given period of time. The insured must also systematically invest the difference between the term and the whole-life premiums for the same amount of coverage in a separate investment such as a mutual fund, money market fund, or bank CD. At the end of the insurance period, the relative success of the decision is judged by the extent to which the after-tax accumulation-value of the separate investment exceeds the guaranteed cash value plus any dividends accumulated which would have been available under a whole-life policy purchased at the same time. There is, of course, the risk that an individual will not systematically (on a yearly basis) invest the difference between the term and whole life premiums, but for those who are disciplined, systematic savers, history has demonstrated that buying term and investing the difference has offered more insurance protection and an after-tax cash accumulation equal to or greater than a purchase of whole life. On the other hand, the newer forms of insurance, such as variable and universal life, appear to be attractive options, although they offer only a limited history on which to make comparative judgments.

It should be remembered that there are Social Security benefits available to the children of deceased adults, and that many employers offer some basic term-insurance coverage as a fringe benefit to employees. The amount of coverage ranges from a nominal amount to cover death expenses to a multiple of three times the annual salary. Although there are many formulas available for suggested life-insurance coverage, a handy rule of thumb is to make sure that for married individuals, total insurance coverage is at least equal to three times their salary. This amount should be supplemented by additional minimum coverage of enough money to pay for four years of college expenses for each child. For example, if the annual salary is $50,000 a year with a nonworking wife and two teenage children, and college costs are expected to average about $15,000 per year for tuition, room and board, then the suggested insurance coverage would be about $270,000. However, one might consider the rising costs of college education. In this case it might be appropriate to round off the insurance coverage to $300,000 or even $350,000 if it can be afforded. Another formula is to buy insurance equal to about six times annual, after-tax income. It should also be remembered that there are budgetary constraints, and that the cost of insurance is an important consideration for many families.

COST VERSUS RISK

The cost of an insurance policy is theoretically determined by the actuarial risk of the event being insured. The cost of the premium is computed by multiplying the probability of an event (such as death) over a particular period of time by the value of the estimated loss. The death rate is calculated from the standard mortality tables. Operating costs and a target profit amount are then added to the expected loss computed above to arrive at a premium for the insurance policy. Life insurance premiums charged are based upon actuarial interpretations of the probability of death, the cost of doing business, investment assumptions germane to interest rates, and the desire for profits and market share by an individual life insurer. The dollar amount of premium per $1,000 of insurance coverage increases rapidly with age.

The life insurance business is founded on the principle of sharing risk. Thousands of policyholders pool their funds (premiums) in an insurance company, each sharing in a portion of the loss which will be incurred each year by a few policyholders due to death, retirement, or medical disability. Insurance works because the risk of financial loss associated with death, disability, retirement, and so forth is actuarially predictable for a large group of individuals.

Life insurance focuses on risks to the well-being of the individual person, while property-casualty companies are concerned primarily with risks involving the ownership of property and the liability of personal injury. Life companies and property-casualty companies are financial intermediaries that raise funds by selling protective policies to the public and receiving premium income, which is invested in securities and real assets.

An insurance company faces four major types of risks: (1) excessive benefit; (2) sales declines; (3) portfolio value loss; and (4) cancellation and policy loan.[4]

Excessive benefit costs can occur because of a natural disaster, because of lower estimates of losses than actually occurred, or because inflation drives claim amounts to excessive levels. Sales declines can occur because of severe economic downturns. Portfolio value loss for bonds and fixed-rate mortgages can occur during periods when interest rates rise. A recession can also bring about a negative impact on portfolio value through declines in stock value and through defaults on bonds and mortgages. Cancellation and policy-loan risks are primarily faced by companies offering endowment and whole-life policies. These withdrawals usually occur during periods of high interest rates. The conditions that might lead to each of the various types of losses are summarized as follows:[5]

Problem	Causes
Excessive claim losses	Natural disaster, inflation
Sales declines	Inflation, recession, competition
Losses in investment portfolio	Inflation, recession
Policy loans	Inflation and double-digit interest rates
Policy cancellations	Recession, competition

FACTORS AFFECTING LIFE INSURERS' NET INCOME

The life insurance business has been reasonably profitable over the years, even though premiums paid by policyholders are eventually returned to them or their beneficiaries in the form of cash benefits. The industry relies heavily on earnings from its investment portfolio. Investment income accounted for $75.4 billion in 1986. During 1986, the net rate of return on the industry's invested assets was 9.35 percent, up substantially from 1980's 8.02 percent, 1975's 6.36 percent, and 1970's net rate of investment income of 5.3 percent.

The majority of net earnings from the investment portfolio flow into the capital account, which serves as a reserve against future needs for funds. Most of the premiums collected from policyholders flow at least initially into policy reserves (amounting to $762 billion in 1986), which are mandated by most state laws to be at a level substantial enough to cover all benefit claims within a reasonable period of time. Other reserves, which are generated from net earnings, flow into a variety of equity accounts to cover future expenses and investment risk. There are some insurers (for example, fraternals and assessment societies) that do not qualify as legal-reserve life insurance companies.

Premiums for life insurance policies accounted for 23.4 percent of gross income in 1986, while premiums from annuities and health insurance accounted for 29.7 and 15.6 percent, respectively. Earnings from the investment portfolio contributed 26.7 percent of gross income, while the other sources contributed 4.5 percent (see Table 13.4). Between 1970 and 1986, the share of total income

260   The New Financial Institutions

derived from investments rose from 21 percent to just under 27 percent. The investment of cash-flow with higher yielding notes and bonds, and the retirement of bonds with low coupons and their reinvestment in issues with higher rates, have all contributed to the importance of investment income growth. It is interesting to note that the proportion of income from premiums for mutual companies is about 74 percent, compared to about 83 percent for stock companies.

Table 13.4
Income of U.S. Life Insurance Companies (000,000 omitted)

Year	Life Insurance Premiums	Annuity Considera-tions	Health Insurance Premiums*	Total Premium Receipts	Investment Income**	Other Income†	Total Income
1911	$ 626	$ 4	—	$ 630	$ 182	$ 24	$ 836
1915	776	6	—	782	241	20	1,043
1920	1,374	7	—	1,381	341	42	1,764
1925	2,340	38	—	2,378	551	89	3,018
1930	3,416	101	—	3,517	891	186	4,594
1935	3,182	491	—	3,673	1,013	386	5,072
1940	3,501	386	—	3,887	1,231	540	5,658
1945	4,589	570	—	5,159	1,445	1,070	7,674
1950	6,249	939	$ 1,001	8,189	2,075	1,073	11,337
1955	8,903	1,288	2,355	12,546	2,801	1,197	16,544
1960	11,998	1,341	4,026	17,365	4,304	1,338	23,007
1965	16,083	2,260	6,261	24,604	6,778	1,785	33,167
1970	21,679	3,721	11,367	36,767	10,144	2,143	49,054
1971	22,935	4,910	12,897	40,742	11,031	2,429	54,202
1972	24,678	5,503	14,318	44,499	12,127	2,222	58,848
1973	26,373	6,771	15,524	48,668	13,670	2,415	64,753
1974	27,750	7,737	17,123	52,610	15,144	2,256	70,010
1975	29,336	10,165	19,074	58,575	16,488	2,959	78,022
1976	31,358	13,962	21,059	66,379	18,758	3,421	88,558
1977	33,765	14,974	23,580	72,319	21,713	3,953	97,985
1978	36,592	16,339	25,829	78,760	25,294	4,152	108,206
1979	39,083	17,939	27,894	84,916	29,562	4,661	119,139
1980	40,829	22,429	29,366	92,624	33,928	4,336	130,888
1981	46,246	27,579	31,803	105,628	39,774	6,464	151,866
1982	50,800	34,644	34,960	120,404	45,532	4,108	170,044
1983	50,265	30,544	38,201	119,010	50,862	6,154	176,026
1984	51,274	42,859	40,671	134,804	59,213	12,092	206,109
1985	60,127	53,899	41,837	155,863	67,952	10,212	234,027
1986	66,213	83,712‡	44,153	194,078	75,435	12,744	282,257

Note: Consideration for supplementary contracts with and without life contingencies are included under "Other Income." Prior to 1947, the business of health departments was not included in this series.

*Includes some premiums for Workers' Compensation and auto and other liability insurance.

**Beginning with 1951, investment income is net of investment expenses in this series.

†Beginning in 1975, "Other Income" includes commissions and expense allowance on reinsurance ceded. In 1975, this amounted to $382 million.

‡Unusually large increase in annuity premiums in 1986 was due to an NAIC-mandated change in statutory reporting methods.

Sources: *Spectator Year Book* and American Council of Life Insurance.

Sources: *Spectator Year Book* and American Council of Life Insurance. Presented in the *1987 Life Insurance Fact Book Update*, p. 27.

ASSETS OF LIFE INSURANCE COMPANIES

The net flow of new money for investment in life insurance companies arises from (1) the excess of premiums over benefit payments, expenses and commissions; and (2) net investment income, the earnings on invested assets and capital gains less expenses and additions to the net flow of new funds. Insurance companies must also invest the large return flow from past investments, such as mortgage payments, interest, and dividends.

The major liabilities of life insurance companies are contractual and long-term in nature. Therefore, the assets of most insurance companies consist of a high proportion of long-term securities such as corporate bonds and mortgages. Corporate bonds have remained the most important component of life insurance portfolios. In 1986, corporate bonds comprised close to 36 percent of portfolio assets. As a matter of fact, life insurance companies hold more than half of all outstanding corporate bonds. Mortgage loans for commercial property accounted for about 21 percent of total assets in 1986, down from 36 percent in 1970. The shift away from mortgage lending in part reflects an increased preference by life companies to make equity investments in real estate; these have more than doubled in the last seven years. Companies also hold common stock and policy loans.

The share of common stocks in the assets of life insurance companies, which was about 4 percent in 1960, had reached just under 10 percent by year-end 1986. Policy loans are loans to policyholders against the cash value of their life insurance policies. Whenever interest rates rise to double-digit levels, policy loans tend to increase and policyholders disintermediate. Policy loans were a serious problem for some life companies at times in the 1960s and 1970s. At year-end 1986, policy loans accounted for just under 6 percent of life insurance company assets. Fully invested companies were often forced to sell bonds at a loss, to increase their borrowings in the commercial paper market, or to utilize their credit lines at commercial banks at rates in excess of the yield on policy loans in order to meet the demand for low-yielding policy loans.

Life insurance companies face additional problems when interest rates increase. Whole life insurance policies include a savings component on which the insurer pays an implicit rate of return. When market rates of interest rise, consumers may choose to hold those savings in the form of financial assets that yield a higher return. An additional problem is that the size of the premiums in relation to the face amount of the policy depends partially on the rate of return on the life insurance company's portfolio of financial assets. When interest rates are increasing it is possible for new companies to enter the industry and offer lower premium rates to consumers. This is because their investment portfolios will have a higher average rate of return than the portfolio of an established insurer which will own many older bonds with lower yields.

Life insurers have tried to adjust to the more volatile interest rate conditions in the money and capital markets by developing new products that are more sensitive to changes in market rates of interest. Newly developed policies such as variable and universal life shift some of the investment risk onto the consumer. These policies separate the savings and insurance components of life insurance and allow the savings component to pay a rate of return comparable to what can be earned on other savings instruments. These new products helped to reduce life insurers' sensitivity to increases in interest rates, though widely volatile rates continue to be a problem.

During the mid-1980s, life companies sought greater liquidity by increasing their holdings of short-term credit market instruments. For example, at year-end 1980, cash and short-term assets held by life companies accounted for about 3 percent of assets, while by year-end 1986 they accounted for just over 4 percent of the total. Life companies also added to their potential liquidity with holdings of readily marketable U.S. government and agency notes and bonds. From 1980 to 1986, holdings of such securities have increased from 3 to 15 percent of total assets. (See Table 13.5.)

The long-term nature of most liabilities, and the generally steady inflow of funds for investment, enables life insurance companies to participate in forward commitments by agreeing to invest a precise amount of money at a stated interest for a specified period, with agreed-upon dates for the disbursement of funds. The insurance company receives a commitment fee and is legally obligated to provide the funds on the terms stated in the commitment: the borrower also has an obligation to meet the terms of agreement. The commitment may, under certain conditions, be cancelled by the borrower at the cost of any commitment fee paid.

The forward commitment process limits the possibilities of following cyclical investment policies, timing investments to take maximum advantage of short-term changes in interest rates. On the other hand, it permits the insurer to earn substantial commitment fees and to lock in interest rates on future investments. The main attractions of private placements were rates higher than those of public-market bonds, attractive call-option features, and protective convenant indentures. In recent years, life companies have committed smaller percentages of their investable cash flows to private placements. For example, life insurance companies invested 25 to 30 percent of their investable cash flow in private placements in 1984, down from a historical level of 40 to 50 percent. The explanation for this lies in a reduced supply of private placements and an increased preference for securities with liquid secondary markets.

Forward commitments are typically firm contracts to buy mortgages of office buildings, apartment complexes, utility plants, and industrial plants. These large projects are usually planned well in advance, and a great deal of money is placed at risk during the development stage. Developers are generally willing to pay a premium (commitment fee) for the assurance that permanent financing will be available when the construction phase is completed.

Insurance companies have broadened their perspectives on investment portfolio philosophy, and have shown a greater interest in nonconventional investment or tangible assets than in the traditional portfolios of publicly held paper

Table 13.5
Distribution of Assets of U.S. Life Insurance Companies

Year	Government Securites	Corporate Securities Bonds	Stocks	Mortgages	Real Estate	Policy Loans	Misc. Assets	Total
AMOUNT (000,000 omitted)								
1917	$ 562	$ 1,975	$ 83	$ 2,021	$ 179	$ 810	$ 311	$ 5,941
1920	1,349	1,949	75	2,442	172	859	474	7,320
1925	1,311	3,022	81	4,808	266	1,446	604	11,538
1930	1,502	4,929	519	7,598	548	2,807	977	18,880
1935	4,727	5,314	583	5,357	1,990	3,540	1,705	23,216
1940	8,447	8,645	605	5,972	2,065	3,091	1,977	30,802
1945	22,545	10,060	999	6,636	857	1,962	1,738	44,797
1950	16,118	23,248	2,103	16,102	1,445	2,413	2,591	64,020
1955	11,829	35,912	3,633	29,445	2,581	3,290	3,742	90,432
1960	11,815	46,740	4,981	41,771	3,765	5,231	5,273	119,576
1965	11,908	58,244	9,126	60,013	4,681	7,678	7,234	158,884
1970	11,068	73,098	15,420	74,375	6,320	16,064	10,909	207,254
1975	15,177	105,837	28,061	89,167	9,621	24,467	16,974	289,304
1976	20,260	120,666	34,262	91,552	10,476	25,834	18,502	321,552
1977	23,555	137,889	33,763	96,848	11,060	27,556	21,051	351,722
1978	26,552	156,044	35,518	106,167	11,764	30,146	23,733	389,924
1979	29,719	168,990	39,757	118,421	13,007	34,825	27,563	432,282
1980	33,015	179,603	47,366	131,080	15,033	41,411	31,702	479,210
1981	39,502	193,806	47,670	137,747	18,278	48,706	40,094	525,803
1982	55,516	212,772	55,730	141,989	20,624	52,961	48,571	588,163
1983	76,615	232,123	64,868	150,999	22,234	54,063	54,046	654,948
1984	99,769	259,128	63,335	156,699	25,767	54,505	63,776	722,979
1985	124,598	296,848	77,496	171,797	28,822	54,369	71,971	825,901
1986	144,616	341,967	90,864	193,842	31,615	54,055	80,592	937,551
PERCENT								
1917	9.6%	33.2%	1.4%	34.0%	3.0%	13.6%	5.2%	100.0%
1920	18.4	26.7	1.0	33.4	2.3	11.7	6.5	100.0
1925	11.3	26.2	.7	41.7	2.3	12.5	5.3	100.0
1930	8.0	26.0	2.8	40.2	2.9	14.9	5.2	100.0
1935	20.4	22.9	2.5	23.1	8.6	15.2	7.3	100.0
1940	27.5	28.1	2.0	19.4	6.7	10.0	6.3	100.0
1945	50.3	22.5	2.2	14.8	1.9	4.4	3.9	100.0
1950	25.2	36.3	3.3	25.1	2.2	3.8	4.1	100.0
1955	13.1	39.7	4.0	32.6	2.9	3.6	4.1	100.0
1960	9.9	39.1	4.2	34.9	3.1	4.4	4.4	100.0
1965	7.5	36.7	5.7	37.8	3.0	4.8	4.5	100.0
1970	5.3	35.3	7.4	35.9	3.0	7.8	5.3	100.0
1975	5.2	36.6	9.7	30.8	3.3	8.5	5.9	100.0
1976	6.3	37.5	10.7	28.5	3.3	8.0	5.7	100.0
1977	6.7	39.2	9.6	27.5	3.2	7.8	6.0	100.0
1978	6.8	40.0	9.1	27.2	3.0	7.8	6.1	100.0
1979	6.9	39.1	9.2	27.4	3.0	8.1	6.3	100.0
1980	6.9	37.5	9.9	27.4	3.1	8.6	6.6	100.0
1981	7.5	36.8	9.1	26.2	3.5	9.3	7.6	100.0
1982	9.4	36.2	9.5	24.1	3.5	9.0	8.3	100.0
1983	11.7	35.4	9.9	23.1	3.4	8.3	8.2	100.0
1984	13.8	35.8	8.8	21.7	3.6	7.5	8.8	100.0
1985	15.0	36.0	9.4	20.8	3.5	6.6	8.7	100.0
1986	15.4	36.5	9.7	20.6	3.4	5.8	8.6	100.0

Note: Beginning with 1962, these data include the assets of separate accounts. For detail on separate accounts, see page 41.

Sources: *Spectator Year Book* and American Council of Life Insurance.

assets such as stocks and bonds. Negative real interest rates in the late 1970s encouraged investments in appreciating tangible assets such as oil, gas, and real estate. Investment in commercial satellites, venture capital projects, leveraged buyout pools, commercial real estate, and commercial lending to corporate clients have heightened the shift in philosophy. As a share of their total investments, "other" investments by life insurance companies have grown from about 6 percent in 1980 to about 8.6 percent in 1986. There was a 130 percent increase from $28 billion to $65 billion in the past five years.

Life insurance companies usually put a high priority on investment quality because of state regulations and because of their fiduciary responsibility. State laws governing the operation of life companies are designed to require diversification of assets and limitation of investment risks. For example, most states limit holdings of common assets and place legal constraints on the quality of investment.

The composition of premium income has changed in recent years as customer demand for different types of risk protection and investment needs have changed. Traditional policy lines, such as whole life, have not been as well received by the public during periods of inflation, high interest rates, and volatile economic activity. For example, premiums from the sale of ordinary life insurance policies represented only 26.6 percent of total premium receipts in 1986, compared to 44 percent in 1981, and 50 percent in 1971. Premium receipts from annuity contracts grew to 43 percent in 1986, compared to 27 percent in 1981 and 10 percent of total premium income in 1971. Variable and universal life insurance have become popular during the 1980s, and together and in various combinations they accounted for 33 percent of the total amount of ordinary life insurance purchases in 1986. Health insurance premiums accounted for about 23 percent of premium income. (See Table 13.3.)

The changing mix of premium income, more competitive pricing of policies and guarantees under annuity contracts, and volatile interest rates, as well as a consumer shift toward investment-related insurance capital market securities, coerced the larger insurers away from their traditional buy-and-hold strategy. Insurance companies responded to these changes with a more flexible, market-sensitive investment policy. This included a shortening of the average maturity of investments, portfolio switching as opposed to a buy-and-hold strategy, more investments with equity kickers, the purchase of real assets instead of just paper securities, and greater participation in higher-yielding private placements. At the same time, the growth of separate accounts created a potential cash outflow less predictable than for conventional life insurance claims, increasing the need for more liquid, shorter-term money market instruments.

Life insurance companies have increased their direct ownershp of real estate, with greater involvement in the construction and direct ownership of apartment complexes, office buildings, and shopping centers. A number of insurance companies such as Prudential, Metropolitan Life, Equitable Life Assurance Society, Cigna, and Aetna Life and Casualty Company have become major real estate developers, either on their own or in partnership with established developers. However, commercial and residential mortgages, corporate notes and bonds, and U.S. government and federal agency securities are still dominant assets in insurance company portfolios.

Life companies classified by different product mixes show small though discernible differences in portfolio mixes. For example, life insurance companies with a high proportion of health insurance policies tend to have relatively high proportions of government bonds and common and preferred stock in their portfolios. This reflects their greater needs for liquidity, and the short-term nature of health insurance liabilities. Life companies with a high proportion of group term insurance policies tend to favor government bonds and hold a lower than average proportion of mortgages in their portfolio, while companies with a high proportion of annuities have a higher than average proportion of mortgage loans and corporate bonds.

Insurance Company Hedging: An Example

Insurance companies have come under pressure by a better educated and informed public to provide more competitive investment rates. For example, insurance companies are under competitive pressure to extend the maturities and improve the yields of the guaranteed investment contracts (GICs). If insurance companies wish to offer more competitive rates, they will either have to assume more rate risk or use financial futures to offset some of that risk. For example, if an insurance company guarantees a forward investment rate to a pension-fund client, the insurance company could lose money if rates decline before actual premiums are received for investment. A long hedge could alleviate much of the exposure to declining rates. The insurance company could also try instruments with a maturity longer than the life of the asset, while protecting the resale value of the asset with short futures positions in a similar maturity but in a different instrument that might correlate highly with the original instrument purchased.

LIABILITIES OF LIFE INSURANCE COMPANIES

Policy reserves, the major liabilities of life insurance companies, are held by these companies to meet the obligations of policyholders and their beneficiaries. The reserve is recognized in the insurance policy as cash surrender value. In a sense, policy reserves are a liquid asset, since whole-life policyholders can take out policy loans or cancel their policies, obtaining the cash surrender value. The amount of life insurance policy reserves that are compiled depends upon the type of policy involved. Greater policy reserves are required for endowment and whole-life policies than for term insurance policies. Group policies create smaller reserves than ordinary life insurance, and produce lower levels of investment earnings relative to the amount of premium income. At the end of 1986, life-insurance-company policy reserves amounted to $762 billion. (See

Table 13.6.) Total policy reserves of the U.S. life insurance companies include life insurance, annuities, and supplemental contracts (agreement by which the life insurance companies retain the cash sum payable to beneficiaries under the insurance policies and make payments in accordance with a particular settlement option).

The ratio of reserves to policyholders' surplus (Table 13.6) can be used as a measure of insurance leverage. Insurance companies have high leverage ratios resulting from reserves because of the long-term nature of their contractual obligations. Traditional leverage ratios are not relevant for insurers because insurance companies do not ordinarily use long-term debt.

Table 13.6
Policy Reserves of U.S. Life Insurance Companies (000,000 omitted)

Year	Amount	Year	Amount	Year	Amount	Year	Amount
1890	$ 670	1910	$3,226	1925	$ 9,927	1940	$27,238
1900	1,443	1915	4,399	1930	16,231	1945	38,667
1905	2,295	1920	6,338	1935	20,404	1950	54,946

| | | | Annuities | | Supplementary Contracts | | |
| | Life | Health | | | With Life Contin- | Without Life Contin- | |
Year	Insurance	Insurance	Individual	Group	gencies	gencies	Total
1955	$ 54,588	$ 575	*	$ 13,216	$1,895	$5,085	$ 75,359
1960	70,791	865	$ 4,327	14,952	2,674	4,864	98,473
1965	90,795	1,432	5,028	22,187	3,281	4,897	127,620
1970	115,442	3,474	6,951	34,009	3,726	4,177	167,779
1971	121,585	3,892	7,655	38,476	3,905	4,136	179,649
1972	128,257	4,347	8,560	43,503	3,937	4,155	192,759
1973	135,292	4,910	9,482	46,607	4,066	4,164	204,521
1974	142,273	5,607	10,511	49,861	4,176	4,079	216,507
1975	150,063	6,293	12,442	59,907	4,280	4,131	237,116
1976	158,359	6,962	15,347	73,393	4,410	4,304	262,775
1977	167,281	8,329	18,932	84,285	4,563	4,542	287,932
1978	177,743	9,596	23,057	98,673	4,751	4,663	318,483
1979	188,177	10,416	27,103	116,443	4,985	4,513	351,637
1980	197,865	11,015	31,543	140,417	5,215	4,284	390,339
1981	206,986	11,931	38,800	160,992	5,364	3,958	428,031
1982	213,783	13,181	51,002	191,898	5,654	3,842	479,360
1983	220,968	14,956	64,661	221,724	5,873	4,259	532,441
1984	225,904	16,552	76,983	254,592	5,831	4,331	584,193
1985	235,854	18,805	96,969	303,021	5,941	4,712	665,302
1986	252,035	21,294	121,146	355,756	6,283	5,410	761,924

Note: Before 1947, the business of health insurance departments of life companies was not included in this series.

*Included with "Group Annuities."

Sources: Spectator Year Book and American Council of Life Insurance.

Declared Dividends

Another important liability of life insurance companies is declared dividends. Declared dividends are refunds to policyholders representing the difference between premiums charged and the actual experience on policies or annuities sold on a participation basis. Essentially, the policyholder receives some of the difference between the premium charged and the actual experience. Life companies owned by stockholders usually sell nonparticipating policies with the annual cost of the policy equal to the premium. However, mutual life companies sell participating policies that pay dividends, and consequently tend to have slightly higher policy rates than rates at stock companies. In actuality, companies that sell participating policies overcharge on their premiums, allowing room for dividends. However, when the dividend is taken into account, the net cost to the insured of the mutual policy is often lower than the net cost of policies issued by stock companies.

MARKETING TRENDS

Mass merchandising, via mail solicitation, television, radio, and group- or association-sponsored business, is a trend that is likely to continue. It is an effort to reduce underwriting costs by eliminating the need for an agent. Another benefit is that if automatic payroll deductions or a credit card are used to collect premiums, the likelihood that customers would let their policy lapse would be reduced. Some banks have also become involved in insurance sales, as have brokerage firms.

New insurance offerings reflecting today's trends include:

1. Charge account insurance that will make payments on outstanding bills in case a worker is laid off;
2. Divorce insurance to cover legal expenses;
3. Small-business package policies;
4. Broadened insurance for dental treatments, vision-care coverage, and legal consultations are being offered on a group basis as company fringe benefits;
5. Homeowner's and personal auto, as well as life and health benefits, are being offered by more employers as part of fringe-benefit packages; and
6. Total asset protection needs for individuals and large business clients are being developed.

Other trends include the increasing popularity of term insurance, guaranteed insurance contracts, and variable and universal life insurance. Premiums on universal and variable life accounted for 42 percent of new premiums on life insurance sales in 1985.

There has also been a structural shift toward the "living concept" or longevity emphasis, and such products as annuities, tax shelters, guaranteed return vehicles, universal life, financial planning, and administration of funds. The life insurance industry continues to suffer from highly competitive pricing (declines of more than 50 percent in premiums per $1,000 of life insurance coverage in the last decade), policy loans, policy cancellations (known as lapses or surrenders), and increased expenses. Highly competitive market conditions have coerced most companies to pass through the benefits received from improved mortality and higher interest returns on their invested assets in the reduced price of insurance. With the prices for new insurance products falling as rapidly as they have, older policies on the books are becoming increasingly vulnerable to replacement. Policy replacement trends have accelerated rapidly during the past few years and have become a significant problem to more mature companies with traditional whole-life bases. This indicates that the existing base of older policies is not immune to a life insurance price war. Though large insurance companies can weather such price wars for long periods, the higher degree of competition is likely to continue to stimulate further consolidation within the life industry. Increased economies of scale in companies with older policy bases have become more of a necessity in order to control rising costs and servicing expenses. Home and field expenses, especially personnel occupancy costs, have been increasing substantially over the last 15 years. Life insurance companies have tried to counteract these rising costs by increased data processing and improved office management in an effort to reduce processing and legal costs.[6] Computers seem to achieve favorable economies of scale for large insurance companies, even though they increase fixed costs.

Insurance companies have also tended to favor group policies which reduce selling expenses and the number of policies written. There are serious problems with the distribution or marketing systems of most insurance companies. There has been a tendency to shift away from the agency system toward mass marketing, group sales and cluster association selling, and specialty product emphasis as a better way of controlling distribution and marketing expenses. It is highly likely that we will see more use of marketing via home computer hookups that will enable financial products, services, and transfers to be sold through the home electronics media. This would cut distribution costs considerably, and allow price-sensitive consumers even better product prices for insurance. Direct marketing through mail, credit cards, telecommunications, and other media represent more efficient distribution systems for smaller life policies and special coverages such as health, disability, and travel accident insurance. They are also a more efficient way of achieving a better market penetration. Another sales method—selling of insurance through financial institutions—also offers the advantage of convenient premium collection because premiums can be added to the mortgage or credit card payment. These alternative distribution methods are thought to be cheaper than maintaining a large sales staff and selling these policies through sales agents, who receive a large initial sales commission and smaller renewal commissions based on premiums paid for the policy. Sales costs at life companies are considerably higher than for other forms of financial investment. Vendors of other financial products have progressively lowered the cost of their marketing strategies through the use of new, lower cost distribution systems, while life insurance companies have retained their high-cost labor intensive marketing and distribution systems.[7]

Also, just as brokerage firms have begun to sell personal line insurance, insurance companies have begun to acquire or establish nonbank banks and brokerage firms in the hopes of tapping into "higher" income streams of brokerage firm clients. They also hope to cross-sell existing and new products to this group of higher income consumers. Most insurance companies have set up money market funds and mutual funds, and have also set up investment departments to manage money for pension funds, retirement plans, and profit-sharing plans. Insurance companies such as Travellers even offer the equivalent of Merrill Lynch's CMA account.

In the keynote address at the World Insurance Congress held in Philadelphia in 1982, Ralph Saul, former chairman of Cigna, described a marketplace where insurers will provide risk management services on a fee basis rather than accept risk themselves for an uncertain reward. He also commented that ATMs and two-way cable television systems are forging electronic links among banks, brokers, and insurers in a process of convergence that "could change totally the way financial services are delivered to individuals. . . . There appears to be little need for direct selling of personal lines."[8] Insurance companies will be under considerable pressure to reduce their costs and to become more efficient producers if they wish to survive and prosper in an era of a more sophisticated, price-conscious consumer shopping for financial services.

PENSION PLANS

Insurance companies, primarily in the life insurance field, compete against bank trust departments and investment companies for the management of pension funds. Insurance companies also compete for the management of IRA, Keogh, and 401(K) accounts. Since 1960, the number of workers covered by pension plans administered by life insurance companies has grown by about 7 percent annually, compared to a 3-percent rate for other private pension plans. At the end of 1986, there were 45.8 million private plans at life insurance companies, with total assets of $441 billion.

SEPARATE ACCOUNTS

Separate accounts are a separate legal entity from traditional, insurance company-owned investment assets. They represent investment accounts managed by a life insurer on behalf of corporate pension plans, mutual funds, partnerships, Keogh Plans, IRAs, and so forth, in return for management of the investment portfolio. Assets acquired in a separate account on behalf of the customer are held apart from all other insurance company assets, and are subject to much less restrictive investment regulations than assets held in the life company's general accounts.

The concept of a separate account arose in the early 1960s when life companies offered to manage pension plans of corporations. Separate accounts have been growing rapidly. For example, they represented $13 billion in 1975, $44 billion in 1981, and $109 billion in 1986. As recently as 1975, income receipts from separate accounts represented less than 10 percent of the industry's investment earnings; they represented close to one-third in 1981 and in 1986.

BANKS VERSUS INSURERS: THE IMPACT ON
THE INDEPENDENT AGENT

Banks will either underwrite personal lines of insurance (particularly life, health, auto, and homeowners) or act as an agent in attempting to sell these insurance lines within their branch systems or through mass marketing campaigns and "envelope stuffers" in monthly deposit or credit card statements (or both). The form they take will be a function of regulatory and congressional guidance, and to some extent, the willingness of bank senior management to expose their institutions to both risk and the cyclicality of underwriting profits in property and casualty lines. It is unlikely that banks will initially try to sell commercial and wholesale insurance lines, because they are more complex and subject to price-cutting. Also, there is less actual selling to do in homeowner's and car insurance, since 92 percent of automobile owners are insured, and 94 percent of homeowners have at least fire insurance coverage. The pricing of these lines is also more standardized and book, list or catalogue oriented. The ability and willingness of the bank to provide a direct loan or credit card financing is another advantage. In addition, since banks make auto, mortgage, and home improvement loans, they often have access to customers before the insurance agent is even contacted.

Essentially then, the potential entry of banks into the insurance business and the increased sale of products and services via cable-TV and home computer modules and modems does not bode well for insurance agents. It will, of course, take years for the banks to become effective sales agents and penetrate the market for personal lines insurance. However, with their enormous customer base and fine reputation for honesty and integrity, their close to 15,000 banks and 45,000 domestic branches represent a potentially powerful competition. Insurance agents may lose customers among price-conscious consumers who do not feel the need for personalized attention. As a precautionary move, independent insurance agents who are strictly in personal lines insurance might want to consider diversifying into commercial lines as well as group coverage. Also, in order to lock the customer in, the insurance agent might also wish to offer the client other insurance company products such as money market funds, mutual funds, and annuities.

DEMUTUALIZATION

A mutual insurance company can enhance its capital base by converting to the stock form of ownership. The advantages of demutualization include:

1. The opportunity for the insurance company to expand its base;
2. The opportunity for greater access to capital markets;
3. The ability to facilitate expansion through acquisitions and mergers;
4. The ability to form an upstream holding company that effectively allows the company to participate in business activities outside of the purview of the state insurance regulatory agency; and
5. The opportunity to attract and to offer management new, equity-linked incentive compensation plans.[9]

However, conversion to the stock form also has a number of disadvantages:

1. The process is arduous, complicated and costly.
2. Complex accounting, actuarial, valuation, ownership, legal, and tax issues must be resolved, while management strategy and operating results will be subject to greater scrutiny.
3. A stock company could become susceptible to an unfriendly takeover, and has the additional regulatory burden of security law compliance and the expense of shareholder reports, communications, and administration.[10]

Demutualization is one way to obtain additional capital that might be used to finance internal growth or to achieve external acquisitions. At the time of this writing, only one major insurance company has demutualized. It looks as if demutualization would be extremely difficult, if not impossible to achieve in certain key mid-Atlantic and New England states. Although the management of numerous insurance companies are favorably inclined toward the concept of demutualization, it is not likely to become an important issue in the decade of the 1980s.

MANAGEMENT ADJUSTMENTS

In order to deal with increasing costs and loss of customers and to strengthen and protect their margins, insurance companies have taken the following positive steps:

1. Continually developing new products and services, such as universal/variable life policies and pension fund and annuity management services.
2. Hedging against interest rate risk by more closely matching maturities of assets and liabilities and making greater use of financial futures, options, and swaps.

3. Strengthening company liquidity positions in the investment portfolio. This was accomplished by increasing investments in money market instruments and purchasing more marketable long-term securities. Insurance companies have more securitized assets such as mortgage pass-through securities and collateralized mortgage obligations, which allow others to turn relatively unliquid mortgages into new sources of cash.

4. Seeking to invest in higher yielding assets like diversified portfolios of junk bonds and direct equity or equity-kicker projects.

5. Decreasing marketing and service delivery costs by moving toward cheaper and more efficient sales programs than the traditional local sales agent method of generating customers. These methods include direct mail offerings, telemarketing, and marketing through branch offices of banks and stock brokerage firms. In addition, some insurance companies have moved their processing and computer operations out of areas where real estate and personnel costs are high to places where these costs are considerably lower.[11]

In addition to these steps, some life insurers have begun to pay benefits before death. For example, under a new Jackson National Life Insurance Company policy that covers six catastrophic illnesses, if the insured suffers a heart attack, a 25 percent advance payment of the death benefit will be paid. In another instance, a First Penn–Pacific Life Insurance Company policy will pay 2 percent of the death benefit each month until the maximum death benefit is reached if the insured is confined to a nursing home for at least six months. Insurance companies hope that these pre-death benefits will make life insurance more marketable to younger people and singles. There is an additional cost for coverage of this type that runs between 2 and 5 percent of the usual life insurance policy premiums.

NOTES

1. F. Yeager and N. Seitz, *Financial Institutions Management, Text and Cases* (Reston, Virginia: Reston Publishing Co., 1982), 187.

2. A. Gart and D. Nye, *Insurance Company Finance* (Malvern, Pa.: Insurance Institute of America, 1986), 95.

3. Ibid., 96.

4. F. Yeager and N. Seitz, *Financial Institutions Management*, 202-203.

5. Ibid., 202.

6. R. O. Edmister, *Financial Institutions, Markets and Management*, 2d ed. (New York, McGraw-Hill Book Co., 1986), 222.

7. T. Curry and M. Warshawsky, "Life Insurance Companies in a Changing Environment," *Federal Reserve Bulletin* (July 1986), 451.

8. A. Gart, *Banks, Thrifts, and Insurance Companies: Surviving the 1980s* (Lexington, Mass.: Lexington Books, 1985), 47.

9. Ibid., 112-113.

10. Ibid., 113.

11. Curry and Warshawsky, "Life Insurance Companies," pp. 449-460.

14

Property and Casualty Insurance Companies

HISTORY

The first insurance company in what is now the United States was established in Charleston, South Carolina, in 1735. Fire insurance companies were established in New York in 1787, and in Philadelphia a few years later. Health insurance has been written in the United States since before the Civil War, when it was first used to provide protection against a loss of income related to accidents and certain diseases. Modern health insurance began in the 1930s with the beginning of associations similar to Blue Cross.

OVERVIEW

The insurance industry has grown in both size and scope, with over 5,000 insurance companies in operation today. These companies employ over 1.8 million people, with close to 500,000 employed by property-casualty companies; 785,000 by life and health companies; and 580,000 by agents, brokers, and service personnel. The largest of the property-casualty insurers include State Farm, Allstate, Aetna, John Hancock, Cigna, and Travellers; while Prudential Metropolitan, Equitable, Aetna, John Hancock, and New York Life are among the leading life companies.

Property-casualty insurers generate premiums by selling protective policies to the public. These protective services cover a wide span of potential losses related to the ownership of property (aircraft, autos, boats, homes, commercial buildings, equipment, agricultural products, recreational vehicles, money, and other valuables) and to legal liabilities that might result from injury or damage to people or their property due to negligence or incompetence. Protection services sold by property-casualty insurance companies cover a much wider span of potential losses than life insurance company products. While they share the common characteristic of financial intermediation with life insurance companies, the term "insurance supermarket" is often applied to the assorted package of policies sold by large property-casualty insurance companies.

Another key difference between life insurers and property-casualty insurers lies in the predictability of the frequency and amount of claims of life insurance companies, and the lack of accurate predictability of the magnitude or frequency of claims that must be honored by property-casualty insurance companies. Most life insurance claims come due when a policy holder reaches retirement or dies, or the policy contract matures. These events are either known in advance or are actuarily predictable. A casualty claim can arise at any time, and the size of the claim is usually uncertain or unpredictable in advance. There is no way to predict the extent of damage due to a fire, the amount of a claim due to theft, or the size of the claim related to injury in an automobile accident. The amount of the claim is not fixed as is the case in the death benefit payable on most life insurance policies. However, there is usually an upper limit on the size of the claim which is a function of the amount of insurance coverage in the contract.

Insurance touches the lives of virtually all people. It provides financial protection for homeowners and renters, families, automobile owners, business owners, employees, and people who suffer property damage and injuries from the actions of others. It would be almost impossible to practice medicine, conduct business, or ship goods without property and liability insurance. With the current structure of American society, the "sue whenever possible" syndrome, and the generous awards given by juries in liability suits, the private insurance sector has become a pivotal industry in the U.S. economy. The basic role of insurance in the economic and social structure is to provide relief from the financial consequences of uncertainty germane to financial loss and, especially, the fear of loss.

Insurance rests on the fact that:

1. Individuals and organizations face potential losses that they may not be able to bear;
2. Such losses, if anticipated and averaged over large groups, are often found to be bearable by organizations;
3. The process of anticipating and averaging is possible through insurers;
4. These insurers agree to pay for all or part of the losses suffered by the insured; and
5. Insurers promise, in return for payments from relatively many (whose payments are expected to enable them to cover the losses), to absorb the expenses of the mechanism. (They also expect this will leave a modest excess for contingencies and possible profits.)

Although a British insurer may be authorized to write any type of insurance throughout the world, U.S. companies are restricted to specific types of insurance such as life insurance, annuities and title insurance, and auto, liability, and homeowner's insurance. The "compartmentalization" of insurance under-writers is unique, and is referred to as the American System.[1]

REGULATION

Insurance is said to be a business "affected with the public interest." Most regulation is at the state level, and involves, among other things, licensing, wording of contracts, rates, investments, accounting, and reporting.

The primary regulators of insurance are the state insurance commissions. Their regulatory attention covers the broad areas of finance, product, business methods, and liquidation or rehabilitation of insurance companies. State insurance commissioners are responsible for regulating insurance rates; establishing minimum standards for reserves; licensing insurers, agents, and brokers; revealing policy forms; setting minimum financial requirements for operating insurance companies, and making periodic audits to see that the firms meet their obligations to policyholders. Insurance investments are regulated by most states through setting limits on how much can be invested in various media and establishing procedures for evaluating investments for accounting purposes. The objective of such control seems to be maintaining the solvency of insurers. It should be noted that laws vary in stringency from state to state. Insurance companies are not subject to the National Bankruptcy Act, and their dissolution is normally within the jurisdiction of the state insurance commissioner. Insurance companies rarely become bankrupt because they are taken into receivership or conservatorship when conditions warrant, and are liquidated either by runoff of claims or by portfolio reinsurance by other insurance companies.

The National Association of Insurance Commissioners (NAIC) is an organization of insurance commissioners who meet regularly to discuss mutual problems and prepare model legislation for the respective legislatures. The commissioners have developed systems for cooperative company audits, simultaneous investigations of interstate problems, and information exchanges that increase efficiency in the regulatory process. The NAIC has helped overcome much of the burden of conflicting regulation in the different states.

TYPES OF PRIVATE PROPERTY AND CASUALTY INSURANCE

While the cost of life insurance has declined over the last decade as a function of competitive market conditions, longer life, and higher yields earned in the bond portfolio, auto and homeowner's insurance have gone up in price at a rate about equal to the inflation rate. On the other hand, commercial fire and multi-peril insurance rates declined substantially in price because of competitive conditions in the market place during the early 1980s, before rising substantially in late 1985 and 1986.

Property-casualty insurance companies protect their policyholders against financial losses associated with the ownership of property, personal or professional negligence, bad weather, crime, and accidents. Liability insurance is concerned with providing financial protection against legal liabilities that might result from injury or damage to people or their property, while property insurance is concerned with providing financial protection against damage and loss to the insured's property because of perils such as fire or burglary. A comparison of the different types of insurance and the amount of premium dollars generated follows (see Table 14.1).

Automobile Insurance

Auto insurance provides for losses related to the damage or theft of the insured's car; legal liabilities related to the ownership or use of a car, truck, or other motorized vehicle; or payment of medical expenses incurred in car

Table 14.1
Net Premiums Written by Line, 1985-1986*

	1986	1985	% Change
Auto Liability, Pvt. Passenger	$ 32,972,920,000	$ 28,243,882,000	+ 16.7%
Auto Liability, Commercial	11,108,002,000	7,842,789,000	+ 41.6
Total Auto Liability	44,080,922,000	36,086,671,000	+ 22.2
Auto Physical Damage, Pvt. Passenger	24,198,891,000	21,180,583,000	+ 14.3
Auto Physical Damage, Commercial	5,106,615,000	4,066,138,000	+ 25.6
Total Auto Physical Damage	29,305,506,000	25,246,721,000	+ 16.1
Total Automobile	73,386,428,000	61,333,392,000	+ 19.7
Medical Malpractice	3,491,905,000	2,769,230,000	+ 26.1
General Liability	19,364,658,000	11,544,152,000	+ 67.7
Total Liability (other than auto)	22,856,563,000	14,313,382,000	+ 59.7
Fire Insurance and Allied Lines**	6,933,221,000	6,173,369,000	+ 12.3
Homeowners Multiple Peril	15,222,027,000	14,066,391,000	+ 8.2
Farmowners Multiple Peril	828,365,000	769,915,000	+ 7.6
Commercial Multiple Peril	16,190,282,000	12,096,578,000	+ 33.8
Workers' Compensation	20,431,215,000	17,047,548,000	+ 19.8
Inland Marine	3,898,591,000	3,672,227,000	+ 6.2
Ocean Marine	1,224,729,000	1,176,528,000	+ 4.1
Surety and Fidelity	2,116,275,000	2,852,680,000	− 25.8
Financial Guaranty***	575,008,000	—	—
Burglary and Theft	121,055,000	122,259,000	− 1.0
Boiler and Machinery	531,319,000	618,358,000	− 14.1
Glass	26,608,000	25,492,000	+ 4.4
Aircraft	711,862,000	508,480,000	+ 40.0
Accident and Health	2,929,510,000	3,205,359,000	− 8.6
Other Lines	8,569,012,000	6,204,462,000	+ 38.1
Total, All Lines	$176,552,070,000	$144,186,420,000	+ 22.4

*Net premiums written represent premium income retained by insurance companies, direct or through reinsurance, less payments made for business reinsured.
**Allied lines include crop-hail insurance premiums, reported separately on page 28, and earthquake insurance premiums.
***Financial guaranty first broken out in 1986.

Source: A. M. Best Company, Inc., Best's Aggregates & Averages. Presented in *Insurance Facts 1987-88 Property Casualty Fact Book,* p. 16.

accidents. Automobile insurance accounts for about 40 percent of the total property-liability premiums, and is the principal service line for property-casualty insurers: about 40 percent of auto insurance premiums are designed to cover any physical damage caused by the operation of motor vehicles, while the remaining 60 percent of the automobile premiums paid by the public are for liability claims such as personal injuries. The bulk of auto insurance coverage is for private passenger cars owned by individuals and families, while just under 20 percent of all auto insurance premiums cover commercial vehicles.

Multiple Peril Insurance

This group represents the combining of what used to be individual policies covering such perils as theft, fire, storms, and liability into one package for the homeowner, tenant, or business concern. This type of insurance accounts for just under 20 percent of total premiums paid. The advantage of the comprehensive policy includes broad and necessary protection without expensive overlaps or dangerous gaps in coverage.

Workers' Compensation

Workers' compensation is compulsory for most employers. The benefits are determined by state law, while the premiums paid by employers are based on recent experience. Workers' compensation insurance provides a procedure for compensating employees for injuries that arise out of and in the course of employment. Insurance is available for the most part through private insurers, although six states have funds that compete with private insurers. Workers' compensation accounts for just under 12 percent of total net premiums written by property and casualty companies.

Liability Insurance

Liability insurance protects the insured against losses arising from personal injury to others and damage to the property of others. Liability insurance provides financial protection against claims arising from negligence or incompetence. The major types of liability insurance are the following:

1. Professional liability, including that of doctors, nurses, dentists, and hospitals, which is often referred to as malpractice insurance for medical personnel. Professional liability refers to liability arising from errors and omissions in the case of accountants or lawyers, and from bodily injury in the case of medical personnel. Because of many malpractice suits, physicians have begun to practice "defensive medicine," the ordering of additional diagnostic tests in order to avoid being sued.

2. Personal liability related to ownership of a residence or animals, or to participation in sports;

3. Contingent liability, which includes owners', contractors' and landlords' protection;

4. Business liability, including that of owners, landlords, tenants, manufacturers, contractors, elevators, products, owners' protection, and employers' contractual; and

5. Comprehensive liability, which covers off-premise as well as on-premise liability, and combines in one contract comprehensive general, personal, and farmers' personal.

The insurance company agrees to pay damages to third parties who have valid claims against the insured.

Fire and Allied

This line provides financial protection against the loss of or damage to buildings or personal property caused by fire, lightning, and other perils. Individual insurance policies have declined in importance because most insurers now write multiple-peril policies that include fire coverage in the package.

Marine Insurance

This line covers loss, theft, liability, or damage in connection with transportation of goods or commodities, covering cargo, freight, ship hulls, bridges, and dams, as well as personal property such as art, furs, jewelry, and silver. Ocean marine insurance covers cargo after it has been loaded onto ships, as well as coverage of the vessel and the shipowner's liability for damage or injury; inland marine covers goods in transit by other than marine vessels. Inland marine insurance protects domestic shipments by ships and barges on inland waterways, railroads, trucks, airplanes, mail, parcel post, messenger, armored car, and other forms of transportation. In addition, inland marine insurance includes personal property floater risks, or property that is mobile, such as clothes, jewelry, furs, animals, and construction equipment. Inland marine contracts also cover tunnels, lighthouses, bridges, and television and radio communication equipment.

Surety and Fidelity

Fidelity bonds are written to cover the possible dishonesty of employees, and to protect the employer against the loss of any kind of property. When bonded employees steal money or embezzle funds, the bonding company pays for the loss. Fidelity bonds are commonly obtained by financial institutions to cover employees who handle cash and marketable securities. Surety bonds differ from fidelity bonds because they insure that a specific obligation of one party to another party will be met, rather than indemnifying against criminal acts. Surety bonds are contracts of indemnity paying to the extent that an obligee has suffered loss. Suretyship protects against losses that may arise because an employee or contractor does not perform as expected because of inability or dishonesty. Most surety bonds are written for those seeking licenses or permits and for individuals doing contract construction.

CONSOLIDATION

Within the last two decades, the insurance industry as a whole has experienced a number of mergers and acquisitions by large conglomerates and holding companies, including ITT, American Express, J.C. Penney, American Brands, Continental Group, General Electric, Connecticut General and INA (forming CIGNA), and American General and NLT Corporation. Industrial companies have been buyers of life insurance companies because of earnings, stability, lower tax rates, and dividends from the insurance company that are 80 percent tax-free. Noninsurance firms have also shown an increasing interest in the acquisition of insurance agencies and brokerage firms. Furthermore, it appears as if large life insurance companies will continue to grow in the personal lines segment of the property and casualty business.

CAPTIVE

A growing number of large American businesses (for example, MMM, Gulf Oil, and Mobil Oil) have set up their own captive insurance affiliates and expanded their self-insurance program. It is estimated that approximately 200 of the largest 500 U.S. companies operate captive insurance subsidiaries or affiliates. These companies feel that they can save on insurance premiums in terms of actual prices paid for coverage, and can receive some tax benefits. Insurance premiums paid to a captive would normally qualify as a tax-deductible business expense. The formation of captives has slowed the growth of net premiums written by domestic companies during the 1980s.

INSURANCE BROKERS

A substantial share of business insurance coverage is sold through insurance brokers who purchase property-casualty insurance protection on behalf of corporate clients at the lowest possible price. Traditionally, insurance brokers collected commissions from insurance companies to whom they directed client business. However, more of the insurance broker's income is coming from direct charges to corporate clients in the form of negotiated commissions. Insurance brokers perform a variety of other insurance-related functions such as consulting, property management, claims processing, and the management of captive insurance companies owned by large manufacturing or industrial corporations.

RISKS AND RATES

Premiums paid by policyholders to property-casualty companies really represent the estimated cost of transferring future risk from the policyholder to the insurance company. Although the policyholder pays a fixed premium based on expected costs for the period of the insurance contract, the true cost to the insurance company of the transference of risk is uncertain until all claims are filed. It is not unusual for there to be a substantial underwriting loss, which must be covered by investment income, policy reserves, or both. If huge underwriting losses continue for a prolonged period of time, it is possible that the insurance company could be driven into bankruptcy.

Insurers set rates with specific objectives in mind. The rate should cover the projected cost of future claims and anticipated expenses, as well as providing for a reasonable profit. The rate-setting process is an attempt by insurers to quantify the unknown. The estimates of the cost of future claims and expenses are determined through an analysis of both past loss experience and projected socio-economic and legal trends that might have a financial impact on the risk covered. Rates usually reflect the cumulative loss experience for a given type of risk, and are adjusted based on actual or individual experience. Insurance companies spread the cost of risks and must properly price their product so that they can pool premiums from many to pay the claims expenses of a few.

In the study of insurance, "risk" is defined as uncertainty regarding the occurrence of an economic loss, while "peril" is defined as a cause of loss, such as fire or fraud. Some risks, such as those caused by fire, windstorm, theft, or auto accident, are typically transferred to private insurers, while risks rising out of social as well as physical phenomena such as unemployment, floods, and war may be insurable, but typically only when the government is an insurer or reinsurer. Risks such as unemployment, nuclear exposures, property expropriation by foreign governments, and the collapse of the banking systems are examples of loss exposures from which private insurance companies usually will not write policies. The federal government, state governments, or both, tend to offer insurance protection when private insurers do not provide insurance on an acceptable basis. One of the objectives of the management of risk is to alleviate the financial consequences of chance losses by using, either singly or in combination, the following techniques:

1. *Avoidance:* when a company refuses to undertake a project because the costs of meeting the insurance premium would result in making the project unprofitable;
2. *Control:* prevention and protection help reduce the probability that loss will occur and, after a loss, the limitation of the extent to which further damage could occur;
3. *Retention:* when a business or individual decides to bear the financial consequences of chance loss out of accumulated assets or current income, or from formal arrangements including self-insurance, use of deductibles, or creation of loss reserves that do not involve segregation of assets for the specific purpose of meeting uninsured losses;
4. *Transfer:* the shifting of the financial consequences of loss to an individual or firm willing to accept the transfer.

REINSURANCE

Reinsurance is the assumption by one insurance company (the reinsurer) of all or a part of a risk undertaken originally by another insurance company (the ceding company). The ceding company buys reinsurance to reduce liability, to gain underwriting capacity, or to provide financial support to the primary company. Reinsurance is both insurance and a management device that is vital to the effective operation of the primary insurance company.[2]

Reinsurance usually can be classified into two categories: treaty and facultative. In treaty reinsurance, the reinsured and the reinsurer agree that the former will cede and the latter will accept liability on a stock of future exposures according to a pattern set forth in the contract. The acceptance of liability by the primary insurer follows a detailed study of each risk. However, the treaty reinsurer knows nothing about the individual risk, and relies almost entirely on the assessment of the primary insurer's management and judgment of the underwriting. The reinsurer follows the fortune of the reinsured under a procedure of summary accounting once a treaty is accepted.

Facultative reinsurance is a transaction involving a specific risk or a well-defined group of risks, and its underwriting is similar to that performed in primary insurance. Both facultative and treaty reinsurance are available in worldwide markets for most commercial lines, and their proper use is essential for the operation of most primary companies.

INVESTMENTS OF PROPERTY-CASUALTY INSURERS

Insurance companies derive funds for investment from three major sources: policyholders' surplus, unearned premium reserves, and loss reserves. Investments of insurance companies totaled $282 billion in 1986. Investments represented close to 75.4 percent of total assets, which totaled more than $374 billion industrywide in 1986. Assets not considered investments include such items as office equipment, supplies, and buildings. The asset mix of property and casualty insurers depends on regulatory requirements and the demands of business. The assets of insurance companies are mainly securities. They have few inventories and fixed assets. Some assets are not recognized for solvency purposes, such as nonadmitted assets. Therefore, insurance companies tend to invest in securities that are acceptable as admitted assets. Insurance companies do not have traditional debt in their capital structure because their main liabilities are reserves. Important differences between the accounting procedures of insurers and those used by other business firms are in the valuation of assets and the treatment of expenses and revenues. Insurers recognize unrealized capital gains in surplus. Expenses are charged when they are incurred, but premium revenues are deferred until earned. Insurance companies "hold" money for their policyholders and invest it in various securities. However, unlike most other financial intermediaries, insurance companies do not explicitly pay for the use of their customers' funds.

Generally speaking, property-casualty companies exhibit a preference for liquid investments to enable them to meet claims when they arise, as well as a preference for at least some tax-exempt income. Consistent with these and other objectives, these companies attempt to maximize income on market investments while attempting to match the maturity of liabilities and assets.

The composition of the portfolio is affected by the nature of the risks insured, the costs of doing business, and taxes. Property-casualty portfolios are generally much shorter in maturity than those of life insurance companies that have actuarially predictable longer-term claims, since the contractual obligations of a property-casualty firm are generally of a short-term nature. The major investments of property-casualty insurers are municipal bonds, common stocks, and government and corporate short- and long-term debt instruments. Investments in mortgages and real estate are limited (see Table 14.2). It is interesting to note that since mortgages and bonds are carried at their amortized values, the book value of the assets of a life insurance company tends to be more stable over time than the assets of property-casualty insurers. The extreme cyclicality of the underwriting cycle in the property-liability industry leads to a different type of investment portfolio from that of life insurance companies. Mortgages represent under 2 percent of investment portfolio holdings, compared to just under 30 percent for life insurance companies. The holdings of corporate bonds are in the neighborhood of 10 percent of assets, compared to more than one-third for the life industry. Common stock holdings are typically much higher, as are the holdings of tax-exempt municipal bonds, the latter representing the biggest percentage of assets held in most property-casualty industry portfolios. Dividends received from common and preferred stock holdings are 80 percent tax-free, while the interest income from state and local municipal bonds are 100 percent free of federal income taxes.

While life insurance companies have a portion of their income exempted from taxation to meet policy reserves, property-casualty companies pay the usual corporate tax on all profits and investment income without exemption. Therefore, when net underwriting profits are positive or only modestly negative, property-casualty companies tend to invest heavily in tax-free municipal bonds in order to shelter income. Depending upon the relative returns on alternate investments and the tax position of the individual company, tax-exempt bonds might consist of between 25 and 50 percent of company investment portfolios. The investments held by these insurance companies reflect the industry's needs for investments having some of the following characteristics: safety, marketability, appreciation potential, and tax benefits.

Top management usually determines the investment strategy of the company. This is typically a function of underwriting losses, expenses, tax position, insurance regulation, cash flow needs, and industry outlook. There is a need to consider the interrelationships between the underwriting and investment operations in order to assure that compatible goals are pursued. The investment department implements the strategy of making portfolio decisions, and conducts primary research into the viability of alternative securities. This research is complemented by guidance and advice from financial analysts and investment bankers.

Table 14.2
Investments of Property/Casualty Insurers

	% in 1986	% in 1981	% in 1976
Bonds	**75.97**	**74.82**	**70.04**
U.S. Government	20.87	11.73	11.82
Other Government	.83	.81	.48
State, Municipal, etc.	11.54	14.90	16.32
Special Revenue, etc.	27.77	33.23	24.78
Railroad	.23	.31	.43
Utility	2.73	3.59	4.69
Miscellaneous	11.81	9.84	10.98
Parent, Subs., Affiliates	.19	.41	.54
Common Stock	**18.86**	**18.67**	**25.74**
Railroad	.16	.15	.03
Utility	1.73	1.52	1.92
Bank	—	.95	1.19
Insurance	—	.86	.33
Bank and Insurance*	1.71	—	—
Miscellaneous	9.70	10.53	10.95
Parent, Subs., Affiliates	5.55	4.66	11.32
Preferred Stock	**2.80**	**4.96**	**3.59**
Railroad	.04	.06	.01
Utility	1.57	3.33	2.83
Bank	—	.11	.02
Insurance	—	.03	.06
Bank and Insurance*	.23	—	—
Miscellaneous	.80	1.36	.59
Parent, Subs., Affiliates	.15	.07	.08
Other	**2.38**	**1.55**	**.63**
Mortgages	1.60	.77	.29
Collateral Loans	.06	.09	.05
Other Invested Assets	.73	.69	.29

*Separate breakout of bank and insurance items no longer available as of 1983.

NOTE: Sums of individual items may not add up to totals because of the effects of rounding.

Source: A.M. Best Company, Inc.

Insurance accounting rules tend to provide some insulation of policyholders' surplus from the risk of fluctuating asset values because insurers can value corporate, government, and municipal bonds in good standing at amortized cost rather than at current market value. This practice reduces one aspect of investment risk.

In managing the investment portfolio, it is extremely important for the insurance company to maintain considerable liquidity in order to meet expenses and loss claims. To maximize their interest income while maintaining liquidity, insurance companies generally move funds above a minimum balance level out of their demand deposit accounts and shift them into money market funds, repurchase agreements, or some other short-term investment. They also attempt to match maturities in the portfolio with known periods when payments or major expenditures are expected.

Portfolio investment decisions are extremely important because property-casualty insurance-company profits have come almost entirely from investment income during the 1980s. Financial models can be used to explore the risk-return trade-offs for different investment allocation strategies. The models can be used to help allocate the optimal mix of short-, intermediate-, and long-term investments to meet cash needs for paying claims and expenses while earning the maximum investment income.

UNDERWRITING RESULTS

Property-casualty insurance is the business of assuming risks, that is, indemnifying others against specific losses in return for premiums paid. If the risks are properly underwritten, then insurance companies earn profits because there are advantages to pooling risks, and because the premiums earned exceed the expected value of all claims. Modest insurance company profits are usually acceptable to individuals and businesses seeking insurance because they are willing to make a small payment (insurance premium) in order to avoid a large loss.

That is the situation in theory. Property-casualty companies have had net underwriting losses in every year since 1979. Their net underwriting losses have ranged from $1.3 billion in 1979 to a peak of $24.8 billion in 1985. Insurance companies can afford modest underwriting losses because of a large income that is generated from their investment portfolios. For example, even though insurance companies suffered an underwriting loss of $1.3 billion in 1979, income of $9.3 billion from investment holdings yielded combined before-tax net income of close to $8.0 billion. The same situation repeated itself in 1980 through 1983 when investment income exceeded net underwriting losses. However, during 1984 and 1985, net underwriting losses exceeded net income from investment holdings by $3.8 and $5.3 billion respectively, while during 1986, investment income exceeded net underwriting losses by $6 billion (see Figures 14.1, 14.2, and 14.3).

One popular measure of insurance underwriting success and efficiency is in the combined ratio, or ratio of losses from claims and operating costs to premiums written. The combined ratio rose from 97.4 in 1978 to 116.5 in 1985, before declining to 108.1 in 1986. These rates suggest that the property-casualty industry as a whole absorbed heavy losses. The overall cost of underwriting operations in 1985 and 1986 amounted to the equivalent of $1.165 and $1.081 for every dollar in premiums received.

The effect of inflation on property repair costs and the costs of medical care have also contributed to the poor underwriting results. In summary, losses and expenses involved in adjusting claims accounted for nearly 89 cents of every premium paid to property and casualty insurance companies in 1985, while sales and administrative expenses, taxes, and dividends to policyholders amounted to approximately 23 cents, 3 cents, and 1.6 cents, respectively for every premium dollar. Since the turn of the century, the insurance industry has been dominated by boom-and-bust pricing cycles brought on largely by the inherent uncertainty of the business and fluctuations in interest rates which affect investment portfolio

Figure 14.1
Underwriting Gains/Losses after Policyholder Dividends
Property/Casualty Insurance Business, 1965-1986

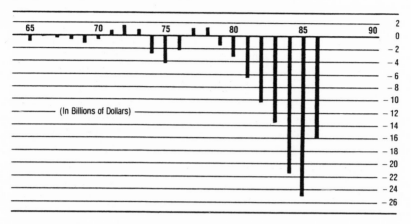

Figure 14.2
Investment Income, Property/Casualty Insurers,* 1965-1986

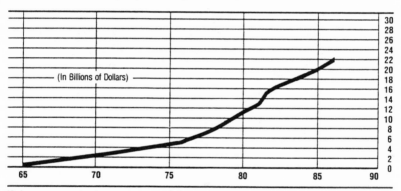

*Industry aggregates less investment expenses; before taxes.

Figure 14.3
Combined Net Income* before Taxes, Property/Casualty Insurers, 1965-1986

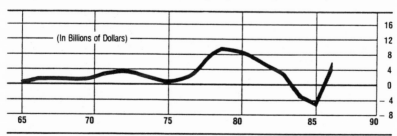

*Includes both underwriting gains or losses and aggregate investment income.

Source: Insurance Facts, 1987-88 Property/Casualty Fact Book, p. 21.

income. Prior to the 1980s, most previous cycles moved within a narrow band between charging too much (using a modest underwriting profit) and charging too little (generating a modest underwriting loss). As a matter of fact, in only five years during the post–World War II era have the underwriting profit margins of U.S. companies approximated the 5-percent profit margin typically figured in premium rates charged the public. The price swing in the 1980s brought about record underwriting losses in 1985, which reached $24.8 billion, while investment reached only $19.5 billion (see Table 14.3).

A record 21 insurance companies became insolvent in 1985, and more than 85 reinsurance companies withdrew from the market in 1984 and 1985. What caused the severity of the underwriting downturn? There are numerous explanations that involve industry structure, inflation, overcapitalization, poor pricing policies, bad underwriting decisions, poor management, and an industry that became absorbed in gaining market share and investment income rather than concentrating on intelligent underwriting practices. According to Myron M. Picoult, an insurance industry analyst with Oppenheimer & Company, "the industry got carried away with high interest rates and didn't pay attention to its knitting." Insurance companies engage in an unending balancing act juggling the risks of underwriting against the benefits of investment income. In a scramble to draw in premium dollars (which grew from $90 billion to $177 billion in 1986) which could be invested at high, double-digit interest rates, many insurers abandoned their conservative underwriting policies. Massive price cutting followed. The actions of insurance companies germane to underwriting and pricing worked for a while until interest rates declined dramatically and investment income could no longer match underwriting losses (for example, in 1984 and 1985). The false security created by the high interest rates led to a breakdown in underwriting practices and prices.

The insurance industry is also highly competitive and fragmented. With 3,600

Table 14.3
Property and Casualty Insurers (Billions of Dollars)

	1981	1982	1983	1984	1985	1986	1987
Investment Income	13.2	14.9	15.9	17.7	19.5	21.9	23.5E
Underwriting Losses	6.3	10.3	13.3	21.5	24.8	15.9	9.8E
Combined Net Income	7.0	4.6	2.7	-3.8	-5.3	6.0	13.7E
Net Premiums Written	99.3	104.3	108.3	117.8	142.3	176.5	n.a.
Total Assets	212.3	231.7	249.1	264.7	311.4	374.1	n.a.

different property and casualty insurers, no one company or group can maintain price discipline. For example, Aetna, one of the largest companies, accounts for less than 5 percent of the total market. As a matter of fact, the 10 largest insurers have a combined market share of 38 percent. As a result, it is difficult for any company to raise prices in a competitive market because it is felt that it would only lose market share. Barriers to entry are low so that almost any cash-rich company or group can gain industry entrance. Record-breaking interest rates lured new and inexperienced players into the business with millions of dollars in new capital. This led to excess capacity in the industry and enormous price cutting in order to capture a larger share of premium dollars.

In addition, there was the increased willingness of the courts to broaden the notion of liabilities, which made underwriting even worse. For example, the average annual size of product liability verdicts was $346,000 in 1979 and $1,247,000 in 1983. Between 1979 and 1983-1984 there was a 16.5 percent increase (to 10,745) in the number of product liability cases commenced in Federal District Courts. Also, in 1983 there were 16 malpractice claims filed for every 100 doctors (contrasted to 3 per 100 in the early 1970s). Deregulation also played a role. It gave insurance companies more freedom to set rates without approval from state regulatory bodies. As a result, the traditional check on insurance-industry pricing eroded at the time of the greatest competitive rate wars on commercial insurance lines.

Insurers were also particularly attracted to policies with "long tails" during the early 1980s. That is the industry's phrase for a business where claims for losses are likely to be filed far into the future rather than immediately, as in auto accidents. Insurance companies liked the "long tails" because of the longer time they had to earn income on the premiums before having to pay any claims. However, the long-tailed policies are coming back to haunt insurers in court, whether it is in the newly uncovered ills caused by asbestos, the Dalkon Shield intrauterine device, drugs, nuclear power, or unknowns yet to come.

During the period from 1984 through the first half of 1987, 67 property-casualty companies declared insolvency. This compared to 81 insolvencies during 1969 through 1983. Compounding the problem, insurers had to pay a record of $532.6 million during 1986 in state-guaranteed funds, which assess surviving insurers for the unpaid claims of insolvent insurance companies. This assessment amounted to a scant $49 million in 1984. Moreover, in June 1987, state regulators placed 516 companies out of 2,000 property and casualty insurance companies they reviewed on their watch list, with 200 flagged for immediate attention.

Behind the high level of insolvencies are the suicidal pricing practices of the early 1980s, when insurers slashed prices to attract premium dollars to invest at high interest rates. Insurance companies were seduced by this strategy since they book income immediately, while losses may not occur until some time in the future. In the commercial insurance lines, rates fell substantially in the early 1980s because of overcapacity in the industry and intense competition from both domestic and foreign competition. The industry has made an effort to protect its remaining profit margins with substantial price increases on commercial insurance and reinsurance lines, and more skillful tax and investment management. The interplay of underwriting losses and investment income in shaping property-casualty insurance profits suggests that the industry's pricing policies and earnings are highly interest-rate sensitive. Rising interest rates, which usually imply increased investment income on newly generated premiums, led many companies to try to increase their market share of written premiums without consideration of the poor underwriting practices and results. The industry is also sensitive to business cycle fluctuations. For example, during recessions there is usually a declining demand for commercial insurance policies and there is usually more arson. This problem is often exacerbated by the fact that insurance premium rates are often increased during these times as companies try to make up for declining dollar sales volume by charging higher prices for insurance coverage.

LIABILITIES AND CAPITAL STRUCTURE

Insurance companies hold reserves to provide for future underwriting claims and as protection against losses of assets resulting from bad investments. In principle, total reserves will increase gradually as an insurer's volume of business grows. However, conditions can change and alter basic actuarial assumptions germane to losses. If poorly handled, reserving decisions can give an insurance company the image of being poorly managed. In some cases, it can even undermine the insurer's solvency. Solvency becomes an issue because an increase to loss reserves comes directly out of earnings and reduces the capital available to protect against insolvency. If an insurance company overreserves, current earnings will be depressed, and it may cause a company to price its products too high and lose market share. On the other hand, inadequate reserves can lead to underpricing, which often increases market share in the short run. However, if larger than anticipated underwriting losses develop, underreserving produces inadequate earnings, which sometimes leads to insolvency.

The major liabilities of an insurance company are, first, the unearned-premium reserve and, second, the loss and loss-adjustment reserve. Loss reserves are created to cover unpaid claims, a matter of fact because insurers collect premiums in advance. The regulatory authorities require them to set up unearned premium reserves to make sure that insurers will fulfill their contractual obligations. These reserves play a key role in the capital structure of insurance companies. In addition, policyholders' surplus is relatively large because of the variability associated with losses from year to year. By examining Table 14.4, it can be seen that policyholders' surplus was $94.3 billion in 1986 and that the premium to surplus ratio was 1.85. It is important to recognize that the level of insurance leverage varies among the different lines of insurance. Property lines have a "short tail" because loss payments tend to be made quickly, while liability lines tend to have larger loss reserves outstanding for a longer period of time relative to property lines. These liability lines are said to have a long tail with respect to loss payout.

The role of reserves as a form of financial leverage explains why an insurer will continue in business even though it is suffering regular underwriting losses. The reserve-to-policyholders' surplus ratio becomes unfavorable to stockholders only when underwriting losses related to reserves exceed the return on the investment portfolios. Therefore, nonequity financing adds to an insurance company's income stream as long as the cost of financing the reserves is less than the returns from invested assets. This latter effect helps to explain the high leverage ratios of insurance companies. It is important to note that insurance companies cannot use debt, so traditional leverage ratios are not relevant.

The loss and loss-adjustment reserve is the main liability of property-casualty insurers, while the second most important liability is the unearned-premium reserve. As a percentage of total assets, the loss reserves have increased from 32.7 percent in 1972 to approximately 50 percent in 1986. This increase reflects the growing importance of liability lines in the business mix. Liability lines are characterized by a relatively long delay in the payment of losses. On the other hand, the importance of the unearned-premium reserve has decreased over time. Because of inflation and rate-adjustment considerations, many insurers have moved to policies with shorter terms, which explains part of the relative decline in these reserves. Policyholders' surplus has also decreased from 36.6 percent of total assets in 1972 to close to 25.2 percent in 1986. Policyholders' surplus is

Table 14.4
Operating Results, Property/Casualty Insurers, 1984-1986
(000 omitted from dollar figures)

	1986	1985	1984	% Change 1985-86	% Change 1984-85
Assets	$374.088.083	$311.364.665	$264.734.722	+ 20.1%	+ 17.6%
Net Premiums Written	176.552.070	144.186.420	118.166.311	+ 22.4	+ 22.0
Premiums Earned	166.381.186	133.341.852	115.009.836	+ 24.8	+ 15.9
Losses and Adjustment Expenses Incurred	135.765.622	118.572.435	101.445.723	+ 14.5	+ 16.9
Loss and Loss Adjustment Ratio	81.60%	88.92%	88.21%	− 8.2	+ 0.8
Underwriting Expenses Incurred	44.542.343	37.585.418	33.184.338	+ 18.5	+ 13.3
Underwriting Expense Ratio	25.23%	25.95%	27.98%	− 2.8	− 7.3
Combined Ratio (before Dividends to Policyholders)	106.83%	114.87%	116.19%	− 7.0	− 1.1
Combined Ratio (after Dividends to Policyholders)	108.13%	116.52%	118.01%	− 7.2	− 1.3
Statutory Underwriting Gain (Loss)	(13.747.925)	(22.597.292)	(19.378.885)	− 39.2	+ 16.6
Dividends to Policyholders	2.164.969	2.196.247	2.098.062	− 1.4	+ 4.7
Net Underwriting Gain (Loss)	(15.912.894)	(24.793.539)	(21.476.947)	− 35.8	+ 15.4
Net Investment Income	21.924.445	19.507.869	17.659.729	+ 12.4	+ 10.5
Operating Earnings after Taxes	6.610.383	(3.327.453)	(2.150.139)	− 298.6	+ 54.8
Policyholders' Surplus	94.288.390	75.511.417	63.809.497	+ 24.9	+ 18.3
Premium to Surplus Ratio	1.87 to 1	1.91 to 1	1.85 to 1		
Dividends to Stockholders	2.806.818	2.723.108	2.342.572	+ 3.1	+ 16.2

Source: A. M. Best Company, Inc., Best's Aggregates & Averages. Presented in *Insurance Facts 1987-88 Property Casualty Fact Book.*

still relatively volatile because of the variability associated with year-to-year losses.

OTHER FINANCIAL RATIOS

A few specific financial ratios for insurance companies have been developed:

1. Capacity or Solvency Ratios

Kenny Fire Ratio = Policyholders' surplus/Unearned premium reserve

Kenny Casualty Ratio = Premiums written/Policyholders' surplus

Cover Ratio = Admitted assets/Premiums written

In evaluating the adequacy of the capitalization of an insurance company relative to the volume of its business, the Kenny Fire Ratio should be greater than or equal to 1, and the Kenny Casualty Ratio should be greater than 2, while the rule-of-thumb for the cover ratio is 1.25 or more.

2. Liquidity Ratio

Liquidity Ratio = Invested assets/Loss reserve and unearned premium reserve

A ratio of 1 or more is considered acceptable.

3. Profitability Ratios

Combined Ratio = Losses + Loss adjustment expense/Premiums earned + Expense incurred/Premiums written

Underwriting Profit = 100 − Combined ratio

Return on Net Worth = Net profit/Policyholders' surplus

A combined ratio of 100 indicates that the insurance company broke even on underwriting results. As long as investment income exceeds underwriting losses, the insurance company is not in danger of being insolvent.

INSURANCE MARKETING

Most marketing experts feel that life and disability insurance coverage must be sold to the public, while auto, fire, homeowner's, workers' compensation, and professional liability insurance are deemed to be bought. Insurance companies can use a direct distribution system for marketing their product (direct writing). In this case, the insurance agent is an exclusive representative of the insurance company, or the insurer uses direct mail or telemarketing. In addition to using direct distribution channels, property-liability insurers also use indirect distribution systems. Under the indirect system, consumers acquire their insurance from an independent agent or intermediary, who represents more than one company.

Agents who work for direct writers are usually exclusive agents of the insurer and work on a commission basis. The agents do not own the business they sell, and cannot bind the insurance company. On the other hand, much of the property-casualty insurance sold in the United States is distributed through the independent agency system. The general agent is usually an independent business person who works on a commission basis and owns the business sold; the agent controls the renewal of contracts and can bind coverage for the insurance company, change the terms of the contract, and negotiate premiums.

Mass marketing is popular in selling some forms of property insurance. One method is distribution through employer payroll deductions. Although underwriting is done on an individual basis, the premiums are usually less expensive because of economies of scale and savings in commissions that arise because of mass marketing. Some insurers have reduced commission costs by distributing their products through mass marketing and through brokerage firms.

BUYING INSURANCE

A general rule of thumb is to insure large potential losses first and to use deductibles to avoid paying premiums for high-frequency, low-severity losses. A good insurance agent can help a customer eliminate some of the errors associated with buying insurance. These errors include:

1. Underinsurance;
2. Excessive insurance costs related to failure to use deductible and coinsurance clauses;
3. Failure to adopt loss-control programs, such as implementing a safety program and installing sprinklers;
4. Uneconomic arrangements of insurance, such as buying collision insurance for old cars, and underinsuring large exposures to loss as in the product or professional liability area; and
5. Selecting an insurance company that is in a weak financial condition and is a candidate for insolvency.

Choosing the appropriate insurance company and the right agent can be a complex and time-consuming effort. Insurance companies differ in types of coverage offered, costs, financial strength, and services provided. It is important to make a careful selection of both agent and company.

NEW YORK INSURANCE EXCHANGE

When the industry-sponsored and -regulated New York Insurance Exchange started up in 1980, the idea was to build a great marketplace, like Lloyd's of London, where insurance buyers could walk from one underwriting syndicate to another, shopping for the best rates and terms for their big and unusual risks.

Most of the coverage written on the exchange is reinsurance, coverage insurers buy from one another to spread the effect of single huge losses. The idea was to keep in the United States much of the $2 billion a year in premiums that had been placed with Lloyd's of London.

Unlike Lloyd's, U.S. syndicates were to have limited liability, and an insolvency fund was established. Each member syndicate deposited $500,000 which was to be part of the syndicates' own reserves backing potential underwriting losses. Beyond that, each syndicate was required to put up $3.5 million in capital.

Policies written on the New York Insurance Exchange reached a level of less than 10 percent of the $6 billion written by Lloyd's in 1984. In addition, a torrent of big hurricanes and huge casualty losses from 1982 through 1984 created such big deficits that many of the fledgling insurance syndicates writing policies at the exchange were in trouble almost from the beginning. At the time of this writing, 8 of the 50 little syndicates that wrote insurance on the exchange have declared insolvency.

Most of the solvency fund to cover their losses has been drawn down, with losses still arriving. Conflict has broken out among the huge corporations, smaller insurers, and individual investors that own the little syndicates over who will pay the mounting bills. Three healthy syndicates have sued to stop the solvency fund from paying out money to customers of the failed syndicates. The prospect of possibly having to ante up still more money to cover additional losses of the insolvent syndicates has caused the New York Exchange to close.

EMERGING FINANCIAL SERVICES INDUSTRY

Historically, insurers concentrated their efforts on selling insurance products rather than a diversified portfolio of financial services. However, during the 1980s, many insurance companies have become more customer-oriented, and have begun to offer their customers financial planning and a variety of new insurance and investment products. Many insurance companies have purchased brokerage and investment management firms, and have set up investment companies and nonbank banks. At the same time, life insurance companies have extended their operations into the property-casualty sector and vice versa; many brokerage firms have purchased insurance companies and set up nonbank banks or savings and loans; and retail stores (for example, J.C. Penney, Sears, and Montgomery Ward) and commercial and savings banks are selling insurance directly to customers.

There has been a tendency toward diversification, mergers and acquisitions, and greater competition within the financial services industry, as well as new product innovation and new modes of distribution.[3] This has been facilitated by technological, regulatory, economic, and social change. As the products sold by insurance companies, brokerage firms, and depository institutions become more homogeneous, it may be difficult to distinguish between functions performed by the various financial intermediaries.

MANAGEMENT ADJUSTMENTS

Property-casualty insurance company managements have begun to follow the following strategies:[4]

1. Diversification into new markets and services in order to reduce risks and lower unit operating costs;

2. careful integration of tax management in both the underwriting and investment sides of the business;

3. avoidance of "price wars" in the commercial insurance field that has historically driven premiums charged customers so low as to make these policies unprofitable even after taking into account investment income generated from premium cash flows;

4. closer and more careful management of operations and computer-based automation attempting to achieve increased employee and agent productivity;

5. greater use of reinsurance to minimize risk from any one particular catastrophe; and

6. increased capitalization by reinsurance companies to enable them to participate in more attractive syndications and to enable them to better absorb losses without catastrophic consequences to the balance sheet of the insurance company.

NOTES

1. R. O. Edmister, *Financial Institutions: Markets and Management,* 2nd ed. (New York: McGraw Hill Book Co., 1986), 222.

2. R. L. Braddock, "Reinsurance," in *Property and Liability Insurance Handbook,* ed. J. D. Long and D. W. Gregg (Homewood, Ill.: Richard D. Irwin, Inc., 1965), 955.

3. R. J. Shima, "Making Money in Insurance," in *The Financial Services Handbook: Executive Insights and Solutions,* ed. E. M. Friars and R. N. Gogel (New York: John Wiley & Sons, 1987), 133-139.

4. M. Williams, "Big Underwriting Losses at Cigna Reflect Serious Earnings Problem Among Insurers," *Wall Street Journal,* May 4, 1984.

15

Investment Banking and the Securities Industry

HISTORICAL PERSPECTIVES

The first investment banking house in the United States was founded by Thomas A. Biddle in Philadelphia in 1764. Alexander Brown set up an investment bank in Baltimore when he left his dry goods business. Other general store proprietors and merchants who had been advancing credit to their customers in domestic trade joined the transition from selling goods to selling credit. They included, among others, Lehman Brothers; Goldman, Sachs and Company; Kuhn, Loeb and Company; Astor and Sons; and Corcoran and Raggis.[1]

Investment banks derive their name from their traditional functions: locating and collecting funds for clients so they can finance new investment products. In the early years, private bankers did little investment banking or securities underwriting. Investment banking remained a small business until well after the Civil War, for the simple reason that raw materials for a securities business did not exist in abundance; even government securities were in short supply. Part of the reason for this was that the U.S. economy was primarily agricultural.[2]

Three types of organizations traditionally compose the securities industry: investment banks perform the service surrounding a public offering of securities; brokers arrange the buying and selling of securities; and exchanges provide a place to actually conduct transactions and a vehicle for setting price. Investment banks can be classified into two categories: originating firms and distribution firms. Originating firms are the major players in the development of securities offerings. Distribution firms come together in syndication, under the guidance of an originating firm to guarantee and sell the securities of an issuer.[3] Brokerage involves bringing together buyers and sellers, facilitating trades through maintaining a marketplace, and assuring that the trade is complete.

The investment banking community is best known for its ability to underwrite and distribute common stock and new corporate, government, and municipal debt issues; arrange private placements; provide funds management and real estate investment advice; and act as marriage brokers and advisers in the merger and acquisition business and in other corporate services in this country and abroad. As a matter of fact, investment banking is becoming more internationally oriented, causing firms such as Goldman Sachs and First Boston to become global in nature.

Many of these investment banking firms also provide brokerage services to both institutional and retail clients. Investment bankers are often referred to as securities dealers. They usually participate in most financial markets, including the money and capital markets, spot and futures markets, foreign exchange markets, real estate markets, commodities markets, and most secondary markets. (See Figure 15.1).

The classic underwriting and corporate finance functions of the investment banking business are going through a period of upheaval and transition as commercial banks and insurance companies are competing in some segments of the business, such as the underwriting of revenue bonds, Eurodollar syndications, and commercial paper, as well as acting as merger and acquisition advisers.

Investment banking has remained fiercely competitive, with a large move toward vertical integration. Companies that were primarily investment bankers, specializing in underwriting and corporate client services, have moved into more broadly based brokerage distribution services, while retail-oriented brokerage firms such as Merrill Lynch acquired White Weld & Co., a prominent investment banking firm in the late 1970s, and the institutional business of A. G. Becker in the early 1980s. The latter acquisition represents an example of backward vertical integration. The nature of competition within investment banking is changing. Price competition has cut underwriting fees to new lows, while the simplification of securities registration requirements could make underwriters less necessary. Fortunately, the need to transfer risk continues to provide a strong incentive for utilizing the services of investment banks.[4] In addition, many nonbrokerage firms acquired either brokerage houses or investment banking firms. For example, Prudential Insurance bought Bache Halsey Stuart Shields; Sears purchased Dean Witter Reynolds; and American Express acquired Shearson Loeb Rhoads, Lehman Brothers, and E.F. Hutton.

The biggest change encompassing the investment banking industry is the consolidation of large financial resources among a few large investment bankers. Table 15.1 shows that underwriting is dominated by Salomon Brothers, First Boston, Merrill Lynch, Goldman Sachs, Drexel Burnham Lambert, Shearson-Lehman American Express, Morgan Stanley, Kidder Peabody, Prudential-Bache, and Paine Webber. What the table does not show is that Salomon was in the first place in underwriting mortgage-backed securities, First Boston in auto-loan-backed securities, Merrill Lynch for common stocks, Drexel for "junk bonds," and Credit Suisse First Boston for Eurodollar financing.

Figure 15.1
Organization of a Typical Investment Bank

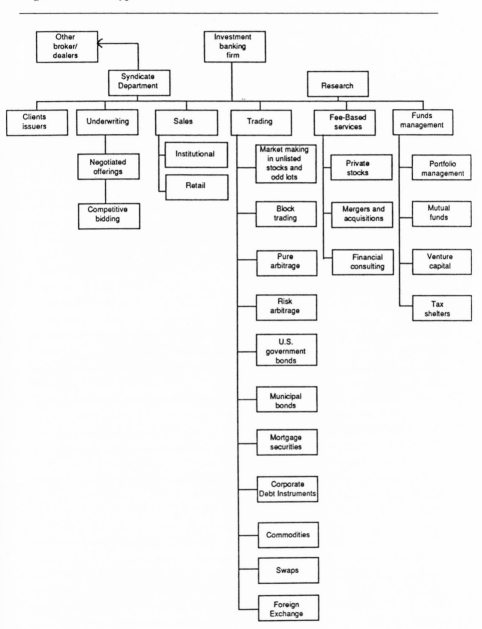

Table 15.1
Leading Underwriters for U.S. Issuers

Manager	Total Amount Managed ($ billions)		
	1987	1986	1985
Salomon Brothers	40.8	53.6	34.2
First Boston	32.6	47.0	25.7
Morgan Stanley	31.8	33.2	12.7
Merrill Lynch	31.8	31.4	17.6
Goldman Sachs	29.2	31.0	19.9
Drexel Burnham Lambert	21.2	30.0	13.3
Shearson Lehman	20.0	19.9	10.3
Kidder Peabody	10.0	10.5	3.9

Source: Select annual reports, newspaper articles, IDD Information Services

The total volume of securities sold in the United States and abroad by U.S. investment banking companies doubled in 1986 to $318.4 billion from the previous record of $171.5 billion in 1985. Most of the gain came in the U.S. market, where volume more than doubled to about $220 billion. The large decline in interest rates produced not only a record volume of new corporate issues, but also a substantial number of debt refinancings, particularly among industrial companies and utilities.

John M. Hennessy, chairman of Credit Suisse First Boston, has stated that "people will look back at the 1980s as the decade when truly global flows became an important impetus to world growth." The economic effect of this integration of the world's capital markets could be as significant as post–World War II liberalization of merchandise trade under the General Agreement on Tariffs and Trade.

Historically, many investment banking firms specialized in one or more products such as institutional brokerage, research, retail brokerage, or the financing of corporations, government agencies, and state and local governments. Some firms focused on a particular geographic region, while others specialized in a particular industry, such as energy, insurance, or banking. Since May Day 1975, many of the large, New York-based securities firms have broadened their lines of business and acquired other firms to strengthen their competitive position.[5]

Although many securities firms offered both investment banking and broker services, by the early 1980s, only a dozen firms provided broker services nationwide, while about 2 dozen firms operated corporate finance departments that were capable of underwriting and distributing sizable new issues for corporations. This concentration of revenue and capacity was evident in 1981, when the leading 25 firms contributed 74.4 percent of the industry gross revenue, while holding 71.5 percent of the capital funds.[6]

INVESTMENT BANKING FUNCTIONS

The Banking Act of 1933, commonly called Glass-Steagall, forbids commercial banks from underwriting corporate securities (except commercial paper) and most types of municipal bonds (except general obligation issues); this role was given to the securities industry. The separation of investment banking from commercial banking was related to the sometimes incongruent objectives and different levels of risks associated with these kinds of organizations. Federal regulations enacted in the 1930s disallowed involvement by depository institutions in securities activities because of concern about the effects of risk associated with these transactions on the stability and soundness of banks. These restrictions separated capital creation from the banking activities of corporations, and were intended to assure that banks acted in the best interests of depositors. However, large commercial banks and other financial institutions have increased their investment banking-related services, and have lobbied hard to have the Glass-Steagall laws modified.

Investment bankers bring new securities to the market by purchasing whole issues of securities from corporate issuers or from public bodies and distributing them to institutional and individual investors. Investment bankers also compute the cost of capital, offer advice on mergers and acquisitions, advise on commodity contracts and foreign transactions, structure investment plans or employee stock-savings plans for client firms, and offer secondary distribution of securities, for example, using the distribution network for the sale by a few holders of large blocks of a security to the investing public.

Investment banking firms that engage primarily in the origination and purchase of new issues of securities are called wholesalers or underwriters. The wholesalers purchase the new securities and market them through retail groups of brokerage firms that sell to client buyers. In most cases, the investment banker will contract to buy securities from the corporation and sell them to other security dealers, institutional investors, and individuals. By making a firm commitment to purchase the securities from the company, the investment banker is said to underwrite any risk that might be associated with a new issue. While the risk is limited in a stable market, this is not the case in a volatile market environment.

The corporation may also choose to arrange a negotiated deal with an investment banker or put out its offering for competitive bid. Competitive bidding requires the investment banker to invest time and effort without any assurance of obtaining the bid. Only about 3 percent of all public-equity offerings and 15 percent of bond and preferred stock public offerings are done through competitive bidding. However, most public utility holding companies are required by the Securities and Exchange Commission (SEC) to choose underwriters by competitive bid. In seeking an investment banker, corporations consider several factors, including the banker's reputation for successfully marketing similar offerings. The choice of the investment banker is important, since an association with a highly regarded banker can enhance a firm's marketplace credibility.

When an investment banking firm agrees to distribute a new issue, it may make either a "firm commitment" to purchase all of the issue outright, a "stand-by commitment" to attempt to purchase part of an issue, or a "best-efforts commitment" to attempt to sell as much of the issue as it possibly can. Most issues are executed with a firm-commitment agreement, which requires that the investment banking firm put up its own capital and borrow the remainder to buy the issue outright from the originating corporation or municipality The "best efforts" commitment accounts for a relatively small portion of total offerings. Some issuing companies choose to sell their own securities directly.

Most of the time, the amount of securities that a firm must sell is too large for a single underwriting firm to distribute by itself. The single firm will then form a temporary partnership with other investment banking firms called a syndicate. The syndicate then attempts to immediately distribute the issue to potential customers in small units at a set price that is slightly higher than the price paid for the issue. While the selling group handles the actual sales, the underwriters accept the risk of the issue not being sold or selling at a price below the investment banker's purchase price. The spread between the investment banker's buying price and selling price determines the gross profits, from which expenses must be subtracted. The spread represents the total compensation for those who participate in the distribution process. The size of the spread decreases with the magnitude of the issue and the size and financial strength of the issuing firm.

Although the investment banker's compensation is negotiated with the company raising the capital, underwriting commissions generally range from 0.75 to 11.0 percent for bonds, 1.4 to 2.0 percent for preferred stock, and 2.3 to 12.0 percent on common stocks. Other expenses, such as lawyer's fees, accountants' costs, printing and engraving, and so forth, range from 0.2 to 4.0 percent for bonds, 0.2 to 9.0 percent for common stock, and 0.2 to 0.7 percent for preferred stocks. Costs as a percentage of proceeds are higher for stocks than for bonds, and higher for smaller issues than larger issues (see Table 15.2). The inverse relationship between size of issue and flotation cost is related primarily to the existence of fixed costs that must be incurred regardless of the size of the issue. Flotation costs as a percentage of proceeds are extremely high for small issues because of this factor.

Costs of flotation depend on the quality of the issue, the type of investment

Table 15.2
Spread by Size and Type of Issue, Total Costs to Issue Common Securities

Size of Issue (millions)	Spread		Common Stock		
	Common Stock	Bonds	Spread	Out-of-Pocket	Total
.1 - .9	9.7-11.3%	7.2-7.4%	9.7-11.3%	4.9-7.3%	14.6-18.6%
1.0 - 4.9	7.4-8.6	4.2-7.0	7.4- 8.6	1.7-3.0	9.1-11.6
5.0 - 9.9	6.7	1.5	6.7	1.0	7.7
10.0 -49.9	4.9-6.2	1.0	4.9- 6.2	0.6-0.8	5.7- 6.8
50 and over	2.3	0.8	2.3	0.3	2.6

banker's commitment, the type of issue (debt or equity), and the size and financial strength of the issuing company. The average flotation cost as a percent of net proceeds was 13.4 percent for equity issues of $0.5 to $1.0 million. For equity issues over $100 million, the average cost was 3.95 percent. On the other hand, issue costs can be under 1 percent for a big bond issue.[7] For example, Bethlehem Steel issued 12 million shares of common stock in October 1987 with a market value of $196.5 million. The gross spread or flotation cost was 4.99 percent. The gross spread of $.82 per share was split as follows:

1. Management fee of $.17 to the lead manager (Salomon Brothers);
2. Underwriting fee of $.17 to members of the syndicate based on amount of commitment to underwrite; and
3. Selling concession of $.48 to members of the syndicate and selling group of investment banks/brokers based on shares actually sold.

In another example, CIGNA issued $250 million of convertible preferred stock in May 1985 at $50 per share. The net to CIGNA was $49 per share with a gross spread or flotation cost of $1 per share or 2 percent of the offering price. The $1 gross spread was split as follows:[8]

1. Management fee of $.20 to the lead manager (Goldman Sachs) and co-managers;
2. Underwriting fee of $.15 to members of the syndicate based on amount of commitment to underwrite; and
3. Selling concession of $.65 to members of the syndicate and selling group of investment banks/brokers based on shares actually sold.

On medium-grade industrial bond issues, the average flotation costs or spread between the public price of the bonds and the proceeds to the issuer is just under 5 percent. An underwriting spread of 2 percent is shared on a pro rata basis by all members of the underwriting syndicate, while the syndicate managers receive an additional fee of 1.75 percent. Another .5 percent is paid to selling group members, while the remainder is paid out as a commission to salespeople. There is a lower underwriting spread on utility issues because of their greater marketability. It should also be noted that in addition to the underwriting spread, there are additional expenses that involve legal, printing, and filing costs related to SEC registration.

The lead bank will keep a much greater percentage of the spread as a commission for arranging the deal, and as compensation for higher administrative costs and the assumption of greater risks. The underwriting spread received by the investment banker is not only for recovery of distribution costs in acting as a retailer, but also for risk-bearing as the investment banker buys the securities from the issuing corporation and attempts to sell them to the public at a profit.

STEPS IN SECURITIES ISSUANCE

Preunderwriting Conference

The company selects and meets with an investment banker to determine the size and type of issue (debt versus equity) and approximate price. An underwriting agreement is then usually signed between the company and the investment banker.

Registration Statement

After the underwriting agreement is signed, the issue is then registered with the SEC. The issue cannot be sold until 20 days after the registration statement is filed, unless the SEC objects or asks for more time. The SEC rules only on whether appropriate information about the investment has been properly disclosed; it does not rule on the quality of the investment. The investment banker cannot sell any of the issues during the SEC examination period, but the issuer is permitted to distribute a preliminary prospectus called a "red herring," which carries a warning in red ink saying that this is not an offer to sell at this time. These preliminary prospectuses contain all the information in the regular prospectus except the price of the offering. The prospectus contains a detailed description of the company financials, management, and history, as well as projections and a statement of the intended use of the funds to be raised. When appropriate, it also contains various convenants of a debt instrument, such as when and how interest is to be paid, restrictions on additional borrowing, and so on. Investment bankers must also be sure that their clients are complying with the laws in the states in which they are operating. Firms that are issuing stock in relatively new, more speculative issues must be cognizant of state "blue-sky laws" which are intended to protect state residents from being misled by untrustworthy securities marketers. In addition, investment bankers will help secure a credit rating, if needed, and coordinate the activities of a bond counsel, who passes an opinion on the legality of the security issue.

Underwriting Syndicate and Selling Group

With the exception of Morgan Stanley, few investment bankers absorb an entire moderate- to large-sized issue, which on occasions can exceed $1 billion. Typically, the originating investment banker will form a syndicate whereby each investment banker buys part of the issue and is responsible for reselling the purchased securities. (See Figure 15.2.)

Membership and participation in a syndicate are typically based upon the financial strength and market image of a firm, its strength in selling new security issues, its ability to work effectively with the manager, the ability to provide reciprocal business, and special requests of the issuing company. Each syndicate

Figure 15.2
The Issuance Process for New Securities in the Primary Market

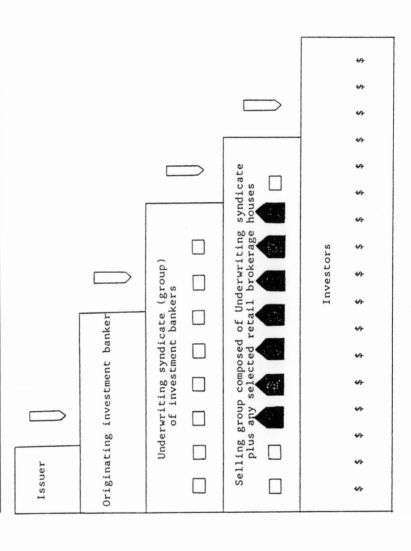

member is assigned a participation or share of the issue. Custom requires that the manager establish several blocks of firms, called "brackets," with each firm in a bracket having the same participation as other firms in that bracket. These syndicate brackets take on a pyramidal structure, with a few leading Wall Street firms in a special bracket with the largest participation, and firms in successively lower brackets having smaller participation. The specific bracket membership of a syndicate is a visible symbol of a firm's standing on Wall Street. There is considerable professional jealousy over syndicate-bracket ranking, which has wide public visibility through the "tombstone" ad that announces the offering in financial publications and lists syndicate members. Tombstone advertisements are newspaper ads that describe the name of the firm selling securities, the amount, the date of offering, and the name of the distributing investment bankers. The investment bankers' names are listed in terms of their relative importance in the particular underwriting syndication, with the names of the lead underwriters at the top. The position of a brokerage firm in the tombstone advertisement depends typically on the amount of the issue it is underwriting for the client firm and the amount that it agrees to sell to potential buyers.[9]

There have been bracketing struggles for as long as Wall Street has been underwriting securities. Tombstones have been and remain Wall Street's scoreboard of prestige, providing a subjective measurement of a firm's strength. In the period from World War II to about 1970, bracket battles did not take place among the genteel investment bankers. There was an unwritten understanding that clients would not be propositioned by other investment banks in the same syndicate. There was a hierarchy of four top firms—First Boston, Morgan Stanley, Kuhn Loeb, and Dillon Reed—followed by the two dozen or so major bracket firms, then the submajors, and then the regionals. Those underwriting participations did not shift from issue to issue. The discipline began to break down in the 1970s, as inflation picked up, the prices of securities changed, the cost of capital rose, and profits eroded because human costs and systems costs rose. Kuhn Loeb was forced to merge into Lehman Brothers, while Dillon Reed, unwillingly or unable to develop sales, trading, and distribution muscle, became more of a niche player. These factors opened the door for Salomon Brothers, Goldman Sachs, Lehman Brothers, and Merrill Lynch to penetrate the top tier of underwriters and to join First Boston and Morgan Stanley as the lead managers.[10]

The choicest position in any tombstone, the one firms battle for, is the upper far left position. The spot is reserved for the lead underwriter, which takes the largest portion of the issue to sell (assumes the largest risk) and manages the underwriting ("runs the book"). Next in prestige are the "co-lead" managers listed to the right of the lead manager. These firms are generally selected because of their proven ability to distribute securities or because their capital base is big enough to assume a degree of risk second only to that of the lead manager. Generally, but not always, firms are listed in tombstone in terms of descending underwriting risk in a deal. Each bracket is usually defined by an alphabetical listing of the firms.

The influence of the lead manager, sometimes in concert with the issuer, not only determines which companies will underwrite the issue and for how much, but also which ones in the syndicate will get the securities to resell to the public (see Figure 15.3). Elevation to major bracket status rests upon such factors as the professional and social standing of the firm's partners, the firm's possession of an adequate capital base, its strength and staying power in distribution, and its ability to generate major business which could be shared with other investment banking houses.

Price Setting and Sale

As soon as the registration becomes effective, the price of the issue is set just before it comes to market. The selling group then proceeds to sell the issue

Figure 15.3
Deciphering a Tombstone

```
1   Salomon Brothers Inc.
                     Goldman Sachs
                                First Boston Corporation

2   Merrill Lynch Capital Markets
                                Bear,Stearns & Co.Inc.

3   Morgan Stanley and Co          Paine Webber

4   ABD Securities Corp.           Daiwa Securities America

5   Dean Witter Capital Markets    Prudential-Bache Securities

6   William Blair & Co  Advest Inc.   Van Kampen Merritt
    Stifel, Nicolaus & Co            McDonald & Co
    Butcher & Singer    Boettcher & Co  Ewing Capital, Inc.
    Prescott, Ball & Turben, Inc.    Dain Bosworth
```

```
1   Lead Managers: Salomon Brothers, lead manager of the entire
    syndicate of firms, underwites $130 million in bonds, with the
    other firms in this bracket each underwriting $128 million.

2   Co-Managers: Each firm underwrites  $60 million in bonds.

3   Special Bracket: Each firm underwites $30 million in bonds.

4   Major Bracket: Each firm underwrites $15 million in bonds.

5   Fifth Bracket: Each firm underwrites $8 million in bonds.

6   Sixth Bracket: Each firm underwrites $5 million in bonds.
```

through investor contact and advertisement in appropriate financial publications. Since many potential investors have been previously contacted, a successful offering is sometimes sold out in a few hours. The investment bankers hope to sell the entire issue as soon as possible because they do not wish to accept the capital commitment and risk of a long-term holding.

The agreement among underwriters typically permits the manager to allocate among the syndicate an aggregate number of shares, which exceeds the total offering. This leaves room for misjudgment about the number of shares that would be sold by individual firms. To provide for market demand when the issue is oversold, the issuing company may agree in advance to give the manager a "Green Shoe" option (named after the shoe company that first used it) under which the company will increase the size of the offering up to an agreed-upon limit at the request of the manager.

Because syndicate members purchase stock for redistribution to the marketing channels, investment bankers must be careful about the pricing of a stock. When a company is going public, the managing investment banker will perform an in-depth study of the company to determine its market value. The analysis should include an industry study, expected company earnings, and dividend-paying capability. Based upon appropriate valuation techniques, a price is tentatively assigned. The price-to-earnings ratio of the company is then compared to the price-to-earnings ratio of similar firms in the same industry. Expected public demand is also a major factor in pricing a new security.

Market Stabilization

The managing underwriter usually stands ready to buy at the offering price any part of the issue that investors attempt to resell before the entire issue is sold; for example, while it remains in syndication. Thus, there is only a limited risk of a decline in market price before the entire issue is sold. Sometimes underwriters are unable to sell the entire issue, and after a few days, upon mutual agreement of the members of the underwriting syndicate, the syndicate is broken and the price is reduced or the investment bankers holds the remainder of the issue hoping the price will rise.

There is always the risk of unanticipated weakness in the stock or bond markets when the actual public distribution starts. Since the selling group usually has a firm commitment to purchase stock at a given price for redistribution, it is important that the price of the stock remains relatively strong. Syndicate members committed to purchase the stock at $25 could be in trouble if the sale price falls to $23. The managing investment banker is usually responsible for stabilizing the offering during the distribution period. This may be accomplished by repurchasing the stock as the market moves below the initial offering price. The period of stabilization normally lasts two or three days after the initial offering for difficult-to-distribute securities. In a bad market environment, stabilization may be difficult to accomplish. For example, when the Federal Reserve announced an extreme credit tightening in October 1979, newly underwritten IBM bond prices fell substantially and investment bankers lost approximately $10 million. A similar situation occurred in 1987 when BP was taken public in England. BP was owned by the British government. In 1987 BP common shares were sold to the investment public through investment bankers.

Aftermarket

During distribution and in later time periods, the investment banker may make a market in a given security by agreeing to buy and sell the security. An investment banker is also interested in how well the underwritten security behaves after the distribution period. The ultimate reputation of the investment banker depends on bringing strong securities to the market. This is particularly true of initial public offerings.

ADDITIONAL SOURCES OF INCOME

Brokerage firms generate revenues from (1) commissions on agency activities; (2) spreads on market-making activities; (3) fees for various activities and services; and (4) margin and position interest and dividends.[11] Although investment bankers make considerable income at underwriting in the primary market, they also generate income from trading and negotiating large block trades of outstanding securities among institutional investors, and in redistributing those blocks more widely through a secondary offering. As a matter of fact, the largest volume of all security trading on the secondary market is on the over-the-counter market by dealers on a negotiated basis. Profits from underwriting are dependent upon the number of new issues in the money and capital markets. However, with the growth of shelf-registrations, there is less need for investment bankers to act as underwriters and it has reduced the underwriting spreads available to investment bankers.

The sources of income for investment banking firms tend to vary as a function of cost containment, interest rates, and market conditions; the number of new issues brought to the market, the volume of trading activity, and merger and acquisition fees earned. Profits are quite volatile and can vary dramatically from year to year.

Stock market trading, while still a vital part of brokerage firm profitability, is shrinking as a source of income for the nation's top securities' firms. The giant institutions that do most of the trading, such as bank trust departments and pension funds, have pushed commissions down to about 5 cents a share on the average. At the same time, deficit-laden governments and cash-hungry corporations have continued to raise huge sums of capital via bonds and other fixed-income securities. Institutions have begun trading these securities at more rapid rates as a function of interest-rate volatility. Thus, bond trading has become one of the most important sources of revenue for the brokerage industry. However, when interest rates are relatively level, there is less institutional bond trading, which affects brokerage firm revenues.

Commissions have dropped from 56 percent of industry revenues in 1973 to 28 percent in 1983 and 21 percent in 1986. Trading and investing has grown in importance from 8 percent in 1973 to 26 percent in 1983 and 27 percent in 1986. Underwriting income has increased from 9 percent in 1973 to 12 percent in both 1983 and 1986. Securities firms have worked diligently to increase the fee-income base, particularly through merger and acquisition service, as illustrated by the growth of other revenues which have risen from 10 percent of total revenues in 1973, to 24 percent in 1983 and 32 percent in 1986. (See Table 15.3.)

Security industry revenues and profits remain volatile and depend on the state of economy, performance of the stock market, and level of interest rates which affect the volume of underwriting activity and the amount of trading activity and profitability. Since May Day 1975, pre-tax profit margins have been volatile: 14 percent in 1980, 5 percent in 1984, and approximately 11 percent in both 1985 and 1986.

The outlook for the securities industries is difficult to predict because the

Table 15.3
Revenue Sources of Investment Banks

Activity	Percent of Total Revenues			
	1973	1983	1985	1986
Commissions	56	28	21	21
Trading and Investing	8	26	28	27
Underwriting	9	12	11	12
Margin Lending	13	7	7	6
Commodities	4	3	3	2
Other *	10	24	30	32
Total	100	100	100	100

* Fees for mutual fund sales, investment advice and counsel, service charges, custodian fees, dividends, and interest on term investments, and miscellaneous other income

Source: NYSE Fact Book, miscellaneous yearly editions

behavior of the markets that directly affect the business is so fickle. Analysts feel that the industry is at least somewhat more solidly grounded than previously, as ownership equity in the ten largest firms was close to $18 billion in 1987, compared to $3.4 billion for the entire industry on December 31, 1978. Many of the privately held firms have gone public, increasing the equity capital in the industry. The volatility of security industry earnings can be seen by looking at the total net profit after taxes of New York Stock Exchange (NYSE) member firms in Table 15.4.

Although it is not a major source of income, many securities brokers and dealers use their available funds to extend margin credit to customers who borrow to buy stocks. Dealers also purchase investment securities for their own accounts and make markets in various securities, buying and selling stocks and bonds from their own inventory positions. It is also interesting to note that dealers and brokers obtain most of their funds by borrowing from banks, usually on call or overnight loans at the dealer rate. They also obtain substantial funds from cash credit balances held by customers in their brokerage accounts.

SECURITIES INDUSTRY

The securities industry includes:

1. The suppliers of securities—the industry's clients, which include federal government, government agencies, state and local governments, private business firms, and individuals;

Table 15.4
Income and Expenses of NYSE Member Firms (Millions)

Year ended December 31	Income			Expenses	Net profit before taxes ■	Estimated net profit after taxes
	From securities commissions	Total				
1971	$3,124	$ 5,807		$ 4,662	$1,145	$ 915
1975	2,949	5,927		5,116	811	415
1976	3,163	6,902		5,919	983	508
1977	2,809	6,730		6,314	416	188
1978	3,779	8,832		8,148	684	339
1979	4,012	11,264		10,164	1,100	557
1980	5,671	15,986		13,721	2,265	1,158
1981	5,346	19,805		17,666	2,139	1,086
1982	6,021	23,212		20,186	3,026	1,550
1983	8,348	29,542		25,732	3,810	1,959
1984	7,082	31,148		29,559	1,589	504
1985	8,249	38,739		34,593	4,146	2,112
1986	10,453	50,036		44,554	5,482	2,900

Source: NYSE Fact Book 1987, p. 81.

2. The buyers of securities—the industry's customers, represented by individuals and institutions. Institutions are responsible for two-thirds of the current public volume on the NYSE, but individuals still own over 60 percent of the value of stock outstanding in this country;

3. The investment community—brokerage firms, exchanges, investment bankers, investment companies, associations;

4. Industry regulators—the SEC and self-regulatory groups;

5. Direct supporting services—transfer of certificates, custodial services, and telecommunication networks; and

6. Other supporting services—legal, accounting, educational, and outside computer support.[12]

The salient functions performed by the securities industry are:

1. To make more orderly the buying and selling of securities by promoting rules and standards, such as hours of operations, mode of payment for transactions, the process for transferring securities, the fee structure to be charged, the description of ethical behavior, and the training and education required for those acting as agents in the marketplace;

2. To promote the raising of new capital for public and private groups;

3. To analyze financial and economic information to assess security values or the proper utilization of new investment flows; and

4. To use such analysis and other tools in managing major capital pools such as mutual funds and pension funds, and for individual brokerage-firm clients.[13]

The modern structure of the securities industry evolved with the enactment of the Securities Exchange Acts (1933-1934), the Trust Indenture Act (1939), the Investment Company Act (1940), and the Investment Advisors Act (1940). This legislation was a direct out-growth of the function of the securities markets in the period 1929-1932. With the collapse of the financial markets during the Great Depression, a series of laws was passed to separate commercial banking from investment banking, and to impose stricter regulatory control on the securities industry. Controls were increased in the registering of new public issues and in professional management of money by investment companies. Regulations were established for avoiding conflicts of interest between a firm and the institution that is trustee for some debt security of the firm. Legislation also established the structural form of operation for mutual funds and closed-end investment companies, as well as the responsibilities of officers, advisers, and others associated with such funds.

Liabilities issued by brokers, dealers, and investment bankers are regulated by the disclosure rules of the Securities and Exchange Commission and by state securities laws. Investment bankers and securities firms are not federally insured and are not directly subject to banking regulation. Most have gone to some length to avoid bank holding company regulation by the Federal Reserve by acquiring or forming only nonbank banks or single savings associations. However, customer accounts are usually insured by the Securities Investors Protection Corporation (SIPC), an agency of the federal government established in 1970. The SIPC was established to protect customer's accounts against the consequences of financial failure of the brokerage firm; it insures customer's accounts for up to $500,000, except that claims for cash are limited to $100,000. The SIPC insurance does not guarantee that the dollar value of the securities will be recovered; it guarantees only that the securities themselves will be returned. A number of brokerage firms have purchased additional private insurance beyond the SIPC's $500,000 to insure customer accounts.

There are about 3,000 firms that are members of the National Association of Securities Dealers, an association that promotes and self-regulates the securities business. Over half of these firms are located in the New York City region. Today, a typical firm has about five employees, a few partners, operates out of one office, and has under $100 million in operating capital. The largest of these firms operate in all or most sectors of the business, while specializing in a limited number of sectors such as in commercial paper, government securities, and municipal revenue bonds. Smaller, specialized firms are commonly called financial boutiques. Some firms have a local, regional, retail, or institutional presence. For example, Morgan Stanley and Salomon Brothers concentrate their activities within the institutional market with only a handful of offices. On the other hand, Merrill Lynch has approximately 525 offices, underwrites and participates in all segments of the securities business, and serves both retail and institutional customers. Merrill Lynch employs over 11,000 registered representatives, about 10 times the number employed at either Salomon Brothers or Morgan Stanley.

As previously mentioned, there have been a large number of mergers and acquisitions in the 1980s, as well as many firm failures. In addition to the previously mentioned acquisitions, John Hancock and Equitable, both large insurers, bought DLJ and Tucker Anthony; Phibro, a large commodity dealer, purchased Salomon Brothers; and GE purchased Kidder Peabody. Commercial banks and insurance companies are threatening some parts of the business through the underwriting of commercial paper and the purchase of either brokerage or discount brokerage firms.

DISCOUNT BROKERS

The brokerage portion of the industry was affected by the abolition of fixed commission rates in 1975. Brokerage firms had competed on the reputation of their research and the quality of their service; price competition has now become a salient factor. Discounters, who concentrate on the transaction side of the business, have entered the market and have attracted a significant portion of both institutional and individual trading. The discounters define their business as executing trades on behalf of customers who know what investments they want to make. Also, the actions by some thrifts and commercial banks to offer discount brokerage should also have a major impact in pricing within the retail segment of the brokerage business.

According to a study by Market Facts, Inc., of Chicago, discount stock-brokerage operations at banks and thrifts could surpass in number the accounts at full-service brokerage houses in the 1990s. Banks and thrifts will capture an increased share of accounts because of consumers' trust in the institutions and their extensive branch networks, rather than because of their lower brokerage commissions. The survey indicates that full-service brokerage firms are likely to retain customers with higher incomes and net worth, while banks and thrifts will attract younger, less wealthy clients with the least experience in the stock market. The less-experienced investors who may be drawn to discount operations at banks and thrifts are the people who need advice. Most discount brokers do not offer advice or recommend stocks. While the discount units at banks cannot offer advice, banks could set up separate operations to distribute investment analyses.

IMPLICATIONS FOR THE DISCOUNT
BROKERAGE INDUSTRY

While banks and thrifts have helped increase the market share of discount brokerage services, they have also intensified the competition, which has caused many independent discount services to expand their branches or services, or both. The motivation of banks for providing discount brokerage services may be seen as either a reaction to market conditions or an attempt to protect market shares. Since most brokerage houses are offering investment opportunities that serve functions similar to depository accounts, the consumer's perceived need for a commercial branch may have decreased. A motivation for providing brokerage services may be to prevent the potential slipping away of other portions of a depositor's business.

At the beginning of 1982, not one bank or thrift offered a discount brokerage service. At the time of this writing, there were approximately 1,200 offering the service in some form. Banks either start their own, acquire an existing discount broker, or contract for agency services. Invest, a brokerage firm owned by about three dozen savings associations, is an additional option for thrifts. It falls between the services of a discounter and a full-service operation. The larger, well-capitalized banks have acquired established discounters or have started their own services.

Competition from banks and thrifts will continue to grow because of attractions such as these:

1. Cross-selling opportunities,
2. Ease of entrance,
3. Possibility for added profit,

4. To retain customers who might otherwise go elsewhere,

5. Lack of geographical limitations,

6. To enhance the distribution system, and

7. To learn brokerage basics before deregulation.

Name recognition, a large customer base, numerous branches, and a local presence give banks both a marketing and a distributing advantage that independent firms do not have.

Independent discount firms have begun to diversify services, to expand their branches, or both, in an effort to survive the growing competition. Quick & Reilly, Inc. estimated that approximately 25 percent of the customers serviced by a branch actually visit that office. Discounters' views regarding diversifying services differ. Quick & Reilly, Inc., Discount Brokerage, and Rose & Co. chose to remain with the basic services. Charles Schwab & Co. has diversified and offers 24-hour quotes, individual retirement accounts, low and no-load mutual funds, automatic transfer of idle cash into a cash-equivalent or tax-exempt money market funds, and a cash management service.

Although Charles Schwab has no stock research department, it offers customers a personal computer software package that provides a valuable source of investment information previously available only to well-heeled institutions. This software offers information from several on-line research facilities, such as the latest investment ideas from Standard & Poor's, *Dow Jones News,* essential information about the company's past and present performance, automatic stock alerts when price limits are reached, useful tax information, and the ability to buy and sell securities via the home computer.

Expanding branches or diversifying services require capital that only the larger firms have, and thus concentration is developing in the industry. Small firms may still find a special market niche keeping their services unique and in demand. Medium-sized firms without the capital or the flexibility may find independent survival difficult if stock market volume declines substantially.

In the future, the discount brokerage industry will probably consist of large independent firms with many branches and some with additional services, and small independent firms with special services not found elsewhere. Medium-sized firms may be required to fold, merge, or be acquired due to the increasing competition from the larger firms and from depository institutions.

By not offering a discount brokerage service, banks and thrifts may find themselves at a competitive disadvantage as more and more depository institutions offer some form of brokerage service. "One-stop financial shopping" has grown popular, and discount brokerage provides a means for developing an image of a full-service institution at little cost, depending on the level of involvement. In response to discounters, many full-service brokerage firms have taken steps to differentiate their services, to improve them, and to increase customer loyalty. Increased efforts have been directed toward product development and promotion. After a decade of growing by adding customers, discounters have reached the point where they must generate additional revenues from existing customers to maintain growth.

It is interesting to note that the pretax profit margin for discounters in the six years from 1980 to 1985 was considerably higher than that of national full-line (NFL) brokerage firms. The average return on equity (ROE) for discounters was also much higher than for the NFLs. Over 85 percent of discounters' revenues come from commissions and margin interest. Investment bankers had even higher ROEs in every year except 1983, and higher pretax margins in every year.[14] (See Table 15.5.)

SHELF REGISTRATIONS

Although the investment banks now have the upper hand on fee services, this lucrative area seems vulnerable to a squeeze in margins from several directions. Falling profits have already occurred in the municipal-revenue bond area as the volume of new issues of these bonds has declined. It is also likely that there will be increased competition in the merger and acquisition business. Expertise outside the investment banking business, such as management consulting and the consulting arms of commercial banks, is beginning to make its presence felt in these lines of business.

The likelihood is that continuing profit pressures will be felt, both indirectly through the fielding of more extensive corporate services, and more directly through such vehicles as the further proliferation of co-managership. There will probably always be assaults on the gross spread, or increased pressure to price aggressively. If corporations succeed in transforming certain types of debt offerings into quasi-commodity business, they may eventually hire investment bankers as financial advisers for issues and may run de facto competitive bidding for them.

Table 15.5
Return on Equity

		1980	1982	1983	1984	1985
Total ROA		10.8%	13.1%	12.9%	5.2%	10.7%
	ROE	35.9	40.5	36.6	13.3	24.6
National Full Lines ROA		6.9	8.8	8.6	-0.9	5.6
	ROE	24.6	29.8	46.7	0.8	21.8
Discounters ROA		12.2	13.6	14.0	3.0	9.9
	ROE	52.2	53.9	46.7	0.8	21.8
Investment Banks ROA		15.4	17.4	16.7	11.4	14.6
	ROE	56.7	54.9	43.8	31.1	33.8

SEC Rule 415, which allows for shelf registration, has, to some extent, changed corporate underwriting techniques. The "shelf registration" process provides a mechanism for employing new options in both the timing and pricing of securities. Large, well-known corporations can file a master registration statement with the SEC and then update it with a short-form statement on short notice just before each individual offering. Essentially, the corporation puts its new securities "on the shelf" for up to two years, and then sells them to investors when it feels the market is right. Once effective, the shelf prospectus can be used for single or multiple offerings through the mailing of a prospectus supplement to the SEC after the pricing of any or all of the registered securities. The process provides issuers with an opportunity to price and offer securities instantly. The size of the offering, maturity, price, and spread can be set at any time without any delay for SEC review. Issuers should be able to cope with the market's volatility and constantly changing investor preference through speed of issuance, customization of terms, and flexibility in the size, type of security, and format of underwriting. Rule 415 specifies that the issuer may designate one or more potential managing underwriters in the shelf filing. As long as one of these underwriters is selected as manager or co-manager for a particular underwriting, the offering can be priced on an instantaneous basis by means of the "sticker" supplement to the effective registration supplement.

It is expected that insurance companies and banks through their merchant banking subsidiaries will eventually attempt to bid directly for these debt instruments. The winning bidder will have the option of holding the bonds in their own investment portfolio or placing them in their trading account for eventual secondary-market sale. Eventually, banks and insurance companies would like to have corporate underwriting privileges. The entry into this field by banks and insurance companies is a distinct threat to the profitability of investment bankers that concentrate on the underwriting of corporate issues. These large intermediaries consider that Rule 415 will enable them to establish a closer rapport with corporate treasurers for decisions that will impact future bank loans and risk-management plans.

After almost two years of experimentation, SEC Rule 415 was made permanent for companies with at least $150 million in stock owned by investors not affiliated with management. However, the SEC banned shelf financings for small- and medium-sized companies offering new issues of stock. The registration proceedings have been quite popular with larger issues because they save on underwriting costs. Companies raising funds in 1982 using 415 filings for equity offerings saved 29 percent on underwriting fees. A total of about $37 billion of shelf-rule offerings were underwritten in 1983, compared to approximately $20 billion in 1982. The controversial rule was adopted over the opposition of many regional brokerage firms, which maintain that the speed with which corporations can sell securities off the shelf severely limits their access to new offerings. Rule 415 tends to favor highly capitalized investment banks with strong trading capabilities because, when using the shelf rule, underwriters tend to buy corporate securities in large blocks and resell them almost immediately to institutional clients. In traditional financing, a lead manager puts together a syndicate of investment banks to help distribute securities, which may take from a few hours to several weeks.

Shelf registration has been most frequently used with debt issues. There has been relatively less usage in the equity market. The introduction of shelf registration and the rising volatility of the market has had the effect of reducing response time. Lead managers cannot wait to obtain underwriting commitments from different firms. After a few years of observing the impact of shelf registration, it appears as if shelf registration has contributed to the concentrated nature of the investment banking business with the strong firms acquiring more business.

The creation of shelf registrations—new issues that are ready to be sold, and for which the final administrative work can be completed within a few days whenever the timing seems right—may lead to a reduction in the underwriting spread to a fee resembling those available in the commercial paper market. For major companies, shelf registration has made it easier to select investment banks on a transaction rather than a relationship basis. Historically, long-term relationships between corporations and investment banks were extremely important in selecting an underwriting manager. However, these relationships have become less important in the current environment, where the comparative advantage for banks lies in the pricing of deals and in the successful market timing of the issue.

Although shelf registration was only a few years old, these issues accounted for almost 60 percent of the debt issues in 1984 and 1985, and less than 2 percent of the equity issues.[15] (See Table 15.6.)

BROKERS MEETING THE PROFIT CHALLENGE

Brokerage firms have broadened and diversified their activities by developing and marketing their own mutual funds, money market funds, and real estate and tax shelters; also, they have developed many new types of mortgage- and installment-loan-backed securities in order to generate additional sources of revenue. Investment bankers also entered the commercial paper and Eurodollar markets as financial intermediaries. The growth of these markets has provided a new source of earnings to participating institutions. Merrill Lynch has gone a step further than most of its investment banking competition by forming its own international bank, which takes credit positions and acts as an underwriter in Euroloan syndications. Companies like Shearson Lehman Hutton, Prudential-Bache, Merrill Lynch, and others may be able to use their large capitalizations to advantage in enlarging and integrating services for the governmental, corporate, and institutional sectors, as well as increasing their penetration of personal lines of insurance.

Some investment bankers provide extensive merger and acquisition services as well as other corporate financial and counseling services. More recently, a

Table 15.6
Public Debt and Common Equity Issues 1/84 through 8/85

Debt Issues	Shelf Registration	Other	Total
Negotiated	881	680	1,561
Competitive	67	18	85
	948	698	1,646
Equity Issues			
Negotiated	18	1,462	1,486
Competitive	2	0	2
	20	1,462	1,488

Source: Securities Data Company

number of the wholesale firms have started in-house brokerage activities aimed at wealthy individuals, whose needs often compare in size with those of the smaller institutional investors. The aim is to provide personalized financial services including insurance and quasi-banking activities to wealthy retail customers.

A number of retail firms are now promoting loans against securities collateral, while most brokerage firms have a cash management service for customers similar to that provided by commercial banks. These accounts make available checks that can be written against a customer's cash balance at the brokerage house. Merrill Lynch and other brokers are also issuing bank credit and debit cards. Merrill Lynch has broadened the spectrum of finance-related service it offers. In its move to establish a nationwide real-estate brokerage network, it has acquired a mortgage insurance firm, a mortgage life insurance company, a real estate financing firm, and an employee relocation business.

The securities industry was subject to tremendous structural strains during the 1970s and 1980s. These pressures included deregulation of pricing (brokerage commission rate deregulation), major new product areas (commodities, options, financial futures, mortgage certificates, insured municipal bonds), a new technology that is causing changes in decades-old processing procedures, and a new level of competition both within the industry and outside it. Over the past ten years, there have been over 300 mergers of securities firms and numerous brokerage firm failures. There are likely to be further mergers within the industry, particularly if there is a significant economic downturn in industry profitability. The operating leverage of most securities firms is still quite high. Periods of high brokerage transactions are associated with exceptional profits, while periods of relatively lower volume can result in substantial losses.

Over the last decade, a large number of well-known investment firms have disappeared as independent entities, as a result of mergers within the industry and acquisition of nonbanks. Intra-industry mergers have been motivated by a need for additional capital in an increasingly capital-intense business and by a desire to go "full-service" by acquiring firms with complementary product lines. In addition, regional firms have been absorbed by large companies wishing to achieve or increase nationwide market penetration. We have also seen the acquisition of a few primarily retail-oriented investment firms by giant nonbanks such as Sears, Prudential, and American Express.

The need for capital and the increasing globalization of markets have led most observers to predict an industry that will essentially resemble the U.S. accounting profession, with a small number of large, fully integrated firms, with worldwide operations but a sizable number of smaller specialist and regional firms. Capital requirements also suggest the eventual demise of the partnership form, which still exists in a few large firms.

The traditional long-standing relationship between an investment banker and a client has eroded in many cases. It has been replaced by "transactional finance," a world in which investment bankers seek each others' clients, primarily by aggressive marketing of new financing ideas. If the corporation being approached likes the idea, the investment banker making the proposal usually gets the deal, regardless of the previous relationship that existed with another investment bank. There is no monopoly on successful ideas; other investment banking firms will copy them or offer improved versions. It is important to note that new investment products seem to come on-line monthly; the number and variety are limited only by the human imagination.

In the 1970s, inflationary pressures exacerbated the high volume "back-office" pressure that affected a number of the distribution firms. This led to a series of liquidations and mergers in the brokerage sector of the industry (for example, Merrill Lynch acquired Goodbody). In addition, the introduction of negotiated brokerage commissions in 1975 altered the economics of the securities industry and precipitated another round of mergers and consolidations. A new generation of leaders took over the management of Wall Street firms. They were less sensitive to institutional loyalties, and challenges mounted to the informal discipline within the investment-banking syndicate system. Distribution capability began to carry more weight in syndicate participation. Foreign securities firms became more competitive, and institutional investors became an even more dominant part of the market. At the same time, corporate treasurers and investment managers became even more sophisticated consumers of financial services.[16]

Another major development is the proliferation of services. This proliferation appears to reflect both the pressures of declining profitability of the early 1980s and also the stimulus of developing opportunities in a rapidly evolving financial system. The abolition of fixed commission rates, in particular, was an important reason for firms in the industry to seek new sources of revenue. However, the enormous changes in the demands for financial services and the growth of computer technology, which made it feasible for many brokers and dealers to meet that demand, have produced opportunities for new financial services. As a result, many brokerage firms are becoming "department stores" of financial services.

There has also been a recent trend among well-capitalized investment bankers to place their own funds at risk in the projects that they helped to finance and in some cases to originate. This has been particularly the case in some recent leveraged buyouts and venture capital investments. Venture capital investments offer a chance to create new clients for future business. Although the risk has been substantially increased, so have the potential rewards and income. With their equity participation, these bankers perform a role familiar to British merchant banks and French Banques d'Affaires. The willingness of an investment banking firm to risk its own funds may act as a catalyst in a deal and persuade other investors to become participants. Competitors have bid actively for human as well as financial resources, even as product, process, application, management, and marketing technologies quickly evolve. An environment of vigorous competition is delivering enormous benefits in the prices and qualities of services and products made available to customers.

In 1985-1986, the American securities industry was highly profitable. Although the fortunes of retail-oriented brokerage firms have fluctuated with the movement of stock prices and the number of shares traded, investment banks in general averaged after-tax returns on equity capital of close to 30 percent in the 1979-1986 period. At the same time, a number of select "wholesale" firms have been remarkably profitable, earning pretax returns of 80 percent or more. Some analysts have predicted that increasing competition will shave these enormous profits, as has happened to institutional brokerage commission rates and underwriting spreads. As a matter of fact, many Wall Street firms announced large layoffs in 1987-1988 in response to some unprofitable business lines, monstrous overhead, enormous trading losses that revealed meager management controls, and plunging bond and stock-market prices. Competitive pressures have squeezed the profit margins of once-successful businesses such as public finance and money market instruments. Some major firms have announced withdrawal from the underwriting of municipal bonds and commercial paper.

Security brokers and dealers have experienced enormous changes in the last two decades. Among the salient changes have been the consolidation in the number of firms and the proliferation in the number of products and services offered. Many brokers and dealers offer check withdrawals of investment funds, credit cards, money market accounts, insured depository accounts through nonbank bank affiliates, sale of CDs of client banks, and mortgage loans through affiliated companies. As a matter of fact, some huge financial conglomerates have been formed with extensive financial powers following the mergers of securities firms with insurance companies, retailers, and other financial service companies such as American Express.

Consolidation may be traced back to the financial difficulties that were encountered by many firms in the late 1960s and early 1970s, and also to the abolition of fixed commission rates in 1975. The expansion in equity trading volume in the late 1960s caused enormous clerical problems for many firms, ultimately leading to financial difficulties in some cases. In addition, the increasing volatility of stock and bond prices produced financial problems at some firms that "guessed wrong" and took incorrect positions in their own inventory positions and investment portfolios. The abolition of fixed-minimum commission rates effective May 1, 1975 (known as May Day in the financial community) also impacted earnings in a negative manner. As a result, commission rates for large transactions fell substantially, making many firms inviable. As a consequence of all these factors, the number of firms in the industry has declined substantially, while the average size of surviving companies has increased dramatically. The abolition of fixed-rate commissions led to the development of discount brokerage firms for small investors. These boutiques provide no research or recommendations to customers but do offer prices at substantial discounts from May Day fixed-rate prices. This has created profit problems for firms that are dependent on the small investor and contributed to the consolidation in the number of firms.

A development related to this consolidation has been the acquisition of broker-dealer firms by companies outside the industry. The trend accelerated in 1982-1984 as rising stock-exchange volume and the resulting higher profitability for brokerage firms made them attractive acquisition candidates.

Technological development in the securities industry has been instrumental in facilitating the processing of transactions, helping to reduce costs, improving marketing efforts, creating new products and services, and stimulating unprecedented competition. Considering that 100 to 200 million shares a day were traded on the New York Stock Exchange (NYSE) in 1986-1987, it is difficult to believe that the NYSE had to close the trading floor early because brokers could not keep up with 10- to 12-million-share days in 1967.

With the complexity of available hedging techniques, and an increase in computerized information, many investment banking firms have recruited traders and researchers with PhDs in mathematics, statistics, operations research, and finance. These researchers help firms to refine immunization techniques and hedge away interest-rate and market risk.

The research activities of most investment banks have supplemented their brokerage and trading operation, as reports, analyses, and opinions on industries and companies have traditionally been prepared and provided to customers in return for brokerage commissions. Today, research has become more integrated with the rest of a firm's strategy. For example, particular industry or company expertise is used to help develop underwriting or merger and acquisition business.

CHANGES TAKING PLACE

In addition to the changing nature of industry participants and the structure of funds, other significant changes are occurring. They include:

1. An array of innovative products and integrated financial services;
2. The development of sophisticated automated systems, not only to process business but also to compete for and retain clients;
3. A growing emphasis on strategic planning as a means of identifying business opportunities;
4. A huge increase in the amount of attention, time, and money spent on management; this is related in part to the recognition that Wall Street has suffered from serious managerial problems;
5. The unfixing of commission rates, and the growth of discount brokerage and shelf registrations;
6. A shrinking network of regional brokerage firms that have been acquired by national brokerage firms and insurance companies;
7. The development of financial supermarkets and new specialty firms or boutiques;
8. The entry of insurance companies, thrifts, and commercial banks into the securities business;
9. Changing government and regulatory attitudes toward the financial services industry;
10. A new computer technology, which is forcing changes in decades-old processing procedures;
11. A decline in ethical standards within the industry;
12. The growth of discount brokerage, which is helping to cut retail commission rates;
13. Patterns of volatility and shrinking margins, which are likely to continue; and
14. A decline in commissions on equity trading, which should continue as institutional investors become more sophisticated and demanding, while underwriting fees are likely to continue in a downward trend as competition intensifies.[17]

There had been a tendency for corporate borrowers to create bidding contests among underwriters, making it difficult for the underwriters to make more than a small underwriting spread. The market was almost entirely based on the execution or distribution capabilities of the underwriters.

Since 1986, we have seen significant transformation in the market where creativity has become as important as distribution. Today, the successful investment banker must be able to create new value products as well as execute them. Many current underwritings are the result of an effort between investment bankers and clients in the area of liability management where an option is incorporated in the deal that provides the issuer and the investor with added flexibility.

Traditionally, an investment banker created a product by staying in close contact with the issuing client, and mostly answering his needs. To a much greater extent today deals are created, often with new instruments, following consistent contact with the investing client.

Communications and computer technology underly the revolution in financial markets. A plethora of new products and services have been developed to meet client needs or to improve existing products. There has been an emphasis on financial engineering in unbundling, repackaging, and securitizing money and capital market instruments where the institutional catalyst has been the investment banker.

Although most of the new products and services developed have been quite successful, there have been flaws in some new instruments. Some quasi-equity instruments were sold with the illusion that there would be a liquid secondary market maintained by the issuing investment banker. For example, during the latter half of the 1980s it was not uncommon for retrenchment to take place in markets where investment bankers were not making enough money. This has led to the drying up of liquidity in some segments of the capital markets. When profit opportunities began to evaporate in one market, investment bankers would shift their funds used to maintain inventory positions to more lucrative markets. This was the case for floating rate preferred stock issues which sold for 15 to 20 percent under par less than a year after they were first issued when market makers withdrew their support from this segment of the market. Market makers can only provide liquidity if there is another investor or buyer. Market makers cannot substitute for investors if an enormous amount of funds are required to support a market, especially when changes in tax laws or fear of default drive investors from a market.

WHERE IS THE INDUSTRY HEADED?

Most of the regulatory barriers now separating tomorrow's competitors in the financial services industry are likely to be eliminated. With this will come increased business opportunities for those who are quick to recognize them and who know how to compete. As these regulatory barriers fade, there will be increased interaction and cooperative efforts between depository institutions, insurance companies, and the securities industry, as each player seeks to bridge current gaps and circumvent current laws and regulations. Also, prudent management decision making will be required lest companies succumb to the temptation to rush into business activities for which they are ill-prepared or ill-suited.[18]

The emerging financial services industry will consist of extremely competitive institutions of all types and sizes. Giant-sized financial supermarkets will coexist with smaller firms that serve the specialized needs of clients. Marketplace participants are expected to strive to develop multiple relationships with clients to satisfy customer needs and to deal with the lack of consumer loyalty to any one institution. There will be the continuation of the current movement to diversify into both financial and nonfinancial areas. State of-the-art technology and telecommunication facilities will be required to retain and attract clients. Technology and instantaneous communications will continue to accelerate transaction speed and information flow to investors, bridging territorial boundaries and creating world markets.

There have been at least 200 mergers involving securities firms in the 1980s to date. It is likely that further consolidation will occur, since the industry still has a low concentration ratio. These consolidations and the increased competition from other financial institutions should continue to make investment banking an extremely competitive activity.[19]

The operating leverage of most securities firms is quite high, so that periods of high brokerage transactions are associated with excellent profits, and periods of low volume can result in substantial losses. There has been a trend for the volume break-even point to increase steadily at most brokerage firms as "permanent employees," leased communications and computer facilities, and other fixed costs grew rapidly in the 1983-1987 period. Although many brokerage firms have attempted to diversify into other industries to offset part of this operating risk, their success has not been tested by a decline in market volume. Successful NFLs and discounters are adding products such as mutual funds and asset management accounts to their previously narrow product lines. Also, NFLs will be working to trim their costs as these firms try to become more efficient distributors. The trend will be toward value-priced products and lower-cost distribution options.[20] Because the exchanges have not been able to diversify very much away from their brokerage functions and have experienced rapidly increasing overhead, one or more of the existing exchanges could be forced out of business.

NOTES

1. M. R. Blyn, "The Evolution of the U.S. Money and Capital Markets and Financial Intermediaries," in *Financial Institutions and Markets,* 2nd ed., ed. M. E. Polakoff and T. A. Durkin (New York: Houghton Mifflin Co., 1981), 35-36.

2. A. Gart, *An Insider's Guide to the Financial Services Revolution* (New York: McGraw-Hill, 1984), 107-108.

3. S. L. Hayes III, "The Transformation of Investment Banking," *Harvard Business Review* (January-February 1979): 153-170.

4. *Effects of Information Technology on Financial Service Systems,* Washington, D.C.: U.S. Congress, Office of Technology Assessment, OTA-CIT-202, September 1984.

5. D. B. Crane, *Trends in the Securities Industry,* Harvard Business School, Case 9-286-029, 1985, 1.

6. Ibid., 1-2.

7. E. F. Brigham, *Financial Management, Theory and Practice,* 4th ed. (Chicago: Dryden Press, 1986), 592-593.

8. Crane, *Trends in the Securities Industry,* 5.

9. W. Law, "Investment Banking," in *Handbook of Financial Markets and Institutions,* 6th ed., ed. E. I. Altman (New York: John Wiley & Sons, 1987), 14.5-14.6.

10. S. L. Hayes III, A. M. Spence, and D. Van Praag Marks, *Competition in the Investment Banking Industry* (Cambridge, Mass.: Harvard University Press, 1983), 24-28.

11. P. Hines, "Making Money in Brokerage," in *The Financial Services Handbook,* ed. E. M. Friars and R. N. Gogel (New York: Wiley-Interscience, 1987), 103.

12. M. Keenan, "The Securities Industry: Securities Trading and Investment Banking," in *The Financial Handbook,* ed. E. I. Altman (New York: John Wiley & Sons, 1981), 53-54.

13. Ibid.

14. P. Hines, "Making Money in Brokerage," 112-124.

15. Crane, *Trends in the Securities Industry,* 3-4.

16. Hayes et al., *Competition in the Investment Banking Industry,* 28.

17. Hines, "Making Money in Brokerage," 124.

18. National Association of Securities Dealers, Inc., *The Financial Services Industry of Tomorrow* (Washington, D.C.: National Association of Securities Dealers, Inc., November 1982), 6-7, 48-49.

19. W. M. Keenan, "The Securities Industry: Securities Trading and Investment Banking," in *Handbook of Financial Markets and Institutions,* 6th ed., ed. E. I. Altman (New York: John Wiley & Sons, 1987), 9-31.

20. P. Hines, "Making Money in Brokerage," 124.

16

The Leasing Industry

Ron Caruso

HISTORICAL DEVELOPMENT

Communications satellites, railroad locomotives, and mining equipment are three diverse types of equipment with specific uses in distinctively different geographical settings. All share a common link, however: they are assets often financed through leasing. Although some sources trace the rudiments of equipment financing to prehistoric times—perhaps as far back as 2000 B.C.—its modern-day structure bears little if any resemblance to its ancestors.

Leasing permeates even our everyday existence, where "convenience" leasing can include copiers, minicomputers, and office furniture; in fact even the family automobile may be leased for economic reasons. Make no mistake about it, leasing is big business. This obviously begs the question, "How big?" As an example, two lease transactions were completed recently wherein the lessee (equipment user) was a major Midwest utility listed on the New York Stock Exchange. Its objective was to obtain financing for its undivided interest in both a coal-fired and a nuclear-fired generating unit. It was seeking a financial alternative that would prevent what is commonly referred to as "customer rate shock." Leasing was the chosen solution; the equipment had a total cost of almost $2 billion.

Equipment leasing has established itself as the single most important financing tool used by American business in the capital formation process in the last 20 years. It was estimated that some $350 billion of plant and equipment was acquired by commercial businesses in 1987. The largest lessor association, the American Association of Equipment Lessors (AAEL) estimated through member surveys and independent sources that the equipment-leasing industry provided some $100 billion, or 29 percent of this total.[1]

THE BASICS OF LEASING

The modern-day development of leasing into what is commonly referred to as "a viable financial alternative" is based on three propositions:

1. Earnings are generated by the usage of equipment, not the ownership;
2. The essence of leasing viewed as a pure financial mechanism is a renting of money; and
3. Leasing as a financial tool allows for the optimal division of ownership and usage of equipment, and can reflect this dichotomy in the ultimate cost for renting the money involved in equipment acquisition.

In order to understand how this optimization takes place in the real world, there are a few basic financial mechanics that must be understood. Leasing in its basic form consists of three elements:

1. *The Equipment.* Leasing involves a complete dichotomy between the user of the equipment and the provider of the equipment financing (the lessor). Independent of any lessor participation, the equipment user will first identify the equipment he or she is seeking to use, and negotiate its price and all attendant terms and conditions (that is, installation, warranties, and all other factors).

2. *Lessee: Evaluation of Financial Alternatives.* The next step in the scenario is for the equipment user to determine what type of financing will be utilized to pay for the equipment. This is commonly referred to as the "lease versus buy decision." Such factors as corporate liquidity, cost of borrowing, projected usage (normally quantifiable in years), implicit tax benefits in ownership and whether or not the corporation can utilize these benefits, and residual value (projected worth of the equipment at the end of the anticipated usage period) are evaluated.

In determining the optimal method of financing the new equipment, one or more of the following lease structures may be considered:

1. A true lease, which meets the qualifications as a lease under the Internal Revenue Code, enabling the lessee to claim the rental payments as tax deductions and the lessor to claim tax benefits of ownership as well as the residual (remaining) value of the equipment at the end of the lease term;
2. A finance lease, which can either be a true lease or a conditional sale with no tax benefits transferred to the lessor. Rentals over the life of the lease are sufficient to enable the lessor to recover the cost of the equipment plus a return on its investment; or
3. An operating lease, which is a short-term lease whereby a lessee can acquire the usage of an asset for a fraction of its useful life. This type of leasing does not allow a lessor to recover his investment during the initial lease term. Because of the short-term nature, the periodic rental payment may be greater than in the above alternatives, but the lessor must look to future rentals to recoup his investment and profit.

3. *Lease Negotiation.* Once the equipment user has determined that leasing is the best financial alternative, he or she will negotiate a lease arrangement. This

will provide full usage of the chosen equipment for a specified lease term, subject to the obligation to pay the lessor (the equipment owner) the contracted periodic rental payments and return the equipment at the expiration of the lease term in good condition (normal wear and tear excepted) or purchase it for either a predetermined or to-be-negotiated amount. This arrangement will normally reflect the fact that the total of the lease payments will enable the lessor to recoup the entire original cost of the equipment plus some additional profit. The amount of profit in total is comprised of these elements:

a. The excess of the rentals over and above the original equipment cost;

b. The value of the tax benefits generated by the ownership of the equipment, if a true lease structure is used; and

c. The projected value of the equipment—referred to as fair market value at the end of the lease term (assuming a true lease structure).

Building upon these elements, it must be understood that leasing transactions are comprised of "hard" and "soft" dollars. The hard-dollar elements are the equipment cost and the rental payments. The soft-dollar elements are the intrinsic tax benefits of ownership and the projected future residual value. It is the availability and utilization of these two elements that distinguishes equipment leasing from other forms of commercial lending. This underlies both its continued popularity and its future growth.

CHANGING THE COSMOS: DEVELOPMENT OF THE LEASING ENVIRONMENT

One of the unique aspects of the financial services industry is its almost total dependence on human creativity for its existence. If one accepts the basic premise that a dollar is a dollar, then the only difference is in the packaging. Viewed from this context, leasing is sheer artistry. To fully understand this, it is helpful to retrace the basic building blocks in the modern development of leasing.

Legal Structure

As discussed above, one of the cornerstones of leasing is the separation between equipment ownership and equipment usage. The legal term used to connote this is "true lease." This is taken to mean (in layman's terms) that the equipment user (our lessee) has no ownership interest in the equipment, and does not develop one during the lease term. The leasing concept of separation of ownership and usage has evolved through several stages.

1870s. The country was expanding westward; railroads were the major transportation link in this growth. To finance their equipment acquisitions, railroads committed to contracts similar to the modern conditional sales contract. Typically, the contract allowed for the equipment cost to be financed over a specified number of years, and called for payments of principal and interest at set intervals during the term. Upon the completion of the required payments, title to the equipment passed to the railroad. This approach had an obvious limitation: the manufacturer was also the financier. Two later approaches, called the New York Plan and the Philadelphia Plan, solved this problem by creating a structure wherein the conditional sale contract (or under the Philadelphia Plan, the direct lease) was assigned to a bank or trust company which issued participation certificates (or equipment trust certificates) to investors calling for payments identical to the underlying conditional sale or direct lease. Equipment title under these arrangements still passed to the user—the "lessee"—upon fulfillment of the contractual obligations.

Post–World War II. Insurance companies were active investors through the financial structures discussed previously. A few became comfortable with the expected life and potential value of railroad equipment at the end of a given term of usage. They began to assume a residual risk: in essence, they began to impute a given residual value and reflect this projected value by reducing lease rentals during the lease term, as compared to the alternative of borrowing. In simple mathematical terms, this is illustrated in Table 16.1. For surrendering the right to continued usage at the expiration of the lease term, the user-lessee has reduced the periodic rental payments to $61,966.20, a savings of more than $10,000 per rental payment compared to the loan alternative. It should be observed that the residual value in the above illustration is not guaranteed—it is a projected value, subject to the vagaries of equipment technology and demand as well as the condition of the equipment when returned. Thus, a prudent lessor, when utilizing a residual estimate, would allow for a cushion between the assumed value and the realistic expectancies. The lessee in this example would do much the same.

However, this new financing structure also had certain additional, intangible benefits:

1. It was not classified as a fixed charge as was interest on conditional sales contracts or equipment trust certificates; thus the entire payment could be expensed; and
2. Since it was not classified as a fixed charge, the financing was considered off-balance-sheet and thus outside the restrictions of loan covenants. It also could not be subject to the open-ended basket security clauses of indentures or classified as "after-acquired property."

In 1949, a rudimentary form of what is now called leveraged leasing was developed by the Equitable Life Assurance Society to finance the purchase of railroad cars, subject to a full-payout lease. In essence, Equitable purchased the equipment from the manufacturer, paying 80 percent of the cost upon delivery. The remaining 20 percent was paid in installments over a five-year period. However, these payments were contingent upon receipt of rental payments from the lessee. The rental payments were sufficient to retire this indebtedness to the

Table 16.1
Loan versus Lease

```
Equipment Cost:  $1,000,000

Lending/Lease Term:  10 years

Assumed Residual Value:  20% of original cost * ($200,000)
                         (At end of lease term)

Assumed Borrowing/Lease Financing:  100% of equipment cost

Assumed ROI:  10% (For either a lessor or lender)

Payments:  Semi-annual Arrears

                        With the assumed residual of 20%
                        imputed at the ROI of 10%, the
                        rental payments are reduced as
                        follows:
                        1)  The present value(P.V.)
                            of $200,000 due ten
                            years in the future
                            imputed at 10% is:      $  144,940

                        2)  Original Equipment
                            Cost:                    1,000,000
                            Less: P.V. of 20%
                            Residual:                 (144,940)
                            Equipment Cost for
                            Rental Basis:              855,060
                            Rental Factor
                            (10% ROI):             x   .072470

Semi-annual loan        3)  Semi-annual rental
payments are: $72,470.90     payments:             $61,966.20
($1,000,000 x .072470)
```

manufacturer and also to enable Equitable to recover its 80 percent investment plus profit.

All these examples served to create and propagate a population of corporate investors increasingly adept in equipment financing. This was to serve as the cornerstone for the further development of leasing as a sophisticated financial tool. However, before this could occur, several other events were required.

Setting the Stage. The initial step was the seemingly innocuous case of *Crane v. Commissioner* (331 U.S.1), which held that the owner of qualifying property could include in the cost basis amounts that had been borrowed on the security of the property and that the owner was not personally obligated to pay. In a later stage, when the tax benefits for lessors in true leases had been considerably enhanced due to accelerated depreciation provisions and investment tax credit (ITC), this precedent would be invaluable.

During the 1950-1970 period, several independent leasing companies were formed. They were not affiliated with either a manufacturer or a parent financial entity. For this reason, they were referred to as independent, third-party lessors. The so-called "granddaddy" of such leasing companies, U.S. Leasing Corporation, was formed in 1954. In quick succession, others such as Boothe Leasing Corporation and Chandler Leasing (later acquired by Pepsi-Cola) followed. Also in the 1950s, General Electric Credit Corporation (GECC), a wholly owned subsidiary of General Electric, commenced leasing of personal property and financing of the parent company's products sold to consumers. At this stage, leasing was a financial structure with limited appeal. Its cost (expressed in the form of lease-rental rates) was a reflection of the leasing company's cost of funds, the perceived credit risk, some minimal residual valuation, and profit. The missing link consisted of substantial tax benefits, plus tax-paying corporations eager to participate in this new financial arena to utilize these tax benefits.

Both these needs were fulfilled in quick succession. In 1962, seeking to promote economic expansion by fostering investment in capital equipment, Congress enacted income tax legislation that created the ITC (then 7 percent) and increased or accelerated the depreciation deduction for tax purposes. This enabled companies such as Greyhound, CIT, and Ford Motor Credit, who quickly realized the potential of this untapped market, to begin offering tax-oriented true leasing. They were able to offer rental rates that reflected the value of the tax benefits and residual value, thus significantly reducing the lessee's cost for equipment usage. Now all three essential elements, rental rates, tax benefits, and projected residual values could be synergistically combined.

Commercial Banks Enter the Arena. The development of this new financial arena and its potential profits did not go unnoticed by the commercial banks. In many instances, the commercial banks were indirectly involved in leasing as either lenders to the leasing companies or the purchasers of equipment trust certificates. Their participation was indirect because of the uncertainty concerning the legality of banks becoming lessors—did their charters allow this financial activity? The issue was resolved when the comptroller of the currency issued an interpretive ruling in 1963 stating that personal-property leasing falling within certain parameters would be viewed as the functional equivalent of extensions of credit.[2] Essentially, this enabled commercial banks to enter into full payout leasing, utilize the tax benefits, and even reflect modest residual estimates in their pricing.

Although the major elements were now in place, the entry of commercial banks into this arena was a gradual process. Leasing still suffered from a general reputation (with the exception of its usage by airlines and railroads) as something of a last-resort financial alternative. Moreover, there was inherently a basic philosophical difference between commercial banking at that time, which was viewed as relationship-oriented, versus leasing, which was transaction-oriented. This distinction, perhaps too subtle for the casual observer to appreciate, was reflected in significant initial resistance to leasing in most bank hierarchies.

Additionally, leasing was perceived as competition to traditonal lending, and thus most financial institutions discouraged their customers from it except as a last resort. Commercial banking at this time still did not face the intensive competition from the myriad of financial options that is so prevalent today. (Noblesse oblige?)

One additional piece of legislation, the Bank Holding Company Act (amended in 1970), created a solution for this internal problem. In essence, it authorized banks to form holding companies and to engage in a number of additional activities (including leasing) beyond traditional lending. This legislation was partially a reaction to perceived competition: commercial banks were observing finance companies such as CIT, GECC, and Ford Motor Credit, making inroads into their traditional lending markets with leasing alternatives. However, it also solved the internal problem: leasing and other activities could now be set up as separate subsidiaries of the holding company, and developed as independent operations with their own personnel.

It must be recognized that for bank lessors, the internal credibility question was as significant as profitability. However, in the early years, bank-lessors were in a situation where it was difficult not to succeed. Their cost of funds, leverage, and tax appetites gave them enormous capability (remember that this was before Latin America and energy-related loan problems reared their ugly heads). It was also a time of increased competition between major commercial banks for asset growth. Most banks were somewhat constrained by legal restrictions pertaining to their geographic scope. While some, however, thought of creative solutions to this issue, most dreamed of (or dreaded) the time when national banking would become a reality.

Finance companies, such as General Electric Credit Corporation (GECC), were not as legally encumbered. Using equipment financing as a primary marketing tool, they expanded their geographic coverage across the country, and correspondingly increased their asset base. For example, in a comparison of the size of GECC's total net earning assets (total finance receivables minus deferred income and bad-debt reserve) and the percentage of this total that true leasing comprises, the results are indicative of the growth of asset-based leasing.[3]

	1970	1980	1986
True Lease Receivables	200MM	1.7Bil	8.3Bil
Leasing as a % of Total Net Earning Assets	8%	20%	36%
Total Net Earning Assets	2.4Bil	8.6Bil	23.3Bil

Although the entry of commercial banks into leasing was not an overnight phenomenon, it soon became apparent that leasing presented two very important possibilities:

1. This new financial structure could attract new customers and increase their asset base and their bottom line; and

2. Leasing operations could be structured in a way that enabled major bank lessors to develop a national equipment financing presence via regional and branch offices in selected cities. This also enhanced the national visibility of the parent, and was a significant step toward national banking.

Leveraged Leasing. The initial thrust by certain money-center banks focused on what is termed "leveraged leasing." This is a true lease structure that embodies three participants:

1. The lessor: the owner of the equipment and the recipient of all the tax benefits allowed for the equipment; in this type of lease structure, the lessor is often called the equity participant, denoting his ownership position;

2. The lessee: the user of the equipment, responsible for the rental payments and lease terms as negotiated; and

3. The debt participant: a major financial institution (typically an insurance company or other long-term lender) who would loan up to 80 percent of the equipment cost on a nonrecourse-to-the-lessor basis, relying strictly on the creditworthiness of the lessee and the collateral of the underlying equipment and lease rentals.

This unique structure combined all the isolated historical elements discussed above in a structure that:

1. Allowed the addition of a third party. This was a debt participant, typically a long-term lender unable to utilize the tax benefits but seeking this type of investment because it offered a slightly higher return than traditional long-term corporate bonds yet embodied a risk factor most were familiar with because of their involvement as investors under either the New York or Philadelphia Plans.

2. Resulted in the lessor calculating his yield based on a 20-percent investment yet receiving:

    a. The excess of rentals net of debt repayment;

    b. The tax benefits of 100 percent of the equipment cost with an equity investment of typically only 20 percent (the amount of equity investment would normally range between 20 and 40 percent dependent upon the availability of investment tax credit and related accounting and cash-return considerations); and

    c. The residual value at the expiration of the lease term.

Leasing versus Lending: Income Comparison

For most financial institutions, one accepted benchmark for measurement of profitability is Return on Assets (ROA). For commercial banks, the goal has been to achieve an ROA of 1 percent. It is an objective that has not often been attained. However, as a recent survey of industry activity by the American Association of Equipment Lessors (AAEL) revealed (see Table 16.2), it has been attained and surpassed by lessors. In fact, comparing results for the period

Table 16.2
ROA

	Return on Total Assets (ROA) in percent	Average Bank Prime Interest Rate in percent
1978	2.4	6.8
1979	2.1	9.1
1980	1.6	12.7
1981 [4]	1.6	15.2
1982	1.9	14.9
1983	2.2	10.8
1984	2.1	12.0
1985	1.8	9.9
1986 [5]	1.9	8.3

1978-1986, the lowest ROA was 1.6 percent in 1980 and 1981 (note that there were significant upturns in the average bank prime interest rate), while the highest was 2.4 percent in 1978. These results reflect the inherently different profit potential for a lessor in a true lease versus a lender for a loan alternative.

Hidden Assets: Residual Values

The ability to accurately project equipment residual value becomes more demanding in the mega-sized leveraged-lease transactions. It is an inexact science at best, yet in considering a transaction involving equipment with an original cost of $100 million dollars or more, this valuation (in some instances projected 20 or more years into the future) can be crucial. Often the difference between winning and losing a transaction can be determined by a few basis points (keep in mind that there are 100 basis points in 1 percent).

In some rare instances, a combination of unusual circumstances can leave a lessor with a potential embarrassment of riches. For example, the introduction of wide-body commercial aircraft in 1970 forced lessors to add another factor—new technology—to such other variables as fuel economy and projected passenger loads, in estimating the future residual value of this equipment. Obviously, if error were inevitable, then to err on the side of conservatism or underestimating the future worth was the prudent course. During the early 1970s, another factor reared its ugly head—inflation, impacting the replacement cost of all equipment. As the popularity of wide-body aircraft increased, its projected life was also enhanced. When double-digit inflation was added to this equation, the results were mind-boggling. The original cost of Boeing's 747 aircraft in 1970 was $18,000,000 for the airframe and $740,000 for each engine (four required). The replacement cost for a new 747 similarly configured in 1986 had risen to $61,300,000 for the airframe and $2,500,000 for each engine. Moreover, the original aircraft with four engines (now 16 years old) had an estimated value of $14,000,000, approximately two-thirds (66 percent) of the initial cost.

Certain lessors, such as Citicorp Industrial Credit (CIC) and GECC were very active in commercial aircraft leasing in the late 1960s and early 1970s. Most of these transactions included an option enabling the lessee to purchase the equipment at the expiration of the lease term for its fair market value. In pricing such transactions, it was not unusual for a lessor to assume a relatively conservative residual value for the reasons stated above. As many of these leases entered their final years, it became apparent there was a wide gap between the assumed residual value and the actual fair market value: the lessors had erred on the side of conservatism.

At this time, most financial institutions were feeling the impact of skyrocketing money costs which were seriously impacting their earnings projections. Most institutions investigated every possibility, seeking ways to impact the bottom line by reducing costs or increasing revenues. Once the significance of the aforementioned scenario had been appreciated, considerable attention was devoted to determining if a solution could be found to bring these untapped millions to the bottom line. The major stumbling blocks were: (1) Generally Accepted Accounting Principles (GAAP) dictated that assets must remain on the books at their original cost on an adjusted cost basis (original cost less depreciation), unless it was determined that their value had decreased, at which point the asset basis had to be adjusted to this diminished value; and (2) no provision existed in GAAP that would allow an increase in value above its adjusted cost basis unless a sale of the asset occurred.

Ultimately, a solution was found. Lindsay McManus, then a vice president of CIC, was instrumental in creating a new financial vehicle called Residual Value Certificates (RVCs). The RVCs transferred to another investor the right to receive some prescribed percentage of the original equipment cost (over and above the lessor's assumed residual) at the expiration of the lease. The transaction involved three parties:

1. The lessor—owner of the leased asset;
2. The investor—typically an insurance company or other financial institution;
3. The insurer—this was the key element—the inclusion of an acceptable insuring entity, ready, willing, and financially able to guarantee the agreed-upon future worth.

The transaction was then completed, with the investor paying some negotiated amount (the insured future residual being sold, present-valued at some agreed percentage) to the lessor. For accounting purposes, the transaction could be treated as a sale, enabling the lessor to immediately bring this income to the bottom line. The financial impact of this solution has been estimated to be in excess of $50 million for each of several lessors in additional profits. The additional earnings enhanced shareholder equity, which of course had a favorable impact on stock and credit analysts, who are always evaluating financial strength and coverage of interest expense, among other factors.

Unfortunately, as inflation played a significant role in this scenario, there is another factor that can have an equally significant (some might say devastating) impact: technology. Computer lessors in the early 1970s were faced with a formidable competitor: IBM. Moreover, the computer leasing industry contained an overabundance of small, thinly capitalized entities. These "minnows" were always attempting to create financial alternatives enabling them to compete against the "giant whale," IBM. Computer leasing firms were typically writing seven-year contracts, but with a so-called "walkaway" option that allowed the lessee to break the lease after three or four years with no financial penalties. The existence of this provision (a competitive necessity) severely limited the ability of computer lessors to obtain financing for these leases. Because they feared IBM might introduce new models that would make the leased computers obsolete overnight, banks were reluctant to provide financing for this equipment for more than four years.

However, in 1973, Lloyd's of London received a request from a small Dallas-based leasing company seeking insurance protection against equipment coming off lease (via this walkaway provision) being worth less than the underlying debt still owed on it. Lloyd's renowned for its ability to offer unique types of insurance coverage, put together a policy called "J" policy to cover this specific risk. This policy insured IBM 370-158s and -168s, which sold for as much as $5 million each. Lloyd's guaranteed to repay the original loan to the funding source used by a leasing company to finance this computer lease if the lessee exercised its walkaway option and the lessor could not release the equipment on a comparable basis. In some instances, contracts were written on the assumption that a machine would be worth 40 percent of its purchase price at the point where the walkaway provision was exercisable. Needless to say, in a field where everyone was fearful of instant financial annihilation at the hands of one announcement by IBM, business was brisk. Between 1974 and 1977, Lloyd's wrote policies on about $2.4 billion worth of computer equipment. Its total exposure reached $600 million on premium income of roughly $75 million.[6]

In late 1977, Lloyd's discontinued issuing the "J" Policy as rumors began circulating concerning improved computers being developed by IBM. The rumors in this instance proved to be true, with IBM announcing in quick succession a new line of 303x large computers, which were two and a half times faster than the machine they were replacing and only 40 percent higher in price; and a new

4300 series of smaller computers vastly more capable than their predecessors. In an industry where cost and performance rule, the results were predictable: the value of the IBM 370s dropped as much as 50 percent.

Although no official figure has ever been released by Lloyd's, the "J" Policy debacle has been classified as the largest disaster in its long history. Prior to this, the record loss was the more than $100 million paid out for damages from Hurricane Betsy in 1965. Although Lloyd's indicated it had earmarked $220 million for anticipated losses from its "J" Policy, some insiders indicated the loss could be as high as $1 billion. As one source aptly summarized, "Lloyd's experts unaccountably underestimated the possibility that computer-leasing contracts, unlike ships, might well all sink together."[7]

As the RVC and "J" Policy examples reflect, predicting future equipment values has its rewards and perils. Although the assumed value can be looked on as an additional element of risk, experience has shown that original assumed values have been fairly accurate, with certain caveats as indicated in this section (see Table 16.3). Enlightened, 20/20 hindsight is helpful in refining the analytical tools, but many elements of this exercise are subjective and difficult to quantify, at times leaving a gap of significant proportions between estimate and reality.

Accounting and Tax[9]

As the leasing industry continued to expand in the mid-1970s, it also began to attract increased regulatory attention from both the Financial Accounting Standards Board (FASB) and Congress. Each had its own distinct concerns.

FASB had been designated in 1973 as the organization in the private sector for establishing the standards of financial accounting and reporting, superseding the Accounting Principles Board (APB). Its pronouncements are recognized as authoritative by both the Securities and Exchange Commission (SEC) and the American Institute of Certified Public Accountants (AICPA). The SEC in particular began to note the growth of leasing as a financial alternative, and became concerned that the current accounting standards (particularly APB Opinions 5, 7, 27, and 31) did not fulfill the following major objectives: (1) Bring about a symmetry in accounting between lessors and lessees, and (2) provide for full disclosure of lease obligations. The SEC went so far as to issue its own "rules" for lease accounting, which were subsequently withdrawn with the promulgation of Financial Accounting Standard (FAS) No. 13, "Accounting for Leases," which was issued in November 1976. FAS No. 13 defined two basic types of leases, capital and operating, and enunciated certain criteria that should be utilized in determining if a lease qualified as one or the other. Initially, this was deemed to be the death knell of the leasing industry. It was felt that FAS No. 13 would require the capitalization of most leases, thus eliminating the ability of the lessee to expense the rental payments as paid, and eliminating the tax benefits for lessors. Upon further investigation, new approaches were discovered that enabled the leasing industry to continue to grow, while meeting the requirements of FAS

Table 16.3
Average Residual Recovery[8]

For financial statement purposes as a percent of the
original estimated book residual value during 1986:

	Number of Respondents	Average Residual Recovery*
Agricultural	23	82.0
Aircraft	**	**
Computers	74	109.7
Construction	35	84.1
Industrial	38	90.1
Manufacturing	52	98.9
Medical	42	90.7
Office machines	51	98.5
Project (multi-asset)	**	**
Railroad	**	**
Telecommunications	50	151.3
Trucks and trailers	46	93.4
Other	49	106.4

*Simple average.
**Five or fewer respondents.

Source: Survey of Industry Activity, 1986, AEEL, p. 11.

13. FASB has continued to refine its initial pronouncement and has promulgated seven additional statements and six additional interpretations pertaining to leasing (see Table 16.4).

Congress and the Internal Revenue Service have since 1955 shown a more than passing interest in the leasing industry. The tenor of this relationship was first defined in 1955 when the IRS issued its first definitive set of rules, seeking to distinguish true leases from conditional sales.[11] The accounting profession dealt with the same issue in seeking to determine which leases must be capitalized (finance or capital leases) and which may be expensed (true or operating lease).

Table 16.4
Leasing Accounting Standards[10]

Statement of Leasing Accounting Standards	
Title	Date Issued
No. 13 -- Accounting for Leases	11/76
No. 17 -- Accounting for Leases -- Initial Direct Costs -- an amendment of FASB Statement No. 13	11/77
No. 22 -- Changes in the Provisions of Lease Agreements Resulting from Refundings of Tax-Exempt Debt -- an amendment of FASB Statement No. 13	6/78
No. 23 -- Inception of the Lease -- an amendment of FASB Statement No. 13	8/78
No. 26 -- Profit Recognition on Sales-Types Leases of Real Estates -- an amendment of FASB Statement No. 13	4/79
No. 27 -- Classification of Renewals or Extensions of Existing Sales-Type or Direct Financing Leases -- an amendment of FASB Statement No. 13	5/79
No. 28 -- Accounting for Sales and Leasebacks -- an amendment of FASB Statement No. 13	5/79
No. 29 -- Determining Contingent Rentals -- an amendment of FASB Statement No. 13	7/79

Interpretations	
Title	Date Issued
No. 19 -- Lessee Guarantee of the Residual Value of Leased Property -- an interpretation of FASB Statement No. 13	10/77
No. 21 -- Accounting for Leases in a Business Combination -- an interpretation of FASB Statement No. 13	4/78
No. 23 -- Leases of Certain Property Owned by a Governmental Unit of Authority -- an interpretation of FASB Statement No. 13	8/78
No. 24 -- Leases involving Only Part of a Building -- an interpretation of FASB Statement No. 13	9/78
No. 26 -- Accounting for Purchase of a Leased Asset by the Lessee during the Term of the Lease -- an interpretation of FASB Statement No. 13	9/78
No. 27 -- Accounting for a Loss on a Sublease -- an interpretation of FASB Statement No. 13 and APB Opionion No. 30	11/78

Source: Financial Accounting Standards Board, *World Leasing Yearbook,* 1980, p. 44. Copyright by Financial Accounting Standards Board, High Ridge Park, Stamford, Connecticut 06905, U.S.A. Reprinted with permission. Copies of the complete document are available from the FASB.

The IRS in 1955 established the standard of "Fair Market Value" for the purchase of equipment by the lessee at the expiration of the lease term. With this new standard, in order to preserve the true lease-tax benefits, any option given to the lessee to purchase the asset at the end of the lease term had to be for an amount not less than its fair market value. Up to this time, the standards for this determination were "flexible," and lessees were sometimes given side letters allowing them to purchase the equipment at the expiration of the lease term for a nominal amount (for example, $1).

As Congress enacted more liberalized tax laws, providing for accelerated depreciation and investment tax credit, a new opportunity was created: the utilization of tax benefits. Congress has since the early 1960s attempted to provide economic stimulation by providing tax incentives to promote capital spending. However, an underlying premise of Congress has been the capability of the equipment-user to utilize the tax benefits attendant on equipment acquisition. This is not always the case. For some companies already in a tax-loss carry-forward position, the tax benefits have no current value. It may also be argued these tax benefits place them at an even greater disadvantage vis-à-vis their competitors, who can use the tax benefits on a current basis and reflect these in their bottom line. Similarly, at a time when the corporate federal income-tax-rate was 46 percent, certain tax-paying financial institutions had a higher effective corporate tax rate due to the cumulative effect of additional state and city taxes. For companies paying high federal income taxes, tax loss carry forwards have a greater importance than for a corporation in a lower tax bracket.

The ability of true leasing to shift the tax benefits to the corporation better able to utilize them, and which in turn can reflect their benefit (commonly called tax pricing) in the lease rental rate, has historically been one of the reasons for the popularity and growth of leasing.[12] It has enabled both high-growth companies and companies not in a tax-paying position to obtain equipment that they may have otherwise been denied. This has not always been viewed as favorable by Congress and the IRS, who are both concerned about total tax revenues. In fact, it has been reported that when Congress was considering the Capital Cost Recovery Act of 1979, the cost of this tax deferral program was estimated at between $19 billion and $50 billion per year in lost tax revenues.[13] It should not come as a surprise that every major tax bill since 1981 has included provisions that have altered the tax consequences of leasing.

The Economic Recovery Tax Act (ERTA) of 1981. This act established the accelerated cost recovery system (ACRS), seeking to relate depreciation to useful life, and decreased the recovery period for ITC. ERTA also introduced a new financial vehicle known as Tax Benefit Transfers (TBTs) as part of its safe-harbor leasing guidelines, which allowed for the transfer of tax benefits through leases without any other economic substance.

The Tax Equity and Fiscal Responsibility Act (TEFRA) of 1982. TEFRA repealed the safe-harbor rules of ERTA (with limited exceptions). The purpose of safe-harbor TBTs was to provide a trading mechanism for major corporations unable to utilize tax benefits, whereby they could transfer them to a tax-paying entity for an up-front cash payment. It was intended that the funds so derived would be utilized for recovery and expansion in existing operations. Instead, many corporations utilized this largesse for diversification via acquisition, arousing the ire of Congress. TEFRA created the "finance lease," which allowed for the transfer of tax benefits while requiring some economic substance beyond tax considerations.

The Deficit Reduction Act (DRA) of 1984. The DRA eliminated the ITC and reduced the depreciation available on property leased to tax-exempt or non-taxpaying entities.

Tax Reform Act (TRA) of 1986. TRA eliminated ITC, modified depreciation allowances, lowered corporate tax rates, and created an alternative minimum tax (AMT). Certain leasing subsidiaries of Fortune 100 companies up to this time were able to shelter not only their own income, but also the entire income of their parent. The AMT eliminated this, and the reduction of the corporate tax rate reduced the value of tax benefits associated with equipment acquisition, thus diminishing one of the advantages of leasing.

Leasing and Capital Equipment Expenditures

The creativity and flexibility of leasing is perhaps best reflected in its growing utilization. As Table 16.5 indicates, leasing has grown more than twice as fast as business investment in equipment since 1978.

For example, equipment leasing comprised 14 percent of business investment in new equipment in 1978. In 1986, the comparable figure was 30 percent. This tremendous growth underscores the versatility and flexibility of leasing. Leasing's ability to offer 100-percent financing, its matching of the lease term to the useful life of the equipment, protection against obsolescence, creation of structures that enable tax-exempt entities (for example, municipalities or hospitals) to obtain equipment without violating their funding restrictions, and provision of an essential marketing tool for vendors seeking customers for their products: all these attributes underscore the diversity of equipment markets for which leasing provides a service, separate from its tax-oriented utilization.

The utilization of leasing will continue to shift, both in participants and concentration, predicated on tax law and capital spending. Whereas tax leasing in the 1970s was dominated by bank-related lessors, the 1980s are dominated by the financial subsidiaries of industrial giants and the "Baby Bells"—offshoots of AT&T. Bank lessors, however, have not dropped out of the picture. As their tax appetites have diminished due to loan losses of their parent entities, they have turned in many instances to leasing products that are less tax-sensitive. They have focused on money-over-money (usually fixed-rate) finance leases, akin to mortgage financing. Some have developed highly successful vendor-finance capabilities, removing the financial and operational problems from the vendors and enabling them to concentrate their resources in product development and sales.

Table 16.5
Historical Trends and Forecast: Equipment Leasing[14]

(in billions of dollars)

	Equipment Leasing [1]	Business Investment In Equipment [2]
1978	26.5	178.0
1979	32.8	203.3
1980	43.5	208.9
1981	55.5	230.7
1982	57.6	223.4
1983	61.2	232.8
1984	74.5	277.3
1985	93.7	303.4
1986 [3]	95.0	309.5
1987 [4]	97.0	321.9

[1]   Estimates of new lease receivables based on survey data from the American Association of Equipment Lessors, except as noted.

[2]   Private nonresidential investment in producers' durable equipment.

[3]   Estimated.

[4]   Forecast.

Source: U.S. Industrial Outlook 1987, U.S. Government Printing Office.

According to a recently completed survey, the transportation sector accounted for $32 billion of all equipment added for leasing in 1986. This represented 38 percent of the $85 billion of equipment leased. Additionally, the computer, office equipment, and communications sectors added an estimated $26 billion of new equipment, while the agriculture, construction, industrial and manufacturing machinery, and medical equipment sectors added $8 billion.[15]

Comparing leasing as a source of funds for business is even more revealing. In 1986, only bonds and commercial mortgages provided more financing for businesses. The amount of bond financing was 19 percent greater than equipment leasing, and commercial mortgages were 6 percent greater. New equipment leases financed 19 percent of the value of business fixed investment (including structures) and 27 percent of producers' durable goods equipment.[16]

As the industry continues to evolve, it also becomes more sophisticated in its approaches. For example, the initial entry of commercial banks into leasing was viewed by regulatory authorities as the functional equivalent of lending. They were in fact restricted from becoming too aggressive by certain requirements pertaining to the amount or percentage of future equipment value they could include in their pricing calculations, because this was viewed as lending, not equipment speculation. Since the time of the original mandate, many things have changed.

1. Money-center banks utilized leasing not only as a means of product diversification and asset growth, but also as a vanguard for national expansion: with leasing offices or representation in most major cities, identification of their name was enhanced, opening the door for future activities.

2. The distinctions within the financial markets between short-term, medium-term, and long-term lenders have blurred, if not ceased. Some financial institutions, by internal growth and acquisition, are becoming all things to all people via one-stop shopping, whereas others are reexamining their historical roles and attempting to remain viable by finding niches where their expertise creates value-added.

3. The leasing industry has developed and refined its capabilities in both the tax and pure financing aspects of leasing. The remaining frontier is estimating future equipment value; that is, residual valuation. As other parts of this discussion have illustrated, this can be either a lucrative opportunity or a disastrous one. Recent changes in the tax code as well as competitive conditions have dictated this. While lessors have enhanced their understanding of equipment usage and future valuation, so too have lessees. Tax-paying lessees in evaluating their lease-versus-buy decisions are also more knowledgeable about future equipment value and less likely to settle for an open-ended fair-market value-purchase option. Both lessors and lessees recognize that the new playing field is going to be focused in equipment residual pricing and realization.

4. Bank lessors have lobbied for a lifting of the residual restrictions they competed within, and recently have been successful in eliminating most of their restraints.[17]

Some lessors believe the trend of the future will be asset management. Lessors will become providers of leasing alternatives as an intermediary between various funding sources and lessees. Unlike brokers, whose responsibility ends when the transaction is consummated, they will continue to play an active role as the administrative and operational center, collecting rents, remitting funds to lessors, providing expertise in equipment appraisal, managing the lease portfolio, and optimizing the amount realized for the equipment at the end of the lease term—all for a fee. This trend closely parallels the emphasis of major financial institutions toward fee-generated services and away from asset-building, as they prefer to emphasize improvement in earnings and restrict asset growth.

Other lessors, seeking to move away from a pure rate-competition environment, are developing a servicing-maintenance capability combined with an operating lease financing alternative (less than full payout) in certain equipment categories such as aircraft and railroad equipment. By bundling several services, they hope to attract lessees and simultaneously insulate themselves from the pure financing arena.

Predicting the future growth of any industry over the long term is speculative at best. However, if the present utilization is any indication, the future of leasing, in whatever forms or structures, seems assured.

NOTES

1. Wiliam J. Montgomery, "The Tax Environment in the United States," presentation at Fifth World Leasing Convention, Toronto, Canada, June 1-3, 1987.

2. Interpretive Ruling No. 400, 12CFR Sec. 7.3100.

3. Annual Reports of GECC, 1970, 1980, 1986.

4. *1981 Survey of Accounting and Business Practices* (Arlington, Va.: American Association of Equipment Lessors, 1981), 7.

5. American Association of Equipment Lessors, *Survey of Industry Activity* (Arlington, Va.: AAEL, 1986), 7.

6. "Lloyd's Biggest Disaster," *Forbes,* May 28, 1979, 38.

7. J. A. Tannenbaum and P. S. Meyer, "At Lloyd's of London a Record Loss Looms on Computer Policies," *Wall Street Journal,* July 10, 1979, 21.

8. American Association of Equipment Lessors, *Survey of Industry Activity,* 1986, 11.

9. The author gratefully acknowledges the assistance of Howard Weber, senior vice president, Shearson, Lehman Bros.

10. *World Leasing Yearbook* (Coqqeshall, Essex: Hawkins Publishers Limited, 1980), 44.

11. Rev. Rul 55-540.

12. Yankelovich, Skelly & White, Inc., *Attitudes Towards the Equipment Leasing Industry* (Arlington, Va.: American Association of Equipment Lessors, 1983), 22.

13. Joe Morald and David Lees, "Capital Cost Recovery Act," in *World Leasing Yearbook,* 46.

14. *U.S. Industrial Outlook 1987—Equipment Leasing,* no. 53 (Washington, D.C.: U.S. Government Printing Office).

15. Robert R. Nathan Associates, Inc., *Equipment Leasing Activity in the United States* (Arlington, Va.: American Association of Equipment Lessors, September 1987), 1.

16. Ibid., 3.

17. John D. Hawke, Jr., and Melanie L. Fein, "Congress Grants New Leasing Powers to National Banks," *Equipment Financing Journal* 9, 5 (September-October 1987), 1.

Glossary

adjustable-rate mortgage (ARM): a mortgage on which the contractual interest rate can be changed prior to maturity. ARMs include VRMs, RRMs, and other forms of mortgages with adjustable rates.

asset-liability management: a management technique designed to provide for a financial institution's funding needs and reduce its net exposure to interest rate risk. It tries to reduce mismatches in an institution's contractual inflows and outflows of interest and principal payments.

asset management: a financial institution's management of its asset structure to provide both liquidity and desirable rates of return.

automatic transfer of savings (ATS) accounts: the automatic transfer of funds from an interest-bearing savings account to a demand deposit account. ATS accounts are functionally similar to NOW accounts.

bank insolvency: a bank is declared insolvent when the value of its liabilities exceeds the value of its assets. Typically, banks become insolvent and fail by incurring losses on their loans or investment holdings.

bank liquidity: the ability of banks to accommodate depositors' requests for withdrawals.

banker's acceptance: a promissory note drawn by a corporation to pay for merchandise on which a bank guarantees payment at maturity. In effect, the bank substitutes its credit standing for that of the issuing corporation.

basis point: one hundred basis points equals 1 percent.

bear market: a market which is declining.

best efforts: an offering of securities to investors where the investment banker provides only a marketing effort and not a guarantee of sale which is normally at the center of a "firm commitment underwriting agreement."

bond: a long-term debt instrument.

borrowed funds: short-term funds borrowed by commercial banks from the wholesale money market or the Federal Reserve. They include Eurodollar borrowings, Federal Funds, and funds obtained through the issuance of repurchase agreements.

branch banking: branch banks can have multiple full-service offices. Some banks can engage in statewide branching; others may only be able to branch on a limited basis within their state.

broker: one who acts as an intermediary between buyers and sellers but does not take title to the securities traded or hold an inventory position or make a market in securities.

bull market: a market which is rising.

call: an option giving the buyer the right to purchase the underlying security at a predetermined price over a stated period of time.

call provision: the right of an issuer of a security to redeem that security for a pre-determined value on or after some future point in time. Call provisions are often used by borrowers to liquidate outstanding debts that carry high interest rates after interest rates fall.

capital: on a balance sheet, an institution's net worth. In terms of physical assets, capital can be used to generate future returns.

capital adequacy: the adequacy of a financial institution's net worth to absorb potential adverse changes in the value of its assets without becoming insolvent.

capital impairment: a situation in which a financial institution holds less capital than is required by law. Such a firm may be forced to acquire new capital, merge, or cease operation.

capital markets: financial markets in which financial claims with maturities greater than one year are traded. Capital markets channel savings into long-term productive investments.

captive finance company: a sales finance company that is owned by a manufacturer and helps finance the sale of the manufacturer's goods.

closed-end investment company: a form of pooled investment alternatives whose capitalization remains fixed. Trading occurs in the shares outstanding.

collateral: assets that are used to secure a loan. Title to them will pass to the lender if the borrower defaults.

collateralized mortgage obligation (CMO): a security issued by a thrift institution's finance subsidiary that is collateralized by participation certificates (issued by federal agencies) that promise to pass through principal and interest payments on pools of underlying mortgages. CMOs are attractive to many investors because they pay principal and interest like bonds and because the securities that serve as collateral are obligations of federal government agencies.

commercial paper: an unsecured, short-term promissory note issued by a large, creditworthy business or financial institution. Commercial paper has maturities ranging from a day to 270 days and is usually issued in denominations of $1 million or more. Direct-placed commercial paper is sold by the seller to the buyer. Terms are negotiable. Dealer-placed commercial paper is sold through dealers with terms similar to those offered on bank CDs.

common stock: ownership claims on a firm. Stockholders share in the distributed earnings and net worth of a firm and select its directors.

compensating balance: a required minimum balance that borrowers must maintain at a bank, usually in the form of noninterest-bearing demand deposits. The required amount is usually 10 to 20 percent of the amount of the loan outstanding. A compensating balance raises the effective rate of interest on a bank loan.

Comptroller of the Currency: an agency of the U.S. government responsible for regulating banks with federal charters. Only federally chartered banks may use the word national in their name.

concentration ratio: measure of competition in banking markets. Typically computed as the percent of total deposits held by the largest banks in the market. Lower concentration ratios imply greater competition.

consumer finance company: a finance company that specializes in making cash loans to consumers.

convertible bond: a bond that can be converted into a predetermined number of shares of stock at the borrower's option.

correspondent balances: deposits banks hold at other banks to clear checks and provide compensation for correspondent services.

correspondent banking: a business arrangement between two banks where one (the correspondent bank) agrees to provide the other (respondent bank) with special services, such as check clearing or trust department services.

country risk: the risk tied to political developments in a country that affect the return on loans or investments. Examples of country risk are foreign government expropriation of the assets of foreigners or prohibition of foreign loan repayments.

coupon rate: the rate of interest on a bond that is determined by dividing the fixed coupon payment by the principal amount of the bond. The coupon rate is established when the bond is issued.

credit risk: the possibility that the borrower will not pay back all or part of principal as promised. The greater the credit risk, the greater the loan rate.

currency risk: risk resulting from changes in currency exchange values that affect the return on loans or investments denominated in other currencies. For example, if the currency in which a loan is made loses value against the dollar, the loan repayment will be worth fewer dollars.

dealer: one who is in the security business acting as a principal rather than as an agent. The dealer buys for his own account and sells to customers from his inventory. The dealer's profit is the difference between the price received and the price paid for a particular security.

default: the failure on the part of a borrower to fulfill any part of a loan contract, generally by not paying the interest or principal as promised.

default risk premium (DRP): the amount of additional compensation investors must receive for purchasing securities that are not free of default risk. The rate on U.S. Treasury securities is used as the default-free rate.

deficient reserves: reserves that fall below those required by law. Banks with deficient reserves must pay a penalty (2 percent above the discount rate) on the amount deficient to the Federal Reserve.

deficit spending unit (DSU): an economic unit that has expenditures exceeding current income. A DSU sells financial claims on itself (liabilities) to borrow needed funds.

demand deposit: deposits held at banks that the owner can withdraw instantly upon demand—either with checks or electronically.

deposit rate ceilings: before April 1, 1986, legal limits under Regulation Q were set on the interest that could be paid on financial institutions' deposits.

Depository Institutions Deregulation and Monetary Control Act (DIDMCA): legislation passed in the spring of 1980 committing the government to deregulation of the banking system. It (1) provided for the elimination of interest rate controls for banks and savings institutions within 6 years; (2) authorized them to offer interest-bearing NOW accounts; (3) overrode many state usury ceilings on mortgage, agricultural, business, and consumer loans; (4) required the Federal Reserve to open up its discount window to all depository institutions subject to reserve requirements and to make its funds transfer payments and clearing services available to all depository institutions at the same price; and (5) gave the Federal Reserve board new powers to control the money supply by establishing reserve requirements for all depository institutions.

direct financing: financing wherein DSUs issue financial claims on themselves and sell them for money directly to SSUs. The SSU's claim is against the DSU and not a financial intermediary.

direct placement: the direct sale by a corporation of its debt to institutional investors. Such sales do not require underwriters.

discount: a security sells at a discount when it sells for less than its face or par value. Treasury bills are sold at a discount and redeemed for face or par value at maturity.

discount rate: financial institutions can borrow from the Federal Reserve. The interest rate charged by the Federal Reserve Bank is called the discount rate and the act of borrowing is called borrowing at the discount window.

disintermediation: the withdrawal of funds that were previously invested through financial intermediaries, so that they can be invested directly in the financial markets.

dual banking system: a term referring to the fact that United States banks can be chartered either by the federal government (national bank) or by state governments—each with different laws.

duration: the point in time when the average present value of a security (or portfolio) is repaid. Duration measures the sensitivity of securities (or portfolios) to interest rate changes. The longer the duration, the greater the security's price will change when interest rates change. It is more useful than maturity for assessing a security's price sensitivity to interest rate changes.

Edge Act corporation: a subsidiary of a U.S. bank formed to engage in international banking and financial activities that domestic banks cannot conduct in the United States. Incorporated in the U.S. under Section 25 of the Federal Reserve Act.

Efficient Market: a theory that public markets for certain stocks are sufficiently liquid and the flow of information about the issue is so quickly and efficiently incorporated into the price of the securities that the value of those securities in the market at any point in time may be presumed to be imbedded in the market price.

Electronic Funds Transfer System (EFTs): a computerized information system that gathers and processes financial information and transfers funds electronically from one financial account to another.

endowment insurance: a life insurance contract that promises to pay the face amount of the policy upon death of the insured or (if the insured survives) at the end of the contract period.

equity kicker: a form of convertible security that is viewed as a form of deferred equity because they are intended to be converted eventually into shares of the company's common stock.

Eurobank: a financial institution that simultaneously bids for time deposits and makes loans in a country other than the one in which it is located.

Eurodollar: a U.S. dollar-denominated deposit issued by a bank located outside the United States.

excess reserves: cash in the vault or deposits at the Fed that exceed the amount of reserves required by law.

exchange rate, or spot exchange rate: the rate at which one nation's currency can be exchanged for another's at the present time.

factor: a firm that specializes in financing and collecting the debts of other firms.

factored accounts receivable: receivables of a firm that have been sold to a factor in exchange for cash.

failing bank: a bank that is declared in imminent danger of being unable to meet its financial or legal obligations by the FDIC. Failing banks are allowed to merge with other banks, even though the mergers may violate the antitrust laws' competitive criteria for business mergers.

"Fannie Mae": see Federal National Mortgage Association.

Federal Deposit Insurance Corporation (FDIC): an agency of the U.S. government that insures bank deposits up to $100,000 per account.

Federal Funds: financial institution deposits held at Federal Reserve banks. Banks may lend their deposits to other financial institutions through the Federal Funds market.

Federal Home Loan Bank Board (FHLBB): the primary regulatory agency for savings and loan associations. It controls the Federal Home Loan Bank system, the Federal Home Loan Mortgage Corporation, and the Federal Savings and Loan Insurance Corporation. Its regulations affect all federally chartered and federally insured savings associations.

Federal Home Loan Mortgage Corporation (FHLMC): "Freddie Mac" provides a secondary market for conventional mortgages. It was established to help savings and loan associations sell their mortgages.

Federal National Mortgage Association (FNMA): "Fannie Mae" provides a secondary market for insured mortgages by issuing and executing purchase commitments for mortgages.

Federal Reserve System: our nation's central bank. Its primary function is to control the money supply and financial markets in the public's best interest. The Fed consists of 12 regional Federal Reserve banks, but primary policy responsibility resides with its Board of Governors in Washington, D.C.

Federal Savings and Loan Insurance Corporation (FSLIC): FSLIC provides deposit insurance to savings and loan associations.

fidelity bond: a contract that covers the infidelity or dishonesty of employees. Fidelity bonds protect employers and others against embezzlement, forgery, and other forms of theft.

financial intermediaries: institutions that issue liabilities to SSUs and use the funds so obtained to acquire liabilities of DSUs. They include banks, savings associations, credit unions, finance companies, insurance companies, pension funds, and investment companies.

financial sector: the sector of the economy that encompasses financial institutions, financial markets, and financial instruments. The role of the financial sector is to collect savings from SSUs and allocate them efficiently to DSUs for investment in productive assets or for current consumption.

fractional reserve banking: refers to the fact that banks hold only a fraction of their deposits in the form of liquid reserves (vault cash or deposits at the Federal Reserve Bank) and loan out the rest to earn interest. For example, a bank that has deposits of $1,000 and reserves of $50 is holding 5 percent reserves (50/1,000).

"Freddie Mac": see Federal Home Loan Mortgage Corporation.

401(K) Plan: refers to a salary reduction plan that allows employees to contribute a portion of their salaries on a tax deferred basis.

GAP: the difference between the maturity or duration of a firm's assets and liabilities.

A maturity GAP is calculated by subtracting the amount of an institution's liabilities that mature or are repriced within a given period of time from the amount of assets that mature or are repriced within the same period. A duration GAP compares the difference between the average duration of an institution's assets and its liabilities, weighted by the market value of each.

Garn-St. Germain Act: passed in 1982, it allowed depository institutions to have deregulated money market accounts and super-NOW accounts.

General Agreements on Tariffs and Trade: GATT was established in 1947. It is a framework of rules for nations to manage their trade policies. It also provides a forum in which disputes can be negotiated.

"Ginnie Mae": see Government National Mortgage Association.

Glass-Steagall Act: the Banking Act of June 16, 1933, which was designed to separate the function of commercial banking and investment banking with the intent of prohibiting a banking entity from both taking public deposits and making commercial loans on the one hand and underwriting issuances of corporate securities to the public on the other.

goodwill: an intangible asset created when one institution purchases another for more than the market value of its assets. Such behavior is considered irrational unless the acquired firm has valuable intangible assets known as goodwill. Goodwill is used to make the purchased institution's balance sheet balance when all assets are restated at market value. It is assumed to depreciate over time. Goodwill created by "purchase accounting" had been used to add to a purchased thrift institution's assets. Some say thrifts' goodwill really reflects the value of federal insurance, which lets them obtain liabilities at low rates, and the "franchise value" associated with being able to provide financial services in specific locations.

Government National Mortgage Association (GNMA): "Ginnie Mae" helps issuers of mortgages obtain capital market financing to support their mortgage holdings. It does so by creating government-guaranteed securities that pass through all interest and principal repayments from pools of mortgages to purchasers of the pass-through securities.

hedger: an individual or firm that engages in futures market transactions to reduce price risk.

holding company: a corporation operated for the purpose of owning the common stock of other companies. Most commercial banks operate as subsidiaries of holding companies.

homeowner's insurance: a combination property-liability insurance coverage for individuals and families.

immunization: a fixed income portfolio management strategy to eliminate the sensitivity of a financial institution's income or a portfolio's net worth to fluctuations in value caused by changes in interest rates.

Individual Retirement Account (IRA): a retirement plan for individuals. The pension contributions are deposited with trustees (usually banks, insurance companies, or mutual funds). Contributions are limited to $2,000 per year for each working adult. In addition, an annual $200 contribution can be made for a nonworking spouse.

industrial bank: a financial institution chartered under industrial banking laws in a state. Industrial banks make loans and issue savings deposits. Finance companies may obtain charters as industrial banks so they can issue savings deposits to obtain funds.

installment loan: a loan that is repaid in a series of fixed payments.

interest rate swap: the exchange of interest payments received on underlying assets. Typically, a fixed-rate interest payment stream will be exchanged for a variable-rate payment stream, or vice versa. Such swaps let institutions match the cash flow of their assets and liabilities more easily.

intermediation: transfer of funds from surplus units (SSUs) to deficit spending units (DSUs) via the services of a financial intermediary. Depository institutions provide denomination intermediation by issuing small-denomination liabilities and buying large-denomination assets. They provide maturity intermediation by issuing short-maturity liabilities and acquiring long-maturity assets. They provide risk intermediation and portfolio diversification by pooling many assets and issuing liabilities that have pro rata claims against the pooled value of those assets.

investment banker: a person who provides financial advice and who underwrites and distributes new investment securities.

investment company: a company or trust fund that uses its capital to invest in other companies. Individuals buy units in the investment company and own part of the portfolio.

Keogh Plan: a plan that allows self-employed persons to establish tax-sheltered retirement programs themselves.

leverage: the ratio of funds supplied by the owner of an asset to the total value of the asset. A firm is said to be highly leveraged when its net worth is small relative to its total assets (and debts). A stock purchase is said to be highly leveraged if the buyer borrows most of the funds used to purchase it.

liabilities: a firm's debt. Liabilities are a source of funds for the firm.

liability insurance: insurance that protects against losses arising from liability for damages to property or personal injury to others.

liability management: a bank's management of its liability structure to increase or decrease its source of funds as needed. Liability management is based on the assumption that certain types of bank liabilities are sensitive to interest rate changes. Examples of interest-sensitive funds are CDs, repos, Eurodollar borrowings, and Fed Funds.

LIBOR: London Interbank Borrowing Rate, the "prime rate" of international lending and the cheapest rate at which funds flow between international banks. Other international rates often are set to vary with LIBOR rates.

limited branching: state laws that restrict a bank's abilities to branch to a limited geographical area, usually to a county or contiguous counties or to a set number of branches.

liquidity of an asset: the ease with which an asset can be quickly converted to money (M1) with negligible cost or risk of loss. The higher the potential cost of rapidly converting an asset into money, the lower its liquidity.

liquidity of an institution: an institution is liquid if it holds sufficient amounts of cash and liquid assets to allow it to easily meet requests from its liability holders for cash payment. It is illiquid if it has difficulty meeting such requests. Bank panics can quickly convert an institution from liquid to illiquid status as depositors withdraw their funds.

loss reserves: liabilities of a firm that are accumulated, in lieu of retained earnings or surplus, to enable the firm to meet future losses. When losses on assets occur, they are written off against a firm's loss reserve accounts rather than its current profits and net worth accounts.

margin loans: loans that brokerage firms extend to their customers to purchase securities.

marine insurance: insurance contracts that cover losses related to all types of transportation. The contract may cover the means of transportation, cargo, or freight.

marketability: the ease with which a financial claim can be resold. The greater the marketability of a financial security, the lower its interest rate.

maturity: the date when the repayment of the principal amount of a financial claim is due.

maturity imbalance: a maturity imbalance occurs when an institution holds assets that do not have maturities similar to the maturities of its liabilities. If an institution suffers from a maturity imbalance, its earnings will be subject to wide swings if the term structure inverts or the general level of interest rates changes.

McFadden Act: in 1927, Congress passed the McFadden Act, which authorized national banks to branch within their home state limits if state laws permitted branching. With a few exceptions, banks are not permitted to establish branches outside the state in which their home office is located.

money market deposit account (MMDA): MMDA and consumer deposit accounts at commercial banks originated in 1982. MMDAs are not subject to deposit rate ceilings or reserve requirements. Customers may use them for no more than six withdrawals (including only three checks) per month.

money market fund: an investment company whose portfolio consists of liquid debt instruments such as Treasury bills and negotiable certificates of deposit.

money markets: financial markets where financial claims with maturities of less than a year are sold.

mortgage: long-term debt secured by real estate.

mortgage banker: an institution that originates and sells mortgages. Most mortgage bankers do not hold the mortgages they originate for long, but rather profit from the service fees they receive for collecting payments on each mortgage for the ultimate purchaser of the mortgage.

municipal securities: securities issued by state and local governments, whose coupon interest is generally exempt from federal income tax.

mutual company: a company that is owned and controlled by its depositors or policyholders.

mutual fund: open end investment company. Fund continually accepts new investment funds and stands ready to redeem shares previously purchased.

NASD: the National Association of Security Dealers is a trade association of brokers and dealers in the over-the-counter market. It is self regulating but subject to SEC jurisdiction and review.

National Credit Union Administration (NCUA): the regulatory body that sets standards for all federally chartered and federally insured credit unions.

negotiable certificates of deposit (CDs): unsecured liabilities of banks that can be resold prior to their maturity in a dealer-operated secondary market.

net worth: the net ownership value of a firm. Net worth equals the value of assets held by a firm minus the value of all its liabilities.

nominal interest rates: the interest rates that are observed in the marketplace.

nonbank bank: the name nonbank bank comes from the confusing wording in the Bank Holding Company Act that defines a bank as a firm that simultaneously makes commercial loans and accepts demand deposits. If the financial institution either does not make commercial loans or does not accept demand deposits it is referred to as a nonbank bank.

NOW accounts: deposit accounts that pay explicit interest and can be withdrawn by "negotiable orders of withdrawal" (checks) upon demand.

OCC: Office of the Comptroller of the Currency. See Comptroller of the Currency.

one-bank holding company: a holding company that holds 25 percent or more of the stock of a single bank. Prior to 1970, one-bank holding companies were excluded from Federal Reserve regulations, and they could engage in a wider range of business activities than either independent banks or multibank holding companies.

open-end investment company: an investment company (mutual fund) that continually accepts new funds and redeems previously issued shares.

open market operations: the purchase or sale of government securities by the Federal Reserve. Open market operations are used to increase or decrease bank reserves and the monetary base. When the Fed purchases securities, the monetary base expands.

option: a contractual agreement that allows the holder to buy (or sell) a specified asset at a predetermined price prior to its expiration date. The predetermined price is called the strike price. Options to buy assets are call options. Options to sell assets are put options.

par value: the stated or face value of a stock or bond. For debt instruments the par value is usually the final principal payment. Most bonds are sold at $1,000 or $5,000 par values.

pass-through securities: securities that pass through the principal and interest payments made on a pool of assets (mortgages) to holders of the securities. Pass-through securities have uniform denominations and set payment dates. They also may carry guarantees of timely and full payment. Thus they are more easily traded in the capital markets than mortgages per se.

Pension Benefit Guarantee Corporation (PBGC): the federal body responsible for administering the plan termination insurance program under ERISA.

pool: the collection of a number of different financial assets into a single unit. Mortgages are pooled before pass-through securities are issued.

preferred stock: corporate stock that has certain "preferences" relative to the interests of common stockholders. Usually, dividend payments are predetermined and must be made before dividends can be distributed to common stock holders.

primary markets: financial markets in which financial claims are first sold as new issues. All financial claims have a primary market.

primary reserves: cash assets on a bank balance sheet that are immediately available to accomodate deposit withdrawals. Primary assets are the most liquid assets held by the bank but earn no interest income. Primary reserves are vault cash, deposits at correspondent banks, and deposits at the Federal Reserve.

prime rate: a commercial bank's lowest posted rate. The prime rate is a short-term rate granted to a bank's most creditworthy customers. Some large bank customers who have access to the commercial paper market may borrow below the prime rate. Smaller or riskier customers often pay more than the prime rate, such as "prime plus two" percent, to borrow.

private mortgage insurance (PMI): a private insurance contract that agrees to make principal and interest payments on a mortgage if the borrower defaults. PMI is often required on conventional mortgage loans with low down payment requirements.

property insurance: insurance that provides coverage for physical damage to or destruction of personal or commercial property that results from a specified peril, such as fire, theft, or negligence.

put: an option giving the buyer the right to sell the underlying security at a predetermined price over a stated period of time.

real interest rate: the nominal rate of interest prevailing in the marketplace less the expected rate of inflation. Real and nominal rates of interest are equal when market participants have no expectation of inflation.

Regulation D: a Federal Reserve regulation that sets required reserves that must be held by depository institutions at the federal reserve bank or as vault cash.

Regulation Q: a Federal Reserve regulation that set a maximum interest rate that banks can charge on time and savings deposits. All interest rate ceilings were phased out on April 1, 1986, by federal law.

renegotiated-rate mortgage (RRM): a mortgage whose rate must be renegotiated periodically. Renewal at the new rate is guaranteed and the maximum rate change is limited.

repo: see repurchase agreements.

repurchase agreements (repo): a form of loan in which the borrower sells securities (usually government securities) and simultaneously contracts to repurchase the same securities, either on call or on a specified date, at a price that will produce a specified yield.

required reserves: financial institutions are required by law to maintain minimum reserves equal to a percent of deposits and other liabilities. Reserve requirements vary with the deposit size of the institution and the type of deposit. They are held at the Federal Reserve banks or as cash in financial institutions' vaults.

rollover mortgage (ROM): a mortgage that matures before it is fully amortized. At that time, the borrower may elect to renew (roll over) the mortgage at the prevailing mortgage rate. Thus the borrower may pay several different rates on the mortgage before it is fully amortized.

run on the bank: bank "runs" or "panics" occur when a large number of depositors try to convert bank liabilities into currency. Since banks hold fractional reserves, it is not possible to satisfy all requests immediately. Bank runs were a major cause of bank failures prior to the 1930s. The establishment of the FDIC has eliminated most bank runs.

SEC: Securities and Exchange Commission, the federal regulatory agency for the securities industry that was established by the Securities Exchange Act of 1934 to carry out the mandate of the Securities Act of 1933.

sales finance company: a company that finances the credit sales of retailers and dealers by purchasing the installment credit contracts that they acquire when they sell goods on credit.

secondary market: a financial market in which existing securities are resold by one buyer to another before the security matures. The secondary market is a "second-hand" market for previously sold securities. The New York Stock Exchange is the best known secondary market.

secondary reserves: short-term assets (often Treasury bills) that can quickly be converted to cash at a price near their purchase price. They provide an institution with liquidity while allowing it to earn safe interest income.

Securities Investor Protection Corporation: SIPC is the federal agency that insures customers' accounts at brokerage firms.

service company: a subsidiary of a thrift institution that may engage in activities that are not allowed to thrifts because of tax considerations and regulations.

share draft accounts: checking accounts offered by credit unions that pay explicit interest. They are equivalent to NOW accounts.

spread: the difference between the price a dealer pays for a security (the bid price) and the price at which the dealer sells the security (the asking price).

stock company: a company that is owned by stockholders.

stock exchange: an organization established to make purchases and sales of stocks easier. Stock exchanges may either bring buyers and sellers together through the auspices of specialists who trade in each stock, or use computer facilities to match buy and sell orders.

surety bond: a contract whereby one party, the surety or guarantor, guarantees the performance of a second party for the benefit of a third party. A bail bond is an example.

surplus: for a mutual institution, net profits that are not distributed as dividends are retained as surplus in the institution's net worth account.

swap: an exchange of assets or income streams for equivalent assets or income streams with slightly different characteristics. A typical mortgage swap may involve an exchange of the payments on a pool of mortgages for "participation certificates" issued by the FNMA or FHLMC that promise to pass through those same payments (less a small service fee) to the holder of the certificates. Thrift institutions may make such swaps to gain marketable securities in exchange for mortgages that cannot be sold easily. See also interest rate swap.

syndicate: an organization of dealers formed to help underwrite and market new security issues.

technical insolvency: an institution is technically insolvent when the market value of its assets is less than its liabilities. However, if the institution is not forced to write off its bad debts or mark down the value of its securities portfolio to market value, the book value of its assets may still exceed its liabilities; thus it will still appear to be solvent. If regulatory authorities are permissive, such institutions can continue to operate, even though, if they were liquidated, not all liability holders could be paid in full.

term life insurance: an insurance contract that provides for payment of benefits to the beneficiary if the insured dies within a specified time. Term life insurance does not provide for the accumulation of any cash value (a form of savings).

term loan: a loan from a bank with a maturity greater than one year.

term structure of interest rates: the relationship between the yield to maturity and term to maturity of otherwise similar securities. Graphically, this relationship is shown by the yield curve.

thrift or thrift institution: a financial institution (savings and loan association, savings bank, or credit union) that obtains a major source of its funds from consumer time and savings deposits. Often credit unions are not included.

trader: an individual who buys or sells futures contracts or stocks in the hope of profiting quickly from expected price movements.

transactions deposit: a deposit that can be used to finance depositors' transactions. Money can be withdrawn on demand by checks, electronic impulses, negotiable orders of withdrawal, share drafts, or other payment devices.

Treasury bills: direct obligations of the federal government with initial maturities ranging from three months to one year. They are considered to have no default risk and are the most marketable of any security issued.

Truth in Lending Act: a law designed to provide consumers with meaningful information about the cost of credit. It requires that both the dollar amount of finance charges and the annual percentage rate (APR) must be disclosed prior to extending credit.

underwriter: a securities firm which commits itself either to sell a proposed securities issuance or portion thereof to investors, or failing that, to acquire it for its own account.

unit banking: allowing banks to operate only a single full-service banking office.

unit trust: a portfolio that is constructed and then sold to the investing public in pieces called units; each unit is a proportional interest in the portfolio.

usury laws: state laws that prohibit the charging of interest above a certain limit—the usury ceiling. Such laws generally apply universally. However, exceptions to these laws may be enacted that establish different rate ceilings for particular types of loans or lenders.

variable-rate mortgage (VRM): a mortgage on which the rate can change (according to a predetermined formula and within certain limits) over the life of the mortgage. When VRM rates are adjusted, either the mortgage maturity is altered or the monthly payment is changed.

whole life insurance: an insurance contract that provides periodic payment of premiums and protection as long as the insured lives. Upon death or a specified age (usually 65), the face amount of the policy is paid to the policyholder or beneficiary. Whole life differs from term insurance in that it has a savings feature.

yield curve: the graph of the relationship between interest rates on particular securities and their yield to maturity. To construct yield curves, bonds must be as similar in all other characteristics (e.g., default risk, tax treatment) as possible. Yield curves are most easily constructed for U.S. government securities.

yield to maturity: the discount rate that equates the present value of all cash flows from a bond (interest payments plus principal) to the market price of the bond.

Suggested Reading

GENERAL REFERENCES

Periodicals

ABA Banking Journal, American Bankers Association.
American Banker (daily banking newspaper).
The Bankers Magazine, Warren, Gorham, and Lamont, Incorporated.
Bank Marketing, Bank Market Association.
CLU Journal, American Society of Chartered Life Underwriters.
CPCU Journal, Society of Chartered Property and Casualty Underwriters.
Federal Reserve Banks, various publications.
Financial Analysts Journal, Financial Analyst Federation.
Financial Management, Financial Management Association.
Issues in Bank Regulation, Bank Administration Institute.
Journal of Bank Research, Bank Administration Institute.
The Journal of Commercial Bank Lending, Robert Morris Associates.
Journal of Finance, American Finance Associates.
Journal of Financial Economics, Elsevier Science Publications (academic publication).
Journal of Money, Credit, and Banking (academic journal).
Journal of Portfolio Management, Institutional Investor.
Journal of Risk and Insurance, American Risk and Insurance Association.
Kaplan Smith Report, Kaplan, Smith Associates.
The Magazine of Bank Administration, Bank Administration Institute.
Savings Institutions, U.S. League of Savings Institutions.

BOOKS

American Bankers Association. *Statistical Information on the Financial Services Industry.*
    4th ed. Washington, D.C.: American Bankers Association, 1987.

Aspinwall, Richard C., and Robert A. Eisenbeis, eds. *Handbook for Banking Strategy.* New York: Wiley Interscience, 1985.

Auerbach, Joseph, and Samuel L. Hayes, III, *Investment Banking and Diligence: What Price Deregulation?* Boston, Mass.: Harvard Business School Press, 1986.

Baughn, William H., and Charles E. Walker, eds. *The Banker's Handbook.* Rev. ed. Homewood, Ill.: Dow Jones-Irwin Inc., 1978.

Beidelman, Carl R. *Financial Swaps.* Homewood, Ill.: Dow Jones-Irwin Inc., 1985.

Black, Tyron, and Bonnie Daniel. *Money and Banking Contemporary Practices, Policies and Issues.* 2nd ed. Plano, Tex.: Business Publications Inc., 1985.

Bowden, Elbert V. *Revolution in Banking.* Houston: Robert F. Dome Inc., 1980.

Brandon, Larry. *Sound a Clear Call.* Malvern, Pa.: CPCU and Harry Loman Foundation, 1984.

Brick, John R. *Bank Management: Concepts and Issues.* Houston: Robert F. Dome Inc., 1980.

Brick, John R., H. Kent Baker, and John Haslem, eds. *Financial Markets: Institutions and Concepts.* 2nd ed. Reston, Va.: Reston Publishing Co., 1986.

Cohen, Kalman J., and Stephen E. Gibson, ed. *Management Science in Banking.* Boston: Warren, Gorham, and Lamont, 1978.

Compton, Eric N. *The New World of Commercial Banking.* Lexington, Mass.: Lexington Books, 1987.

Cooper, K., and D. R. Fraser. *Banking Deregulation and the Competition in Financial Services.* Cambridge, Mass.: Ballinger Publishing, 1986.

Crosse, Howard D., and George H. Hempel. *Management Policies for Commercial Banks.* 3rd ed. Englewood Cliffs, N.J.: Prentice-Hall, Inc., 1980.

Darst, David M. *The Handbook of the Bond and Money Markets.* New York: McGraw-Hill, 1981.

Edmister, Robert O. *Financial Institutions: Markets and Management.* New York: McGraw-Hill, 1980.

Eitman, David K., and Arthur I. Stonehill. *Multinational Business Finance.* 4th ed. Reading, Mass.: Addison-Wesley, 1986.

Elliot, J. Walter. *Money, Banking and Financial Markets.* St. Paul, Minn.: West Publishing Co., 1983.

Fabozzi, Frank J. *The Handbook of Mortgage-Backed Securities.* Chicago: Probus Publishing, 1985.

————. *Readings in Investment Management.* Homewood, Ill.: Richard D. Irwin, 1983.

Fabozzi, Frank J., and Irving Pollack, eds. *The Handbook of Fixed Income Securities.* Homewood, Ill.: Dow Jones-Irwin Inc., 1983.

———— *The Municipal Bond Handbook.* Vols. I and II. Homewood, Ill.: Dow Jones-Irwin Inc., 1985.

Fabozzi, Frank J., and Frank G. Zarb, eds. *Selected Topics in Investment Management.* Homewood, Ill.: Dow Jones-Irwin Inc., 1981.

Federal Reserve Bank of Atlanta. *The Future of the Financial Services Industry.* Atlanta, Ga., 1981.

Feldstein, Slyvan G., Frank J. Fabozzi, and Irving M. Pollack. *The Municipal Bond Handbook.* Homewood, Ill.: Dow Jones-Irwin Inc., 1983.

First Boston Corporation. *Handbook of Securities of the U.S. Government and Federal Agencies.* New York: biannually.

Francis, Jack Clark. *Investment Analysis and Management.* 4th ed. New York: McGraw-Hill, 1986.

Friars, Eileen M., and Robert N. Gogel. *The Financial Services Handbook: Executive Insights and Solutions.* New York: Wiley-Interscience, 1987.

Gart, Alan. *Banks, Thrifts and Insurance Companies: Surviving the 1980s.* Lexington, Mass.: Lexington Books, 1985.

_____. *An Insider's Guide to the Financial Services Revolution.* New York: McGraw-Hill, 1984.

_____. *Handbook of the Money and Capital Markets.* Westport, Conn.: Quorum Books, 1988.

Gart, Alan, and Nye, David. *Finance for Insurance.* Malvern, Pa.: The American Institute, 1986.

Gup, Benton E. *Financial Intermediaries: An Introduction.* 2d ed. Boston: Houghton Mifflin, 1980.

Hammond, Bray. *Banks and Politics in America from the Revolution to the Civil War.* Princeton, N.J.: Princeton University Press, 1957.

Havrilesky, Thomas M., and John T. Boorman. *Current Perspectives in Banking: Operations, Management, and Regulation.* 2d ed. Arlington Heights, Ill.: AHM Publishing Corporation, 1980.

Havrilesky, Thomas M., Robert Schweitzer, and John T. Boorman, eds. *Dynamics of Banking.* Arlington Heights, Ill.: Hirlan Davidson Inc., 1980.

Hayes, Douglas A. *Bank Funds Management.* Ann Arbor: University of Michigan Press, 1980.

Hempel, George H. *Bank Capital: Determining and Meeting Your Bank's Capital Needs.* Boston: Bankers Publishing Co., 1978.

Hempel, George H., Alan B. Coleman, and Donald Simonson. *Bank Management: Text and Cases.* New York: John Wiley & Sons, 1983.

Hempel, George H., and Jess B. Yawitz. *Financial Management of Financial Institutions.* Englewood Cliffs, N.J.: Prentice-Hall Inc., 1978.

Henning, Charles N., William Pigott, and Robert Scott. *Financial Markets and the Economy.* 2d ed. Englewood Cliffs, N.J.: Prentice-Hall Inc., 1978.

Herrick, Tracy G. *Bank Analyst Handbook.* New York: John Wiley & Sons, Inc., 1978.

Horvitz, Paul M., and Richard A. Ward. *Monetary Policy and the Financial System.* 5th ed. Englewood Cliffs, N.J.: Prentice-Hall Inc., 1983.

Jessup, Paul F. *Modern Bank Management.* St. Paul: West Publishing Company, 1980.

Kaufman, George G. *The U.S. Financial System.* 3d ed. Englewood Cliffs, N.J.: Prentice-Hall, 1980.

Kidwell, David, and Richard Peterson. *Financial Institutions, Markets, and Money.* 3d ed. Hinsdale, Ill.: Dryden Press, 1987.

Krebaner, Benjamin. *Commercial Banking in the United States: A History.* Hinsdale, Ill.: Dryden Press, 1974.

Kroose, Herman E., and Martin R. Blyn. *A History of Financial Intermediaries.* New York: Random House, 1971.

Lamb, Robert, and Rappaport, Stephen P. *Municipal Bonds, The Comprehensive Review of Tax-Exempt Securities and Public Finance.* New York: McGraw-Hill, 1980.

Lash, Nicholas A. *Banking, Laws and Regulations.* Englewood Cliffs, N.J.: Prentice-Hall, 1987.

Light, J. O., and William L. White. *The Financial System.* Homewood, Ill.: Richard D. Irwin Inc., 1979.

McKinney, George W., Jr., and William J. Brown. *Management of Commercial Bank Funds.* Washington, D.C.: American Institute of Banking, 1974.

Malkiel, Burton G. *A Random Walk down Wall Street.* 4th ed. New York: W. W. Norton & Co., 1985.

Mason, John M. *Financial Management of Commercial Banks.* Boston: Warren, Gorham and Lamont, 1979.

Mayer, Martin. *The Bankers.* New York: Weybright and Talley, 1974.

Mishkin, Frederick. *The Economics of Money, Banking, and Financial Markets.* Boston: Little Brown, 1986.

Nadler, Paul S. *Commercial Banking in the Economy.* 3d ed. New York: Random House, 1979.

Prager, Jones. *Fundamentals of Money, Banking, and Financial Institutions.* New York: Harper & Row, 1982.

Recent Innovations in International Banking, Basle, Switzerland: Bank for International Settlements, 1986.

Robinson, Roland I., and Dwayne Wrightsman. *Financial Markets: The Accumulation and Allocation of Wealth.* 2d ed. New York: McGraw-Hill, 1980.

Rose, Peter S. *Money and Capital Markets.* Plano, Tex.: Business Publications, Inc., 1980.

Rose, Peter S., and Donald R. Fraser. *Financial Institutions.* 3d ed. Homewood, Ill.: Business Publications Inc., 1988.

Siegal, Barry N. *Money, Banking, and the Economy: A Monetarist View.* New York: Academic Press, 1982.

Sinkey, Joseph F., Jr. *Commercial Bank Financial Management: In the Financial Service Industry.* 2d ed. New York: Macmillan, 1986.

Spellman, Lewis J. *The Depository Firm and Industry: Theory, History, and Regulation.* New York: Academic Press, 1982.

Studenski, Paul, and Herman E. Kross. *Financial History of the United States.* New York: McGraw-Hill, 1963.

Teweles, Richard J., and Edward S. Bradley. *The Stock Market.* 5th ed. New York: John Wiley & Sons, 1987.

Walter, Ingo, ed. *Deregulating Wall Street.* New York: John Wiley Interscience, 1985.

Woerheide, Walter J. *The Savings and Loan Industry,* Westport, Conn.: Quorum Books, 1984.

Wood, Oliver G., Jr., and Robert J. Porter. *Analysis of Bank Financial Statements.* New York: Von Nostrand Reinhold, 1979.

BANK PERFORMANCE: MEASURING RETURNS AND RISKS

Arahood, Dale. "NBSS Measures of Banking Industry Performance: A Long-Term View." *Magazine of Bank Administration* (Sept. 1978): 40-46.

"Bank Scoreboard," *Business Week.* (Annual feature.)

Binder, Barrett F. "A Look at 1979 Commercial Bank Performance." *Journal of Bank Administration* (Aug. 1980): 20-24.

Cole, David W. "Return on Equity Model for Banks." *The Bankers Magazine* (Summer 1972).

Eiseman, Peter C. "Inflation's Impact on Bank Earnings." *The Bankers Magazine* (Jan.–Feb. 1980): 47-49.

Falkenberg, John H. "Practical Profitability Analysis: Opportunities for Improvement." *Magazine of Bank Administration* (Nov. 1977): 34-37.

Feldman, Stephen, and Angelico A. Gropelli. "Bank Trust Departments." In *The Hand-*

book of Financial Markets, ed. F. Fabozzi, and F. G. Zarb. Homewood, Ill.: Dow Jones, 1981.

Flannery, Mark J. "How Do Changes in Market Interest Rates Affect Bank Profits?" *Business Review.* Federal Reserve Bank of Philadelphia (Sept.–Oct. 1980): 13-22.

Ford, William F. "Using 'High-Performance' Data to Plan Your Bank's Future." *Banking* (Oct. 1978): 40-41, 43-44, 46, 48, 162.

Gillis, Harvey N., Rufus W. Lumry, and Thomas J. Oswold. "A New Approach to Analyzing Bank Performance." *The Bankers Magazine* (March-April 1980): 67-73.

Giroux, Gary, and Steven Grossman. "How Does Inflation Affect a Bank Holding Company's Rate of Return?" *Issues in Bank Regulation* (Winter 1981): 24-31.

Gup, Benton, and Linda Mitchusson. "Portfolios and Profits Shape Bank Attitudes." *The Bankers Magazine* (Sept.–Oct. 1978): 46-49.

Howard, Timothy, and William F. Ford. "Story behind Banking Industry's Profits and Losses, 1972-1980." *ABA Banking Journal* (July 1979): 54-62.

Johnson, Bradford M. "Are Bank Stocks Undervalued?" *Magazine of Bank Administration* (April 1981): 38-45.

Kimball, Ralph. "Commercial Bank Profitability in New England: A Comparative Study." *New England Economic Review* (Nov.–Dec. 1978): 5-24.

Matthews, William M., and John J. Pepin. "Corporate Cash Management + Prime Pricing = Lower Regional Bank Earnings." *The Bankers Magazine* (May–June 1978): 16-23.

Metzker, Paul F. "Future System Technology: Can Small Financial Institutions Compete?" *Economic Review.* Federal Reserve Board of Atlanta (Nov. 1982): 58-67.

Meyer, Philip C. "DIDC Is Off to a Stormy Start." *Bank Marketing* (Aug. 1980): 5-6.

Olson, Ronald L., and Ralph H. Sprague, Jr. "Financial Planning in Action." *Magazine of Bank Administration* (Feb. 1981): 54-64.

Polanis, Mark F., and Barret F. Binder. "The Top 50 Profit Performing Banks." *Journal of Bank Administration* (Aug. 1980): 25-27.

Robinson, Roland I. "Toward Improved Analysis of Bank Management." *The Bankers Magazine* (Sept.–Oct. 1980): 82-87.

Spong, Kenneth, Larry Meeker, and Forest Myers. "The Paradox of Record Bank Earnings and Declining Capital." *Magazine of Bank Administration* (Oct. 1980): 22-27.

Turner, William D. "A Better Way to Measure Retail Banking Performance." *The Bankers Magazine* (Nov.–Dec. 1978): 69-75.

Wallich, Henry C. "Bank Profits and Inflation." *Economic Review.* Federal Reserve Bank of Richmond (May–June 1980): 27-30.

MANAGING THE SECURITIES PORTFOLIO

Broaddus, Alfred. "Linear Programming: A New Approach to Bank Portfolio Management." *Monthly Review.* Federal Reserve Bank of Richmond (Nov. 1972): 3-11.

Brown, W. W., and G. J. Santoni. "Unreal Estimates of the Real Rate of Interest." *Review.* Federal Reserve Bank of St. Louis (Jan. 1981): 18-26.

Cook, Timothy Q. "Changing Yield Spreads in the U.S. Government Bond Market." *Economic Review.* Federal Reserve Bank of Richmond (March–April 1977): 3-8.

Ederington, Louis. "The Hedging Performance of the New Futures Market." *Journal of Finance* (March 1979): 57-70.

Grandstaff, Mary C. "Profitability of Bank Loan and Investment Functions: Large Variations Among Banks." *Voice.* Federal Reserve Bank of Dallas (Oct. 1979): 16-23.

Grant, Dwight, and George H. Hempel. "Bank Portfolio Management: The Role of Financial Futures." Banking Structures Conference Proceedings (April 1982): 127-139.

Hayes, Douglas A. "Bank Portfolio Management: Revolution in Portfolio Policies." *The Bankers Magazine* (Sept.–Oct. 1980): 21-24.

Hempel, George H. "Basic Ingredients of Commercial Bank's Investment Policies." *The Bankers Magazine* (Autumn 1972): 50-59.

———. "Quantitative Borrower Characteristics Associated with Defaults on Municipal General Obligations." *Journal of Finance* (May 1973): 523-530.

Hempel, George H., and Stephen R. Kretschman. "Comparative Performance of Portfolio Maturity Policies of Commercial Banks." *Journal of Business and Economics* (Fall 1973): 55-57.

Hempel, George H., and Jess B. Yawitz. "Maximizing Bond Returns." *The Bankers Magazine* (Summer 1974): 103-114.

Nelson, Jane F. "Federal Agency Securities." In *Instruments of the Money Markets.* Federal Reserve Bank of Richmond (1977): 85-93.

Ratti, Ronald. "Pledging Requirements and Bank Asset Portfolios." *Economics Review.* Federal Reserve Bank of Kansas City (Sept.–Oct. 1979): 13-23.

Santoni, G. J., and C. Courtnay. "Navigating through the Interest Rate Morass: Some Basic Principles." *Review.* Federal Reserve Bank of St. Louis (March 1981): 11-18.

Simonson, Donald G., and George H. Hempel. "Public Deposit Policies: Trends and Issues." *Issues in Bank Regulation* (Spring 1978): 14-19.

Sivesind, Charles M. "Mortgage-Backed Securities: The Revolution in Real Estate Finance." *Quarterly Review.* Federal Reserve Bank of New York (Autumn 1979): 1-10.

Wood, John H. "Interest Rates and Inflation." *Economic Perspectives.* Federal Reserve Bank of Chicago (May-June 1981): 3-12.

Yawitz, Jess, George H. Hempel, and William J. Marshall. "A Risk-Return Approach to the Selection of Optimal Government Bond Portfolios." *Financial Management* (Autumn 1976): 36-45.

———. "The Use of Average Maturity as a Risk Proxy in Investment Portfolios." *Journal of Finance,* vol. 30, no. 2 (May 1975): 325-333.

ASSET AND LIABILITY MANAGEMENT

Baker, James. *Asset/Liability Management.* Washington, D.C.: American Bankers Association, 1981.

Beidelman, Carl. *Financial Swaps.* Homewood, Ill.: Dow Jones-Irwin, 1985.

Belongia, Michael. "Predicting Interest Rates: A Comparison of Professional and Market-Based Forecasts." *Review.* Federal Reserve Bank of St. Louis, vol. 69, no. 3 (March 1987): 9-15.

Bierwag, Gerald. *Duration Analysis.* Cambridge, Mass.: Ballinger Publishing Co., 1987.

Binder, Barrett. "Asset/Liability Management—Part 1." *Magazine of Bank Administration* (November 1980): 42-48.

_____. "Asset/Liability Management—Part 2." *Magazine of Bank Administration* (December 1980): 31-35.

_____. "Asset/Liability Management—Part 3." *Magazine of Bank Administration* (January 1981): 42-50.

_____. "New Initiatives in Asset/Liability Management." *Magazine of Bank Administration* (June 1981): 56-64.

Binder, Barrett, and Thomas Lindquist. *Asset/Liability and Funds Management at U.S. Commercial Banks.* Rolling Meadows, Ill.: Bank Administration Institute, 1982.

Brewer, Elijah. "Bank Gap Management and the Use of Financial Futures." *Economic Perspectives.* Federal Reserve Bank of Chicago (March–April 1985): 12-21.

Clifford, John. "A Perspective on Asset-Liability Management: Part I." *Magazine of Bank Administration* (March 1975): 16-21.

_____. "A Perspective on Asset-Liability Management: Part II." *Magazine of Bank Administration* (April 1975): 32-36.

Harrington, R. *Asset and Liability Management by Banks.* Paris, France: Organization for Economic Co-operation and Development, 1987.

Kaufman, George. "Measuring and Managing Interest Rate Risk: A Primer." *Economic Perspectives.* Federal Reserve Bank of Chicago (January–February 1984): 16-29.

Koppenhaver, G. D. "Futures Options and Their Use by Financial Intermediaries." *Economic Perspectives.* Federal Reserve Bank of Chicago (January–February 1986): 18-31.

Melton, Carroll, and Terry Pukula. *Financial Futures.* Reston, Va.: Reston Publishing Co., 1984.

Patton, Kenneth, and Z. Christopher Mercer. "Asset/Liability Management Today." In *Bank Performance Annual 1987.* ed. Edwin B. Cox. Boston: Warren, Gorham, & Lamont, 1987, 85-100.

Platt, Robert. *Controlling Interest Rate Risk.* New York: John Wiley & Sons, 1986.

Stigum, Marcia, and Rene Branch. *Managing Bank Assets and Liabilities.* Homewood, Ill.: Dow Jones-Irwin, 1983.

Toevs, Alden. "Gap Management: Managing Interest Rate Risk in Banks and Thrifts." *Economic Review.* Federal Reserve Bank of San Francisco (Spring 1983): 20-35.

Van Horne, James. *Financial Market Rates and Flows.* Englewood Cliffs, N.J.: Prentice Hall, 1984.

SEPARATION OF COMMERCIAL AND INVESTMENT BANKING

Bierwag, G. O., G. G. Kaufman, and P. H. Leonard. "Interest Rate Effects of Commercial Bank Underwriting of Municipal Revenue Bonds: Additional Evidence." *Journal of Banking and Finance* (March 1984): 35-50.

Carosso, Vincent. *Investment Banking in America: A History.* Cambridge, Mass.: Harvard University Press, 1970.

_____. "Washington and Wall Street: The New Deal and Investment Bankers, 1933-1940," *Business History Review* (Winter 1970): 425-445.

Felgran, Steven D. "Bank Entry into Securities Brokerage: Competitive and Legal Aspects." *New England Economic Review.* Federal Reserve Bank of Boston (November–December 1984): 12-33.

Fischer, Thomas G., William H. Graim, George G. Kaufman, and Larry R. Mote. "The Securities Activities of Commercial Banks: A Legal and Economic Analysis." *Tennessee Law Review* (Spring 1984): 467-518.

Hayes, Samuel L., III. "The Transformation of Investment Banking." *Harvard Business Review* (January-February 1979): 153-170.

———. "Is This Any Way to Run an Investment Bank? Citicorp Thinks So." *Business Week,* July 28, 1986, 56-58.

Hayes, Samuel L., III, A. M. Spence, and D. V. Marks. *Competition in the Investment Banking Industry.* Cambridge, Mass.: Harvard University Press, 1983.

Kaufman, George G. "The Securities Activities of Commercial Banks," in *Handbook for Banking Strategy,* ed. Richard C. Aspinwall and Robert A. Eisenbeis. New York: Wiley Interscience, 1985.

———. "The Securities Activities of Commercial Banks: A Legal and Economic Analysis." *Tennessee Law Review* (Spring 1984): 12-33.

Krooss, Herman, and Martin Blyn. *A History of Financial Intermediaries.* New York: Random House, 1971.

Mote, Larry R. "Banks and the Securities Market: The Controversy," *Economic Perspectives.* Federal Reserve Bank of Chicago (March–April 1979): 14-20.

Peach, W. Nelson, "The Security Affiliates of National Banks." *Johns Hopkins University Studies in Historical and Political Science,* 58, no. 3, 1941.

Perkins, Edwin J. "The Divorce of Commercial and Investment Banking: A History." *Banking Law Journal* (June 1971): 483-528.

Sametz, Arnold W., ed. *Securities Activities of Commercial Banks.* Lexington, Mass.: Lexington Books, 1981.

Securities Industry Association. "Bank Securities Activities: Memorandum for Study and Discussion," *San Diego Law Review* (November 1977): 751-822.

U.S. Congress, House Committee on Government Operations, "Confusion in the Legal Framework of the American Financial System and Services Industry: Hearings." 98th Cong., 1st sess., July 19-21, 1983.

U.S. Congress, Senate Committee on Banking, Housing and Urban Affairs, "Financial Institutions Restructuring and Services Act of 1981: Hearings" (Parts I, II, and III). 97th Cong., 1st sess., October 1981.

Willis, H. Parker, and J. I. Bogen. *Investment Banking.* New York: Harper, 1929.

THRIFT INSTITUTIONS AND CREDIT UNIONS

Brookings Institution. *The Rescue of the Thrift Industry.* Washington, D.C.: Brookings Institution, 1983.

Carran, Andrew S. *The Plight of Thrift Institutions.* Washington, D.C.: Brookings Institution, 1982.

Credit Union National Association. *Credit Union Report.* Madison, Wisc.: annually.

Durham, Constance R. "Mutual to Stock Conversion by Thrifts: Implications for Soundness." *New England Economic Review.* Federal Reserve Bank of Boston (January-February 1985): 31-45.

———. "Recent Developments in Thrift Commercial Lending." *New England Economic Review.* Federal Reserve Bank of Boston (November-December 1985): 41-48.

Federal Home Loan Bank of San Francisco, "Thrift Financial Performance and Capital Adequacy," Proceedings of the Twelfth Annual Conference, December 11-12, 1986.

Heaton, Gary, G. and Constance Dunham. "The Growing Competitiveness of Credit Unions." *New England Economic Review.* Federal Reserve Bank of Boston (May-June 1985): 19-34.

Kane, Edward J. "The Role of Government in the Thrift Industry's Net Worth Crisis." In *Financial Services: The Changing Institutions and Government Policy,* ed. George Benston. Englewood Cliffs, N.J.: Prentice Hall, 1983.

Kawalle, Ira, and James Freund. "Mortgage Lending at Savings and Loan Associations: A Further Inquiry." *Business Economics* (January 1981): 39-49.

Loeys, Jan G. "Deregulation: A New Future for Thrifts." *Business Review.* Federal Reserve Bank of Philadelphia (January–February 1983): 15-26.

Mahoney, Patrick I., and Alice White. "The Thrift Industry in Transition." *Federal Reserve Bulletin* (December 1983): 137-156.

Marcis, Richard T. "Savings and Loan Planning for the New Competitive Environment," *Federal Home Loan Bank Board Journal,* vol. 14, no. 7. (July 1981), 5-14.

Moran, Michael J. "Thrift Institutions in Recent Years." *Federal Reserve Bulletin* (December 1983): 725-738.

Pearce, Douglas K. "Recent Developments in the Credit Union Industry." *Economic Review.* Federal Reserve Bank of Kansas City (June 1984): 3-19.

Pratt, Richard T. "The Savings and Loan Industry, Past, Present and Future." *Federal Home Loan Bank Board Journal.* vol. 15, no. 11 (November 1982): 3-8.

United States League of Savings Institutions. *Savings Institution Sourcebook.* Chicago: published annually.

Vrabac, Daniel J. "Savings and Loan Associations: An Analysis of Recent Declines in Profitability." *Economic Review.* Federal Reserve Bank of Kansas City (July-August 1982): 3-19.

FINANCE COMPANIES

Benston, George. "The Costs to Consumer Finance Companies of Extending Consumer Credit." *The National Commission on Consumer Finance,* Technical Studies, Vol. 2. Washington, D.C.: U.S. Government Printing Office, 1975.

Durkin, Thomas A., and Ysabel Burns McAleer. *Finance Companies in 1986.* American Financial Services Association Research Report and Second Mortgage Lending Report, Washington, D.C., 1987.

———. *Finance Companies 1977-1986.* American Financial Services Association Research Report and Second Mortgage Lending Report, 1987.

Harris, Maury. "Finance Companies as Business Lenders." *Quarterly Review.* Federal Reserve Bank of New York (Summer 1979): 35-39.

Hurley, Evelyn M. "Survey of Finance Companies, 1980." *Federal Reserve Bulletin,* 67 (May 1981): 398-409.

Luckett, Charles A., and James D. August. "The Growth of Consumer Debt." *Federal Reserve Bulletin* (June 1985): 389-404.

Swift, John R. "Consumer Finance Companies: A Step Back and a Look Forward." *Journal of Commercial Bank Lending* (1982): 50-55.

INSURANCE COMPANIES

American Council of Life Insurance. *Life Insurance Fact Book.* Washington, D.C.: published annually.

Best's Review: Life and Health Edition and *Property/Casualty Edition.* Oldwich, N.J.:
    A. M. Best, weekly.
"The Changing Life Insurers." *Business Week,* September 14, 1981, 66-71.
Cummins, J. David, and David J. Nye. "The Stochastic Characteristics of Property-
    Liability Insurance Company Underwriting Profits." *Journal of Risk and Insurance*
    (March 1980): 61-77.
Insurance Information Institute, *Insurance Facts,* New York: Insurance Information
    Institute, published annually.
National Underwriter Co. *Life and Health Edition* and *Property and Casualty Edition.*
    Cincinnati, Ohio: National Underwriter Co., monthly.
Vaughan, Emmett J. *Fundamentals of Risk and Insurance.* New York: John Wiley, 1986.

INVESTMENT COMPANIES

Friend, Irwin, Marshall Blum, and Jean Crockett. *Mutual Funds and Other Institutional
    Investors.* New York: McGraw-Hill, 1970.
Investment Company Institute. *Mutual Fund Fact Book.* Washington, D.C.: Investment
    Company Institute, published annually.
Litzenberg, Robert, and Howard Sossin. "The Structure and Management of Dual
    Purpose Funds." *Journal of Financial Economics* (March 1977): 203-230.
Malkiel, Burton. "The Valuation of Closed-End Investment Company Shares." *Journal
    of Finance* (June 1977): 847-859.
Richards, Malcolm, John Growth, and Donald Fraser. "Closed-End Funds and Market
    Efficiency." *Journal of Portfolio Management* (Fall 1980): 50-55.
Weisenberger Investment Companies Service. *Investment Companies.* New York:
    Warren, Gorham and Lamont, annual.

PENSION FUNDS

Allen, Everett, Jr., J. Melone, and J. Rosenbloom. *Pension Planning.* Homewood, Ill.:
    Richard D. Irwin, 1984.
American Council of Life Insurance. *Pension Facts.* Washington, D.C.: American
    Council of Life Insurance, annual.
Bodie, Zvi, and John Shoven, eds. *Financial Aspects of the U.S. Pension System.*
    Chicago: University of Chicago Press, 1983.
Bogle, John C., and Jan M. Twardowski. "Institutional Investment Performance Com-
    pared." *Financial Analysts Journal* (January–February 1980): 33-41.
Munnel, Alice H. *The Economics of Private Pensions.* Washington, D.C.: Brookings
    Institution, 1982.
_____. "ERISA—The First Decade." *New England Economic Review.* Federal Reserve
    Bank of Boston (November-December 1984): 44-63.
Kotlikoff, Lawrence T., and Daniel Smith. *Pensions in the American Economy.* Chicago:
    University of Chicago Press, 1984.
Nektarius, Militidis. *Public Pensions: Capital Formation and Economic Growth.* Boulder,
    Colo.: Westview Press, 1982.
Schotland, Roy A. "Divergent Trends For Pension Funds." *Financial Analysts Journal*
    (September-October 1980): 29-33.

Index

About the Author

ALAN GART, Professor of Finance at Lehman College of the City University of New York and a Visiting Professor at the Graduate School of Business at Columbia University, received his B.A., M.A., and Ph.D. degrees from the University of Pennsylvania. He is the author of *An Insider's Guide to the Financial Services Revolution; Banks, Thrifts and Insurance Companies: Survival in the 1980s; Insurance Company Finance* (with D. Nye); and *Handbook of the Money and Capital Markets* as well as numerous journal and magazine articles. He is a former senior vice president of a family of mutual funds, senior vice president of the Girard Bank, vice president of Manufacturers Hanover Trust and chief economist of INA.

About the Contributors

RON CARUSO, editor of the *Equipment Financing Journal,* is president of an executive recruiting and consulting firm that specializes in the leasing and financial services industry. He received his B.A. from Fordham University, an M.B.A. from Columbia University, and a J.D. from Fordham University.

DAVID LEAHIGH, Assistant Professor of Finance at Lehigh University, specializes in commercial bank management and financial institutions. He received his B.A., M.A., and Ph.D. in economics from Georgetown University.

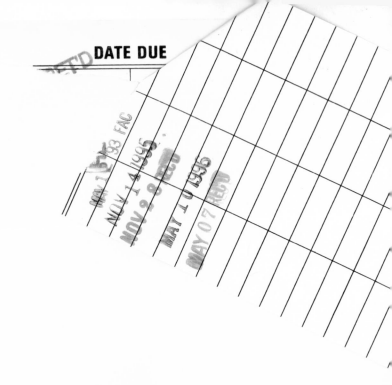